The Complete Sophie Grigson Cookbook

Published by BBC Worldwide Limited,
Woodlands, 80 Wood Lane,
London W12 0TT

First published 2001
Copyright © Sophie Grigson, 2001
The moral right of the author has
been asserted.

ISBN 0 563 53428 1

All recipes in this book first published in *Eat
Your Greens*, *Travels à la Carte*, *Meat Course*
and *Taste of the Times*.

Commisioning Editor: Nicky Copeland
Project Editor: Sarah Miles
Copy-editor: Gilly Cubitt
Art Editor: Lisa Pettibone
Designer: Paul Welti

Set in Helvetica light
Printed and bound in Britain by
Butler & Tanner Ltd, Frome and London
Cover printed by Belmont Press, Northampton

About the author

Sophie Grigson, as daughter of the prolific cookery writer Jane Grigson, was brought up in a household that revolved around cooking and food. Sophie, however, had no intention of following in her mother's footsteps. She studied Maths at university and worked in pop video production for a while, but slowly and surely, her love of cooking took over. Fascinated by the small ethnic food shops in Manchester and on the Portobello Road in London, Sophie began to experiment in her cooking and discovered a natural talent for writing about the food she loved.

Sophie wrote her first article, *Fifty Ways with Potatoes*, for the *Sunday Express* in 1983. The article grew into a column and by the end of 1986, Sophie was a full-time food writer, contributing a daily recipe column to London's *Evening Standard*. She later became a regular cookery writer for the *Independent* and wrote a weekly cookery feature for *The Sunday Times*. In 2001, she won the Guild of Food Writers Cookery Journalist Award.

Sophie's first television series *Grow Your Greens/Eat Your Greens*, and the accompanying bestselling book on cooking with vegetables, *Eat Your Greens*, published in 1993, firmly established her reputation as one of the best new cookery writers. In 1994, Sophie combined forces with her husband, William Black, for *Travels à la Carte*, which explores Europe's rich culinary traditions. *Meat Course*, an in-depth guide for the carniverous cook, followed in 1995. Two years later, she published *Taste of the Times*, with its wealth of ideas for using the huge variety of unusual ingredients available in Britain today. In total, Sophie has written 16 cookery books, the most recent being *Herbs*, *Feasts for a Fiver* and her bestselling book on Mediterranean cookery, *Sunshine Food*.

Sophie's books are much more than collections of recipes – her writing reflects a deep-rooted passion for the people she meets and the culinary traditions of the places she visits. She has been writing professionally about food for 18 years and has been cooking for herself much longer. Sophie's other passions include reading and travelling, but above all she just loves to cook, for herself, for her friends and, most importantly, for her children.

Contents

Introduction

Long before I began to earn a living from writing about food, my mother, the food writer Jane Grigson, jested in passing that the fantastically useful thing about writing your own cookbooks was that you always knew where to find those special recipes that you particularly liked. She was right (mothers usually are, something I admit far more readily now that I've joined the maternal mafia). It's really just an elaboration of the age-old feminine habit of keeping a scrapbook of favourite recipes, the ones that never fail to please family and friends, so that you don't have to go scrabbling around through five cookery books, a drawer full of newspaper clippings, that pile of old magazines gathering dust in the corner, and scrawled notes jotted down speedily and often too succinctly for anyone but the author to comprehend.

When I eventually followed suit and first wrote my own cookery books, I really appreciated being able to locate readily both simple techniques – the right proportions of flour, butter and egg for shortcrust pastry, say, or basic quantities of yolks, oil, vinegar and mustard for a mayonnaise – and those more complicated recipes which were firm household favourites.

What my mother never warned me about was that there comes a point where the whole process trundles into reverse. 'Now then,' I wonder, 'which book was it that this recipe or that one appeared in?' These days, I have a pretty good idea where to locate fine dishes in the last two or three books, but those that came before that? Forget it! Of course, this may have something to do with age and my dismally useless memory, but let's not delve into that murky area.

So, the pleasure of this particular collection of recipes for me, is that I have rediscovered some real gems that I shall return to with considerable enthusiasm. They will, I believe, regain their rightful place in our family pantheon of fab meals, and we will all benefit, as will, I hope, you, the reader. Gathered together in this tome are a wealth of recipes pulled from the first four books I wrote for Network Books, an imprint of BBC Worldwide Publishing: *Eat Your Greens*, *Travels à la Carte*, *Meat Course* and *Taste of the Times*. All four of them published in the last decade of the last century. I think they've stood the test of time – not very much time, to be sure, but food fashions rumble on so very fast these days that it is hard to keep up. Not that I am a dedicated follower of foodie fashion. I take what seems useful and interesting from new developments and new obsessions, but don't like to abandon dishes that are good but not totally 'à la mode'.

So, in here you will find an eclectic mixture of recipes, including simple, classic British dishes, souvenirs from trips around the Mediterranean and a fair share of coconut milk, chillis and lime, of which I am more than passing fond. I hope that you will enjoy them as much as I have enjoyed rediscovering them and re-incorporating many of them into my regular repertoire.

Best wishes,

Sophie

Cook's notes

Although most recipes are really nothing more than a set of guidelines and recommendations, open to variation as the cook-in-charge (i.e. you) sees fit, there are some basic rules that can make a difference. In general, it is probably a good idea to stick with either the metric or the imperial weights and measures. This is particularly true when baking cakes or biscuits, where small variations can change or even ruin the final result dramatically.

All the eggs I use are large, unless otherwise stated, and, for preference, free-range. My spoon measurements are always rounded, again, unless otherwise stated. I use a standard 5 ml teaspoon and a 15 ml tablespoon. To get the proper flavour with dishes from or inspired by the Mediterranean, you should always use extra virgin olive oil. Herbs are always fresh, except for bay leaves and oregano, both of which dry very well. Pepper and nutmeg are always, always, always freshly ground. Tubs of ready ground nutmeg and pepper lose their flavour (and therefore any culinary value) very quickly, and after two or three uses are good for nothing but the bin.

Above all, enjoy yourself and relax when cooking, and trust your instincts, particularly when it comes to seasonings.

Soups

Watercress Soup

In France watercress soup is sometimes called 'potage santé' – health soup – which suggests that it is dull and worthy. Nothing could be further from the truth. This is a soup which is as good served cold as hot. Whenever I can, I buy watercress in tight bunches rather than sealed plastic bags. I like the look of it – far more aesthetically pleasing – but that's not the only reason. It's easy to tell at a glance the state of the watercress. There's no hiding yellowing leaves or smelly slimy stalks. Back in the kitchen the preparation is quick. To separate leaves from stalks is a simple matter of slicing down in a single stroke, close to the leaves for soups and sauces, a couple of inches down for longer sprigs. All they need then is a good rinse, thorough draining and to be dried gently with kitchen paper or a clean tea towel.

SERVES 4

1 bunch watercress
50 g (2 oz) butter
1 onion, chopped
1 clove garlic, peeled and chopped
1 bouquet garni (1 bay leaf, 2 sprigs parsley and 2 sprigs thyme, tied together with string)

450g (1 lb) potatoes, peeled and diced
600 ml (1 pint) water from cooking vegetables or light stock
Salt and freshly ground black pepper
600 ml (1 pint) milk

Pick over and wash the watercress and discard any damaged leaves. Cut off the leaves, chop roughly and reserve. Chop the stalks. Melt the butter in a large saucepan, and add the onion, garlic, watercress stalks and bouquet garni. Stir to coat nicely in butter, then cover and sweat over a low heat for 10 minutes. Now add the potatoes, water or stock, salt and pepper. Bring to the boil, and simmer for 20 minutes or so until the potatoes are tender. Remove the herbs.

Stir in half the milk and then the reserved watercress leaves. Process in batches until smooth. If you don't have a food processor, sieve the potato mixture, minus the leaves and milk. Mix in the milk, chop the watercress leaves finely and then add them too. Either way, return the mixture to the pan just before serving, adding the rest of the milk. Taste and adjust the seasoning, then re-heat without boiling or serve chilled.

Lovage Soup

Some things in life are hard to fathom and one of them is the virtual disappearance of lovage from common culinary knowledge. Lovage is a sensational herb, with just about everything going for it. It makes an early appearance in the spring, ready to enliven cold-weather soups and stews, but carries on growing and thriving right into the late autumn. It grows remarkably easily, tolerating considerable neglect and maltreatment without complaint. It looks majestic and grand at full height, with long, leafy stems and great umbels of yellow flowers stretching as high as your shoulder. And, most importantly of all, it has a superb flavour, underlined by celery tones but more spicy and with a distinct lemon-zest warmth.

Lovage is a powerful herb and perhaps that contributed to its downfall: too strong, too dominant, too daring. The fact is that, where once it was widely grown in this country, now it is confined to knowing cooks who have room enough in their garden for its striking form. The scene is set to change, however. Flat packs of lovage have at last been glimpsed on the market, though complete with a ridiculously high price tag. Try it once, to see if it pleases you (if you hate celery, you'll probably loathe lovage), and then nip round to any good plant nursery, buy a plant at a reasonable rate and grow it yourself. The best showcase for the pure flavour of lovage is this traditional soup that has been reappraised and reappreciated over the past few years. The potato softens the intensity of the herb, without reducing it to pale insignificance.

SERVES 4–6

60 g (2 oz) butter
1 onion, chopped
250–300 g (9–10 oz) floury potatoes, peeled and diced
1 large carrot, diced

A handful of fresh lovage leaves
1–1.2 litres (1¾–2 pints) chicken, light game or vegetable stock
Salt and freshly ground black pepper
6 tablespoons double cream
Cayenne pepper, to serve

Melt the butter in a large pan and add the onion, potatoes, carrot and lovage. Stir and then cover and sweat over a low heat for 10–15 minutes. Add the stock and a little salt and pepper. Bring to the boil and leave to simmer for 15 minutes, until all the vegetables are very tender. Cool slightly, liquidize and sieve. Taste and adjust the seasoning. Re-heat when needed and stir in the cream. Serve with a dusting of cayenne pepper.

Asparagus and Sorrel Soup

When preparing asparagus don't throw anything away. Save the trimmings (stringy stalk ends and parings) and cooking water which will be loaded with the flavour of fresh asparagus. Then you can make this simple but very delicious soup.

SERVES 2–3

175 g (6 oz) asparagus trimmings
40 g (1½ oz) butter
1 onion, chopped
1 clove garlic, peeled and chopped
1 handful of sorrel, shredded
1 tablespoon plain flour

600 ml (1 pint) water left from cooking asparagus or asparagus water and chicken stock
Salt and freshly ground black pepper
50 ml (2 fl oz) whipping or double cream (optional)
1 tablespoon chopped fresh chervil or chives

Chop the asparagus trimmings roughly. Melt the butter in a saucepan and cook the onion and garlic until tender, without browning. Add the shredded sorrel and stir until it collapses to a mush. Sprinkle the flour over, stir for a few seconds, then, a little at a time, mix in the asparagus water and/or stock. Add the asparagus trimmings and salt and pepper. Simmer for 20 minutes.

Process or purée until smooth, then sieve to get rid of stringy fibres. Just before serving, re-heat to just under boiling point. Stir in the cream, if using, and chervil (or chives). Taste, adjust the seasoning and serve.

Marrow, Potato and Sage Soup

Marrow is not a deeply inspiring vegetable. Not unpleasant, either, but it just doesn't set the pulse racing. Even the name sounds dull and heavy. As you will have gathered, I am not a fan. I buy them once in a while, I get given them occasionally, and I've learnt to make the most of them, but I'm not enthusiastic. The key to cooking marrow is to turn its unassuming character into a virtue. Forget plain boiled marrow, or boiled marrow in a white sauce – both culinary disasters. You need to make more effort than that. Made with a good stock, and fresh herbs, marrow soup can be soothing and most welcome. It's never going to hit the headlines, but when you want something warming and gentle, you could do much, much worse. If you have time, deep-fry a handful of sage leaves for a few seconds, to scatter over the soup just before serving.

SERVES 6
1 onion, chopped
1 clove garlic, peeled and chopped
40 g (1¹/₂ oz) butter
750 g (1 lb 8 oz) marrow, peeled and diced
340 g (12 oz) potato, peeled and diced
4 fresh sage leaves

2 teaspoons sugar
1.2 litres (2 pints) vegetable or chicken stock
Salt and freshly ground black pepper
150 ml (5 fl oz) single cream

TO GARNISH
Fresh parsley or sage leaves, chopped

In a large saucepan cook the onion and garlic gently in the butter until tender, without browning. Add the marrow, potato and sage leaves, turn to coat in the butter, then cover tightly and sweat over a low heat for 10 minutes, stirring occasionally. Now add the sugar, stock, salt and pepper and bring to the boil. Simmer for 20–30 minutes until the vegetables are very tender. Cool slightly, fish out the sage leaves and discard, and then liquidize the soup in several batches. Return to the pan, adding extra stock or water, if necessary. Adjust the seasoning.

When ready to serve, bring back to the boil, draw off the heat and stir in the single cream. Garnish with chopped parsley or sage leaves.

Sweet Potato and Broccoli Soup

The first potatoes to be planted in Britain were probably sweet potatoes. In other words, not real potatoes at all but Ipomoea batatas, *a relation of that garden pest, the wild convolvulus (bindweed) and of the morning glory. The crop failed miserably; the climate here is not conducive to a tuber that hails from tropical America. Potatoes, real potatoes, from the chillier heights of the Andes, eventually fared far better once we got used to the idea of them, but that is another story.*

To this day, our sweet potatoes have to be imported and they wing their way here not only from their native Americas but from all around the hotter parts of the world too. What you can't tell from the outer appearance is the colour of the flesh inside. There are two quite distinct types of sweet potato – orange-fleshed, which seems to be the easier to find at the moment, and white-fleshed. Orange-fleshed sweet potatoes have a smoother, denser, waxier texture and a chestnut-like flavour. White-fleshed sweet potatoes are mealier, more like a mature King Edward in texture, still sweet but not quite as sugary as the orange ones. Broccoli and sweet potato are an unexpected but well-matched pair. Though the colour given by orange-fleshed potatoes is jazzier, white ones work extremely well.

SERVES 6
1 medium-sized onion, chopped
45 g (1 1/2 oz) butter
350 g (12 1/2 oz) broccoli, trimmed and
  sliced
3 whole garlic cloves, peeled
675 g (1 lb 8 oz) orange- or white-
  fleshed sweet potatoes, peeled and
  cubed
2 fresh marjoram sprigs or 1/2 teaspoon
  dried marjoram
Salt and freshly ground black pepper

**FOR THE PASTRY CROÛTONS
(OPTIONAL)**
Small amount of left-over puff or
  shortcrust pastry
1 egg, beaten
Poppy, caraway or sesame seeds or
  finely grated Gruyère cheese or
  coarse salt

TO SERVE
Buttermilk or soured cream
Fresh chives or parsley, chopped

Sweat the onion in the butter, covered, over a low heat, for 5 minutes. Add the broccoli, garlic, sweet potatoes and marjoram, stir and then leave to sweat for another 10 minutes. Add 1.2 litres (2 pints) of water, salt and pepper and bring to the boil. Simmer gently for 20–30 minutes, until all the vegetables are tender.

Liquidize and sieve the soup, or pass it through the fine blade of a vegetable mill. Add extra water, if it is on the thick side, taste and adjust the seasonings.

If you're making the croûtons, pre-heat the oven to 230°C/450°F/Gas Mark 8. Roll the pastry out thinly. Cut into small diamonds or other shapes, arrange on a baking tray and leave to rest for 15 minutes in the fridge. Brush with beaten egg. Scatter the seeds, Gruyère or coarse salt lightly over the top. Bake for 5–10 minutes, until golden brown.

When you are nearly ready to eat, re-heat the soup and quickly crisp up the croûtons in the oven. Ladle the soup into bowls and add a spoonful of buttermilk or soured cream and a scattering of chopped chives or parsley. Serve the pastry croûtons in a separate bowl, so your guests can help themselves.

Portuguese Potato and Coriander Soup

In Portugal, the coriander leaf is among the most widely used of herbs. It is a particulary popular ingredient in soups and stews. How big is a small bunch of coriander? Well, that depends on how much you like it. My bunch would be a comfortable handful, but that may not help you a great deal. See how you feel, and how much coriander you have.

SERVES 4–6

1 small bunch of coriander
2 onions, chopped
2 cloves garlic, chopped
3 tablespoons olive oil

900 g (2 lb) potatoes, peeled and diced
1.2 litres (2 pints) chicken stock or water
Salt and freshly ground black pepper

Cut the stalks from the coriander and tie them in a bundle with string. Chop the leaves and reserve.

Fry the onions and garlic gently in the oil until tender without browning. Add the diced potatoes and coriander stalks, stir, then cover and sweat over a low heat for 5 minutes. Now add the stock, salt and pepper and bring to the boil. Simmer until the potatoes are very tender. Remove the bundle of coriander stalks. Pass the potatoes through a *mouli-légumes* (vegetable mill). You can process them instead, but only if you've got time to let them rest for a couple of hours afterwards, as processing produces a gluey texture.

Stir in the coriander leaves and re-heat gently without boiling. Serve hot.

VARIATION

Pea and Coriander Soup is a simple spring-time variation on the preceding soup. Replace half of the potatoes with 275 g (10 oz) shelled peas. For preference these should be freshly shelled, but frozen ones (thaw before use) do a perfectly acceptable job. Their natural sweetness is lovely with coriander. Make as the Portuguese Potato and Coriander Soup, adding the peas to the pan with the potatoes if using fresh ones. If you're using frozen peas, wait until the potatoes are almost done before adding them.

Rocket and Potato Soup

This is a peasant soup from Apulia, the heel of Italy. Filling and thick with potatoes and bread, it's the peppery rocket and the final touch of garlic fried in olive oil that hoists it into the realms of truly satisfying food. When made with water it's good, but it's even better with a good stock.

SERVES 4

1 kg (2 lb) potatoes, peeled and diced
Salt
900 ml (1 1/2 pints) water or light chicken stock or water left over from cooking vegetables
75 g (3 oz) rocket leaves, roughly chopped

Cayenne pepper
4 thick slices of stale bread (about 100 g/4 oz)
3 cloves garlic, peeled and sliced
5 tablespoons olive oil

Put the potatoes into a saucepan with the water or stock, and salt. Bring to the boil and simmer for 10 minutes. Add the rocket and continue cooking for 15 minutes. Taste and add more salt if needed and a shake of cayenne pepper. Draw off the heat, add the bread, and leave to stand, covered, for 10 minutes.

While the soup is standing, fry the garlic in the olive oil until golden brown. Pour over the soup, dust lightly with a little more cayenne, and serve, stirring garlicky oil into the soup as you spoon it into bowls.

Bread and Tomato Soup

This marvellous bread and tomato soup from Tuscany is only worth making if you use good-quality country-style bread. It's thick and filling, so serve in small quantities. I like it best hot, but it can be served cold (you may have to add extra stock to thin it down).

SERVES 6–8

350 g (12 oz) stale bread with crusts, thickly sliced
1 large onion, chopped
150 ml (5 fl oz) olive oil
4 cloves garlic, peeled and finely chopped
1 kg (2 lb) ripe tomatoes, skinned and roughly chopped

Salt and freshly ground black pepper
1.5 litres (2 1/2 pints) light chicken or vegetable stock
1 small bunch of fresh basil, shredded

TO SERVE
Extra virgin olive oil
Freshly grated Parmesan (optional)

Pre-heat the oven to 150°C/300°F/Gas Mark 2.

Spread the bread out on a baking sheet and dry in the oven for 10–15 minutes. Break into pieces.

Fry the onion in 2 tablespoons of olive oil until just tender. Add the garlic and raise the heat slightly. As soon as the garlic begins to brown add the tomatoes, salt and pepper. Simmer for 10 minutes. Cool slightly, then pass through the fine plate of a *mouli-légumes* (vegetable mill) or liquidize and sieve.

Bring the stock to the boil and add the puréed tomato mixture, bread, remaining olive oil, basil, salt and pepper. Simmer for 20–30 minutes, stirring occasionally, until the soup is very thick. Taste and adjust seasonings. Serve hot or cold, with a drizzle of olive oil and, if you wish, a scattering of Parmesan.

Winter Squash Soup with Star Anise and Basil and Lime Cream

An excellent autumn or winter soup, with a beautiful, rich orange colour. The sweetness of winter squash carries the scent of star anise, ginger and basil well. For a more everyday supper leave out the finishing swirl of whipped flavoured cream, if you like, but this sharp basil and lime cream melting into the soup is a perfect finish for a smarter occasion. Though it is widely available, I do my best to buy star anise from a specialist spice shop, or from an oriental food store, rather than a supermarket. I like to buy it whole in its proper, charming stars (or at least mostly whole – there are bound to be a few broken pieces in any packet), not squashed into small jars willy-nilly, section by section. Since it keeps for months, and probably years in an airtight jar, I reckon it's worth waiting for the opportunity to buy the best you can get.

SERVES 6–8

1.5 kg (3 lb) piece winter squash
5 garlic cloves
1 large onion, chopped
3 cm (1 1/2 in) piece of fresh ginger, chopped
3 tablespoons sunflower oil
1 bouquet garni (1 bay leaf, 2 sprigs parsley and 1 sprig thyme, tied together with string)
3 star anise

340 g (12 oz) tomatoes, skinned, seeded and roughly chopped
2 litres (3 1/2 pints) vegetable or chicken stock
Salt and freshly ground black pepper

FOR THE BASIL AND LIME CREAM
300 ml (10 fl oz) whipping cream
Juice of 1 lime
Fresh basil leaves

Remove the seeds and rind from the winter squash and chop roughly into cubes. You should end up with about 1 kg (2 lb 4 oz) of cubed squash flesh. Chop two of the garlic cloves but leave the rest whole. Put the chopped and whole garlic into a large pan, with the onion, ginger, oil, squash and bouquet garni. Cover the pan and leave to sweat over a low heat for 10 minutes, stirring once or twice.

Uncover the pan and add the star anise, tomatoes and stock. Season with salt and pepper and bring to the boil. Leave to simmer for 20 minutes, until the squash is just tender.

Pick out and discard the bundle of herbs and the pieces of star anise. Either pass the soup through a *mouli-légumes* (vegetable mill), or liquidize and sieve it. Taste and adjust the seasoning. Re-heat, if necessary, when needed.

Shortly before serving, make the basil and lime cream. Pour the cream into a bowl and add the lime juice. Whisk until it holds its shape loosely. Chop a small handful of basil leaves and fold in. As you ladle the soup into bowls, top with a floating crown of the cream.

Pumpkin Soup in a Pumpkin

I've always liked soup with plenty of bits and bobs in it, and this one has its fair share. Once you've prepared the pumpkin, all there is to do is fill it up and pop it into the oven to get on with the cooking all by itself. Exact cooking time depends on the size of the pumpkin, but if it seems to be almost done and you are not yet ready to eat, turn the oven down low to prevent the shell softening too much.

SERVES 4
1 × 1.75–2.25 kg (4–5 lb) pumpkin
15 g (^{1}/$_2$ oz) butter
Salt and freshly ground black pepper
50 g (2 oz) long-grained rice
2 shallots, finely chopped
2 cloves garlic, peeled and finely chopped
2 sprigs of fresh thyme
1 sprig of fresh rosemary
1 tablespoon finely chopped fresh parsley
600–900 ml (1–1^1/$_2$ pints) milk
25g (1 oz) freshly grated Parmesan cheese
Crisp croûtons to serve

Pre-heat the oven to 180°C/350°F/Gas Mark 4

Using a sharp knife, cut a lid off the pumpkin. Scrape out the seeds and threads inside and discard. Rub the butter around the inside of the pumpkin and season generously with salt and pepper. Place rice, shallots, and garlic in the pumpkin. Add the thyme, rosemary, and parsley. Bring the milk to the boil, and pour enough into the pumpkin to almost fill it. Cover with its lid, then wrap foil loosely around it, taking care not to spill the contents. Stand it in a roasting tin and bake for 1^3/$_4$–2^1/$_2$ hours until the inside is tender.

If you can find them, fish out the herb twigs, then stir the Parmesan into the soup, taste and adjust the seasoning. As you serve the soup, scrape out some of the softened pumpkin with each spoonful. Pass croûtons around separately.

Red Lentil and Bulgur Soup

When I visited Nesrin Ilter's flat in Istanbul, for my Travels à la Carte *television series, I sat down for a quick coffee and we started talking food – a dangerous subject. Within minutes I had been given tastes of this and that, among them this lentil and bulgur soup, made slightly out of the ordinary by the last-minute addition of lemon juice. Nesrin's version was also enriched with a little cream, but when I made it at home, I decided that I preferred the soup without.*

Bulgur is cracked wheat, sold by larger supermarkets here, but failing that by most wholefood shops. It may also be labelled 'burgul'.

SERVES 4–6
1 large onion, finely chopped
40 g (1 1/2 oz) butter
175 g (6 oz) red lentils
100 g (4 oz) bulgur (cracked wheat)
1.5 litres (2 1/2 pints) chicken, meat or
    vegetable stock
2 tablespoons tomato purée
Generous pinch of ground chilli
1/2 teaspoon dried mint
1/2 teaspoon ground cumin
Salt and freshly ground black pepper
3–4 tablespoons lemon juice

Cook the onion in the butter in a large pan until tender and golden. Add all the remaining ingredients except the lemon juice. Bring to the boil, then simmer gently, covered, until the lentils have dissolved to a mush – around 30 minutes, though this varies from one batch of lentils to another. Stir occasionally to prevent catching. Stir in the lemon juice – the soup should have a slightly sour flavour, but it shouldn't be overwhelming. Adjust the seasoning and serve.

Swiss Barley Soup

This is a delicious recipe I picked up whilst visiting Switzerland. It's a meal-in-a-bowl sort of soup, full of bits and pieces, and very welcome when the weather is bad.

SERVES 6–8 AS A MAIN COURSE
2 carrots, diced
1/2 celeriac root, diced
1 onion, chopped
2 leeks, sliced
2 tablespoons lard
2 tablespoons flour
175 g (6 oz) pearl barley
2 celery leaves, chopped
275 g (10 oz) smoked speck or smoked
    streaky bacon, thickly sliced and
    cut into 1 cm (1/2 in) strips
100 g (4 oz) air-dried beef or ham
    (Parma ham can be used), thickly
    sliced and cut into 1 cm (1/2 in)
    strips
175 g (6 oz) pork rind, cut into wide
    strips
1 bay leaf
2 sprigs of fresh parsley
Salt and freshly ground black pepper
2 large potatoes, diced
1/4 cabbage, finely shredded

In a covered pan, sweat the carrots, celeriac, onion and leeks in the lard over a low heat for 10 minutes. Sprinkle over the flour and stir to mix. Add all the remaining ingredients except the potatoes and cabbage. Pour in 2 litres (3¹/₂ pints) water, bring to the boil and simmer gently for about 1¹/₂–2 hours, until the barley and meats are very tender. Add salt and pepper to taste, then add the cabbage and potatoes and simmer for a further 15–20 minutes, until the potatoes are cooked. Serve with lots of good bread.

Minestra di Riso e Castagne

This rice and chestnut soup comes from the mountains of northern Italy and has long been a favourite of mine. This is a quick version, made with pre-cooked, vacuum-packed chestnuts that dispense with the tedium of peeling chestnuts (and the pain of catching a splinter of chestnut husk under a fingernail), without sacrificing too much of the flavour. If you prefer to use fresh chestnuts (and you will gain a little in flavour), peel about 450 g (1 lb) and cook for an extra half an hour in the stock.

The starchiness of risotto rice makes it a marvellous addition to soups, imparting a quiet and digestible creaminess that doesn't interfere with other ingredients.

SERVES 6
340 g (12 oz) vacuum-packed chestnuts, halved or quartered roughly
1 fresh thyme sprig
1 fresh rosemary sprig
1 bay leaf
1.5 litres (2¹/₂ pints) chicken or vegetable stock
Salt and freshly ground black pepper
100 g (3¹/₂ oz) risotto rice
30 g (1 oz) butter
300 ml (10 fl oz) creamy milk

Put the chestnuts in a pan with the herbs tied together with a length of string. Add the stock, salt and pepper and bring to the boil. Leave to simmer gently, uncovered, for 40 minutes.

Now add the rice and continue simmering for another 10 minutes. Next, add the butter and milk and simmer away until the rice is just cooked but still *al dente* (another 10 minutes or so). Taste and adjust the seasoning and serve.

Prawn, Chicken, Lemon Grass and Coconut Soup

Coriander is now as easy to buy as basil and even lemon grass has made its way into supermarkets. For all that, lemon grass still seems a magical substance to me, with its hidden fragrance of lemon oil mixed with a hint of ginger and mint.

The fullest flavour lies in the lower, fatter 10 cm (4 in) or so of the stem and this is what I use for most recipes. First of all, you will need to peel away one or two of the toughest outer layers. For soups and stews, cut in half and then bash and bruise it flat, with either a wooden rolling pin or the flat of a knife or cleaver. This method releases the juices but means that the chunks of lemon grass can easily be located (think of them rather like bay leaves) and removed when their job is done.

Try it for yourself in this marvellously aromatic soup which can be made in a matter of minutes if you use canned coconut milk and have chicken stock in the freezer. It is filling enough to constitute lunch in itself but could also form the first course of a more substantial meal.

SERVES 4

Two 400 ml (14 fl oz) cans of coconut milk

300 ml (10 fl oz) chicken stock

350 g (12 oz) boneless, skinless chicken, cut into thin slivers

3 lemon grass stems, trimmed and heavily bruised

1.5 cm ($^1/_2$ in) piece of galangal or fresh ginger, cut into thin matchsticks

225 g (8 oz) shelled prawns

1 fresh red chilli, seeded and thinly sliced

5 spring onions, sliced

Juice of 1–2 limes

3 tablespoons roughly chopped fresh coriander

3 tablespoons Thai fish sauce

Put the coconut milk and stock into a pan and bring to the boil. Add the chicken, lemon grass and galangal or ginger and reduce the heat to a gentle simmer. Cook for 10 minutes, uncovered.

Add the prawns and cook for a further 2 minutes. Finally, add all the remaining ingredients. Taste and add more lime juice, if needed, then serve.

Henningsvaer Fish Soup

This is a scandalously rich and delicious fish soup. I ate it at Otto Åsheim's restaurant, Fiskekrogen, in Henningsvaer, Norway, where inevitably fish is what it's all about, then just had to go back a few days later for more. I was told that Otto would never give me the recipe, apparently a closely guarded secret, but when it came down to it, he didn't bat an eyelid. It's really a version of the more southerly Bergen fish soup, and the real secret is the addition of vinegar and sugar, which cleverly cuts through the creaminess.

SERVES 6–8

FOR THE FISH STOCK
450 g (1 lb) bones and skin from white
    fish
1 carrot, sliced
1 large leek, quartered
1 stick celery, sliced
1 glass dry white wine
1 bay leaf
2 sprigs of fresh parsley
4 black peppercorns

FOR THE SOUP
350 g (12 oz) cod fillet
50 g (2 oz) butter

1 onion, finely chopped
1 large carrot, finely chopped
1 large leek (both white and green
    parts), finely chopped
2 teaspoons caster sugar
2 tablespoons white wine vinegar
Salt and freshly ground black pepper
300 ml (10 fl oz) crème fraîche, or
    soured cream mixed with double
    cream

TO SERVE
Fresh parsley, chopped

First make the stock. Put all the ingredients in a large pan and add 1.75 litres (3 pints) of water. Bring to the boil and simmer for 20 minutes. Cool and strain.

Bring the stock to the boil. Add the cod, bring gently back to the boil and then draw off the heat. When tepid, lift out the cod and flake, discarding the skin and any stray bones. Reserve the flesh and stock.

Melt the butter in a large pan and add the vegetables. Stir to coat nicely in fat, then cover the pan, reduce the heat to very low and leave to sweat for 20 minutes, stirring once or twice. Add the stock, sugar, vinegar, salt and pepper and bring to the boil. Simmer for 10 minutes. Stir in the crème fraîche (or soured cream mixture) and the flaked fish. Taste and adjust the seasoning, then re-heat gently without boiling. Serve immediately, sprinkled with a little chopped parsley.

Cock-a-Leekie

One of Scotland's finest culinary creations and more than a match for the haggis, even if it does sound the most unlikely collection of ingredients. Cock-a-Leekie requires long simmering but very little effort. It actually tastes much better if re-heated the day after it is made though, inevitably, you lose some of the freshness of the sliced leeks.

Prunes, like fresh plums, are very good with all kinds of meat, and are an essential ingredient here. You must use whole prunes, with stones in. Stoned prunes will go mushy at best and may well collapse.

SERVES 8
1 kg (2 lb 4 oz) piece of shin of beef
2 bay leaves
2 fresh thyme sprigs
4 fresh parsley sprigs
1 kg (2 lb 4 oz) leeks

1 large free-range chicken
675 g (1 lb 8 oz) prunes with stones in
Salt and freshly ground black pepper

TO GARNISH
Fresh parsley, chopped

Put the shin of beef into a large pan and add enough water to cover it generously (at least 3.5 litres/6 pints and probably more, depending on the shape of your pan). Tie the herbs together with a piece of string and drop those in, too. Trim and clean half the leeks, leaving them whole. Tie them together with a piece of string and tuck them into the pot alongside the beef. Bring up to the boil, skim off any scum, season with salt and pepper and then leave to simmer for 2 hours. If the water level drops, exposing the beef and leeks too much, top up with hot water. Skim again, if necessary.

Now add the chicken and continue simmering for another hour or so, until the chicken and beef are very tender. Lift out and discard the bundles of herbs and leeks.

While the meats are cooking, trim and clean the remaining leeks and slice them into rings about 1.5 cm (1/2 in) thick. Add these and the prunes to the broth, once you have discarded the tired bundle of whole leeks. Leave to simmer for another 30 minutes.

Some 5 minutes or so before the soup has finished simmering, lift out the chicken and beef and cut the meat into small pieces, discarding the bones and carcass. Return to the pan of simmering soup (or to a warmed tureen, if you are dishing this up smartly). To serve, ladle the soup into big soup plates, making sure everyone gets a good share of meats, prunes and leeks. Scatter with a little chopped parsley and serve.

Duck Noodle Soup

A big bowl of lightly spiced duck noodle soup, packed with little bits and bobs, makes a most soothing and satisfying meal, squeezing the last of the goodness out of a duck.

SERVES 4
1.2 litres (2 pints) of well-flavoured duck or chicken stock
1¹/₂ tablespoons soy sauce
1¹/₂ tablespoons rice wine or dry sherry
1 tablespoon rice vinegar or cider vinegar
1¹/₂ tablespoons demerara sugar
1 star anise
1 clove
5 cm (2 in) cinnamon stick
1 cm (¹/₂ in) piece fresh root ginger, cut into matchsticks
1 carrot, cut into fine matchsticks
1 red chilli, seeded and cut into rings
4 spring onions, shredded
1 layer Chinese egg thread noodles
Scraps of duck from the carcass used for stock
100 g (4 oz) bean curd, cubed

Skim or blot as much fat as you can from the surface of the stock, then put it into a pan with the soy sauce, rice wine or dry sherry, vinegar, sugar, star anise, clove, cinnamon and ginger. Bring gently to the boil. Add the carrot and simmer for 2 minutes.

Now add the chilli, spring onions and noodles. Simmer for 2 minutes or so until the noodles are done. Stir in the scraps of duck and the bean curd. Give it one more minute to heat through, then taste and adjust the seasonings. Serve in deep bowls.

Gazpacho

Gazpacho, the 'liquid salad', is a soup I never tire of. Pounding it by hand is a long tedious job but, with a processor, preparing it is just a matter of minutes. Remember that the proportions of vegetables and other ingredients that I give below are there merely to serve as a starting point. Tomatoes, peppers, garlic and all will vary in flavour from one batch to another, so it's important to keep tasting and to adjust the seasonings accordingly. To intensify both the tomato flavour and colour of the soup you can replace some of the water with tomato juice, or add a tablespoon or two of tomato purée.

SERVES 6

750 g (1 lb 8 oz) ripe, richly flavoured tomatoes, skinned, seeded and roughly chopped

1 medium-sized cucumber, peeled and roughly chopped

1 large green pepper, seeded and roughly chopped

1/2 red onion, chopped

2–2 1/2 tablespoons red wine vinegar

5 tablespoons olive oil

100 g (4 oz) fresh white breadcrumbs

2 cloves garlic, roughly chopped (optional)

1/2–1 teaspoon sugar

Salt and freshly ground black pepper

FOR THE GARNISH

Diced, seeded tomato

Diced cucumber

Diced red onion

Diced green pepper

Diced *jamón serrano*

Put all the soup ingredients in a processor with a small slurp of iced water. Process to a fairly smooth sludge (you may have to do this in 2 batches if your processor bowl is small). Gradually stir in enough water to give a soupy consistency: 300–450 ml (10–15 fl oz) should do it. Taste and adjust the seasoning, adding a little more salt, vinegar or sugar as necessary to highlight the flavours.

Chill, and adjust the seasoning again just before serving. Place all the garnishes in small bowls and pass around for people to help themselves.

Chilled Yoghurt and Cucumber Soup

This soup demands precious little effort and no cooking whatsoever. What more could you ask for on a hot summer's day? Present it well chilled with a flourish of fresh mint and you have a first course fit for kings.

SERVES 6
1 cucumber
600 ml (1 pint) Greek-style yoghurt
1–2 cloves garlic, peeled and crushed
Finely grated zest of 1 lemon

2 tablespoons chopped fresh mint
Salt and freshly ground black pepper
Lemon juice
6 sprigs of fresh mint to garnish

Grate the cucumber, peel and all. Beat the yoghurt with 150 ml (5 fl oz) of water. Stir in the cucumber, garlic (I like this soup good and garlicky, so prefer two cloves, but that's a matter of taste), lemon zest, chopped mint, salt and pepper. Taste and add a squeeze or two of lemon juice if you think it could do with sharpening up. Chill for at least 1 hour, then stir and adjust the seasonings. Spoon into bowls and garnish with sprigs of mint before serving.

Starters and Light Meals

VEGETABLES

Baba Ganoush

Aubergines, along with peppers, tomatoes and courgettes, make up the essential quartet of Mediterranean vegetables that have become so beloved of British cooks in recent times. Because the aubergine is uniquely adaptable, even promiscuous. It has spawned recipes by the dozen. No, probably by the hundred. Every country that has fallen prey to its charms has developed an amazing repertoire of aubergine dishes. It is a truly cosmopolitan character.

Now for the big question ... do they really need salting? Yes and no is about the best answer I can come up with. These days, it is rare to come across an aubergine that is truly bitter, so you don't have to salt them before use, if you are short of time. However, I do think that salting aubergines improves the flavour, by drawing out the tinny juices that can otherwise linger, slightly uncomfortably, in the mouth. Salted aubergines will also absorb less oil when fried, which is an undoubted plus.

The salting process is simple. Just slice or dice the aubergine, spread the pieces out on baking trays or in a colander, whichever is more appropriate, and sprinkle lightly with salt. Leave for at least half an hour, longer if possible, and then wipe clean of all the brown juice (or rinse under the tap). If aubergines are to be cooked whole and then mashed or cut up, drain the cooked aubergine flesh thoroughly in a colander, pressing out as much liquid as possible. It will look a bit mangled but in most recipes this won't matter at all.

There's many a form of aubergine purée to be found around the Mediterranean but this Middle Eastern one is, perhaps, the king of them all. Tahina (sesame seed paste) and cumin are the distinguishing factors. Serve it with warm pitta bread, or other good bread, and/or batons of raw vegetables.

SERVES 6

2 medium-sized aubergines, weighing about 450 g (1 lb) in total
1–2 garlic cloves, roughly chopped
4 tablespoons tahina
Juice of 1 lemon
1–1¹/₂ teaspoons ground cumin
6 tablespoons olive oil
10 fresh mint leaves (optional)
Salt and cayenne pepper

Grill the aubergines close to the heat, turning them fairly frequently, until the skin is charred all over and they feel squishy and soft. Drop into a plastic bag, knot loosely and leave until cool enough to handle. Quarter lengthways, strip off the skin and leave the pulp to drain in a colander for 15 minutes or so. Press to squeeze out the last of the juice.

Process the aubergine flesh with the garlic, tahina, lemon juice, cumin and salt. Trickle in 5 tablespoons of oil. Taste and adjust the seasonings, adding more cumin, lemon or salt as the will takes you (the purée shouldn't actually taste sharp but there should be enough lemon juice to prevent it seeming insipid). Shred all but two of the mint leaves and stir the shreds into the mixture. Pile into a bowl. Just before serving, drizzle over the last tablespoon of olive oil, dust lightly with cayenne and decorate with the last two mint leaves. Serve at room temperature.

Caponata

I can think of no other cold aubergine dish that surpasses sweet and sour caponata. *I've been making it for years, but was rather upset to learn that I'd been getting it wrong! In Sicily they use green olives in* caponata, *not black as I always do. So, if you want to do it properly, use green ones – though, to be honest, I'm going to continue in my same mistaken way. Serve* caponata *as part of an antipasto, or as a cross between a relish and a side-dish.*

SERVES 4–6

1 large aubergine, diced
6 tablespoons olive oil
6 sticks celery, chopped
1 onion, chopped
400 g (14 oz) can chopped tomatoes or
  450 g (1 lb) fresh tomatoes, skinned
  and chopped

2 tablespoons caster sugar
4 tablespoons red wine vinegar
1 teaspoon grated nutmeg
Salt and freshly ground black pepper
1 heaped teaspoon capers
12 green or black olives, pitted and
  roughly chopped
2 tablespoons chopped fresh parsley

Spread out the aubergine dice in a colander, sprinkle with salt and set aside for 1/2–1 hour. Press gently to extract as much water as possible. Dry on kitchen paper or a clean tea-towel.

Heat 4 tablespoons of the olive oil in a heavy-based frying-pan. Sauté the celery until browned. Scoop out and set aside. Fry the aubergine in the same oil until browned and tender, adding a little extra oil if necessary. Scoop out and leave to cool.

Add the remaining oil to the pan and sauté the onion until golden. Add the tomatoes and simmer for 15 minutes until thick. Next add the sugar, vinegar and nutmeg and cook for a further 10 minutes, until you have a rich sweet-and-sour sauce. Add a little salt and plenty of pepper. Stir in the capers, olives, parsley, aubergine and celery. Taste and adjust the seasoning – the flavours will soften as the *caponata* cools. Serve in a dish when cool.

Grilled Aubergine Sandwich with Mascarpone and Sun-Dried Tomatoes

We filmed the titles for the television series Taste of the Times *one chilly November day, popping in and out of shops and calling at food stalls the length of London's Portobello Road and the adjoining Golborne Road (a Mecca for anyone who likes Moroccan or Portuguese food). At lunchtime, we dived into the Portobello Café for a quick lunch. The grilled aubergine sandwich with mascarpone and sun-dried tomatoes, sluiced down by a big mug of very British tea, was exactly what I needed to get me through the rest of the day.*

SERVES 1

2 slices of aubergine, cut about 2 cm
   (^{3}/4 in) thick, from stalk to stem end
Olive oil
2 generous tablespoons mascarpone
^{1}/3–^{1}/2 ciabatta loaf, split in half and
   warmed through in the oven, or
   2 large slices of sturdy *pain de
   campagne* or sour-dough bread,
   lightly toasted

Salt and lots of freshly ground black
   pepper
4 halves of sun-dried tomatoes, cut
   into strips

If you have time, salt the slices of aubergine lightly and leave for 30–60 minutes, to degorge (draw out some of the juices to improve the flavour). Wipe dry, and then brush with olive oil and grill under a thoroughly pre-heated grill, fairly close to the heat, until browned on both sides and tender through and through. Leave to cool until tepid. Spread the mascarpone on the cut sides of the ciabatta, or on each slice of bread. Season with salt and pepper. Sandwich the aubergine and the sun-dried tomatoes between the pieces of bread. Eat quickly, while still warm.

Hummus bi Tahina

It is worth making your own hummus? Now if you were to ask about taramasalata instead, the answer is an unhesitant, loud 'yes'. When it comes to hummus, I think that these days I have to admit to a rather quieter 'just about'. Commercial hummus is so good, for the most part, that there is no great impetus to cook your own, but if you do have the time, you will end up with something even more delectable and more-ish than the best bought hummus.

SERVES 6–8
150 g (5 oz) chickpeas, soaked
   overnight
2 cloves garlic, roughly chopped
Juice of 2 lemons
4 tablespoons light tahina paste
A pinch of salt

TO SERVE
A little olive oil
Paprika or cayenne pepper
Ground cumin

Drain the chickpeas and put into a pan with enough water to cover by about 7.5 cm (3 in). Bring to the boil and simmer gently until they are very tender, adding extra hot water if the level drops too low. Drain, reserving a little of the cooking water.

Put the chickpeas into the processor with 2 tablespoons of their cooking water, the garlic, lemon juice, tahina and salt. Process to a smooth cream, adding a little more of the cooking water if necessary. Don't leave it too heavy and claggy like damp clay – all too often the problem with home-made hummus. Taste and add more lemon juice or salt as needed.

Spoon into a bowl. Shortly before serving, drizzle a little olive oil over the top and dust lightly with a little paprika or cayenne and ground cumin. Serve with warm pitta bread or *crudités*, spoon over salads or serve with grilled fish, meat or vegetables. Thin down the hummus a little, if necessary, and use as a particularly wonderful dressing-cum-sauce.

Falafel

There's a street in Tel Aviv which is home to a clutch of falafel stalls, all vying to take the falafel makers' crown, all with their own courtiers and admirers. Were the falafel that I tasted here the best ever? I'm inclined to think so, though it may have been partly the fun of the occasion, and the enthusiasm of the hordes of falafel snackers around me that added an extra dose of deliciousness.

Falafel are deep-fried balls of ground chickpeas flavoured with garlic and parsley. Cheap snack food in the Middle East, they're now becoming rather fashion-able in this country. Unfortunately, they are all too often rather poorly made – too large and stodgy, or cooked far too early and re-heated in the microwave, which makes them soggy and greasy. They should be crisp on the outside, soft on the inside. Piled hot from frying into a warm pitta bread, with simple fresh salad and oodles of tahina dressing to smooth the whole lot together, they are quite sensational.

If you want a rather more defined presentation, dispense with the pitta bread (or serve this on the side), and arrange the falafel on a bed of salad, drizzling the tahina dressing over the top. Perch a sprig or two of coriander on top, and tuck a wedge of lemon in, too.

If you must cook the falafel themselves in advance, re-heat them in hot oil to restore the crisp exterior.

SERVES 4–8 DEPENDING ON HUNGER AND GREED

FOR THE FALAFEL

220 g (8 oz) chickpeas, soaked for 24
    hours in cold water
1 tablespoon cumin seeds
2 teaspoons coriander seeds
1 small onion, chopped
2 cloves garlic, chopped
3 heaped tablespoons chopped fresh
    coriander
1 tablespoon flour
1/4 teaspoon baking powder
Salt and freshly ground black pepper
Sunflower oil for deep frying

FOR THE TAHINA DRESSING

180 g (6 oz) light tahina paste
3 cloves garlic, crushed
Juice of 1 1/2–2 lemons

TO SERVE

8 pitta bread
4 tomatoes, seeded and roughly
    chopped
1/2 cucumber, peeled and diced
6 cos or Webb's or other firm lettuce
    leaves, shredded
Salt and freshly ground black pepper

To make the falafel, begin by draining the chickpeas and tipping them into the bowl of a processor. Dry-fry the cumin and coriander seeds in a small, heavy frying-pan over a high heat until they turn a little darker and their scent wafts through the kitchen. Cool and grind to a fine powder. Process together until smooth. To test for seasoning, break off a small knob of the mixture and shallow fry in a little oil. Taste and add more spices or salt if needed. Wet your hands and roll the remaining mixture into small balls – no bigger than a walnut, and even smaller for a higher ratio of crisp exterior to soft interior. Set aside until you are ready to fry them.

To make the tahina dressing, put the tahina into a bowl with the crushed garlic and lemon juice. Start to mix, gradually beating in enough water to make a creamy mixture with the consistency of double cream (90–150 ml or 3–5 fl oz should be about right). Don't worry that the tahina seizes up like cement at first. Keep adding water and beating and it will smooth out. Season with salt, and add a little more lemon juice if needed. Cover and set aside until required.

Put the pitta in a low oven or under the grill to warm through and place the tomatoes, cucumber and lettuce in individual bowls on the table so that everyone can help themselves. Heat up a panful of sunflower oil (I actually use my wok for most deep frying) over a moderate heat, until a small cube of bread dropped into the oil sizzles immediately, but doesn't start to brown straight away. Fry the falafel a few at a time, taking care not to overcrowd the pan. When they are richly browned (they should take about 8 minutes – any quicker and the interior won't be properly cooked), drain briefly on kitchen paper. Season with a little salt and take to the table for everyone to start making up their pittas, while you cook the remaining falafel.

The rough order to fill pitta breads is this: slit open the pitta bread along one of the long curved sides, first put a little of the diced tomato in and maybe a shred or three of lettuce. Now drop in four or five falafel, then drizzle over some tahina. Then add some more tomato and cucumber and stuff in more lettuce and finish with more tahina dressing if you can!

Asparagus with Hollandaise Sauce

There's no finer way to celebrate the arrival of the asparagus season than by tucking into a plate of hot, steamed asparagus with a rich Hollandaise sauce. With tender asparagus I usually steam the whole stem and tip in a normal steamer, but the accepted wisdom is that asparagus should be part-boiled, part-steamed, standing upright, with the tougher parts of the stems immersed in water, while the tender tips cook in the heat of the steam. If you don't have a proper asparagus steamer, use the tallest pan you have, tie the asparagus in a bundle with string and secure it in an upright position with scrumpled balls of foil tucked around the base to keep it steady or, better still, with halved new potatoes which will absorb the asparagus flavour as they cook.

Pour in enough water to come about 4–5 cm (1$\frac{1}{2}$–2 in) up the stems of the asparagus, bring to the boil, then cover the pan with a dome of foil to trap the steam. Reduce the heat slightly and simmer until the bases are tender. Lift out carefully and drain. If you are serving asparagus cold, run under the cold tap as soon as the spears are tender to halt cooking, and then drain thoroughly.

The classic method for making Hollandaise is not that difficult, but it can occasionally go wrong. I always play safe and make my Hollandaise in the food processor while the asparagus is cooking.

SERVES 6

1 kg (2 lb) asparagus

FOR THE HOLLANDAISE SAUCE
4 egg yolks

2 tablespoons lemon juice
225 g (8 oz) unsalted butter, diced
Salt and freshly ground black pepper

Trim and steam the asparagus. While it is cooking, make the Hollandaise.

Put the egg yolks into the bowl of a food processor or liquidizer with a pinch of salt and whizz for a few seconds. Heat the lemon juice and 1 tablespoon of water in a small saucepan until just boiling. At the same time, put the butter into another saucepan and heat gently until foaming.

Turn on the processor and trickle in the hot lemon and water, keeping the machine whirring until it is all incorporated. Turn off. As soon as the butter is foaming, turn the processor on again and start adding the butter drop by drop. Once about a third of the butter is incorporated, accelerate the adding of the butter to a slow but continuous trickle. After two thirds of the butter has been incorporated you can increase the flow slightly more. Stop short of the white sediment lurking at the bottom of the pan. Taste and adjust the seasoning, adding a little more lemon juice if needed. Serve immediately with the asparagus, or keep warm in a bowl over a pan of barely simmering water until required.

Asparagus and New Potatoes with Parmesan

Asparagus and new potatoes are perfect bedfellows, each benefiting from the other's presence. In this dish both can be cooked in advance, leaving only the final re-heating and browning to be done just before serving.

SERVES 4 AS A FIRST COURSE OR SIDE DISH
225 g (8 oz) asparagus
225 g (8 oz) new potatoes
3 tablespoons olive oil

2 cloves garlic, peeled and chopped
$^{1}/_{2}$–$^{3}/_{4}$ teaspoon chilli flakes
25 g (1 oz) Parmesan, cut into paper-thin slivers

Trim the asparagus, discarding the woody ends. Cut into 2.5 cm (1 in) lengths, keeping tips and stalks separate. Bring a pan of lightly salted water to the boil. Add the stems and simmer for 5 minutes. Now add the tips and simmer for a further 3–4 minutes until tender. Drain and rinse under the cold tap. Drain and dry on kitchen paper.

Halve the potatoes or quarter if large. Steam or boil in the asparagus water, until just tender, topping up with extra water if necessary. Drain well and dry.

Turn on the grill so that it has time to heat up. Heat the oil in a wide frying-pan and add the garlic and chilli. Cook gently for 2–3 minutes. Raise the heat slightly and add the asparagus and potatoes. Toss in the oil for a few minutes to heat through. Tip into a shallow heatproof dish, scatter over the Parmesan and whisk under the grill. Grill until lightly patched with brown and serve.

Asparagus, Poached Egg and Pine Nut Salad

A fresh-tasting spring salad to serve as a first course or a light lunch. Pine nuts are one of the nicest nuts to add to a salad and dry-frying them brings out their distinctive flavour.

SERVES 2
250 g (9 oz) medium-sized asparagus spears
Salt
45 g (1$^{1}/_{2}$ oz) pine nuts
30 g (1 oz) Parmesan
2 eggs
A handful of rocket leaves

2 slices of air-dried ham, e.g. Parma, *jamón serrano* or Cumbrian

FOR THE DRESSING
2–3 tablespoons olive oil
$^{1}/_{2}$ tablespoon balsamic or sherry vinegar
Salt and freshly ground black pepper

Trim off the tough, woody ends of the asparagus and, if necessary, peel the lower parts. Cut off the top 2.5 cm (1 in) of the tips. Cut the rest into 2.5 cm (1 in) lengths. Drop these into a pan of salted, boiling water, simmer for 2 minutes and then add the tips. Cook for a further 2–3 minutes. Drain, run under the cold tap and drain again thoroughly.

Dry-fry the pine nuts in a heavy frying-pan over a medium heat, until browned. Tip into a bowl before they burn.

For the dressing, whisk the oil into the vinegar and season with salt and pepper. Meanwhile use a vegetable peeler to make thin shavings or flakes of Parmesan.

Shortly before serving, poach the eggs. Toss the rocket and asparagus in just enough of the dressing to coat them evenly. Arrange on two plates. Drape a slice of air-dried ham over each one, scatter with pine nuts, nestle a poached egg on top and, finally, strew with Parmesan. Serve immediately.

Grilled Spring Onions and Asparagus with Lime and Coarse Sea Salt

The classic method is not the only way of cooking asparagus. It can be roasted in the oven or grilled if it is not too thick. Be bold – you'll be surprised at the results. Grilling spring onions (or very thin baby leeks) and asparagus gives them a smoky flavour that is enhanced by the spicy sharpness of lime. Serve a mixture of the two, or make it even simpler by using just asparagus or just spring onions. The asparagus should be fairly thin, no more than 1 cm (1/2 in) in diameter.

PER PERSON
4 fat spring onions, trimmed
4 asparagus spears, trimmed

Olive oil or sunflower oil
Wedges of lime
Coarse sea salt

Brush the spring onions and asparagus with the oil and grill, turning until patched with brown. Serve immediately with lime and sea salt.

Pajon

One of the many Korean dishes I enjoy is pajon, a thick 'pancake' of spring onions and other vegetables. It's not a pancake in the European sense, as it is solidly chunky and packed full of bits and pieces. I found this recipe in Mark and Kim Millon's book, The Flavours of Korea (André Deutsch). Once you've chopped all the vegetables and made the dipping sauce, the cooking is speedy. Serve the pancake as a snack, or in small squares with drinks, passing around the sauce for frequent dunkings.

SERVES 4–6 (MAKES 3 PANCAKES)

FOR THE BATTER
2 eggs, beaten
225 g (8 oz) flour
1 tablespoon sunflower or vegetable oil
200 ml (7 fl oz) water

FOR THE DIPPING SAUCE
3 tablespoons rice or cider vinegar
225 ml (7$^{1}/_{2}$ fl oz) soy sauce
1 heaped teaspoon toasted sesame seeds
1 cm ($^{1}/_{2}$ in) piece fresh ginger, peeled, bruised and finely chopped

1 teaspoon ground chilli or chilli flakes
1 teaspoon sugar

FOR THE FILLING
Oil for frying
10 large spring onions or 20 small ones, split lengthways and cut into 10 cm (4 in) pieces
1 courgette, cut into 10 cm (4 in) matchsticks
1 large carrot, peeled and cut into 10 cm (4 in) matchsticks
100 g (4 oz) peeled cooked prawns
Handful of fresh chives, chopped
4 eggs, beaten

First make the batter: mix the eggs with the flour, oil and enough water to make a medium-thick batter. Let it rest for 15–20 minutes while you prepare the filling ingredients and the dipping sauce.

To make the sauce mix all the ingredients.

To make the pancakes coat a large frying-pan with oil and heat. Ladle in a third of the batter. Lay about a third of the spring onions, courgette, carrot, prawns and chives on the pancakes. Cook for about 5–7 minutes over a medium-hot heat. As the pancake cooks, spoon beaten egg over the filling, to fill in the gaps between the vegetables. When the egg has set and the pancake is well-browned underneath, flip it over. Don't worry if it breaks or tears as it will be torn into pieces before eating. Cook for a further 5–7 minutes, pressing down with a spatula to ensure that the batter cooks through.

Remove from the frying-pan, drain on kitchen paper and either serve whole or cut into small squares. Use the remaining ingredients to make another 2 pancakes. Serve with dipping sauce.

Globe Artichokes Filled with Lemon Scrambled Eggs

Globe artichoke cups filled with lemony scrambled eggs make an elegant and substantial first course. Convenient too, as both artichokes and eggs can be prepared several hours in advance.

SERVES 4
4 globe artichokes
Juice of 1/2 lemon

FOR THE EGGS
6 eggs
2 tablespoons lemon juice

Finely grated zest of 1/2 lemon
Salt and freshly ground black pepper
15 g (1/2 oz) butter
2 tablespoons double cream
1 tablespoon chopped fresh dill

To make the artichoke cups slice off the top inch or so of the leaves with a sharp knife. Snap off the stems of the artichokes close to the base. Rub the cut with lemon juice. Boil the artichokes in water acidulated with the juice of 1/2 lemon for 30–50 minutes depending on size. Or wrap individually in clingfilm, and microwave two at a time on full power for 9–12 minutes, again depending on the size of the artichoke and power of the oven.

When cool enough to handle, gently ease open the leaves, exposing the tight, purplish cone of thin leaves in the centre. Twist this out to expose the hairy choke, which can then be scraped away with a teaspoon, leaving a well to be filled with the scrambled eggs.

Beat the eggs in a bowl with the lemon juice and zest, salt and pepper. Set the bowl over a pan of simmering water and add the butter and cream. Stir until the eggs are creamy (but not setting into hard lumps). Draw off the heat and stir in the dill. Cool slightly, then spoon into the artichoke cups. Serve cold.

Normally when you eat a globe artichoke you work from the outside inwards, pull leaves off one at a time, dip the base into the sauce (melted butter, vinaigrette or Sauce Rougette, see p. 360) and nibble off the nugget of soft artichoke at the base. Artichoke cups require a slightly different technique. The filling is all there, ready and waiting inside the artichoke, but in order to prevent it seeping out at quite the wrong moment, you must start with the upper leaves, gradually working your way outwards. Last of all eat the best bit, the sweet nutty base, spearing chunks of it and mopping up the remaining egg.

Chicory with Roquefort

Chicory with a blue cheese dressing is a common hors d'oeuvre in the small restaurants of Barcelona. There they may use French Roquefort, or a Spanish blue cheese called Cabrales which has a similar flavour. Wash the heads of chicory or chicons briefly and dry, then trim the base. Some cooks whittle a small cone out of the base which is supposed to reduce the bitterness, but I've never found that it makes any noticeable difference.

SERVES 4–6
3 heads of chicory (chicons)

FOR THE DRESSING
40 g (1¹/₂ oz) Roquefort or Cabrales
5 tablespoons mayonnaise

2–3 tablespoons milk
Squeeze of lemon
2 tablespoons chopped fresh parsley
Cayenne pepper

Either quarter the heads of chicory lengthwise, or separate into individual leaves. Arrange on a serving plate, and cover.

Mash the cheese to a paste, and then beat in the mayonnaise, followed by the milk. Stir in the lemon juice, parsley and cayenne pepper. Taste and adjust the seasonings, adding more lemon juice or cayenne if you think it needs it. Spoon over the quartered chicory. If you've separated out the leaves, place a spoonful of dressing in the curve of each leaf at the widest end. Serve.

Chicory with Ham

As far as I'm concerned, this is the way to cook chicory. I was brought up on endive au jambon, and can eat it until the cows come home. Choose the best cooked ham, simmer the sauce until thick, and bake the gratin until browned and bubbling, and you will have before you one of the true French classics.

Notice, too, the curious linguistic twist: what we call chicory in English is 'endive' in French, while our endive is … yes, that's right, 'chicorée'.

SERVES 4 AS A FIRST COURSE,
    2 AS A MAIN COURSE
4 heads of chicory (chicons)
Squeeze of lemon juice
2 teaspoons Dijon mustard
4 slices cooked ham
40 g (1¹/₂ oz) butter
¹/₂ onion, finely chopped

2 tablespoons plain flour
450 ml (15 fl oz) milk
25 g (1 oz) grated Gruyère cheese
50 g (2 oz) freshly grated Parmesan
    cheese
Salt, freshly ground black pepper and
    ground nutmeg
5 tablespoons breadcrumbs

Trim the chicory and cook in boiling salted water, acidulated with the lemon juice, until just tender but still firm at the centre. Drain really well, to expel all the water that gathers amongst the leaves. It is a good idea to squeeze them gently with your hands, working from the base down to the tip. Spread the mustard over the ham, and roll each head of chicory in a slice of ham, with the mustard inside. Arrange closely together in a buttered ovenproof dish.

Pre-heat the oven to 200°C/400°F/Gas Mark 6.

Melt 25 g (1 oz) of the butter in a saucepan and add the onion. Cook gently until tender, without browning. Sprinkle over the flour and stir to mix evenly. Cook for 1 minute, stirring. Gradually stir in the milk to give a smooth white sauce. Bring to the boil, and simmer for 10 minutes or so, stirring frequently, until thick and creamy. Stir in the Gruyère and half the Parmesan, salt, pepper and nutmeg to taste (season fairly generously). Pour over the chicory.

Mix the remaining Parmesan with the breadcrumbs, and sprinkle evenly over the top. Dot with the remaining butter. Bake until nicely browned and sizzling. Serve immediately.

Roast Garlic with Herbs

With slow cooking, the hot pungency of garlic mutes down into soft sweetness, still garlicky, but no longer aggressive. I can't promise that your breath won't smell of garlic after you've eaten, say, an entire roast bulb of garlic, but it will have been so delicious that you probably won't care. Cancel the next day's business meeting or romantic tryst if needs be. Whenever I've dished up this first course, my guests have looked horrified at first, but they are soon tucking in gleefully, occasionally complaining that there are no seconds! It has to be eaten with fingers, so provide plenty of napkins.

SERVES 4
4 heads of garlic
6 tablespoons olive oil
2 sprigs of fresh thyme
2 sprigs of fresh rosemary
Coarse salt

TO SERVE
2 × 150 g (5 oz) young fresh goats' cheese
A handful of fresh herbs (e.g. basil, parsley, chives, chervil), finely chopped (optional)
Salt and freshly ground black pepper
Rye bread or other good bread, lightly toasted

Pre-heat the oven to 170°C/325°F/Gas Mark 3.

Neaten up the heads of garlic by removing any loose pieces of papery skin. Trim the roots. With a sharp knife cut the papery skin off the top of the garlic, just exposing the very tips of the cloves.

Arrange the garlic heads fairly close together in a small ovenproof dish and pour 6 tablespoons of water around them. Drizzle the olive oil over the garlic heads and tuck the rosemary and thyme around them. Sprinkle with coarse salt. Cover with foil and bake for 30 minutes. Uncover and bake for a further 15–30 minutes, basting occasionally with their own juices, until the garlic is tender and gives when pressed. Add a little extra water if it is drying out.

Beat the goats' cheese with the herbs, salt and pepper to taste, and pile into a bowl. To serve, give everyone their head of garlic and some of the herby cooking oil, slices of toast, napkins and finger-bowls. Using fingers, guests should squeeze the individual creamy cloves of garlic like tubes of toothpaste onto their toast, drizzle with the herby oil, and eat with a dab of soft cheese.

Sweet-and-sour Pearl Onions

There are many agrodolce (sweet-and-sour dishes) in Sicilian cookery, often picking up on the natural sweetness of vegetables. Though these little sweet-and-sour onions are usually part and parcel of the antipasto selection, they also go very well with cold meats, such as ham, or even with a nice piece of mature Cheddar! – not remotely a Sicilian combination, but worth trying anyway. Once cooked, they will keep, covered of course, in the refrigerator for three or four days.

SERVES 4–6
750 g (1 lb 8 oz) pearl onions
2 tablespoons olive oil
4 tablespoons tomato purée
2 tablespoons caster or granulated
sugar
3 tablespoons red or white wine
vinegar

1 bay leaf
2 sprigs of fresh thyme
Salt and freshly ground black pepper

TO SERVE
1 1/2 tablespoons chopped fresh parsley

To skin the onions, first top and tail them, then cover with boiling water. Leave for 1–2 minutes, drain and slip off the skins. Dry on kitchen paper.

Heat the oil in a wide frying-pan and add the onions. Brown briskly, then add all the remaining ingredients. Pour in enough water to cover the onions. Bring to the boil, reduce the heat and half-cover. Simmer gently for 40–45 minutes, stirring occasionally, until the onions are tender and bathed in a sweet-and-sour sauce. Serve cold, sprinkled with parsley.

Pissaladière

Pissaladière is made throughout Provence and parts of northern Italy, but it belongs above all to Nice, where you can buy big squares of it, wrapped in a piece of waxed paper, to eat as you walk through the streets.

Although it is often made with a bread dough, more like a pizza, I prefer a short-crust base. The sweetness of the slowly cooked onion and the saltiness of anchovies and olives are set off to perfection by the crumbly texture of the pastry. Some recipes for pissaladière mix tomato with the onion and, good though they are, I think the simpler onion-only topping better. Save the tomatoes to make a salad to serve alongside.

Pissaladière is perfect for a summer lunch or supper party, or for a picnic. It can be eaten still warm, or cold, as a main course or cut into smaller squares as a starter.

SERVES 6–8 AS A MAIN COURSE
350 g (12 oz) shortcrust pastry
  (see p. 344)
Flour for rolling out

FOR THE FILLING
3 tablespoons olive oil
1 kg (2 lb) onions, thinly sliced
2 cloves garlic, peeled and finely
  chopped
3 sprigs of fresh thyme or 1/2 teaspoon
  dried

2 sprigs of fresh rosemary or
  1 teaspoon dried
1 bay leaf
2 sprigs of fresh parsley
Salt and freshly ground black pepper
1 can anchovy fillets, drained and
  halved lengthwise
50 g (2 oz) black olives (preferably
  Niçoise), pitted

Roll the pastry out on a lightly floured board to form a rectangle large enough to line a 23 × 30 cm (9 × 12 in) baking tray. Line the tray with the pastry and prick the base with a fork, then cover and rest in the fridge for 30 minutes to 1 hour while you prepare the filling.

Warm the oil in a saucepan large enough to take all the onions. Add the onions, garlic, herbs and a little salt and pepper. Cover tightly and stew gently over a low heat for 30–40 minutes, stirring occasionally, until the onions are meltingly tender. Discard the herbs. Cool slightly, and add plenty of pepper (no more salt, as the olives and anchovies will ensure that there is no shortage).

Put a baking tray, the same size as the one lined with pastry, in the oven and heat to 200°C/400°F/Gas Mark 6. Spread the onion thickly on the pastry, arrange the anchovy fillets in a lattice on top and place an olive in the centre of each diamond. Sit the *pissaladière* on the hot baking tray in the oven (this helps give a crisper base), and bake for 20–25 minutes until browned. Serve cut into squares, hot, warm or cold.

Sweet Potato Fritters

Lime, sweet potato and chilli are a magic combination, so I make no excuses for repeating it, though in a very different guise from the recipe for Sautéd Sweet Potatoes with Lamb and Mint (see p. 152). This makes a great first course.

SERVES 6–8
3 sweet potatoes, preferably orange-
  fleshed
85 g (3 oz) plain flour
Salt and freshly ground black pepper
1 teaspoon ground coriander
2 eggs, lightly beaten
Sunflower oil, for deep-frying

TO SERVE
4 spring onions, finely chopped
1–2 fresh red chillies, seeded and
  finely shredded or chopped
1 lime, cut into wedges

Boil the sweet potatoes in salted water until barely tender. Drain and leave until cool enough to handle. Do not peel. Slice into discs about 5 mm (1/4 in) thick. Season the flour generously with salt, pepper and the ground coriander, then spread out on a plate. Pour the eggs into a shallow bowl or plate.

Heat the oil to 180°C/350°F. One by one, using a fork, dip the sweet potato slices into the flour and then into the beaten egg, and then back into the flour to coat them evenly. At each stage, make sure they are completely coated – excess is better than parsimony here. Fry in small batches until golden brown – about 5 minutes, turning occasionally. Drain briefly on kitchen paper. Serve hot, scattered with spring onions and chillies and a wedge of lime to squeeze over.

Mushrooms in Cider Batter with a Coriander Vinaigrette

Deep-fried mushrooms with garlic has become something of a cliché on pub and restaurant menus, but when the mushrooms include wild ones and the batter is light and airy, and they are served with a coriander vinaigrette like this one, they are transformed into a sophisticated starter that is hard to beat.

Of course, it can only be cooked at the last minute, as the mushrooms must be eaten post-haste, before their juices seep out into the batter. When choosing the mushrooms, buy at least three different kinds – a few button mushrooms to save your purse, maybe some shiitake or oyster mushrooms and then, if possible, one or two truly wild mushrooms, such as chanterelles, trompettes de la mort, *ceps (which will have to be sliced thickly) and so on.*

SERVES 4
450 g (1 lb) assorted mushrooms
Plain flour
Sunflower oil for frying

FOR THE CORIANDER VINAIGRETTE
6 tablespoons chopped fresh coriander
1 1/2 tablespoons cider vinegar
1/2 tablespoon caster sugar
2 garlic cloves, roughly chopped
6 tablespoons groundnut or sunflower oil
Salt and freshly ground black pepper

FOR THE BATTER
200 g (7 oz) plain flour
1 level teaspoon baking powder
1/2 teaspoon salt
2 tablespoons olive oil
230–300 ml (8–10 fl oz) dry cider
2 egg whites

Trim the mushrooms, removing any very thick, chunky stalks and slicing large mushrooms in half. Wipe clean but make sure that they are thoroughly dry before you start cooking. Lay them out on a dish.

To make the coriander vinaigrette, put all the ingredients into a food processor with 1 1/2 tablespoons of water and process until smooth. Spoon into a serving bowl.

The batter can be made an hour in advance, though the egg whites should only be added just before using. Sift the flour with the baking powder and salt. Make a well in the centre and add the oil and cider. Mix to a smooth batter. Just before using, stir the batter. It should have the consistency of double cream so, if it seems on the thick side, dilute it with a little more cider. Whisk the egg whites and fold them into the batter.

Heat the oil to 190°C/375°F. Put the flour on a plate. One at a time, coat the mushrooms in flour, shake off any excess and then dip them into the batter, making sure that they are completely covered. Lift them out on a fork and slide into the hot oil. Deep-fry until the batter is puffed, golden brown and crisp, turning once or twice. Drain briefly on kitchen paper and then serve with the coriander vinaigrette.

Baked Fennel with Parmesan

To my mind, there is no better way to cook fennel than this. It is simple; it is Italian; it is a classic; it is unbeatable. Serve this sizzling dish of fennel on its own, as a first course, with good bread, or as a side dish with game, poultry or fish.

SERVES 4–6
3 large or 4 medium-sized fennel bulbs
45 g (1 1/2 oz) butter
60 g (2 oz) Parmesan, freshly grated
Salt and freshly ground black pepper

Pre-heat the oven to 200°C/400°F/Gas Mark 6. Trim the tough stalks off each fennel bulb, slice off a thin disc from each base and remove the outer layer, if it is damaged. Quarter the bulbs from top to base. Steam or simmer the fennel in salted water until just tender. Drain thoroughly (all those curved and interleaved layers can trap a fair amount of water).

Butter a shallow, ovenproof dish that is large enough to take the fennel in a single, densely packed layer. Pack in the fennel and season with pepper. Dot with butter and scatter evenly with Parmesan. Bake in the oven for 20–30 minutes, until the cheese is browned and the butter is sizzling. Serve hot or warm.

Gratin of Courgettes with Potatoes and Tomatoes

This gratin looks enchantingly pretty with its closely packed bands of green, red and white, patched with brown from the heat of the oven. As the vegetables cook they will shrink, so it is important to pack them tightly into the baking dish. Overlap them snugly, leaving only about 5 mm (1/4 in) of each slice peeking out. That way, you will get a good balance of tenderness to crispness.

SERVES 4

225 g (8 oz) tomatoes

225 g (8 oz) courgettes

225 g (8 oz) waxy potatoes

Salt and freshly ground black pepper

1 medium-sized red onion

1/2 tablespoon dried oregano

3 tablespoons olive oil

Slice the tomatoes and courgettes into discs about 5 mm (1/4 in) thick, then sprinkle them lightly with salt and leave for 30 minutes. Wipe dry. Peel the potatoes, and slice them thinly. Halve the onion lengthways and slice each half thinly.

Pre-heat the oven to 180°C/350°F/Gas Mark 4. Arrange the vegetables in a single closely overlapping layer like the tiles on a roof, alternating potato, tomatoes, courgettes and onion, in an oiled heatproof dish. Season slightly with salt but add plenty of pepper. Sprinkle over the oregano. Drizzle over the olive oil.

Bake for 50–60 minutes, until the potatoes are tender. As the gratin cooks baste 2 or 3 times with its juices, trying not to disturb the arrangement too much. If the gratin threatens to burn, cover with foil towards the end of the cooking time. Serve hot.

Tomato and Pesto Terrine

This is a recipe for high summer, when tomatoes are cheap (or fully ripened, if you grow your own), full of flavour and plentiful. It is very simple and makes a light, fresh-tasting first course for a summer dinner party. Skinning and preparing all the tomatoes takes time, but you will be glad you did it when you slice through the terrine to reveal bands of red separated with thin lines of pesto. Set aside the evening before your do and settle down to work in the knowledge that you are creating a tearaway success of a dish.

The bigger the tomatoes, the more you'll need, as they contain a higher ratio of seeds and pulp to flesh (so for beef tomatoes, you'll probably need the full 3 kg/6 lb).

SERVES 8

1 quantity of Pesto (see p. 361)

Olive oil

2–3 kg (4–6 lb) ripe tomatoes

1 tablespoon white wine vinegar

Sugar

Salt and freshly ground black pepper

TO GARNISH

8 fresh basil sprigs

Put 1 tablespoon of the pesto into a small pot, cover with 2 tablespoons of olive oil and then with cling film and reserve for the dressing.

Pour boiling water over the tomatoes, leave for about 30 seconds and then drain and skin. If the skin on some of the tomatoes remains reluctant to part company, bathe the offending tomatoes again in boiling water and then try again. Cut the tomatoes into quarters (or eighths if they are very large) and seed. Use a small, sharp knife to slice away the inner ridges and knobs, to leave neat flat sheets of tomato. Lay them out on wire racks (or baking sheets if you're short of racks) and sprinkle lightly with a little salt and sugar. Leave to drain for half an hour.

Line a 500 g (1 lb) loaf tin with cling film, allowing some of the film to trail over the sides. Brush the inside lightly with olive oil. Pat the tomato pieces dry and then arrange a layer, tightly snuggled together, over the base. Spread with a little of the pesto. Repeat these layers until the tomato is all used up, finishing with a layer of tomato. Fold the trailing cling film over loosely. Sit another loaf tin of the same size on top and weigh it down (use cans of food or bags of rice or whatever is handy and heavy). Stand it on a dish and leave overnight in the fridge, draining off the pressed out liquid whenever you dive into the fridge to get something else out (you'll be amazed by how much oozes out but don't let it unnerve you).

To make the dressing, whisk the vinegar with the reserved pesto and oil. Gradually whisk in another 1–2 tablespoons of olive oil and a touch of sugar. Taste and adjust the seasoning and then set aside until needed.

To serve, carefully drain any remaining juice from the tomato terrine and then turn it out onto a chopping board or serving dish, gently peeling away the cling film. Either take it to the table as it is or, if you can rely on a really good, sharp-as-a-razor knife, cut into 2.5 cm (1 in) slices. Lay each one on a plate and drizzle some of the pesto vinaigrette around it. Garnish with basil sprigs. Serve immediately.

CHEESE AND EGGS

Chèvre Tourangelle

In the Saturday market in the little French town that I have known since I was a child, the cheesemonger always has a big vat of chèvre frais à l'ail: *young, milky curds of goats' cheese flavoured with garlic and fresh herbs. I always buy some and wolf it down at supper with big hunks of* pain bâtard, *the equally excellent sturdy bread made by the baker on the corner. My friends there eat it either as a cheese course or, occasionally, as a simple first course, putting it on the table with lots of slices of salami.*

The soft goats' cheese that we can buy here is not the same as the less processed, local French cheese but it still makes an excellent creamy version of chèvre Tourangelle, *to give it its fancy name.*

SERVES 4
200 g (7 oz) young, fresh goats' cheese
4 tablespoons creamy milk or single cream
1 tablespoon chopped fresh chives

1 tablespoon chopped fresh tarragon
1 tablespoon chopped fresh parsley
2 teaspoons chopped fresh chervil, if available
2 garlic cloves, crushed

Mix the whole lot together. Eat.

Marinated Parmesan and Mozzarella with Garlic, Capers and Lemon

Parmesan and mozzarella marinated together in a green dressing make a sensational first course served with ciabatta bread.

SERVES 4–6
1 buffalo-milk mozzarella
150–200 g (5–7 oz) Parmesan

FOR THE DRESSING
5 tablespoons olive oil
1 tablespoon lemon juice

Finely grated zest of 1 lemon
1 garlic clove, crushed
2 tablespoons small capers
2 tablespoons finely chopped fresh parsley
Salt and freshly ground black pepper

Slice the mozzarella and Parmesan and arrange alternately on a serving dish.

To make the dressing, whisk the oil into the lemon juice slowly, then stir in all the remaining ingredients. Or put the whole lot into a screw-topped jar, seal and shake to mix. Taste and adjust the seasoning. Spoon over the cheeses, cover and leave for at least an hour before serving.

Neapolitan Crostini

Anchovies, mozzarella and blood-red tomatoes are all part and parcel of southern Italian cooking. Essential flavours for the hot sun, and well met on these baked crostini. They could be served as a first course, as a pre-dinner taste-tickler with drinks or even as the focus of a light lunch, accompanied by salads. It's very difficult to be precise about the amount of bread you will need, as this is dictated more by the size of the loaf than anything else: you need as many slices as will allow you to cut 16 broad fingers.

Although I've suggested cutting the bread into fingers, there's absolutely no reason why you shouldn't take liberties and make your crostini whatever shape takes your fancy.

SERVES 4–8

4–8 thick slices of good bread, crusts removed
Butter, softened
8 anchovy fillets
2 × 140 g (5 oz) mozzarella cheeses, sliced
3 ripe tomatoes, skinned, seeded and cut into long strips
Salt and freshly ground black pepper
Dried oregano

Pre-heat the oven to 180°C/350°F/Gas Mark 4. Butter the bread slices generously on one side and cut them into 16 fingers. Butter a baking tray and lay the bread, butter-side up, on it. Cut the anchovy fillets in half lengthways. Now lay slices of mozzarella, trimmed to fit, on each piece of bread, and put a couple of strips of tomato and a strip of anchovy across the mozzarella. Season with a little salt and pepper and a pinch or two of oregano. Bake for 20–30 minutes, until the mozzarella is melting and the bread crisp. Eat while the crostini are as hot as is bearable.

Goats' Cheese and Sun-dried Tomato Pesto Money Bags

Hot from the oven, these goats' cheese purses make an irresistible first course (serve three or four each), or go down a treat at parties. You can make them several hours in advance and leave them in the fridge until needed. You may then need to give them an extra minute or so in the oven.

MAKES 10–12
6–12 sheets of filo pastry, depending on size
85–100 g (3–4 oz) unsalted butter, melted

FOR THE FILLING
110 g (4 oz) goats' cheese, de-rinded and mashed

2 tomatoes, skinned, seeded and cut into small pieces
4 teaspoons Sun-Dried Tomato and Toasted Walnut Pesto (see p. 362), bought red pesto or sun-dried tomato purée

Cut the filo pastry into 12 cm (5 in) squares. Keep them covered with a sheet of greaseproof paper and a tea-towel wrung out in cold water. Take a square at a time, brush with melted butter and lay a second square on that, twisted round to look like an eight-pointed star. Brush with butter. Place a scant teaspoon of goats' cheese in the centre, top with a piece or two of tomato and finish the whole lot with 1/3 teaspoon of pesto or sun-dried tomato purée. Gather all the points and edges of the star up and twist them together, to enclose the filling. On your first attempt, you will probably discover that you have overfilled your money bag. Backtrack and remove a little filling. Place the filled money bags on a buttered baking tray. Continue until filling and filo are all used up. Brush any extra butter over the bags. Chill until needed.

To cook, pre-heat the oven to 200°C/400°F/Gas Mark 6. Bake the money bags for about 7–10 minutes, until they are browned and crisp. Serve hot or warm.

Fried Stuffed Rice Balls

Fried stuffed rice balls or arancini, *which literally means little oranges, have long been one of my favourite snacks when I'm in the south of Italy. You can always get them at railway station buffets, and often at cafés. They are a little fiddly to make at home, but worth it in my book. Though they taste best when hot, they're not at all bad cold – just the thing for a picnic or packed lunch.*

MAKES 12
12 oz (350 g) risotto rice (such as arborio)
Salt, pepper and nutmeg
4 eggs
3 oz (75 g) Caciocavallo or Parmesan cheese, freshly grated
1 oz (25 g) butter
5 tablespoons very thick tomato sauce (see Basic Tomato Sauce, p. 353)

2 oz (50 g) green peas (shelled weight), cooked
2 oz (50 g) Mozzarella cheese, cubed
Flour
3 oz (75 g) fine dry breadcrumbs
Sunflower or vegetable oil for deep-frying

Cook the rice in plenty of boiling salted water until tender. Drain thoroughly. Mix with 2 of the eggs, the Caciocavallo or Parmesan cheese, the butter, salt, pepper and nutmeg. Work well with your hands until the mixture holds together, then leave to cool. Meanwhile simmer the tomato sauce and peas together for 5 minutes, then leave to cool.

Working on one at a time, divide the rice into 12 portions and roll into balls (wet your hands first to prevent sticking). Make a fairly capacious hole in the centre with your finger and insert a teaspoonful of the tomato/pea mixture and a cube of Mozzarella. Carefully cover the filling with a knob of rice, sealing it in completely. Mould back into a ball.

Beat the remaining eggs lightly. Roll the *arancini* first in flour, then dip into beaten egg, shaking off the excess, and finally roll in breadcrumbs, making sure that each one is thoroughly and evenly coated. Deep-fry a few balls at a time in plenty of oil, pre-heated to about 160°C/325°F, until richly browned. Drain on kitchen paper. Serve hot or warm.

To re-heat, either pop back into the oil for a few minutes or heat through, uncovered, in a warm oven.

Cigar Börek

Cigar börek *are the easiest of the many forms of* börek *(savoury pastries) to make at home, taking their name from their shape. Fillings can vary, but feta cheese and herbs is the one we came across most frequently in Istanbul. Be warned:* Cigar Börek *are very more-ish, and though two dozen may sound like a fair number, they'll soon be snapped up and eaten.*

MAKES 22–24
About 6 sheets filo pastry
55 g (2 oz) unsalted butter, melted

FOR THE FILLING
225 g (8 oz) feta cheese, crumbled
1 egg, lightly beaten
2 tablespoons finely chopped fresh parsley
2 tablespoons finely chopped fresh dill

Pre-heat the oven to 190°C/375°F/Gas Mark 5.

To make the filling, mash the cheese and beat with the egg to form a cream. Stir in the herbs. Whatever you do, don't add any salt, as you'll find the feta is already quite salty enough.

Cut the filo into strips about 10 × 25 cm (4 × 10 in) or a close approximation that fits the size of your filo sheets. Keep the filo from drying out while you work by covering first with a sheet of greaseproof paper and then with a tea-towel wrung out in cold water.

Take the first strip of filo, brush with butter, then place a generous teaspoon of the filling close to one of the short ends, shaping it into a small sausage parallel to the edge. Flip over the long sides to cover the ends of the filling, then roll up neatly to form a little cigar shape. Repeat with the remaining filling until used up.

Lay the *börek* on greased baking sheets and brush with melted butter. (They can be stored in the refrigerator for up to 8 hours at this stage, or frozen.) Bake for 10–15 minutes, until golden-brown. Serve hot or warm, and don't worry if a little filling oozes out here or there: just tidy it away and no one will be any the wiser.

Gratin of Cauliflower with Anchovies

Cauliflower has a special affinity with anchovies and here, both as fillets and as essence, they come into play to upgrade cauliflower cheese to a much more stylish dish than usual, more than good enough to eat all on its own.

SERVES 4
1 small cauliflower, trimmed and broken into florets (about 370 g/13 oz prepared weight)
4 tablespoons fine breadcrumbs
2 tablespoons very finely chopped fresh parsley
2 tablespoons freshly grated Parmesan
6 canned anchovy fillets, halved lengthways
15 g (1/2 oz) butter
Salt

FOR THE SAUCE
1 small shallot, chopped
2 tablespoons oil from the can of anchovies, or olive oil
30 g (1 oz) plain flour
450 ml (15 fl oz) milk
1 1/2 tablespoons freshly grated Parmesan
1–2 teaspoons anchovy essence or purée
Salt and freshly ground black pepper

Pre-heat the oven to 200°C/400°F/Gas Mark 6. Cook the cauliflower florets in salted, boiling water until just *al dente*. Take great care not to overcook the cauliflower to a grey grimness. Drain thoroughly and place in a shallow, greased baking dish, in as even a layer as you can manage.

To make the sauce, cook the shallot gently in the oil, until tender. Sprinkle over the flour and stir in. Cook for a minute, stirring, and then draw the pan off the heat and gradually mix in the milk, a little at a time. Bring to the boil, then reduce the heat and leave to simmer very gently for 5–10 minutes, until the sauce is good and thick. Stir in the Parmesan and anchovy essence or purée. Season with pepper and then taste and add salt if needed.

Pour the sauce evenly over the cauliflower. Mix the breadcrumbs, parsley and Parmesan and sprinkle evenly over the surface. Arrange the anchovy fillets in a lattice pattern over the surface and then dot with butter. Bake for 25–30 minutes, until browned and sizzling. Serve immediately.

Fried Eggs with Coriander, Cumin and Balsamic Vinegar

This dish of fried eggs, Latin-American style (with a dash of Italian vinegar), is totally sublime and very quick to make. It is perfect, reinvigorating supper material.

SERVES 1
Olive oil
2 eggs
¹/₄ fresh red chilli, seeded and finely
   sliced
¹/₄ teaspoon cumin seeds

¹/₂ garlic clove, chopped
1 or 2 slices of bread, toasted, to
   serve
¹/₂ teaspoon balsamic vinegar
Coarse salt
Chopped fresh coriander

Pour enough olive oil into a heavy frying-pan to cover the base. Heat over a moderate heat and then carefully break the eggs into it. Fry as usual, spooning hot oil over the eggs to help them set. When they are about half-cooked, add the chilli, cumin and garlic to the pan and continue cooking until the white is set. Lift the eggs out on to the bread, together with the bits of chilli and garlic, and then spoon over a little of the oil. Drizzle over the balsamic vinegar, season with salt and scatter over lots of chopped coriander. Eat immediately.

Baked Eggs with Sorrel

The mildness of baked eggs is lifted by the hidden layer of sorrel at the bottom of each ramekin. This is a lovely first course for a simple May dinner.

SERVES 4 AS A FIRST COURSE
60 g (2 oz) sorrel
15 g (¹/₂ oz) butter

4 eggs
4 dessertspoons double cream
Salt and freshly ground black pepper

Make a *chiffonade* (fine shreds) of the sorrel. Melt the butter in a small saucepan and add the sorrel. Stir over a medium heat for around 3–5 minutes, until the shreds have collapsed to a dark khaki sludge.

Pre-heat the oven to 190°C/375°F/Gas Mark 5. Set four ramekins in a roasting tin and heat them through in the oven for 5 minutes. Meanwhile, boil a kettle of water.

Take out the ramekins and quickly divide the sorrel purée amongst them. Break an egg gently into each one and spoon over a dessertspoon of cream. Season with pepper only (salt hardens the white in the oven). Pour about 2 cm (1 in) of hot water around the ramekins, cover loosely with foil and rush back into the oven. They should be cooked within 7–10 minutes: the whites just set but the yolks tender and runny. Season with salt and serve at once.

Courgette Omelette

This is a chunky omelette, packed with pieces of tender courgette. The final addition of soured cream or, better still, crème fraîche is entirely optional, but it does make it doubly delicious.

SERVES 2
225 g (8 oz) courgettes
Salt and freshly ground black pepper
5 eggs, beaten
2 tablespoons Gruyère cheese, grated
1 tablespoon chopped fresh chives
1 tablespoon chopped fresh parsley

1 tablespoon olive oil
1 large clove garlic, peeled and finely chopped
15 g (1/2 oz) butter

TO SERVE
Soured cream or crème fraîche (optional)

Quarter the courgettes lengthwise, then cut into 2.5 cm (1 in) lengths. Spread out in a colander, sprinkle with salt and leave to drain for 30 minutes. Rinse and pat dry on kitchen paper. Beat the eggs with the Gruyère, herbs, salt and pepper.

Heat the olive oil in a wide frying-pan over a brisk heat. Add the courgettes and sauté until just beginning to brown. Add the garlic and continue frying until browned and tender. Add the butter and stir until it is melted and foaming. Pour in the egg mixture, and cook as for a normal omelette over a moderate heat, pulling up the edges to allow the liquid egg to trickle underneath.

When the omelette is just done – set but still moist on the surface – spoon a couple of large dollops of soured cream or crème fraîche, if using, down the centre, then flip the sides of the omelette over to cover them, and slide out onto a serving dish.

Chinese Scrambled Egg with Squash

When a friend of mine, Frances Bendixon, was buying the pumpkin for her pumpkin pie her Chinese grocer told her how she liked to cook winter squash with eggs. Frances didn't get round to trying it, but she passed the idea on to me. It turns out to be an excellent, if unusual, way to turn squash into a light main course.

SERVES 2
175–225 g (6–8 oz) piece of pumpkin or other winter squash (e.g. butternut)
4 eggs

Salt and freshly ground black pepper
2 tablespoons oil
1 clove garlic, peeled and chopped
1 cm (1/2 in) piece of fresh ginger, peeled and finely chopped

Cut off the rind and remove seeds and fibres from the pumpkin or squash. You should end up with around 100 g (4 oz) of flesh. Slice very thinly, then cut the slices into narrow batons, about 2.5–4 cm (1–1½ in) long. Beat the eggs, adding salt and pepper.

Heat the oil in a wok over a high heat until hazy. Add the garlic and ginger and stir-fry for a few seconds. Add the squash and stir-fry until lightly browned and tender. Pour in the beaten egg and quickly stir and scramble until beginning to set. Scoop into a dish and serve.

Smoked Salmon with Lovage Cream Cheese, on Bagels

This is a spin on the traditional, much-loved salmon and cream cheese bagel. The lovage adds a lemony, celery flavour which makes this an intriguing combination.

SERVES 3

3 bagels, split open

4 tablespoons cream cheese

1 tablespoon chopped fresh lovage
   leaves

2 teaspoons creamed horseradish
   (optional)

Lots of sliced smoked salmon

Freshly ground black pepper

Toast the cut sides of the bagels, if you wish. Mash the cream cheese with the lovage and horseradish, if using, and smear thickly over the cut sides of the bagels. Sandwich as much smoked salmon as is humanly decent (or available) between the two halves of each bagel, seasoning generously with freshly ground black pepper. Eat greedily.

Asparagus with Smoked Salmon and Sauce Mousseline

Dunworley Cottage Restaurant in West Cork is hard to find, but worth getting lost for once or twice. Perched on a headland with its wonderful views of the sea, it is run by Swede Katherine Noren who, with her chef Mikka, creates the most delicious food. She uses the best Irish produce and prepares it with a Swedish accent – like local black and white puddings with a lingonberry sauce. Katherine grows her own vegetables and herbs, bakes her own delicious bread and pickles her own excellent herrings. She buys superb smoked salmon from a fish smoker a few miles down the coast and when asparagus is in season she serves them together with this luxuriously rich sauce mousseline – Hollandaise sauce lightened with whipped cream.

SERVES 6

1 quantity of Hollandaise sauce (see
   Asparagus with Hollandaise Sauce,
   p. 30)

150 ml (5 fl oz) whipping cream,
   whipped

750 g (1 lb 8 oz) asparagus,
   trimmed, steamed and allowed
   to cool

6 slices smoked salmon

TO GARNISH

6 sprigs fresh parsley

Shortly before serving make the Hollandaise sauce, then fold in the whipped cream. Taste and adjust the seasoning if necessary and keep warm. Arrange the cold, cooked asparagus and smoked salmon on 6 individual plates. Spoon a little of the sauce on to each plate and garnish with a sprig of parsley. Serve the remaining sauce in a bowl for those who really want to indulge themselves.

Gravlaks

I know that gravlaks, or gravad lax – cured salmon with a mustard and dill sauce – is originally Swedish. But now salmon from all parts of Scandinavia, and indeed the entire world, is of sterling quality, although it is still cured following the Swedish method. Some recipes add a tot of brandy to the curing mixture, but I prefer the simpler blend of salt, sugar, pepper and dill.

We tend to serve it, rather like smoked salmon, as a first course with thin slices of buttered bread, and the mustard and dill sauce which is somewhere between a vinaigrette and a mayonnaise, with lots of mustard and dill and a little sugar. (You can leave out the raw egg yolk if you prefer, but the sauce won't be quite so thick and luscious.) The Norwegians go for a more robust and generous presentation. Thickly sliced, it may come out with a plate of salad and hot boiled potatoes; or it can be fried in butter for a hot supper dish.

SERVES 8
900 g (2 lb) very fresh salmon fillet
1 tablespoon coarse sea salt
2 level tablespoons sugar
2 tablespoons finely chopped fresh dill
   or 1 tablespoon dried
1 tablespoon black peppercorns,
   coarsely crushed

FOR THE MUSTARD AND DILL SAUCE
2 tablespoons Dijon mustard
1 egg yolk (optional, but a good
   addition)
1 level tablespoon caster sugar
150 ml (5 fl oz) sunflower or groundnut
   oil
1 tablespoon white wine vinegar
3 tablespoons chopped fresh dill
Salt and freshly ground black pepper

If you conveniently have 2 (or 4) portions of fillet all of roughly the same shape, leave them as they are. If you have 1 large piece or, say, 3 smaller ones, cut them so that they can be sandwiched together neatly.

Find a shallow dish that will take the pieces of salmon fillet sandwiched together in a snug layer. Mix all the remaining ingredients. Sprinkle 2 tablespoons of this mixture over the base of the dish and lay the first salmon pieces, skin-side down, on top. Spread most of the remaining mixture over the salmon and lay the second pieces, skin-side up, on top. Scatter over the remaining seasoning mix. Cover with cling film or foil, weigh down with a board or plate and leave for 24 hours in the refrigerator, turning the salmon sandwich once or twice. It can be stored like this for up to 4 days in the refrigerator.

To make the sauce, mix the mustard, egg yolk (if using) and sugar. Gradually whisk in the oil as if you were making a mayonnaise (though it's not quite such a temperamental process). Stir in the vinegar, dill, salt and pepper. Taste and adjust the seasoning.

To serve, wipe the salmon clean and slice thinly, like smoked salmon. A very sharp knife is essential, and it helps to pop the salmon into the freezer for 10–15 minutes beforehand to firm it up. Accompany with the mustard and dill sauce.

Scallops with Sherry Vinegar and Fresh Tomato Sauce

This dish of scallops makes a very quick, very chic starter. Ask for scallops that have not been soaked in water to make them look plumper and weigh more!

SERVES 3–4
8 medium-large scallops, cleaned
Salt and freshly ground black pepper
2 tablespoons olive oil
3 tablespoons sherry vinegar
4 tablespoons fish or light chicken stock

1 tablespoon caster sugar
350 g (12 oz) firm tomatoes, skinned, seeded and cut into 3 mm ($1/8$ in) dice
$1^1/2$ tablespoons finely shredded fresh basil

Separate the corals from the whites of the scallops. Depending on the size of the scallops, cut each white into two or three discs horizontally. Season with salt and pepper.

Shortly before you sit down to eat, put a heavy-based pan on to heat through thoroughly. Let it get good and hot and then add the oil. Leave for a few seconds and then lay the scallop discs and the corals in the oil, one by one. If the oil is hot enough, they will be cooked through within seconds. Lift out and keep warm. Tip excess oil from the pan, reduce the heat to moderate and then spoon in the sherry vinegar and stock. Tip and tilt the pan about, scraping up the residues from frying. Stir in the sugar and the tomatoes, give the whole lot a few seconds to heat and then taste and adjust the seasoning. Stir in all but a few shreds of the basil and serve with the scallops, draping the reserved basil over the top.

Filo Cigars Filled with Crab and Coriander

Here, the crisp filo pastry encloses a blissfully oozy filling of crab, coriander and cream cheese. Shaped like a cigar, this is probably the easiest of ways to use filo pastry. Serve as a first course, allowing three or four cigars per person (add a little mixed green salad to the plates), or just as something to savour with drinks. Use fresh crab meat, not frozen, which isn't worth its price. One fairly large dressed crab will contain about the right amount.

MAKES ABOUT 18

220 g (8 oz) mixed white and brown crab meat
110 g (4 oz) cream cheese
1 tablespoon chopped fresh coriander
1 tablespoon chopped fresh parsley
1 tablespoon lemon juice
Salt and freshly ground black pepper
6–10 sheets of filo pastry, depending on size
60 g (2 oz) unsalted butter, melted

Flake the large pieces of white crab meat, if necessary. Beat the cream cheese with the herbs, lemon juice, salt and pepper. Mix in all the crab meat.

Cut each sheet of filo pastry into long strips about 13–15 cm (5–6 in) wide. Cover with a sheet of greaseproof paper and cover that with a tea-towel wrung out in cold water.

Pre-heat the oven to 200°C/400°F/Gas Mark 6. One at a time, take a strip of filo, brush with melted butter and place a teaspoon of the crab mixture at one end, shaping it into a neat sausage but leaving a good 2 cm (3/4 in) border. Roll the strip of filo up, to form a neat cylinder, flipping over the edges as you go, to prevent the filling from falling out. Place on a greased baking sheet. Repeat until filling and filo are all used up. Brush the cigars with any remaining butter. Chill until needed.

Bake for 10 minutes, until golden brown. Eat as soon as they've cooled enough not to burn your mouth.

Three Suns Sandwich

Here we have Italy meets France meets Spain all in one sandwich, and a big, picnic-worthy one at that. We start with an idea from the south of France – the pan bagna, a stuffed loaf of a sandwich, compressed overnight so that dressing and juices ooze invitingly into the crumb of the bread. For the bread, I've chosen the lovely, chewy, open-crumbed Italian ciabatta and, for the filling, I've headed to Spain with Manchego cheese and sherry vinegar. And there's more – olives and olive oil from whichever hot weather country you fancy, and air-dried ham from Italy, Spain or Portugal or, indeed, Britain, if you want to anchor your flights of fantasy on home territory.

SERVES 3–4

FOR THE DRESSING
1 tablespoon sherry vinegar
7 tablespoons olive oil
60 g (2 oz) black or green olives, pitted
1 fresh red chilli, seeded and roughly
  chopped
1 level teaspoon chopped fresh
  oregano
2 tablespoons chopped fresh parsley
1 tablespoon capers
2 *cornichons* (baby gherkins) or
  1 small pickled gherkin, roughly
  chopped
1–2 garlic cloves, chopped
Salt and freshly ground black pepper

FOR THE SANDWICH
1 ciabatta loaf, split in half
  lengthways
4–6 slices of air-dried ham, e.g. Parma,
  San Daniele, *jamón serrano*, or
  Cumberland
85 g (3 oz) Manchego, thinly sliced
2 ripe tomatoes, thinly sliced
A handful of frisée lettuce leaves
Freshly ground black pepper

Begin with the dressing. Put all the ingredients into a food processor and process until finely mixed and chopped, adding a little more oil or vinegar, if necessary. If you don't have a processor, chop all the solid ingredients together very, very finely and then mix them with the oil and vinegar and season with salt and pepper.

Drizzle a few spoonfuls of the dressing over both the cut sides of the ciabatta. Now build up layers of ham, cheese, tomato and frisée on one half, anointing each layer with a little more of the dressing and seasoning with pepper. Finally, clamp on the second half of the loaf and press down firmly. Wrap tightly in cling film and then lay on a board or plate and weigh down with heavy weights (bags of dried beans, cans of tomatoes or whatever else is to hand). Leave overnight in the fridge. Unwrap and cut into chunks just before eating.

Crostini di Fegatini di Pollo

Toasted bread (preferably grilled over a barbecue for a hint of smokiness) topped with a hash of chicken livers is one of the most appetizing of all Italian crostini, served as a preamble to a meal, with drinks, or as a rustic first course.

It is essential to use absolutely the best-quality bread, cut fairly thickly, so that it can soak up the juice. Sometimes, instead of grilling, I brush the bread generously with olive oil and bake it in a moderate oven until golden brown and crisp through and through. If you like garlic, then you can highlight it by rubbing the toasted or baked bread with a cut clove of garlic, before piling on the livers. The chicken liver sauce doesn't look too attractive, but you can prettify the finished crostini with a few sprigs of parsley and, I can assure you, they will taste superb.

SERVES 4
4 large or 8 small slices good bread,
**   cut thickly**
Olive oil

FOR THE SAUCE
225 g (8 oz) chicken livers
3 tablespoons olive oil
1 onion, chopped finely
2 garlic cloves, crushed

2 sage leaves
5 anchovy fillets, chopped
1 tablespoon capers, rinsed and
**   chopped**
85 ml (3 fl oz) Marsala or dry white
**   wine**
Salt and freshly ground black pepper

TO SERVE
A little chopped parsley

Pick over the chicken livers, removing any greenish-yellow bits. Cut any large livers in half or quarters then fry in 2 tablespoons of the olive oil until they are just firm. Scoop out and chop finely.

Add the remaining oil to the pan and fry the onion and garlic gently until tender but without browning. Return the chicken livers to the pan with all the remaining sauce ingredients (adding only a little salt as the anchovies will provide some) and simmer for about 4 minutes, mashing the livers down to a coarse purée.

Grill the bread, moisten with a trickle of olive oil and spread with the hot chicken liver sauce. Scatter over a little chopped parsley and serve immediately.

Chicken Liver Pâté

I've been making chicken liver pâté for donkey's years, and it never fails to please. It's quick and easy, and makes a lovely first course served with little French cornichons or pickled caper berries (from smart delis) and toast, though usually we just dig into it for lunch, smearing it on bread or crackers with unwonted abandon.

It is also a most adaptable pâté. I usually flavour it with nothing more than a shot of sweet sherry, or Madeira or port, or whatever sweetish fortified wine I can find a few slurps of, but some people prefer a shot of brandy in it or like to add some crushed green peppercorns, a hint of garlic or a smattering of thyme leaves. Of course, you could leave the alcohol out altogether, but it wouldn't be half so nice.

When I'm lucky enough to have a few livers from game birds or a rabbit, I use them instead of, or as well as, chicken livers. These gamey livers are highly flavoured, so I add a little more butter to soften the edge, and smear it on toast with a modicum of restraint.

SERVES 4
225 g (8 oz) chicken livers
100 g (4 oz) butter

1 tablespoon sweet sherry, Madeira,
**   port or brandy**
Salt and freshly ground black pepper

Pick over the chicken livers, removing any greenish-yellow bits. Cut any larger livers in half. Melt 40 g (1½ oz) of the butter and fry the livers over a moderate heat until browned on the outside but still pink inside. Tip the contents of the pan either into a food processor or into a pestle and mortar (depending on whether you want a smooth- or rough-textured pâté), scraping out all the butter and brown frying residues. Add the alcohol and remaining butter, salt and pepper and pound together until roughly amalgamated or blend until smooth.

Taste and adjust the seasoning, transfer the mixture to a bowl, smooth down and leave to set in the fridge.

Pâté de Campagne

This is about the easiest of pâtés to make, with a fine robust flavour. If you wish, you can embellish it by lining the terrine with strips of bacon, though I think it's nicer without. Too much salty bacon can be overwhelming.

SERVES 8–10

450 g (1 lb) belly of pork	**1 tablespoon flour**
350 g (12 oz) raw, boned chicken or veal	**1 large egg**
	1/4 teaspoon ground allspice
225 g (8 oz) pork liver	**1 teaspoon thyme leaves**
225 g (8 oz) flair fat (body fat) or back fat	**1 1/2 tablespoons chopped parsley**
2 garlic cloves, crushed	**Salt and freshly ground black pepper**
85 ml (3 fl oz) dry white wine	**Caul fat (fine lacy fat) to line the mould**
2 tablespoons brandy	**4 bay leaves (optional)**

If you have a helpful butcher, ask him to mince the belly of pork *coarsely* with the chicken or veal, liver and flair or back fat. If you don't and you are landed with the work, either chop them all very finely, or chop roughly and process in brief spurts so that the mixture is lumpily minced – continuous processing risks producing a smooth paste, which is not what you want.

Mix the minced meats with all the remaining ingredients except the bay leaves and caul fat. To check the seasoning, fry a small knob and taste, then adjust the salt and pepper etc. accordingly. If you have time, leave the mixture to sit for an hour or two then mix again with your hands.

Line a 1.2 litre (2 pint) or two 500 ml (1 pint) terrines or loaf tins with caul fat, leaving the ends trailing over the sides. Pack the pâté mixture into the moulds and, if you wish, lay a few decorative bay leaves on top. Fold the trailing caul fat neatly over the pâté. Cover the terrines with their lid or foil.

Stand the terrines in a roasting tin of hot water, which should come about half-way up each terrine. Bake at 170°C/325°F/Gas Mark 3 for 1 1/2–2 hours, uncovering the pâté for the last 30 minutes so that it can brown. The pâté is done when it has shrunk well away from the sides of the dish and the juices run clear and yellow-white, rather than pink.

Cool the pâté for an hour, cover with a layer of foil, then weigh it down with cans or whatever is handy and leave until completely cool before slicing. The pâté will taste even better if left in the fridge for a day or two.

If you want to make the pâté look a little neater and less gappy around the edges, melt 100 g (4 oz) butter. Pour off the clear yellow butter, leaving the milky solids behind in the pan. Pour the yellow 'clarified' butter over the pâté and leave to set.

Chicken and Pork Pâté Studded with Olives

Chicken and pork form the basis of this pâté, which is studded with green olives and flavoured with brandy and orange. Like all pâtés, its flavour improves with keeping for a day or two; in any case, you need to begin at least two days before you want to eat it, to allow for overnight marinating and then pressing. Serve sliced, with hot toast and a fruity chutney or pickled caper berries or cornichons *(baby gherkins).*

SERVES 8–10

1 boned, skinned chicken breast
Juice of 1 orange
1 tablespoon brandy
3 strips of orange zest
1 bay leaf
2 tablespoons olive oil
340 g (12 oz) de-rinded belly of pork, small bones removed
6 boned, skinned chicken thighs
3 tablespoons chopped fresh parsley
1^1/$_2$ tablespoons finely chopped fresh chives
1 teaspoon fresh thyme leaves
1 tablespoon plain flour
Salt and freshly ground black pepper
100 g (3^1/$_2$ oz) green olives, stoned and sliced

Cut the chicken breast into two long, fat strips. Marinate overnight with the orange juice, brandy, orange zest, bay leaf and olive oil.

Pre-heat the oven to 170°C/325°F/Gas Mark 3. If you buy your meat from a friendly butcher, ask him to mince the belly of pork with the chicken thighs for you. If he can't or won't do that, mince them yourself, if you have a mincer. If you don't, either chop the two meats together very, very finely, which is laborious but gives an excellent texture, or chop them roughly and then process in brief bursts in a processor, scraping the mixture down frequently and trying your best not to reduce it to a totally smooth mush.

Take the chicken breast out of the marinade. Discard the orange zest and bay leaf and then mix about half the marinade into the minced meats, along with the parsley, chives, thyme, flour, salt and pepper. Use your hands to get it all thoroughly and evenly mixed and then break off a small knob and fry quickly. Taste it to assess the seasoning situation – add more salt and pepper to the mixture if it seems a bit bland. Finally, work in the olives.

Smooth half the mixture in a china terrine, or 500–750 g (1–1 1/2 lb) loaf tin. Nestle the strips of chicken breast down the centre and then cover with the remaining mixture, pressing it down firmly. Cover the terrine with its lid or foil and stand it in a roasting tin. Pour enough hot water into the tin to come about halfway up. Bake for 1 1/2–2 hours, until the pâté has pulled away from the sides of the tin and the fat runs clear. Give it a final test by plunging a skewer into the centre: if the juices run clear, it is done. Let the pâté cool.

Cover the pâté with a clean piece of foil and weigh it down with cans or weights. Leave overnight in the fridge. Serve cut into thick slices.

Albanian Liver

Despite the name, this is actually a Turkish recipe, usually served as part of a mixed meze or hors d'oeuvre. The briefly fried liver is piled up with sweet fried onions, lashings of thick yoghurt and lots of fresh mint leaves. I usually serve it as a first course on its own and it has been known to convert non-liver eaters to rampant enthusiasm, clearing the last slivers before anyone else can lay their hands on them. If you want to turn it into a light main course for a summery lunch, then accompany it with a tomato and olive salad, perhaps a green salad too and lots of hunks of sturdy peasant-type bread.

All the Turkish cookbooks I own give a very simple recipe for Albanian Liver – the strips are tossed in flour seasoned generously with paprika, fried, and served at room temperature. This version is based on one described to me by my friend Martin Lam at Ransome's Dock restaurant in Battersea, south London.

SERVES 4 AS A FIRST COURSE
450 g (1 lb) lamb's liver, trimmed
2 tablespoons flour
1 tablespoon paprika, plus extra to
  garnish

Salt and freshly ground black pepper
85 ml (3 fl oz) olive oil
1 large onion, thinly sliced
150 ml (5 fl oz) Greek yoghurt
12 mint leaves, roughly torn up

Cut the liver into long strips, about 2 cm (3/4 in) wide. Mix the flour with the paprika, salt and pepper. Coat the strips of liver in the seasoned flour. Heat 4 tablespoons of the olive oil in a wide frying-pan over a brisk heat. Fry the strips of liver, in two batches if necessary, for about 2–3 minutes, until browned, but still pink in the centre. Drain briefly on kitchen paper. Fry the sliced onion in the same oil, adding more if needed, gently at first then raising the heat, once they are tender, to brown them. Drain on kitchen paper.

Place the warm liver in a shallow dish, top with a generous dollop of yoghurt, then scatter over the fried onion and the mint leaves. Drizzle a tablespoon or so of fresh olive oil over the top, dust with a little paprika and serve.

Rillettes and Rillons

These are two rustic, minimalist and essential French charcuterie dishes that are most economically made in tandem, though if you wish you can separate them out.

Rillons are slow-baked cubes of belly of pork, gently roasted until deep brown and meltingly tender. They can be eaten cold, sliced and served with cornichons or chutney and a tomato salad, though many people may, I suspect, find them a little too greasy. I've always preferred them hot (when I was a child, they were a regular mid-week treat when we were in France), simply re-heated in the oven then dished up with mashed potatoes and fried slices of apple.

Rillettes (always in the plural) are also made from belly of pork, but they demand a little more application and patience on the part of the cook. The cooked meat is torn into fine, fine shreds (a processor makes them too smooth) and potted down with the fat from cooking. When we walked back from school in France, we all looked forward to our goûter – tea-time snack – of a hunk of baguette smeared with rillettes. Many of our neighbours made their own, not only from pork, but often with mixtures of pork and rabbit or pork and goose. I remember M. Deroin's massive black cauldron that came out every year for the creation of rillettes. It was so big that it had to simmer over an outdoor fire, frequently stirred, sending its rich fragrance wafting across the village. Again, cornichons and other pickles go down well with rillettes.

This is my version of my mother's recipe for the pair, taken from her very first book, Charcuterie (Macmillan).

SERVES ABOUT 8
675 g (1 lb 8 oz) belly of pork, cut into
    10 cm (4 in) cubes
675 g (1 lb 8 oz) belly of pork, cut into
    2.5 cm × 5 mm (1 × $^{1}/_{4}$ in) wide strips
350 g (12 oz) flair fat (the softer body
    fat), cut into smallish pieces
4 sprigs of thyme
1 bayleaf
Salt

FOR THE QUATRE EPICES
2 tablespoons black peppercorns
1 teaspoon freshly ground nutmeg
1 teaspoon ground cloves
1 teaspoon ground cinnamon

Pre-heat the oven to 140°C/275°F/Gas Mark 1. Put all of the meats and fat into a shallow, heavy oven-proof dish, adding about 4 tablespoons of water to prevent them from sticking. Cover with foil and bake for about 4 hours. Remove from the oven and increase the temperature to about 200°C/400°F/Gas Mark 6. Pick out the large chunks of meat (these will make the *rillons*) and place them in a dish in the hot oven, uncovered, turning occasionally until they are richly browned. Once cooked, they can be eaten hot or cold.

The rest of the meat and fat will make the *rillettes*. Strain the meat, pressing through all the liquid fat. Save it and put it in the fridge to solidify. Transfer the strained meat (including small pieces of fat) to a mortar and pound to break down into a fibrous mush (unless you have a massive mortar, you'll have to do this in several batches). Return the *rillettes* to the dish and use a pair of forks to shred any lumps that remain – if you've pounded vigorously enough, there won't be many.

Make the Quatre Epices seasoning. Grind the peppercorns to a powder and mix with the remaining spices. Add 1 teaspoon to the meat along with the herbs and plenty of salt. (Store the remainder in an airtight jar.) Place over a low heat and cook gently for a further 10–15 minutes, stirring now and then to meld in the flavourings. Discard the bay leaf and thyme. Taste and adjust the seasoning, then pack the meat into small ramekins.

Lift the solidified fat out of the bowl in the fridge, leaving behind the juice. Melt and pour over enough to cover the meat shreds. Leave to cool, cover with foil or cling film and store in the fridge. Eat within 5 days.

Potato and Pepper Stew

This makes a perfect supper dish, as long as you can get good chorizo *to enliven the mixture of potatoes and peppers.*

SERVES 4

1.25 kg (2 lb 8 oz) potatoes
3 tablespoons olive oil
100 g (4 oz) cooking *chorizo*, skinned and roughly sliced
1 red pepper, seeded and diced

1 green pepper, seeded and diced
2 cloves garlic, crushed
1/2 teaspoon Spanish paprika (*pimentón*)
1 bay leaf
Salt and freshly ground black pepper

Peel the potatoes and cut into roughly 1 in (2.5 cm) chunks.

Warm the oil over a moderate heat in an earthenware *cazuela* or a wide heavy frying-pan. Add the *chorizo* and fry briskly until lightly browned. It will fall to pieces, but this doesn't matter. Reduce the heat and add all the remaining ingredients. Pour over just enough water to cover. Bring to the boil and simmer, stirring occasionally, for 20–30 minutes, until the potatoes are cooked and the liquid has reduced by about half. Taste and adjust the seasoning. Serve with plenty of good bread to mop up the juices.

Fish and Shellfish

Grilled Mackerel with Lemon, Tomato and Black Pepper Chutney

This sweet, sharp, peppery and slightly bitter chutney combines cooked and fresh ingredients and goes particularly well with the rich flesh of mackerel, touched with the smokiness that grilling or barbecuing brings.

SERVES 4

FOR THE CHUTNEY
2 lemons
4 tablespoons caster sugar
1/2 tablespoon black mustard seeds
1 teaspoon coriander seeds, coarsely crushed
1/2 teaspoon black peppercorns, coarsely crushed

2 plum tomatoes, seeded and finely diced

FOR THE MACKEREL
4 mackerel
Salt and freshly ground black pepper
1 lemon, quartered
Olive or sunflower oil

To make the chutney, slice the lemons thinly with a sharp knife, discarding the ends. Save all the juice that is squeezed out as you cut. Lay the lemon slices in a shallow dish in a single layer. Pour over enough boiling water just to cover. Leave for 3 minutes and then drain and repeat. Drain again. Cut the blanched lemon pieces into quarters. Put the sugar into a saucepan with 6 tablespoons of water. Stir over a medium heat, until the sugar has dissolved. Now add the quartered lemon slices, any juice and the spices. Simmer for about 20 minutes, stirring occasionally, until the liquid is reduced and syrupy, and the lemon is translucent and tender. Draw off the heat and stir in the tomatoes. Leave to cool.

For the mackerel, make two or three deep slashes across the fattest part of the body on each side. Season inside and out with salt and pepper and slip a wedge of lemon inside each fish. Brush with oil and grill, close to the heat, for 4–5 minutes on each side, until just cooked through. Serve with the tomtato and lemon chutney.

Sardines Stuffed with Currants and Pine Nuts

To the uninitiated this reads as Sicily's most baroque and unfathomable of dishes – sardines with dried currants and pine nuts and orange juice? But this is a genuine triumph. Once the sardines are boned the rest is easy going, and they take no time at all to cook. I like them hot, but it is more correct, I am told, to leave them to cool.

SERVES 4
12 small sardines, scaled and cleaned
75 g (3 oz) stale white breadcrumbs
4 tablespoons olive oil
50 g (2 oz) currants, soaked in warm
  water for 10 minutes and drained
50 g (2 oz) pine nuts
6 canned anchovy fillets, finely
  chopped

2 tablespoons finely chopped fresh
  parsley
Salt and freshly ground black pepper
6 bay leaves
Juice of $1/2$ lemon
Juice of $1/2$ orange

TO SERVE
Orange wedges

Pre-heat the oven to 180°C/350°F/Gas Mark 4.

The first task is to bone the sardines. Cut off the heads and dorsal fins and discard. Extend the cut along the belly right down to the tail end of each fish with a small knife. Open out the flaps and sit the fish on its belly with its back upwards. Press firmly down along the backbone with the heel of your hand, flattening the fish out. Turn it over and pull out the backbone. Rinse the fish and pat dry.

Brown the breadcrumbs in $2^1/2$ tablespoons of the olive oil over a low heat, stirring constantly. Draw off the heat and add the drained currants, pine nuts, chopped anchovies, parsley and some pepper. Lay the sardines cut side up, put a generous teaspoon of the filling on the wide end of each one and roll up towards the tail. Place in an oiled heatproof dish with the tails sticking up in the air, packing them in fairly tightly so that they don't unwind. Tuck the bay leaves in among them. Sprinkle over the lemon and orange juice and the remaining oil and season with salt and pepper. Bake in the oven for 15–25 minutes, until just cooked through. Serve hot or cold with orange wedges.

Marinated Fried Trout

Fresh fish may be a rarity in the Extremadura region of south-west central Spain, but every now and then it might be bought from the market or fished a few miles away in one of the burbling streams of the foothills of the Sierra Morena. As a result it is treated with great respect, cooked carefully with only the best of spices and aromatics. Preservation is of utmost importance if it isn't to be eaten immediately.

This dish fulfils all requirements. The fried fish is marinated with enough vinegar to preserve it for a few days, without overwhelming the delicate flavour. Golden saffron, cloves, bay leaves and oranges scent the flesh.

SERVES 4–8
4 small trout, scaled and cleaned
Salt and freshly ground black pepper
4 cloves garlic, unpeeled
1 bay leaf
Generous pinch of saffron threads

Seasoned flour
Olive oil for frying
2 oranges
6 cloves
4 tablespoons white wine vinegar

Cut the heads and fins off the fish. Season inside and out with salt and pepper, then leave in a cool place for 2 hours.

Heat a heavy iron griddle or frying-pan over a high flame until searingly hot. Lay the garlic in it and reduce the heat slightly. Roast the garlic, turning occasionally, until black on the outside but soft inside. Set aside.

Quickly toast the bay leaf, turning once and whipping it out before it can burn. Toast the saffron threads for a few seconds, then scrape out into a mortar. Crush the bay leaf and saffron threads to as fine a powder as possible. Peel the cloves of garlic and add the pulp to the mortar. Pound to a smooth paste. Sieve to remove the fibres, and reserve.

Coat the trout in seasoned flour, then fry in hot olive oil, turning once, until just cooked. Lay in a non-metallic dish that takes the fish snugly with little room to spare. Slice the oranges, skin and all, then stick the cloves into some of the slices and lay over the fish. Sprinkle with half the vinegar. Dilute the garlic paste with a little water and spoon over, then add enough water barely to cover the fish. Taste and see if you think it needs a little more vinegar to sharpen up, though the vinegar shouldn't be too intrusive. Cover and leave to marinate in the refrigerator for at least 24 hours before serving.

Red Mullet with Chicory and Orange

With its strong, gamey taste, red mullet is a fish that can carry the equally strong, bitter flavour of chicory in easy partnership. The chicory is cooked down to a moist sweet-bitter citrussy mass and served as an essential element with the fish.

SERVES 2

1/2 large orange	1 teaspoon sugar
15 g (1/2 oz) butter	2 × 175–225 g (6–8 oz) red mullet,
1 tablespoon finely chopped onion	scaled and cleaned
2 heads of chicory, sliced 5 mm (1/4 in)	Salt and freshly ground black pepper
thick	Olive oil for brushing
1 tablespoon lemon juice	A little chopped fresh parsley

Pare 4 wide strips of zest from the half orange, and cut into thin shreds. Blanch in boiling water for 2 minutes. Drain and set aside. Squeeze the juice from the orange and set aside.

Melt the butter in a small saucepan over a fairly low heat. Add the onion and cook gently until tender, without browning. Add the chicory and continue cooking, stirring, for a further 2 minutes or so. Mix in the orange juice, lemon juice, and sugar. Simmer, stirring occasionally, until the mixture is moist, rather than liquid – about 5 minutes. Season, and keep warm.

Meanwhile, make two deep slashes on each side of the mullet, brush with oil and season. Grill the mullet under a pre-heated grill, for about 4 minutes on each side until just cooked through. Serve with the chicory, scattered with the orange zest and a little chopped parsley.

Roast Red Mullet with Fennel and Olives

Red mullet and fennel are often cooked together in the south of France, although it is usually the wild herb fennel from the hills, rather than Florence fennel. The soft anise flavour of the vegetable is milder but works just as well.

SERVES 4

2 large or 3 medium-sized fennel bulbs

4 medium-sized red mullet, scaled and
   cleaned

Salt and freshly ground black pepper

2 lemons

4 tablespoons olive oil

12–16 black olives

Pre-heat the oven to 180°C/350°F/Gas Mark 4. Trim the stalks from each fennel bulb, saving all the feathery green fronds. Trim each base and discard the outer layer, if damaged. Halve and slice thinly and then blanch the slices in salted, boiling water for 2 minutes. Drain well.

Season the red mullet inside and out with salt and pepper. Tuck the feathery fennel leaves inside the mullet. Make a bed of fennel slices in an oiled, shallow oven-proof dish that is large enough to take the four mullet. Season the fennel. Lay the mullet on top, snuggling them down into the fennel. Squeeze the juice of one of the lemons over them and drizzle over the olive oil, making sure that the fennel gets bathed in oil as well. Roast for about 20 minutes, until the mullet are almost cooked, basting them with the juices every now and then.

Add the olives to the dish, dotting them around amongst the fennel, and return the dish to the oven for a final 5 minutes or so, to finish cooking. Serve hot from the oven, with the remaining lemon cut into wedges.

Salmon and Sorrel Parcels

Sorrel and fish were made for each other, a natural partnership if ever there was one. The usual way to prepare sorrel for cooking is to wash the leaves, dry them roughly and then make a chiffonade. *In other words, shred them very finely. Snip off thicker stalks, pile up five or six leaves at a time and roll them tightly into a cigar shape, then slice thinly to make fine ribbons of sorrel.*

The earthiness and richness of salmon are blessed by the acidity of sorrel. Make a quick sorrel sauce to go with grilled or baked salmon but if you have a little more time, try these parcels of salmon and sorrel wrapped in pastry. Get the upper portion of salmon, if possible, as it will be thicker and chunkier.

SERVES 4

450 g (1 lb) salmon fillet, skin removed,
**   cut into four portions**
60 g (2 oz) sorrel
1 egg yolk

340 g (12 oz) shortcrust pastry (see
**   p. 342)**
45 g (1^{1}/$_{2}$ oz) butter, softened
Salt and freshly ground black pepper

Season the salmon with salt and pepper. Finely shred the sorrel to make a *chiffonade*. Beat the egg yolk with a tablespoon of water.

Divide the pastry into four and roll each piece out thinly into a rectangle. Smear a quarter of the butter over the centre of each rectangle, covering a square roughly the same size as the salmon portion. Pile a quarter of the sorrel over the butter and lay a portion of salmon on top. Wrap up neatly, to form a parcel, trimming off excess pastry and pressing the edges together to seal. Set the parcels on a greased baking tray, turning them the right way up, with the joins neatly tucked away underneath. If you wish, cut little shapes out of the trimmings of the pastry – leaves, fish or whatever – and arrange them artfully on each parcel, gluing them in place with a little of the egg-yolk glaze. Leave to rest in the fridge for half an hour (or longer, if necessary). Pre-heat the oven to 220°C/425°F/Gas Mark 7.

Brush the parcels generously with the egg-yolk glaze and bake for about 20 minutes.

Grilled Marinated Tuna

This is how the Italians like to eat tuna on the island of Favignana, off the Sicilian coast. Salmoriglio *is the name given to the simple, fresh-tasting marinade of lemon juice, olive oil, garlic and oregano. When it comes to the grilling part, treat the tuna a little like steak, leaving it pink and juicy in the centre.*

SERVES 4

900 g (2 lb) tuna steaks, about 2 cm
**   (^{3}/$_{4}$ in) thick**
Juice of 1 large lemon
8 tablespoons olive oil
Salt and freshly ground black pepper

1 tablespoon dried oregano
1 clove garlic, crushed (optional)

TO SERVE
Lemon wedges

Divide the tuna into 4 portions if necessary, discarding the skin. Whisk the lemon juice with the olive oil, salt and pepper, then stir in the oregano and garlic if using. Pour over the tuna steaks and leave to marinate for at least 30 minutes, but preferably for a good 1–2 hours, turning once or twice.

Take the steaks out of the marinade and grill them, close to the heat, for about 4 minutes on each side, until browned outside but still slightly pink at the centre. Serve immediately with lemon wedges.

Seared Tuna with Anchovy and Tomato Sauce

Although inspired by Sicilian ingredients, this dish has more to do with my own kitchen than any traditional recipe from Sicily. The tuna is cooked rare, like steak, so that it retains its moistness and fresh flavour. The simple anchovy and tomato sauce makes a great partner.

SERVES 4

900 g (2 lb) tuna steaks, about 2 cm (3/4 in) thick
Juice of 1/2 lemon
150 ml (5 fl oz) olive oil
Salt and freshly ground black pepper

6 canned anchovy fillets, roughly chopped
2 cloves garlic, finely chopped
2 tomatoes, seeded and diced small
2 tablespoons chopped fresh parsley

Divide the tuna into 4 portions and marinate in the lemon juice, 4 tablespoons of the olive oil, salt and pepper, for at least 30 minutes.

Begin the sauce while you wait. Warm the remaining oil in a small saucepan and add the anchovies and garlic. Cook over a low heat, mashing in the anchovies with a fork, until they have melted down and the garlic is lightly browned. Then draw off the heat.

To cook the tuna, grease a heavy-based frying-pan with a little hot oil, then set over a high heat for about 5 minutes until searingly hot. Shake the excess marinade from the tuna and slap the pieces on to the hot metal (you may have to do this in 2 batches). Leave for 1 minute, then turn over and give the other side a minute too. With a sharp knife check the interior, which should still be rosy pink at the heart. If it is just too raw for your liking, reduce the heat and cook for a little longer.

As soon as the tuna is done, transfer it to a warm serving dish and keep warm. Add the tomato dice and parsley to the anchovy sauce, re-heat briefly and spoon over the tuna. Serve immediately.

Tuna with Onions and Chorizo

The sweetness of slowly fried onions is lovely with meaty tuna. Here a third element comes into play: spicy chorizo. The tuna itself picks up a hint of the chorizo flavour from the fat that it is cooked in.

SERVES 2
2 portions of tuna steak, cut 2 cm
    ($3/4$ in) thick, weighing about
    170–200 g (6–7 oz) each
1 garlic clove, cut into slivers
1 small fresh rosemary sprig
Olive oil
1 large onion, sliced

$1/2$ tablespoon sugar
$1/2$ tablespoon sherry vinegar
Salt and freshly ground black pepper
80 g (3 oz) cooking chorizo, sliced (but
    not peeled)

TO SERVE
Lemon wedges

Make slits all over the tuna and push in slivers of garlic and a few leaves of rosemary. Season and set aside until needed.

Heat 2 tablespoons of olive oil in a frying-pan and add the onion. Cook gently, stirring frequently, for about 10 minutes, until very tender and golden brown. Now add the sugar and vinegar and cook for a further 2–3 minutes, until the onions are nicely caramelized, tender and sweet and sour. Season lightly with salt and pepper. Re-heat, if necessary, when needed.

When you are almost ready to eat, wipe a heavy cast-iron frying pan or griddle with a little olive oil. Set over a high heat and leave to heat through for 5 minutes. Add the sliced chorizo and cook, turning once or twice, until browned and sizzling. Lift out, leaving its fat in the pan or griddle. Keep the chorizo warm. Lay the tuna steaks in the pan. Cook for about 1–1$1/2$ minutes on each side, so that they are browned on the outside but still pink inside. Serve immediately, with a mound of onions and a few pieces of browned chorizo and, of course, a wedge of lemon on each plate.

Grilled Tuna Salade Niçoise

Usually made with canned tuna, salade Niçoise is even nicer with fresh, dressed with balsamic or sherry vinegar instead of ordinary wine vinegar. All the elements can be prepared in advance (unless you want to serve the tuna hot from the grill), but don't put the salad together until the last possible moment. If you can get them, use the tiny, wrinkled olives from Nice.

SERVES 4 AS A MAIN COURSE
450 g (1 lb) tuna steaks, cut 2–3 cm
    ($3/4$–1 in) thick
Olive oil

FOR THE VINAIGRETTE
1–2 garlic cloves, crushed
1 tablespoon balsamic or sherry
    vinegar
4–5 tablespoons olive oil
2 tablespoons chopped fresh chives
Salt and freshly ground black pepper

FOR THE SALAD
340 g (12 oz) small new potatoes,
    boiled
110 g (4 oz) green beans, topped and
    tailed and cut in half
8 leaves cos lettuce, torn up
3 hard-boiled eggs, quartered
220 g (8 oz) cherry tomatoes, halved
8 canned or marinated anchovy fillets,
    cut in half lengthways
12–16 black olives

Grill or griddle the tuna steaks, brushed first with a little oil, for about 1–1$\frac{1}{2}$ minutes on each side. They should still be clearly pink in the middle. Meanwhile make the vinaigrette by mixing all the ingredients together. If necessary, skin and bone the tuna and then cut it into large chunks. Toss in a little of the dressing and leave to cool.

Slice the potatoes thickly while still hot, removing stray wisps of skin – if they are very small, leave them whole – and then toss in a little more of the dressing and leave them to cool.

Boil the green beans for about 4 minutes, until they are just on the soft side of *al dente*. Drain, run under the cold tap and then drain again thoroughly and mix with the potatoes.

Place the remaining dressing in the bottom of a large salad bowl. Just before serving, compile the salad in the bowl, starting with the lettuce and adding all the other ingredients, mixing lightly with your fingers as you do. Toss at the table.

Brill with Melted Onions and Cucumber

The mild flavour of cucumber makes it a natural to serve with delicately flavoured fish. Here it is cooked with slowly stewed, sweet onions, to form a bed for the fillets of brill.

SERVES 4
4 large brill fillets
Salt and freshly ground black pepper
$^1/_2$ cucumber, cut into 1 cm ($^1/_2$ in) cubes
50 g (2 oz) butter
2 large onions, thinly sliced

1 tablespoon sherry vinegar or red wine vinegar
$^1/_2$ tablespoon light muscovado sugar

TO SERVE
1 tablespoon chopped fresh parsley

Season the brill fillets lightly with salt and pepper and set aside in the fridge. Put the cucumber into a colander and sprinkle with a teaspoon of salt. Leave for 30 minutes to drain. Rinse, then pat dry on kitchen paper.

Melt the butter in a large frying-pan. Add the onions, and stir to coat in butter. Cover (use a large plate if you don't have a lid to fit) and cook very gently for 20 minutes, stirring occasionally. Add the cucumber, vinegar, sugar and some pepper, stir again, then cook uncovered over a gentle heat for another 20 minutes until the onion is meltingly tender. Check occasionally and if absolutely necessary add a tablespoon or so of water to prevent burning.

Lay the brill fillets on top of the onion and cucumber mixture, cover the pan again, and continue cooking gently for 12–15 minutes until the fish is just cooked. Sprinkle with parsley and serve immediately.

Brill with Saffron Sauce

Once you've made and reduced the fish stock (which can be done in advance), this is a brilliantly easy dish to make. The pale fish surrounded by golden sauce, dotted with capers and bright green parsley, looks and tastes magnificent. Lemon sole or plaice makes a more everyday substitute for brill.

SERVES 4

FOR THE FISH STOCK
Bones and trimmings from the fish
100 ml (3¹/₂ fl oz) Noilly Prat or dry white wine
1 tablespoon Pernod
1 carrot, quartered
1 leek, thickly sliced, or ¹/₂ onion, quartered
1 celery stick, thickly sliced
6 peppercorns
1 bay leaf
2 fresh parsley sprigs

FOR THE FISH
2 brill, lemon sole or plaice, weighing about 1.5 kg (3 lb) each, filleted and skinned
3 tablespoons plain flour
Salt and freshly ground black pepper
1 heaped teaspoon ground cumin
30 g (1 oz) butter
1 tablespoon sunflower oil
¹/₈ teaspoon ground saffron
Lemon juice

TO SERVE
1 tablespoon small capers
Chopped fresh parsley
Lemon or lime wedges

Begin by making the fish stock. Put all the ingredients into a pan, with enough water to cover generously. Bring to the boil and leave to simmer for 20 minutes. Skim any scum off the stock. Strain the stock and discard the debris. Pour it into a wide frying-pan and boil hard, until syrupy and reduced by about three-quarters. Measure out 150 ml (5 fl oz) and reserve (any left-over stock can be frozen). Season the fish fillets lightly with salt and set aside for half an hour.

Pat the fillets dry. Mix the flour with a little salt and pepper and the cumin. Heat half the butter and all the oil until foaming, in a frying-pan that is large enough to take all the fillets. Dust the fish fillets with the seasoned flour, shake off any excess and lay them in the pan. Fry for about 2 minutes on each side, or until just cooked through. Transfer the fish to a warm serving dish and keep warm while you finish the sauce.

Tip excess fat out of the pan and add the reduced fish stock. Sprinkle over the saffron and stir over a moderate heat until very hot. Season with salt and pepper and a dash of lemon juice. Add the remaining butter in small knobs and swirl, tip and tilt the pan until the butter has melted into the sauce, thickening it lightly and giving it a rich gloss. Taste and adjust the seasoning.

Serve the fish surrounded by a pool of saffron sauce, scattered with capers and parsley and accompanied by lemon or lime wedges.

Three-minute Fish with Cucumber Celery Relish

The crunchy spiced relish is a great complement to the pure flavour of the briefly cooked fish, but there's no good reason not to serve the relish with other things. I like it with chicken, too, or even with bread and cheese.

SERVES 4–6

FOR THE RELISH
1/2 cucumber, finely diced
Salt
2 stalks celery, finely diced
4 tablespoons rice vinegar or
    white wine vinegar or tarragon
    vinegar
1 1/2 teaspoons peeled and grated fresh
    ginger
2 teaspoons caster sugar
1 1/2 teaspoons mustard seeds

1 teaspoon dill seed
1/2 medium onion, very finely diced
1/2–1 green chilli, seeded and very
    finely chopped

FOR THE FISH
500–750 g (1 1/4–1 1/2 lb) fillet of cod,
    halibut or other firm white fish or
    salmon
Olive oil for brushing

TO GARNISH
Chopped fresh chives

Start with the relish. Spread the cucumber dice out in a colander and sprinkle with 1/2 teaspoon of salt. Leave to drain for 30 minutes, then rinse and pat dry. Mix with the celery.

Place the vinegar, ginger, sugar and seeds in a small saucepan and bring to the boil, stirring to dissolve the sugar. Simmer for 2 minutes, then add the onion and chilli, stir and draw off the heat. Mix with the cucumber and celery. Cool and leave for 30 minutes or up to 24 hours, covered and in the fridge.

Place the fish in the freezer for 15–30 minutes to firm up (not absolutely necessary, but it makes the slicing easier). Slice the fish as thinly as you can. Brush 1 large or 4 individual heatproof dishes with olive oil. Arrange the fish slices on top overlapping as little as possible. Brush with olive oil.

Pre-heat the oven to its highest setting and when everyone is gathered at table, whizz the fish into the oven for 3 minutes, or until the slices begin to turn opaque. Scatter over a few chives and serve quickly with the cool relish.

Roast Cod with a Coriander Crust

This use of coriander in a breadcrumb crust is the kind of thing that has become very fashionable in Britain over recent years. If you can lay your hands on a really fresh bit of cod, this recipe will show it off at its very best.

SERVES 4
675 g (1 lb 8 oz) freshest cod fillet
Salt and freshly ground black pepper
85 g (3 oz) soft or slightly stale white
    breadcrumbs
3 generous tablespoons chopped fresh
    coriander

3 garlic cloves, crushed
Finely grated zest of $1/2$ lemon
60 g (2 oz) butter, melted
Lemon wedges, to serve

Pre-heat the oven to 220°C/425°F/Gas Mark 7. Season the cod with salt and pepper. Mix the breadcrumbs with the coriander, garlic, lemon zest, salt and pepper and then add the butter and mix thoroughly with your fingers. Place the cod in a shallow, oven-proof dish and press the buttered crumbs firmly on to the cod, to form an even crust. Bake for 20–30 minutes, until the crust is browned and the fish just about cooked through. Serve immediately.

Salt Cod Fritters with Spring Onion Aïoli

They fry up fabulous salt cod fritters in Spain and Jamaica, but the best in the world are the ones made by my friend Martin Lam, chef-patron of Ransome's Dock Restaurant in Battersea, south London. This is his recipe, though the spring onions in the aïoli are my idea. Crisp on the outside, tender inside, these fritters are good enough to convert the dubious and even those who profess to dislike salt cod.

Good dried salt cod is creamy-white and fairly thick in the centre. The best quality is to be found in Italian, Spanish and Portuguese delicatessens. West Indian shops and some supermarkets also stock salt cod. Try to buy it from a shop where they stock the whole flat, salty triangle of cod and will slice it for you with a purpose-made salt cod guillotine. The best cut is from the upper, wider part of the breast, where the flesh is thickest.

Remember that cheap salt cod is likely to be bad salt cod. The triangles will prob-ably be small, mean and scrawny, the flesh yellowing (a particularly bad sign) and thin, with a high ratio of waste to flesh and often over-salty. No bargain there. In fact, you'll be hard put to turn out anything edible at all. Most dried salt cod will require 24 hours' soaking to rehydrate it and draw out the salt, but every now and then you hit on a piece that will take a bit more time, so always allow 36 hours to be on the safe side. After all, it doesn't matter if it is soaked for longer than necessary but over salty cod can ruin an entire dish and a terrible waste that would be, too.

To prepare salt cod, begin by rinsing thoroughly under the tap, to remove surface salt. Lay in a shallow dish in a single layer, cut up into chunks with scissors or a saw if necessary, and cover with cold water. Soak for 24–36 hours, changing the water as frequently as practicable. It must be at least three times but more is better. After

24 hours, nibble a small corner of the cod to get some idea of its remaining saltiness. Change the water again and give it more time if it still seems overpowering.

To cook wet-cured salt cod, put the cod into a shallow pan and cover with water or milk. Bring gently up to a rolling boil and then draw off the heat, cover and leave to stand for 15–20 minutes, by which time the cod will be beautifully cooked through. Dried salt cod will need longer cooking – poach it, either in water or milk, for about 10–15 minutes, until it flakes easily. Check regularly, as timing can vary considerably from one batch to another. Poorer-quality salt cod can take as much as 20 minutes. Take care to keep the heat gentle: boiling makes the cod stringy and tough. Once cooked, drain the cod and flake and skin it as necessary, discarding any bones.

SERVES 6 AS A FIRST COURSE
500 g (1 lb 2 oz) floury potatoes
400 g (14 oz) salt cod, soaked
Milk
2 tablespoons double cream
1 teaspoon paprika
1/2 tablespoon lemon juice
Freshly ground black pepper
1–2 eggs
Sunflower or vegetable oil for
**   deep-frying**

FOR THE AÏOLI
2 garlic cloves, crushed
2 egg yolks
1 tablespoon Dijon mustard
1 tablespoon white wine vinegar
200 ml (6 fl oz) sunflower oil
100 ml (4 fl oz) olive oil
5 spring onions, very finely chopped
Salt and freshly ground black pepper

TO SERVE
Lemon wedges

Bake the potatoes in their skins.

To cook salt cod, put the cod into a shallow pan and cover with water or milk. Bring gently up to a bare simmer and poach for 10–15 minutes until it flakes easily. Check regularly.

To make the aïoli, mix the garlic, egg yolks, mustard and white wine vinegar. Mix the two oils in a jug. Whisking continuously, trickle the oils very slowly into the egg yolk mixture. When about half has been incorporated, increase the flow to a steady stream, still whisking away non-stop. When all the oil has gone, you will have a wonderful golden, creamy mass of garlicky mayonnaise. Stir in the spring onions and then taste and adjust the seasonings.

Drain and flake the salt cod, discarding skin and bones. Weigh the prepared cod.

Scrape out the potato flesh and weigh out an equal quantity to the salt cod. Put into a bowl together, and add the cream, paprika, lemon juice, pepper and one of the eggs. Beat together with a wooden spoon and plenty of elbow grease (if you have a Kenwood Chef or a Kitchenaid, use that. You can use a food processor, but it will make the mixture gluey and too smooth). Beat the remaining egg lightly and, if necessary, add it gradually until you have a mixture that is soft and holds together well but is not too sloppy to roll into balls. You may not need it at all. Flour your hands and roll into balls about 2.5 cm (1 in) across.

Heat the oil to 170°C/325°F and deep-fry the balls, a few at a time, until they are a rich even brown. Drain briefly on kitchen paper and serve with wedges of lemon and the aïoli.

Portuguese Salt Cod Croquettes

When they are freshly cooked, with a generous proportion of salt cod to potato, these croquettes are absolutely irresistible. If you've tried them in Portugal, and rejected them as far too heavy and stodgy and over-salty, then I suggest you try making your own. You'll soon notice the difference.

MAKES 16–18

225 g (8 oz) salt cod, soaked and drained (see Salt Cod Fritters with Spring Onion Aïoli, p. 73)
350 g (12 oz) floury potatoes, boiled in their skins
1 small onion, finely chopped
2 cloves garlic, finely chopped
2 tablespoons finely chopped fresh parsley
Salt and freshly ground black pepper
1–2 eggs, lightly beaten
Sunflower or olive oil for deep-frying

Place the salt cod in a wide pan and cover with water. Bring slowly to a quiet simmer, and simmer for 5–10 minutes depending on thickness, until it flakes easily. Drain, and flake with your fingers, discarding the skin and bones. Using a fork and your fingers, tear the fish into fine threads. Peel the potatoes and mash thoroughly or, even better, pass through the fine blade of a *mouli-légumes* (vegetable mill).

Mix the cod and potatoes with the onion, garlic, parsley, pepper and salt if needed. Add enough egg to form a cohesive stiff mass – at this stage use your hands to mix and work the paste. Let it cool completely.

Take egg-sized pieces of the mixture and, using 2 tablespoons, shape them into small rugby-ball croquettes. Deep-fry a few at a time in hot oil at 182°C/360°F until richly browned. Drain briefly on kitchen paper and eat straight away.

If you want to re-heat any, pop them back in hot oil for a few minutes to crisp up.

Salt Cod with Potatoes and Olives

This is quite possibly the best ever way of cooking salt cod. I tucked into it gleefully when Maria Jose showed me how to make it for the television series Travels à la Carte, *eating far more than was good for me. It's one of those dishes that is somehow more than the sum of its parts, a blessed blend of tastes and textures, brought together with plenty of rich olive oil – don't be tempted to reduce the quantity for the sake of a few calories.*

SERVES 4–6

450 g (1 lb) salt cod, soaked and
    drained (see Salt Cod Fritters with
    Spring Onion Aïoli, p. 73)
4 eggs
4 medium potatoes, boiled in their
    skins

150 ml (5 fl oz) olive oil
3 cloves garlic, chopped
2 large onions, chopped
3 tablespoons finely chopped fresh
    parsley
Salt and freshly ground black pepper
20 black olives

Put the salt cod and eggs (still in their shells) into a pan and add enough water to cover. Bring to the boil and simmer for 8 minutes. Remove the eggs and check on the cod to see how it is doing. If it flakes easily, drain it. If it doesn't, simmer gently for a few more minutes until it's done, then drain. Flake the cod, discarding the skin and bones. Shell the eggs and slice. Peel the cooked potatoes and cut into 2.5 cm (1 in) chunks.

Put the olive oil and garlic into a wide, deep frying-pan and warm over a gentle heat for a minute or so, then add the onions. Cook until the onions are translucent and tender, without browning. Now add the flaked salt cod, stir for a minute and add the potatoes. Continue stirring until piping hot, then stir in the parsley and pepper. Add a little salt if it is needed, but be careful as the cod may have already provided quite enough. Tip into a warm serving dish and garnish with the sliced eggs and olives. Serve immediately.

Cold Roast Swordfish with Caper, Tuna and Sun-dried Tomato Mayonnaise

Inspired by vitello tonnato, *that magnificent Italian dish of veal with tuna mayonnaise, (see p. 146) this takes the fishy theme one step further, by replacing veal with a great hunk of swordfish. Roast swordfish is far nicer cold than hot and better still with this zesty mayonnaise. An excellent cold dish for a summer party.*

SERVES 4–6

1 kg (2 lb 4 oz) piece of swordfish
2 garlic cloves, cut into long, thin
    slivers
110 ml (4 fl oz) dry white wine
2 tablespoons olive oil
Salt and freshly ground black pepper

FOR THE MAYONNAISE
1¹/₂ tablespoons capers

3 anchovy fillets, roughly chopped
100 g (3¹/₂ oz) canned tuna, drained
2 tablespoons sun-dried tomato purée
8 tablespoons mayonnaise
Salt and freshly ground black pepper
A dash of lemon juice

TO GARNISH
Chopped fresh parsley

Pre-heat the oven to 190°C/375°F/Gas Mark 5. Don't muck around with the swordfish: leave it in one big chunk with the skin on. The one thing you should do is to make small slits here and there through the skin and push in slivers of garlic. Place the joint of swordfish, skin-side up, in a shallow, lightly oiled baking dish. Pour over the white wine, drizzle with olive oil and season with salt and pepper. Roast, basting frequently, for 40–45 minutes, until just cooked through but no more than that. Leave to cool, basting occasionally with its own juices.

Meanwhile, make the mayonnaise by processing all the ingredients except the seasoning together until smooth. Taste and adjust the seasoning with salt, pepper and a dash of lemon juice.

To serve, slice the swordfish as thinly as you can with a very sharp knife, discarding the skin, and arrange the slices on a dish. Serve straight away, with the mayonnaise in a separate bowl. Alternatively, spread the mayonnaise over the fish before serving and scatter with a little chopped parsley.

Baked Monkfish with Coriander and Red Peppers

This special-occasion-only recipe brings together a whole host of my favourite ingredients: grilled red peppers, monkfish, coriander, garlic, soy sauce and olive oil. Bliss.

SERVES 4
2 red peppers
750 g–1 kg (1 lb 8 oz–2 lb) monkfish tail
8 spring onions, cut into 5 cm (2 in) lengths
2 tablespoons roughly chopped fresh coriander

2 cloves garlic, finely chopped
1 tablespoon dark soy sauce
Juice of 1/2 lemon
5 tablespoons olive oil
Salt and freshly ground black pepper

Quarter the red peppers and grill, skin-side up, as close as possible to the heat, until they are blackened and blistered all over. Drop into a plastic bag, knot the end, and leave until cool enough to handle whilst you get on with organizing the rest of the dish.

Pre-heat the oven to 190°C/375°F/Gas Mark 5. Pull off the thin membrane covering the monkfish tail if the fishmonger hasn't already done it. Place the tail in an oiled ovenproof dish. Scatter the spring onions, coriander and garlic around and over the fish. Return to the peppers, and strip off the blackened skins. Cut into strips and scatter over the fish, along with any juice from the peppers. Pour 4 tablespoons water around the fish, then trickle the soy sauce, lemon juice and olive oil evenly over it. Season lightly with salt and pepper.

Roast the fish, uncovered, for 25–30 minutes, basting occasionally with its own juices, until cooked through. Serve immediately.

Fish Gratin

Mmm, this is a wickedly creamy, luxurious sort of gratin, the type one shouldn't eat too often, tempting though it is. The cream and egg yolks give the sauce a voluptuous texture, and the pungency of Parmesan sets it all off brilliantly. Shrimps or prawns may be optional, but I'd be loath to leave them out.

SERVES 4 GENEROUSLY
750 g (1 lb 8 oz) white fish fillets (such as cod or haddock)
Salt and freshly ground black pepper
1 tablespoon lemon juice
45 g (1¹/₂ oz) butter
25 g (1 oz) flour
300 ml (10 fl oz) milk

150 ml (5 fl oz) single cream
100 g (4 oz) cooked shrimps or prawns (shelled weight), roughly chopped (optional)
2 egg yolks
50 g (2 oz) Parmesan or other full-flavoured hard cheese, freshly grated

Pre-heat the oven to 180°C/350°F/Gas Mark 4.

Put the fish fillets into a lightly buttered ovenproof dish and season with salt, pepper and lemon juice. Cover with foil and bake in the oven for about 20 minutes, until just cooked. Drain off any liquid and quickly flake the fish, discarding the skin. Place in a shallow gratin dish.

Meanwhile melt the butter in a saucepan and stir in the flour. Stir for a minute, then draw off the heat and gradually mix in the milk, a little at a time, followed by the cream. Bring to the boil and simmer for 5–10 minutes, until thick, with no trace of raw flour taste. Draw off the heat again and stir in the shrimps or prawns (if using), then the egg yolks, salt and pepper. Pour over the cooked fish and sprinkle with Parmesan. Whip under a pre-heated grill until nicely browned.

If you've cooked the fish in advance, or are using left-overs from another meal, prepare as above, but finish the gratin in the oven at about 190°C/375°F/Gas Mark 5, baking until nicely browned – about 20–25 minutes.

Stir-fried Prawns with Honey and Spices

This is a marvellous treat of a first course or light main course for a special occasion. I can see that you might have doubts. I quite agree that honey and prawns don't sound too promising together but, believe me, in this instance, it is a combination that really works. The honey plays a relatively quiet, but not unimportant, role tempered by the saltiness of soy sauce, garlic and spices. This is definitely not breakfast with prawns on top.

For a starter, serve the prawns just as they are, with some good bread to mop up the juices. For a main course, serve them with rice and maybe some stir-fried mangetout or broccoli.

SERVES 4

16 large, raw, shell-on prawns (tiger prawns or king prawns)
1¹/₂ tablespoons sunflower oil

FOR THE MARINADE
2 generous tablespoons honey

4 tablespoons dry sherry
2 tablespoons dark soy sauce
¹/₂ teaspoon Chinese five-spice powder
2 garlic cloves, finely chopped
2.5 cm (1 in) piece of fresh ginger, grated

Mix together the marinade ingredients and pour them over the prawns. Turn to coat evenly, then cover and marinate for at least an hour, or longer, in which case, be sure to put them in the fridge. If necessary, bring back to room temperature before cooking. Turn the prawns once in a while as they marinate.

Take the prawns out of the marinade. Heat a wok or a wide frying-pan over a high heat until it smokes and then add the oil. Give it a couple of seconds, then add the prawns and stir-fry for about 1 minute, until they have all turned pink. Pour in the marinade and 2 tablespoons of water. Let the liquids bubble down until they are well reduced and syrupy, stirring constantly – a matter of a few minutes – and serve immediately.

Don't forget to pass round plenty of napkins for all those sticky fingers.

Stir-fried Squid with Onions and Black Beans

This is so delicious, particularly if you can find fresh squid (instead of frozen) which is as tender as butter. The quickly fried onion provides sweetness which contrasts beautifully with the salty black beans. Preparing the squid takes a little time, though it isn't difficult, but once that's done the rest is quick and straightforward.

Salted black beans are available from Chinese food stores, but make sure you are buying the whole beans and not the cans of black bean sauce. Stored in a tightly closed screw-top jar, they will keep for months.

SERVES 4

450 g (1 lb) squid
2 dried red chillies
2 tablespoons Chinese salted black beans
2 tablespoons dry sherry
¹/₂ tablespoon sugar
1 teaspoon cornflour

2 tablespoons oil
2 cloves garlic, peeled and chopped
1 cm (¹/₂ in) piece fresh ginger, peeled and finely chopped
2 large red onions, halved and thinly sliced
Salt and freshly ground black pepper

Prepare the squid. For each one, pull the head away from the body sac, bringing with it the insides. Discard the head and innards. Chop off the tentacles and reserve. Pull the thin purply black skin off the body sac. Split each sac open and discard the quill and any gunk left inside. Cut off the 'wings'. Score the insides of all the sacs and the wings in a criss-cross fashion. Cut the sacs into pieces about 2.5 cm (1 in) across and 5 cm (2 in) long.

Soak the chillies in warm water for 10 minutes, drain, remove the seeds and chop. Mash the black beans roughly with the sherry and sugar, and stir in the cornflour.

Heat the oil in a wok (or large frying-pan) over a high heat. When just beginning to smoke, add the garlic, chilli and ginger and stir-fry for a few seconds. Add the red onions and stir-fry for about 2 minutes, until they are patched with brown and softening. Now add the squid and stir-fry for 30 seconds to 1 minute until opaque and curled. Stir the black bean sauce, then tip it into the wok. Stir to coat the squid and onion and simmer for about 1 minute until the liquid is thickened. Serve immediately.

Poultry and Game

Chicken with Watercress Sauce

This is an elegant cream-and-green-coloured dish, with a fresh gently peppery taste. I sometimes use the same method with fish, adjusting the timing to cook fillets or steaks as appropriate.

SERVES 4

1 bunch of watercress
25 g (1 oz) butter
1 tablespoon oil
4 chicken breasts, boned and skinned

1 shallot, finely chopped
Wine glass of dry white wine
150 ml (5 fl oz) double cream
Salt, freshly ground black pepper and nutmeg

Strip the leaves off the watercress stalks, discarding any damaged leaves (save the stalks for soup). Set aside a dozen or so leaves for decoration, and chop the remainder fairly finely.

Melt the butter with the oil in a frying-pan just large enough to take the chicken breasts. When it is foaming, lay the chicken in the pan. Brown lightly, then cover and cook over a moderate heat for 15–20 minutes, until just cooked through. Remove the chicken and keep to one side.

Now add the chopped shallot to the pan and cook gently for 2–3 minutes until tender, without browning. Pour in the wine and let it bubble, scraping up the residues in the pan, until it is reduced to a scant tablespoonful or two. Draw off the heat, let the bubbles subside and then stir in the cream and the chopped watercress. Simmer for 5 minutes until reduced by about half. Season with salt, pepper, and a little nutmeg, then return the chicken to the pan and let it simmer for about 3 minutes so that it is thoroughly re-heated. Serve, scattered with reserved watercress leaves.

Thai Stir-fried Chicken with Basil

I first tasted this in a market in northern Thailand where holy basil is cheap enough to use with unfettered abandon. It is cooked in two shakes and makes a marvellously quick lunch with a bowl of rice. If you can't get holy basil, then ordinary sweet basil does just fine as a stand-in.

SERVES 4

50 g (2 oz) basil leaves
4 tablespoons vegetable oil
450 g (1 lb) boned, skinned chicken, coarsely minced or finely chopped
4 shallots, finely sliced
4 garlic cloves, chopped

3 red chillies, seeded and thinly shredded
1 cm ($^{1}/_{2}$ in) piece fresh root ginger, finely chopped
2 tablespoons Thai fish sauce (*nam pla*)
2 teaspoons dark muscovado sugar
Salt, if needed

Set aside 5 or 6 basil leaves for a final garnish and tear up the rest roughly. Heat a wok over a high heat for a couple of minutes, then add 2 tablespoons of oil. Wait a few seconds for the oil to get really hot, then add the chicken and stir-fry until just cooked through – this will take no more than a minute or two. Scrape the chicken out into a bowl.

Add the remaining oil to the wok and heat thoroughly. Add the shallots and stir-fry for about 30 seconds. Now add the garlic, chillies and ginger and stir-fry for another minute. Add the torn-up basil leaves and stir-fry for a further 1 minute. Finally, return the chicken and its juices to the pan along with the fish sauce and sugar. Stir-fry briefly to heat the chicken again until piping hot. Scoop into a serving dish, top with the reserved basil and serve with rice.

Savoy-wrapped Chicken Breasts

Steaming keeps chicken moist and tender, but leaves it looking rather pallid. A jacket of green Savoy cabbage covers its nakedness and tastes good too. Interior colour comes in the form of sun-dried tomatoes and chives.

SERVES 4
4 chicken breasts, boned and skinned
6 sun-dried tomatoes in oil, chopped
100 g (4 oz) goats' cheese

2 tablespoons chopped chives
Salt and freshly ground black pepper
8 large Savoy cabbage leaves

Season the chicken breasts lightly. Mash the sun-dried tomatoes with the goats' cheese, chives, plenty of freshly ground pepper and a little salt, if needed. Smear the stuffing between the fillet and the main breast.

Blanch the cabbage leaves in boiling water for about 1 minute until pliable. Drain and run under cold water. Drain again and pat dry. Snip out the thick part of the stem then wrap them around the chicken breasts, enclosing them completely (you may not need all of the leaves).

Steam for 15–20 minutes, until just cooked through.

Devilled Drumsticks

In summertime, devilling sauces are perfect for smearing over chicken that is about to be grilled over the barbecue (or under the kitchen grill if barbecues are out of the question). The anointed drumsticks can also be cooked in the oven – very handy if you are preparing them for a large party of people, though of course you won't get the extra smoky flavour that comes with the barbecue or grill.

SERVES 4
8 chicken drumsticks
A little sunflower oil for baking

FOR THE DEVILLED SAUCE
1 tablespoon clear honey

1 tablespoon Worcestershire sauce
1 tablespoon Dijon mustard
2 tablespoons sunflower oil
A generous pinch of cayenne pepper
1/2 teaspoon salt

Pre-heat the oven to 200°C/400°F/Gas Mark 6 if baking. Mix together the sauce ingredients, then brush or smear all over the drumsticks.

To bake, arrange the drumsticks on a lightly oiled shallow baking tray. Place in the oven for 30 minutes, turning occasionally, until well browned and cooked right through to the bone. Serve hot or cold.

To grill, pre-heat the grill thoroughly. Line the grill pan with foil, then arrange the drumsticks on the rack and grill, about 10 cm (4 in) from the heat, turning frequently until dark brown and cooked through to the bone. Brush the drumsticks with any left-over sauce as they cook.

To barbecue, keep the drumsticks about 10–12 cm (4–5 in) away from the glowing charcoal so that they cook through before they burn to a frazzle. Brush with any left-over sauce as they cook.

Marinated Drumsticks with Salsa Mexicana

Salsa Mexicana is the most fundamental of all salsas, the prototype for a hundred and one variations. It is very easy to make – just a matter of chopping really – and can be served with everything, from grilled beef steak to fish and chicken. I usually make a double batch because I will always use it up in one way or another. I like it with bread and cheese, and one or two spoonfuls scattered over a dull soup can work wonders.

SERVES 4
8 chicken drumsticks

FOR THE MARINADE
Juice of 1 lime
4 tablespoons olive oil
1 teaspoon ground cumin
1 tablespoon tomato ketchup
1 tablespoon honey
1 medium-hot fresh red chilli, seeded and finely chopped
2 thyme sprigs, bruised
Salt and freshly ground black pepper

FOR THE SALSA
500 g (1 lb 2 oz) tomatoes, skinned, seeded and finely diced
1/2 fresh red Scotch Bonnet or *habanero* chilli (very hot) or 1 milder red or green chilli, seeded and finely chopped
Juice of 1/2–1 lime
1/2 red onion, finely chopped
2 garlic cloves, crushed
4–5 tablespoons chopped fresh coriander
Salt
Sugar

Mix all the ingredients for the marinade and smear them over the chicken drumsticks. Leave to marinate for an hour or two.

Mix together all the salsa ingredients and then taste and adjust the seasoning, adding salt and a pinch or two of sugar, to taste. Cover and set aside until needed.

Pre-heat the oven to 190°C/375°F/Gas Mark 5 or pre-heat the grill to hot. Either roast the drumsticks for 20–30 minutes, turning occasionally, until browned and cooked through, or else grill them gently, turning frequently, until browned and perfectly cooked. Pierce the thickest part with a skewer to make sure the juices run clear and the flesh isn't pink.

Serve the drumsticks as a family supper or as part of a barbecue. Make sure you have lots of napkins to hand!

Grilled Chicken Thighs with Lemon Grass

A simple recipe from Vietnam, where lemon grass is used extensively and joyfully. Pork chops can be substituted for the chicken thighs.

SERVES 4
8 boneless, skinless chicken thighs

FOR THE MARINADE
2 garlic cloves, chopped
2 small shallots, chopped
1 tablespoon caster sugar
3 lemon grass stems, trimmed, bruised and finely chopped
1 tablespoon Thai fish sauce (*nam pla*)
Salt and freshly ground black pepper

FOR THE DIPPING SAUCE
2 garlic cloves, chopped
1 fresh red chilli, seeded and finely chopped
1 cm (¹/2 in) piece of fresh ginger, roughly chopped
2 tablespoons caster sugar
Juice of 1 lime
4 tablespoons rice vinegar or cider vinegar
4 tablespoons Thai fish sauce (*nam pla*)

For the marinade, pound the garlic with the shallots and the sugar. Add the lemon grass and give that a few poundings as well. Mix in the remaining ingredients and spoon over the chicken thighs. Leave to marinate for at least an hour or, better still, overnight, turning occasionally.

To make the dipping sauce, pound the garlic, chilli, ginger and sugar to a paste in a mortar, with a pestle. Stir in the remaining ingredients, adding 3 tablespoons of water.

Cook the meat under a thoroughly pre-heated grill (or on the barbecue) for about 5–8 minutes on each side, until cooked through and patched with brown. Serve immediately, with the dipping sauce.

African Chicken in Peanut Sauce

Ground peanuts (plain, not salted or dry-roasted, please) are what thicken the sauce of this African chicken stew. It's the kind of dish that will please both children (as long as you keep the cayenne pepper to a minimum) and adults. The original recipe I was given called for the chicken to be cut into four, though I prefer smaller pieces – say eight altogether. I leave the choice to you.

SERVES 4

100 g (4 oz) raw, shelled peanuts (unsalted)
1.5–1.75 kg (3–4 lb) chicken, jointed
2 tablespoons oil
1 onion, finely chopped
100 g (4 oz) tomatoes, skinned and roughly chopped
1 tablespoon tomato purée
$1/2$–1 teaspoon cayenne pepper
1 tablespoon paprika
$1/2$ teaspoon each ground ginger, cinnamon and coriander
Salt
450 ml (15 fl oz) chicken stock

Spread the peanuts out on a baking tray and toast in a hot oven – 200°C/400°F/Gas Mark 6 – for 5–8 minutes until lightly browned, shaking and checking frequently. Cool, then grind to a powdery paste.

Brown the chicken in the oil and transfer to a flame-proof casserole. Cook the onion gently in the same oil until golden. Add the tomatoes, tomato purée, spices and salt. Stir for about 3 minutes, then add the stock. Bring to the boil, stirring, then pour over the chicken. Cover, reduce the heat and simmer for 30 minutes.

Stir in the ground peanuts, breaking up the larger lumps (the small ones will dissolve as the sauce simmers). Continue to simmer, covered, for a further 10–15 minutes, until the chicken is tender and the sauce has thickened. Skim the fat from the surface, then taste and adjust the seasonings before serving.

Chicken Marengo

The battle of Marengo took place in June 1800. Napoleon, ravenous after a hard day's slaughter and tactics, asked his chef, Dunand, for a good, satisfying supper. All that Dunand could lay his hands on was a chicken, a bottle of white wine, tomatoes, garlic and mushrooms (not bad going, if you ask me), and with these ingredients he created Poulet à la Marengo.

SERVES 4

1.5–2 kg (3 lb 8 oz–4 lb) chicken, cut into
   8 pieces
50 g (2 oz) butter
2 tablespoons sunflower oil
1 onion, chopped
1 tablespoon flour
1 generous glass white wine

400 g (14 oz) can chopped tomatoes
2 garlic cloves, chopped
1 bouquet garni (1 bay leaf, 2 sprigs
   parsley and 2 sprigs thyme, tied
   together with string)
Salt and freshly ground black pepper
175 g (6 oz) button mushrooms, halved
   or quartered if large

Brown the chicken briskly in half the butter and oil then set aside. Add the onion to the pan and fry gently until tender. Sprinkle over the flour, stir for a few seconds then add the wine. Bring to the boil, stirring and scraping in all the residues stuck to the bottom of the pan. Now add the tomatoes, garlic, bouquet garni, salt and pepper and return the chicken to the pan. Add enough hot water to cover the chicken then bring to the boil. Simmer for 40–60 minutes, half-covered, until the chicken is cooked through and the sauce is reduced to a rich consistency. If it seems watery, remove the lid towards the end of the cooking time and let the sauce reduce.

Meanwhile, sauté the mushrooms in the remaining butter and oil, then drain briefly on kitchen paper. When the chicken is done, stir in the mushrooms, simmer for a minute or two longer, then taste and adjust the seasoning.

Burmese Dry Chicken Curry

This 'dry' curry, i.e. one that's not swilling in sauce, is a fragrant affair, scented right at the end of the cooking time with freshly ground cardamom and green coriander leaves. I can't claim to be at all knowledgeable about Burmese cooking, but the two Burmese meals I have eaten, in a small restaurant in Greenwich, London, (then the Mandalay, though when it moved to Herne Hill the name changed to the Maymyo), were altogether different in flavour and style from the food of neighbouring countries such as Thailand or India, though many of the same ingredients are used.

SERVES 4–6

2 onions, roughly chopped
5 garlic cloves, roughly chopped
1 cm (^{1}/$_2$ in) piece root ginger, chopped
2 sticks lemon grass, roughly chopped
1–2 red chillies, seeded and roughly
   chopped
1 tablespoon Thai fish sauce (*nam pla*)

1 teaspoon turmeric
4 tablespoons vegetable oil
1.5–1.75 kg (3–4 lb) chicken, cut into
   8 pieces
4 green cardamom pods
2 tablespoons roughly chopped
   coriander leaves
Salt and freshly ground black pepper

Process the first 7 ingredients together to form a smooth paste. Heat the oil in a wide frying-pan and add the paste. Stir until all the moisture has evaporated and the paste begins to brown.

Now add the chicken pieces, stirring well to ensure that they are all coated evenly. As you stir, scrape the base of the pan to prevent burning. Cover tightly and simmer for 35–45 minutes – the juices from the chicken will provide enough liquid for this type of curry. When the chicken is nearly cooked, stir occasionally.

While it cooks, slit open the cardamom pods, extract the black seeds and crush. Once the chicken is just about cooked through, stir in the cardamom and the coriander leaves. Cover again for a minute or so, then taste and adjust the seasoning. Serve with rice.

Thai Barbecued Chicken

In Thailand this is cooked out on the streets over open braziers. When you hand over your money, you are given in return a portion of chicken along with a small plastic bag full of sauce. Unless there's an adjacent table or ledge to sit on, it can be a messy business dipping and eating as you walk along the street, but it is worth the sticky fingers and chin.

The only special ingredient you really need is fish sauce or nam pla, *which is available from most oriental food stores and now even from some larger supermarkets. If you really can't find any, use light soy sauce in its place. Fresh red chillies are not always available either, but if needs be, replace them with dried red chillies, crumbled or chopped very finely. The spice paste can also be used for fish and prawns.*

SERVES 4
1 plump chicken, cut into 8 pieces

FOR THE SPICE PASTE
1 tablespoon black peppercorns
1 tablespoon chopped garlic
1 tablespoon chopped coriander root
or stem
$^1/_2$ tablespoon sugar
Juice of $^1/_2$ lemon
1 tablespoon Thai fish sauce (*nam pla*)
1 tablespoon oil

FOR THE SWEET CHILLI SAUCE
75 g (3 oz) sugar
85 ml (3 fl oz) rice vinegar or cider
vinegar
2 red chillies, seeded and very finely
chopped
A pinch of salt

TO GARNISH
Coriander leaves

To make the spice paste, crush the peppercorns, pound to a paste with the garlic and coriander, then work in the remaining ingredients. Alternatively, process or liquidize with a hand-held blender.

Make a few deep slashes across the fattest portions of the chicken, then rub the spice paste all over the chicken pieces. Leave for at least 1 hour, preferably overnight.

To make the sweet chilli sauce, stir the sugar and vinegar over a moderate heat until the sugar has completely dissolved. Bring up to the boil and simmer for 5 minutes. Draw off the heat, stir in the chillies and salt and cool.

To cook the chicken, grill over a moderately hot barbecue until well-browned and cooked through to the bone, turning occasionally. Be patient and don't rush this, since you want to end up with chicken that is cooked all the way through, not burnt on the outside and raw on the inside. Serve, sprinkled with coriander leaves, with bowls of the chilli sauce for dipping.

Coq au Vin

A dinner-party favourite of the 1970s, now sadly and foolishly neglected, though I suspect it is on the brink of returning to fashionable plates. It is certainly a dish worth mastering.

SERVES 4–5
225 g (8 oz) small pickling or pearl
   onions
40 g (1 1/2 oz) butter
1 tablespoon sunflower oil
100 g (4 oz) lardons (thick batons of
   bacon)
1 × 1.75 kg (4 lb) chicken, cut into
   8 pieces
Seasoned flour
3 tablespoons brandy
450 ml (15 fl oz) red wine
600 ml (1 pint) chicken stock

Salt and freshly ground black pepper
1 bouquet garni (2 sprigs thyme, 1 bay
   leaf and 3 sprigs parsley, tied
   together with string)
2 garlic cloves, finely chopped
1/2 tablespoon tomato purée
225 g (8 oz) button mushrooms, halved
   or quartered if large

FOR THE BEURRE MANIÉ
25 g (1 oz) butter
25 g (1 oz) flour

To skin the onions, top and tail them, then cover with boiling water. Leave for a couple of minutes, then drain. The skins should now slip off easily. Heat 15 g (1/2 oz) of the butter with the oil and fry the lardons of bacon until lightly browned. Scoop out and transfer to a flame-proof casserole. Brown the pickling onions in the same fat, turning them so that they fry to a rich and more or less even brown colour all over. Pour into the casserole. Add a little more butter to the pan. Dust the chicken with flour and brown briskly all over. Pour over the brandy, swirl the pan around, then set light to it with a match if you have an electric hob, or by tilting the pan toward the flame if you cook on gas. Once the flames have died down, put the chicken and juices into the casserole.

Return the frying-pan to the heat and pour in the wine. Bring to the boil, scraping in the residues from frying, then let it boil down until reduced by half. Pour over the chicken. Bring the stock to the boil in the frying-pan, then pour that over the chicken too. Season with salt and pepper, add the bouquet garni, garlic and tomato purée. Simmer gently, covered, for about 40 minutes until the chicken is tender.

Meanwhile, fry the mushrooms in the remaining butter. Mash the butter and flour for the beurre manié together evenly.

Once the chicken is cooked, lift out with as many of the onions and lardons as you can locate. Boil the sauce down, uncovered, until reduced by half. Throw away the bouquet garni. Stir in about half the beurre manié, in small knobs, and let it cook, without letting it boil hard, for a few minutes to thicken slightly. If necessary add a little more, though the sauce is not meant to be heavily thickened, just given a little more substance. Taste and adjust the seasoning. Return the chicken, onions and lardons to the pan along with the mushrooms and let them heat through for a few minutes.

Serve with boiled buttered potatoes, sprinkled with parsley, and green peas.

Grilled Spiced Chicken with Mango Salsa

To spatchcock a bird (and any bird can be spatchcocked, wild or domesticated, small or large) simply means to open it out flat. A spatchcocked bird can be roasted or grilled whole.

The process is straightforward enough. Turn the bird breast-side down and, using a sharp knife or better still a pair of poultry shears or strong scissors, cut along each side of the backbone from neck to tail. Snip out the backbone completely. Remove the wishbone. Turn the bird skin-side up and flatten out firmly with the heel of your hand to form a sort of butterfly shape.

To keep the bird flat as it cooks, thread a skewer, or several, through from one side to the other. The number and way you do this will depend on the size of the bird.

SERVES 4
1 chicken, spatchcocked

FOR THE MARINADE
$1/2$ teaspoon cumin seeds
$1/2$ teaspoon coriander seeds
$1/4$ teaspoon black peppercorns
Juice of 1 lime or $1/2$ large lemon
3 tablespoons olive oil

FOR THE SALSA
2 ripe mangoes, peeled, stoned and finely diced
$1/2$ red onion, finely diced
$1/2$ red or green chilli, seeded and finely chopped
2 tablespoons chopped coriander
Juice of $1/2$–1 lime
Salt

First make the marinade: mix together the cumin, coriander and peppercorns. Dry-fry over a high heat until they give off a rich aromatic scent. Cool, then crush coarsely. Mix with the lime or lemon juice and olive oil. Make a couple of slashes across the thickest parts of the chicken, then lay flat, skin-side up, in a shallow dish or tin. Pour over the marinade and smear it over the chicken so that it is fairly evenly distributed. Cover loosely and leave for at least 2 hours and up to 24 hours, turning occasionally.

To make the salsa, mix together all the ingredients. Cover and set aside for at least half an hour and up to 4 hours. Taste and adjust the seasoning, adding a little more lime juice, if necessary. If it is stored in the fridge, remove 20 minutes or so before serving so that it can come back to room temperature.

Heat the grill (or better still, barbecue) and grill the chicken, skin-side up, keeping it a good 10–12 cm (4–5 in) from the heat so that it doesn't cook too quickly. Turn every now and then and brush with any marinade left in the dish. Take it slowly and don't be tempted to rush. The skill of grilling a chicken is to get it cooked through to the bone without burning the outside and that demands a degree of patience. All in all, it will probably take a good 25–30 minutes to cook. To check whether it's done, plunge a skewer into the thickest part of the thigh, where it nestles up against the breast. If the juices run pink, return it to the heat.

Once it is cooked, cut the chicken up as best you can and serve it immediately with the salsa.

Poulet à l'Estragon

Tarragon-scented roast chicken with a creamy sauce makes a perfect Sunday lunch main-piece. To enjoy it at its best you will need a real free-range bird, with flesh that has some flavour and resistance to it. The tarragon, stuffed into its body cavity and in the sauce, has such a strong affinity with chicken that it is surprising we don't use them together more. However, that doesn't mean you should go overboard with the herb. It's fairly powerful and a little goes a fair old way. The amount I've added to the sauce seems about right to me, though since all herbs vary in intensity, you may want to add a little more. Keep tasting (no problem in this case, as long as you don't guzzle more than your fair share) to get it right.

SERVES 4
1.75 kg (4 lb) free-range chicken
1/2 lemon
4 branches of tarragon
50 g (2 oz) unsalted butter
Salt and freshly ground black pepper

50 ml (2 fl oz) vermouth, or a small glass dry white wine
300 ml (10 fl oz) crème fraîche or double cream
Lemon juice

Pre-heat the oven to 200°C/400°F/Gas Mark 6. Rub the skin of the chicken all over with the lemon half. Stuff the spent lemon half into the stomach cavity of the chicken along with 3 of the branches of tarragon. Chop the leaves of the remaining tarragon, discarding the stalk. Sit the bird in a roasting tin, smear the butter thickly over its skin and season generously with salt and pepper. Roast for 1–1¼ hours until cooked through. Transfer the bird to a serving dish and let it rest in the oven with the heat turned off and the door ajar, while you make the sauce.

Skim off as much fat as you can from the roasting tin, leaving behind the roasting juices. Put the tin on the hob and pour in the vermouth or wine. Bring to the boil, scraping in any residues from roasting, and boil until reduced to a few spoonfuls. Now add the crème fraîche or cream and stir, and let it return to the boil. Continue to cook hard until reduced to a good consistency. Draw off the heat and add 2–3 teaspoons of the chopped tarragon. Season with salt and pepper and a dash of lemon juice. Taste and adjust the seasoning, then serve the sauce with the chicken.

Roast Chicken with Porcini

This is a nifty way of lifting ordinary roast chicken right out of the ordinary ... and keeping it moist while it cooks. Butter, flavoured with dried porcini mushrooms, parsley and lemons, is smeared between the flesh and the skin before the chicken goes into the oven. And that's all there is to it.

Even if you don't have the porcini mushrooms, plain unadulterated butter smeared under the skin will effectively create a more or less self-basting extra-juicy chicken.

SERVES 4

15 g (^{1}/2 oz) dried porcini mushrooms
2 tablespoons chopped parsley
1 garlic clove, roughly chopped
Finely grated zest of 1 lemon
Juice of ^{1}/2 lemon

50 g (2 oz) butter, softened
Salt and freshly ground black pepper
1.5–2 kg (3 lb 8 oz–4 lb)
 free-range chicken
1 small onion, quartered

Pre-heat the oven to 220°C/425°F/Gas Mark 7. Place the porcini a small bowl and cover with hot water. Leave for at least 20 minutes to soak and soften. Pick the pieces out carefully and pat dry on kitchen paper or a clean tea towel. Strain the soaking water and save to use as mushroom stock in a soup or sauce. It freezes well.

Chop the porcini, parsley, garlic and lemon zest together very finely. Mash with the lemon juice, butter, salt and pepper.

Gently wiggle your fingers under the skin of the chicken, easing it away from the flesh on the breast and upper thighs without pulling it right off. Now – and I find this easiest with fingers, but you may prefer to use a spoon as well or instead – push the flavoured butter between the skin and flesh, smearing it around as evenly as possible. Put the onion quarters inside the cavity of the chicken.

Weigh the chicken and calculate the roasting time. Allow 17 minutes per 500 g (15 minutes per lb), adding 10 minutes extra on top. Roast in the oven, basting frequently with the juices. If it threatens to burn, cover with foil.

Once cooked, set the chicken aside in a warm place for 10–15 minutes before serving. Carve in the usual way, making sure everyone gets their fair share of the top slices, flavoured with the porcini butter.

Roast Chicken with Bananas and Orange

Recipes like this one, which require minimal work and emerge from the oven tasting as if you'd slaved for ages over them, are heaven-sent. This recipe came about more by accident than deliberation (you know the scene – what on earth have we got left in the house for supper tonight?), then was polished by frequent repeats. The alcohol in the rum burns off in the oven, so you can safely offer this to children, who love it, as well as to adults.

There's just one slightly technical bit of preparation to do, and that is separating out the orange segments, minus skin. To do this you will need a small but sharp knife. Cut the peel off the orange, taking it right down to the flesh and leaving no bitter white pith behind. Stand the orange upright, then carefully slice down between each orange segment and the white skin that separates it from its next-door neighbour. This way you will be able to ease out the segments neatly skinned and ready to use. Save the juice that is squeezed out of the orange as you do this and add to the roasting tin when you add the fruit.

The chicken is best served with plain rice to soak up the juices, rather than with potatoes or noodles.

SERVES 4

1.5–1.75 kg (3–4 lb) chicken, cut into 4, or 4 chicken joints
Salt and freshly ground black pepper
25 g (1 oz) butter
4 bananas
2 oranges
3 tablespoons rum

Pre-heat the oven to 190°C/375°F/Gas Mark 5. Place the chicken joints in a roasting tin, season with salt and pepper and dot with the butter. Spoon 4 tablespoons of water around them. Roast in the oven for 20 minutes. Meanwhile, peel the bananas and oranges and divide the oranges into skinned segments (see above). Save any orange juice that is squeezed out as you work.

After the first 20 minutes in the oven, add the whole peeled bananas along with the orange segments and their juice. Spoon over the rum. Return to the oven for 15–20 minutes, basting occasionally, until the chicken is cooked through. Set aside in a warm place for 10–15 minutes before serving.

Roast Chicken with Potato and Chorizo Stuffing

Turn a quiet chicken into a flamenco bird with a stuffing made of piccante chorizo *and potato, and sherry gravy. It will need to be a sturdier, free-range bird to live up to its dancing partners but what wonders it will learn to perform.*

If your bird is bereft of its giblets, as most seem to be these days, it is worth buying a pack of chicken livers for the stuffing as they add an extra richness to it.

SERVES 4
1.5 kg (3 lb) free-range chicken, with livers if possible
Olive oil
1/2 lemon
1 medium-sized glass of sweet sherry
Salt and freshly ground black pepper

FOR THE STUFFING
250 g (9 oz) potatoes

2 tablespoons olive oil
1/2 onion, chopped
2 garlic cloves, chopped
2 chicken livers, chopped
110 g (4 oz) *piccante* cooking chorizo, peeled and sliced
1 level teaspoon fennel seeds or cumin seeds
Salt and freshly ground black pepper

Pre-heat the oven to 200°C/400°F/Gas Mark 6. To make the stuffing, first boil the potatoes in their skins, until just tender. Peel and roughly dice the potatoes. Heat the olive oil in a wide frying-pan and add the onion. Fry over a moderately high heat, until beginning to brown. Now add the garlic, chicken livers, chorizo and fennel or cumin seeds. Fry for another 4 minutes, allowing the bits of chorizo to crumble. Draw off the heat, tip the potatoes into the pan and mix up, mashing them down slightly to give a lumpy stuffing mixture. Season if you wish. Fill the cavity of the chicken about two-thirds full with the mixture.

Place the bird in a roasting tin and rub with olive oil and lemon juice. Season with salt and pepper. Roast for 1–1 1/2 hours, until the chicken is done. About halfway through the cooking time, pour the sherry over the bird, and add an equal quantity of water to the tin. To test if the chicken is done, insert a skewer into the thickest part of the thigh, snug against the body. If the juices run clear, it is ready to eat. While you're at it, give the leg a little wiggle – it should wobble freely on its joint. Set the chicken aside in a warm place for 10–15 minutes to rest. Carve the chicken, spoon the stuffing from the inside and serve with the chicken's own pan-juices, suitably seasoned, for a gravy.

Soy Sauce Chicken

In this Chinese recipe the chicken is cooked whole in an intense, spiced sauce made largely with soy sauce. The chicken, sitting in its pond of inky liquid, is half poached, half steamed. It needs to be turned and basted frequently to ensure that it is evenly cooked and that every part has time and occasion to soak up the flavours. Though it is good hot, it really tastes far better cold. Either way the sauce is powerfully salty and should be treated as a dipping sauce, not ladled over like a Western gravy.

SERVES 4–6
1.5–1.75 kg (3–4 lb) chicken
4 slices unpeeled fresh root ginger
6 spring onions, trimmed
1 teaspoon salt
1 teaspoon coarsely crushed black
   peppercorns

FOR THE SAUCE
3 whole star anise
2 cinnamon sticks
2 strips dried orange peel
300 ml (10 fl oz) dark soy sauce
150 ml (5 fl oz) Shaoxing wine or dry
   sherry
5 tablespoons light muscovado sugar
600 ml (1 pint) water

Stuff the cavity of the chicken with the ginger, spring onions, salt and pepper. Put all the sauce ingredients into a large pan or flame-proof casserole, just big enough to take the chicken. Bring to the boil slowly, stirring until the sugar has dissolved.

Now put the chicken into the pan, breast side down, and baste a few times with the sauce. Reduce the heat to low, cover tightly and leave to simmer for 20 minutes, basting frequently. Turn the chicken onto its side, baste, then cover and cook for a further 10 minutes, basting once or twice. Now turn onto the other side and repeat. Finally, sit the chicken breast side up, cover and cook for a final 20 minutes, again basting frequently. Test for doneness by pushing a skewer into the thickest part of the chicken. If the juices run clear then it is done. If they are pinkish, cook for a further 10 minutes or so and then test again.

To serve hot, carefully lift the chicken out of the pan, tilting it so that the juices trapped inside can pour out and back into the sauce. Carve the chicken and place bowls of sauce strategically around the table.

To serve cold, leave the chicken in the pan, in its sauce, still covered, for at least an hour or until cold, basting every now and then. Lift out, draining off the sauce from the cavity, and cut into suitable pieces. Skim any fat from the sauce, then spoon a little over the chicken to keep it moist.

Turkey Escalopes in Leek and Lemon Sauce

Turkey escalopes or turkey breast steaks take no time at all to cook (far quicker than, say, a whole chicken breast) and, as long as they are not overdone, are a most useful basis for a mid-week supper. They do need a sauce with a bit of oomph, though, since more often than not they are almost as light on taste as they are in colour. Here they are served with leeks and lemon, and scattered with a few chives just before serving.

SERVES 4

4 turkey escalopes
Salt and freshly ground black pepper
25 g (1 oz) butter
1 tablespoon sunflower oil
2 leeks, white part only, cut into
   matchsticks

$1^1/_2$ tablespoons flour
300 ml (10 fl oz) milk
$^1/_2$ tablespoon Dijon mustard
Finely grated zest and juice of
   $^1/_2$ lemon
Freshly grated nutmeg
Chopped chives

Season the escalopes with salt and pepper. Melt the butter and oil in a wide frying-pan. When foaming, add the escalopes and fry for about 3–4 minutes on each side, until lightly browned and just cooked through. If necessary, cook them in two batches. Remove from the pan and set aside.

Add the leeks to the pan and stir until they begin to wilt. Now sprinkle over the flour and stir for about 30 seconds. Gradually whisk in the milk, bringing the sauce to the boil and simmering for about 5 minutes, stirring occasionally, until the sauce is thick and smooth.

Stir in the mustard, lemon zest, salt, pepper and nutmeg and return the escalopes to the pan, nestling them down into the sauce and overlapping slightly if necessary. Simmer for about 2 minutes, long enough to heat the turkey through thoroughly. Draw the pan off the heat and add enough of the lemon juice to sharpen the sauce without making it overwhelmingly acidic. Serve at once, scattered with chives.

Roasted Boned and Stuffed Turkey Thigh

A boned turkey thigh is big enough, when filled with a stuffing, to feed 4–6 people quite generously. Like a boned stuffed chicken, it is a boon for those of us who've never been too skilled with the carving knife. To bone the thigh, cut along the length of the main thigh bone, with a sharp knife, cutting right down to the bone. Carefully scrape the meat away from the bone to expose the joint. Sever the joint and lift out the bone so the thigh can be opened out flat.

The stuffing I've used here is laden with dried wild mushrooms – porcini – and meaty flat-cap mushrooms. Buying muslin by the yard from fabric shops or department stores works out very cheap. It is also sold in many kitchen shops, at a comparatively high price. If you don't have any you can always substitute a clean J-cloth, but boil it first for 5 minutes and rinse well.

SERVES 4–6

1 turkey thigh, boned

25 g (1 oz) butter

FOR THE STUFFING

15 g ($^{1}/_{2}$ oz) dried porcini mushrooms

2 tablespoons oloroso sherry or Marsala

$^{1}/_{2}$ onion, chopped

25 g (1 oz) butter

1 garlic clove, crushed

100 g (4 oz) flat-cap mushrooms, diced

175 g (6 oz) pork sausagemeat

2 tablespoons breadcrumbs

2 tablespoons chopped parsley

Salt and freshly ground black pepper

1 egg, lightly beaten

First make the stuffing. Soak the dried mushrooms in the sherry for half an hour. Pick out the pieces of mushroom and chop finely. Let the sherry settle for 5 minutes or so, then carefully pour off, leaving the grit behind.

Fry the onion gently in the butter until tender. Now add the garlic and the fresh mushrooms and fry over a fairly high heat until the mushrooms are tender and any liquid thrown off has evaporated. Add the dried mushrooms and the sherry and cook hard until all the liquid has evaporated leaving just a moist mush. Cool slightly then mix with the sausagemeat, breadcrumbs, parsley, salt, pepper and just enough egg to bind.

Pre-heat the oven to 200°C/400°F/Gas Mark 6.

Now for that turkey thigh. Melt the butter in a small pan and dunk a large square of muslin right into it, so that it is thoroughly soaked. Lay it open on the worksurface and place the thigh, opened out, flat on it, skin-side down. Spoon the stuffing down the centre and draw the sides up and round. Roll up tightly in the buttered muslin and tie up both ends firmly with a piece of string.

Roast the turkey for 50–60 minutes. If you wish to serve it hot, unwrap the turkey thigh just before it goes on to the table. For a cold dish, leave the muslin *in situ* as it cools, and unwrap just before slicing.

Roast Poussins with Fennel

Technically there is a slight difference between a poussin and a spring chicken, though in general the terms are used interchangeably. A poussin is 4–6 weeks old and weighs around 450–675 g (1–1 lb 8 oz), while a spring chicken can be a smidgen older and heftier. Certainly when it comes to cooking they are much of a muchness.

There's no getting round the fact that poussins taste of precious little at all or, if you want to be polite about it, that they are 'delicately flavoured'. Hardly surprising, given their immaturity and size. However, they do score well on other counts. The main one, as you might well expect, is tenderness. They've barely had time to flex their muscles, so the meat is pale as ivory, soft and moist.

They're small, so they don't take that much time to cook, but big enough to f-urnish a more than generous main course for one, or a light bite for two. They look quite glamorous enough to grace a smart dinner plate, and they do away with the need for carving, a plus for those of us who are less than proficient in this sphere.

Fennel provides the essential boost that mild-flavoured poussins need if they are to be at all interesting. The fennel is used to flavour not only the birds as they roast but also the sauce that will be served with them.

SERVES 2 GENEROUSLY

1 large fennel bulb
2 poussins
40 g (1 1/2 oz) butter
Salt and freshly ground black pepper

1 tablespoon plain flour
250 ml (8 fl oz) milk
85 ml (3 fl oz) single cream
Freshly grated nutmeg

Pre-heat the oven to 200°C/400°F/Gas Mark 6.

Trim the fennel, reserving the green leaves, and quarter. Place one quarter inside each poussin, and dice the remaining two quarters finely. Smear the breasts of the poussins with half the butter, and season with salt and pepper. Sit them in a roasting tin and roast for 30–40 minutes until cooked through.

While they cook, melt the remaining butter and add the diced fennel (but not the fronds). Stir, then cover and sweat over a low heat for 15 minutes. Remove the lid and sprinkle in the flour. Cook for 1 minute, stirring. Gradually add the milk a little at a time, stirring well, to make a smooth sauce. Add the cream. Bring to the boil and simmer gently for 5–8 minutes, stirring occasionally. Season with salt, pepper and nutmeg to taste.

If not serving immediately spear a small knob of cold butter on a fork and rub over the surface of the sauce to prevent a skin forming. Just before serving, re-heat the sauce adding a little extra milk if it seems over-thick when warmed through. Stir in the fennel fronds. Serve with the poussins.

Spatchcocked Poussins with Orange and Lemon

In this recipe, two methods are employed to enhance the taste of young poussins and to keep them tender and juicy. First they are marinated, then given a protective smear of butter flavoured with ground coriander, orange and lemon.

With all that to keep them from drying out, they can be quickly roasted in a hot oven, to emerge glistening and brown.

SERVES 2 GENEROUSLY
25 g (1 oz) butter, softened
Finely grated zest and juice of
    1 orange
Finely grated zest and juice of 1 lemon
½ teaspoon ground coriander
1 tablespoon finely chopped parsley
2 poussins, spatchcocked (see Grilled
    Spiced Chicken with Mango Salsa,
    p. 90)
1 tablespoon honey
Salt and freshly ground black pepper

Process or beat the butter with the zest of the orange and lemon, 1 tablespoon of lemon juice, the coriander, parsley and some pepper. Place the poussins in a shallow dish. Warm the orange juice with the remaining lemon juice and the honey very gently, without letting it get anywhere near boiling, stirring until the honey has dissolved. Add salt and pepper, cool, then pour over the poussins. Leave to marinate, basting and turning occasionally, for at least 1 hour and up to 8 hours.

Pre-heat the oven to 200°C/400°F/Gas Mark 6.

If you've kept the flavoured butter in the fridge, bring it out and let it warm up to room temperature. Now the messy bit. Using your fingers, loosen the skin of the poussins without detaching it completely. Smear the butter between the flesh and the skin, making sure that the breast is evenly coated. Pat the skin back into shape.

Set the poussins flat in a roasting tin and pour over the remaining marinade. Bake for 20–25 minutes until browned and cooked through. Baste occasionally with the pan juices as they cook.

Guinea Fowl with Celery and Dill

When I was a child, guinea fowl was a great rarity in Britain, a treat that came only with our annual trips to France, where it was more widely reared and greatly appreciated. The situation hasn't changed much, except that guinea fowl is gradually making itself a small niche in this country, sold now by good poulterers and in a few select larger supermarkets.

When it comes to cooking, the first thing to note is that guinea fowl are smaller and more meagerly fleshed than chicken. One plump bird is just about enough to stretch around four at a pinch (accompanied by plenty of vegetables) as long as you are not serving rapacious meat-eaters.

Though they can be cooked in any way that you might cook chicken or pheasant, the flesh has a tendency to be dry. If roasting, make sure that the breast is well protected from the heat with thin sheets of pork fat or at least covered with rashers of streaky bacon – and frequently basted as it cooks. As a rule, I usually opt for pot-roasting, casseroling or poaching guinea fowl, by far the best ways to keep it moist.

Based on various French recipes, this casserole brings together guinea fowl and celery in a rich sauce – a perfect dish for a family Sunday lunch.

SERVES 4

1 plump guinea fowl

30 g (1 oz) butter

1 tablespoon sunflower oil

1 onion, chopped

2 cloves garlic, peeled and chopped

3 sprigs fresh dill or $^1/_2$ tablespoon
  dried

1 bouquet garni (2 sprigs thyme, 1 bay
  leaf and 3 sprigs parsley, tied
  together with string)

150 ml (5 fl oz) dry white wine

Salt and freshly ground black pepper

1 head of celery, sliced

15 g ($^1/_2$ oz) plain flour

150 ml (5 fl oz) double cream

Squeeze of lemon juice

TO GARNISH

1 tablespoon chopped fresh dill

Brown the guinea fowl briskly in 15 g ($^1/_2$ oz) butter and the oil and set aside. Fry the onion and garlic gently in the same fat without browning. Make a bed of the onion and garlic in a flameproof casserole just large enough to take the guinea fowl and, eventually, the celery. Add the dill. Set the guinea fowl on top, breast-side down. Tuck the bouquet garni in alongside and pour over the wine and 150 ml (5 fl oz) of water. Season with salt and pepper. Bring to a simmer, then reduce heat and cover tightly. Simmer lazily for 30 minutes. Turn the bird the right way up and snuggle the celery tightly around it. Cover tightly again, and continue cooking for a further 40 minutes until both guinea fowl and celery are tender. Place the bird on a serving dish, scoop out the celery with a slotted spoon and place around it. Keep warm. Discard the bouquet garni and bedraggled sprigs of dill.

Make *beurre manié* by mashing the remaining 15 g ($^1/_2$ oz) of butter thoroughly with the flour. Stir small knobs of it into the cooking juices left in the casserole, and cook at just under a simmer for 4 minutes until thickened. Stir in the cream, bring back to a simmer, then stir in a squeeze of lemon juice. Taste and adjust the seasoning. Pour a little of the sauce over the celery, and sprinkle with chopped dill. Serve the remaining sauce separately.

Pot-roasted Guinea Fowl with Onions and Thyme

Terrifically easy and terrifically good. Pot-roasting keeps guinea fowl from drying out and the lengthily cooked onions melt to a soft sweetness, absorbing the flavours of the guinea fowl and thyme.

SERVES 4

1 guinea fowl

1 tablespoon sunflower oil

40 g (1$^1/_2$ oz) butter

900 g (2 lb) onions, thinly sliced

1 bouquet garni (see Guinea Fowl with
  Celery and Dill, p. 99)

Salt and freshly ground black pepper

1$^1/_2$ teaspoons thyme leaves

Brown the guinea fowl all over in the oil and 15 g (¹/₂ oz) of the butter, over a brisk heat. Melt the remaining butter in a flame-proof casserole. Add the onions and stir briefly. Cover and cook over a gentle heat for 10 minutes, until they are beginning to soften. Bury the bouquet garni amongst them, then sit the guinea fowl, breast-side down, on top and season with salt and pepper.

Cover the casserole tightly and cook over a low to moderate heat for 30 minutes. Turn the guinea fowl the right way up, and sprinkle with the thyme leaves. Continue cooking, still tightly covered, for another 20 minutes or so or until cooked through and the onions are meltingly tender. Remove the bouquet garni and serve.

Guinea Fowl with Green Peppercorns

This takes me straight back to my childhood and to France. My mother cut this recipe, originally for duck, from the local newspaper. Made with guinea fowl, it quickly became a family favourite. Use green peppercorns preserved in brine rather than freeze-dried ones.

SERVES 3–4
550 g (1 lb 4 oz) pearl onions
1 guinea fowl
50 g (2 oz) butter
1 tablespoon sunflower oil
**1 rounded tablespoon green
   peppercorns with their brine**

**1¹/₂ tablespoons each of brandy and
   Benedictine, or 3 tablespoons of
   brandy**
250 ml (8 fl oz) chicken stock
Salt

To skin the onions, top and tail, then cover with boiling water. Leave for 1–2 minutes, then drain. The skins should now slip off readily. Brown first the guinea fowl and then the onions in the butter and oil, then transfer them to a deep, flame-proof casserole. Add the peppercorns, alcohol and 3–4 tablespoons of the stock. Sprinkle with a little salt, cover and cook gently until the bird is done, turning it occasionally and basting it with more stock – but keep the liquid level low.

After about 45–60 minutes, remove the bird from the casserole and carve, arranging it on a warm shallow serving dish with the onions. Season with salt.

Skim the fat from the pan juices, taste and adjust the seasoning. Add a little more stock, but only enough to lighten the sauce, which should not be copious. Pour over the bird and serve.

Grilled Duck Breasts with Plum Sauce

Grilled duck breasts are just the ticket for a dinner party when you've not much time to prepare and cook. I like to dish them up with a tartly fruity plum sauce to counter-balance the richness of the duck.

These days, you can buy prepared duck breasts, but if you are partial to duck, then it may make more sense to invest in a couple of whole birds. You can get two or three meals for four out of the brace and each one will taste totally different.

The great advantage of cooking breasts separately from the rest of the bird is that you can keep them rare, like a steak, as in this recipe. The legs are better cooked thoroughly, long and slow, in a small stew such as the Duck, Tomato and Pepper Stew on p. 105. The carcass of the duck can be turned into stock which might then be used for a meal-in-a-bowl Duck Noodle Soup (see p. 21) and, last but not least, the excess fat can be saved for sautéing potatoes.

If you don't want to grill the breasts, you can roast them in a hot oven instead, though you lose out on the hint of smokiness that grilling gives.

SERVES 4

FOR THE PLUM SAUCE
450 g (1 lb) plums, halved and pitted
1 cinnamon stick
1 glass white wine
1 bay leaf

1 tablespoon sherry vinegar
Sugar, to taste

FOR THE DUCK
4 duck breasts
Olive oil
Salt and freshly ground black pepper

Make the sauce first. Put the plums into a pan with the cinnamon, white wine and bay leaf. Place over a medium heat and bring gently to the boil. Half cover and simmer quietly until the plums have all collapsed to a purée. Either pass through the fine blade of a *mouli-légumes* (vegetable mill) or rub through a sieve. While still warm, stir in the sherry vinegar, sugar to taste (3–4 tablespoons should be ample) and plenty of fresh ground black pepper. Set aside until needed.

Pre-heat the grill. When your guests are assembled, start grilling the duck. Place the breasts, skin-side up, on a rack, fairly close to the grill – 7.5 cm (3 in) or so away. Grill until well-browned and crisp. Turn the breasts over, brush quickly with oil and sprinkle with salt and pepper, then grill the cut side for 4 minutes. Let them rest in a warm place for 5 minutes while you re-heat the plum sauce.

To roast the breasts pre-heat the oven to 230°C/450°F/Gas Mark 8, brush the cut sides with oil and rub salt and pepper into the skin. Lay on a rack, skin-side up, for 10–15 minutes, until well-browned. Rest for 5 minutes before slicing.

If you are the patient sort, slice each duck breast and fan out on individual plates (stir any juices from the duck into the plum sauce), with a spoonful of sauce elegantly drizzled over. Or serve them up whole with the sauce on the side.

Lacquered Duck Breasts

Double-brushing ensures that the glaze of soy sauce and honey cooks to a burnished, chestnut lacquer in the heat of the oven – a welcome contrast to the richness of the meat. Don't be tempted to use a classy high-price honey for this recipe. The intense heat will destroy its subtleties. A good, everyday honey will work just as well.

SERVES 2
1¹/₂ tablespoons clear honey
1 tablespoon soy sauce

¹/₄ teaspoon Chinese 5-spice powder
2 boned duck breasts
Salt and freshly ground black pepper

Mix the honey and the soy sauce with the 5-spice powder and a generous grinding of pepper. Brush the mixture over the skin of the duck breasts. Leave for half an hour and then brush again with any remaining mixture. Place the breasts, skin-side up, on a rack over a roasting tin.

Pre-heat the oven to 230°C/450°F/Gas Mark 8 and roast the duck for 10–15 minutes, if necessary covering with foil towards the end of the cooking time to prevent burning. Once they are cooked, leave the breasts to rest for 5 minutes in a warm place. Just before serving, slice each one and arrange on a warm serving plate.

Roast Duck with Marmalade

One might call this the 'cheat's duck à l'orange', if it weren't for the fact that it is actually rather nicer than nine out of ten versions of that over-exposed restaurant fall-back.

Use one of the high-fruit-content 'extra jams' or better still a completely sugar-free marmalade from a healthfood shop. If you prefer to do without the cream in the sauce, add a little extra stock to soften the flavour.

SERVES 4
2–2.25 kg (4–5 lb) duck
1 orange
175 g (6 oz) fine-cut marmalade
150 ml (5 fl oz) orange juice

150 ml (5 fl oz) duck or chicken
  stock
1¹/₂ teaspoons sugar
150 ml (5 fl oz) double cream
Salt and freshly ground black pepper

Pre-heat the oven to 190°C/375°F/Gas Mark 5. Wipe the duck skin and prick all over with a sharp-pronged fork. Halve the orange and place both halves in the central cavity. Roast the duck breast-side down on a rack over a roasting tin for 40 minutes.

Remove from the oven, turn the duck breast-side up and smear 1 generous tablespoon of the marmalade over the bird. Return to the oven and roast for a further 40–50 minutes until cooked. Check from time to time, and if the marmalade is blackening too fast cover with foil. Aim to finish up with a very dark brown duck, with the odd piece of orange caught and slightly blackened by the heat.

To make the sauce, bring the remaining marmalade, orange juice, stock and sugar gently to the boil, stirring occasionally. Simmer together for 10 minutes, checking to make sure it isn't burning on the bottom of the pan (if using a sugar-free jam this is much less likely to happen). When the duck is cooked, re-heat the sauce, if necessary, remove from the heat and allow to cool for a minute or so. Then stir in the cream and season.

Carve the duck or cut it into portions with poultry shears and serve with the sauce.

Roast Duck with Ginger and Lemon Stuffing

Roast duck is, I think, one of life's luxuries, as long as it is not overcooked. Roast duck, brushed with a mixture of honey and brandy as it cooks so that the skin crisps to a crackling sweetness, is even better.

SERVES 4
2–2.25 kg (4–5 lb) duck
1 tablespoon honey
1 tablespoon brandy

FOR THE STUFFING
25 g (1 oz) currants
1/2 onion, chopped
15 g (1/2 oz) butter
75 g (3 oz) breadcrumbs

Finely grated zest of 1 lemon
2 tablespoons lemon juice
2 spheres preserved stem ginger, chopped
1 tablespoon chopped parsley
Leaves of 1 large sprig of thyme
1/2 teaspoon chopped rosemary
1 egg, beaten
Salt and freshly ground black pepper

Pre-heat the oven to 190°C/375°F/Gas Mark 5. Prick the skin of the duck all over with a fork. Calculate the cooking time of the duck by weighing it, and allowing 22 minutes per 500 g (20 minutes per lb).

To make the stuffing, soak the currants in water for half an hour to plump them up, then drain. Cook the onion gently in the butter without browning. Mix the breadcrumbs with the onion and butter, currants, and all the remaining ingredients, adding just enough of the egg to bind. Fill the cavity of the duck about two-thirds full with the stuffing. Roll any left-overs into golf-ball-sized balls.

Roast the duck, breast-side down for two-thirds of the cooking time (if the fat in the roasting pan threatens to burn, add a tablespoon or two of water – carefully, as the fat will spit). Warm the honey and brandy in a small pan until just runny. Brush over the skin of the duck and season with salt and pepper. Return the duck to the oven, right way up this time. Set the extra stuffing balls around it, turning first to coat them in fat, then roast for the final third of the cooking time.

Carve the duck, spoon the stuffing from the inside and serve with the duck.

Duck, Tomato and Pepper Stew

I happen to like duck legs cooked patiently until the meat is extremely tender, which is exactly what happens here. They are gently stewed in a tomatoey, peppery sauce, but the unusual touch is a final enrichment of chocolate. Don't worry that you'll end up with a duck-flavoured chocolate pud. All this small amount will do is add an unidentifiable depth and richness to the sauce.

SERVES 4

4 duck legs, each cut into 2 pieces
3 tablespoons olive oil
1 small red onion, chopped
3 garlic cloves, finely chopped
1 small red pepper, cut into strips
1 small green pepper, cut into strips
675 g (1 lb 8 oz) tomatoes, skinned, seeded and roughly chopped

2 sprigs of thyme
1 small sprig of rosemary
Salt and freshly ground black pepper
15 g (1/2 oz) plain chocolate, finely chopped
100 g (4 oz) fresh or frozen shelled peas, thawed if frozen

Brown the duck legs briskly in the oil over a high heat in a wide, deep frying-pan. Set aside. Reduce the heat and cook the onion, garlic and pepper strips gently in the oil until tender. Now add the tomatoes, thyme, rosemary, salt and pepper and about 150 ml (5 fl oz) water. Bring to the boil. Return the duck legs to the pan and simmer for around 40 minutes.

Stir in the chocolate and the peas and cook for a final 5 minutes. Taste and adjust the seasoning. Serve with rice.

Roast Goose with Prune, Apple and Apricot Stuffing

My aunt always used to cook a magnificent goose for our pre-Christmas family gathering if we weren't actually going to spend the big day together. She stuffed one end with fruit, the other with a forcemeat stuffing. This isn't exactly her recipe, but it is inspired by it. Some of her quince and apple compote, which she had made when the fruit of her quince tree were ripe in the autumn, was defrosted to accompany the bird. It's a lovely partnership if you can find some quinces, but otherwise a straightforward apple sauce, or even better the French Canadian Roast Apple Sauce on p. 358, is excellent served with the bird.

SERVES 8

4–5.5 kg (9–12 lb) goose, with liver if
   possible

FOR THE FRUIT STUFFING

100 g (4 oz) stoned prunes, roughly
   chopped

100 g (4 oz) dried apricots, roughly
   chopped

85 ml (3 fl oz) port

2 eating apples, peeled, cored and
   diced

1 small red onion, chopped

1/2 teaspoon ground cinnamon

1/4 teaspoon ground nutmeg

Salt and freshly ground black
   pepper

FOR THE FORCEMEAT STUFFING

1 small onion, chopped

1 celery stick, chopped

The goose liver, finely chopped

Finely grated zest and juice of
   1 orange

225 g (8 oz) highest-quality pork
   sausagemeat

1 teaspoon fresh thyme leaves, or
   1 level teaspoon dried

3 tablespoons chopped parsley

50 g (2 oz) soft breadcrumbs

1 egg, lightly beaten

Freshly grated nutmeg

Salt and freshly ground black pepper

**FOR THE QUINCE AND APPLE
SAUCE**

2 quinces, peeled, cored and diced

675 g (1 lb 8 oz) cooking apples, peeled,
   cored and cut into chunks

Juice of 1 orange

A generous slug of port

1 cinnamon stick

Sugar, to taste

First make the fruit stuffing. Soak the prunes and apricots for as long as possible in the port – overnight or even a couple of days if you remember. Mix with all the remaining fruit stuffing ingredients (don't worry that it seems sloppy – as the goose has a long, slow cooking time, it will all meld together loosely in the oven).

To make the forcemeat stuffing mix together all the ingredients, adding just enough egg to bind.

Trim the excess fat from inside the goose. Put the forcemeat stuffing into the neck end of the goose, pressing it in firmly and then tucking the flap of skin neatly down around it. Secure firmly underneath with wooden cocktail sticks or a metal skewer. Put the fruit stuffing into the body cavity.

Pre-heat the oven to 190°C/375°F/Gas Mark 5.

Prick the skin of the goose all over with a fork. Season with salt and pepper. Lay some of the fat from the cavity over the thighs to keep them moist. Cover with foil and place on a rack in the oven with a tray underneath, so that you can empty out the fat regularly. Roast a 4 kg (9 lb) goose for 3 hours, a 4.5–5 kg (10–11 lb) goose for 3 1/2 hours, and a 5.5 kg (12 lb) goose for 4 hours. Remove the foil 30–40 minutes before the end of the cooking time so that the skin can brown and crisp. To test, pierce the fattest part of the thigh with a skewer. If the juices run clear, then the bird is done.

Meanwhile, make the quince and apple sauce. Put the quinces into a pan with just enough water to cover. Simmer gently for about 30–40 minutes until barely tender. If necessary, boil hard to reduce the cooking liquid down to a scant few tablespoons. Add all the remaining sauce ingredients, except the sugar. Cover and cook until the apples have collapsed, then add sugar to taste. Serve hot or cold.

Pheasant à la Normande

This is an old favourite from Normandy, where cream, apples, cider and Calvados flow freely. It is rich and delicious and worthy of a fine Sunday lunch party. Pheasant are only in season from 1st October to 1st February, so if you don't have pheasant, guinea fowl is the next best thing, but a free-range chicken will do in its stead.

SERVES 6
75 g (3 oz) butter
A brace of pheasant (a hen and a cock pheasant)
85 ml (3 fl oz) Calvados, apple brandy, or brandy if all else fails
5 eating apples, peeled, cored and cut into 8 slices each
Salt and freshly ground black pepper
150 ml (5 fl oz) medium cider
150 ml (5 fl oz) crème fraîche or double cream
A squeeze of lemon juice

Melt 50 g (2 oz) of the butter in a flameproof casserole large enough to take the two pheasant whole. Brown the birds briefly but thoroughly in the butter, then reduce the heat. Pour in the Calvados or brandy and set alight at arm's length with a match. When the flames have died down, nestle both birds breast-side down in the casserole. Add 2 apples' worth of slices and season with salt and pepper. Pour in the cider, then cover and leave to cook slowly for about 45 minutes, turning the birds upright after half an hour.

While the birds cook, fry the remaining slices of apple briskly in the rest of the butter until browned. Set aside until needed.

When the pheasant are cooked through, transfer them to a serving dish, tuck the fried apple slices around them and keep warm. Set the casserole over the hob and add the crème fraîche or cream. Bring up to the boil, stirring, and let it reduce to a good consistency. Rub the sauce through a sieve, pushing through some of the disintegrating pulp from the apples, then taste and adjust the seasoning, adding a dash or two of lemon juice to heighten the flavours. Pour a little of the sauce around the pheasants and serve the rest separately.

Perdices Estofadas con Chocolate

Partridges are small birds, the hen weighing in at around 350–400 g (12–14 oz), the cock not much heftier at 375–425 g (13–15 oz). I've always considered this a rather cussed, in-between size, since they are on the large size for a single portion yet on the small side for a two-person helping unless you bulk out the meal with plenty of other bits and bobs. The birds are in season from 1st September until 1st February.

This is a robust sort of stew from Spain. You can use young partridges, but it is admirably suited to older birds. It is a pretty straightforward recipe, the one twist being the final enrichment of the sauce with a square or two of dark chocolate. This adds an almost unfathomable richness and depth. Though in Spain the fried potatoes are considered part and parcel of the dish, I'm not sure that I wouldn't prefer to eat it with a tangled heap of buttered and parsleyed noodles.

SERVES 2–4

2 good-sized partridges, cut in half
About 2 tablespoons olive oil
1 large onion, chopped
8–12 garlic cloves, peeled but whole
2 cloves
1 bay leaf

300 ml (10 fl oz) dry white wine
1 tablespoon sherry vinegar
Salt and freshly ground black pepper
20 g ($^3/_4$ oz) bitter or plain chocolate, grated

TO SERVE
Fried potato slices (optional)

Brown the partridges in 2 tablespoons of oil in a frying-pan over a high heat. Transfer to a casserole. Fry the onion in the same oil, adding a little more if needed, then transfer to the casserole. Add all the remaining ingredients except the chocolate and potatoes. Bring up to a gentle simmer, cover tightly and continue simmering for about 45–60 minutes (or longer if necessary), until the partridges are tender. Transfer to a warm serving dish, surround with fried potato slices, if using, and keep warm while you finish the sauce.

Stir the chocolate into the remaining liquid in the pan and simmer for another 2–3 minutes. Rub the contents of the pan through a sieve, pushing through as much of the onion and garlic as you can to thicken and flavour the sauce. Stir, then taste and adjust the seasoning. Pour the sauce over the partridges and potatoes and serve.

Quaglie al Diavolo

Farmed quail are available all year round. Despite its wee size, the quail is remarkably well-endowed. One alone makes a generous first course or a light main course for one person. They respond well to all manner of cooking, from grilling to roasting to casseroling and, being relatively lean, make good eating hot or cold.

This is a fingers job, par excellence. *The quails, opened out flat, are marinated with paprika and cayenne (*al diavolo *means devilled, from both the colour and the heat), then grilled. You can use the same recipe for partridge, though you'll have to allow a little more cooking time.*

Either way, these devilish quails are extra nice served with mashed potato and celeriac or parsnip in winter, or with hot rice mixed with a couple of spoonfuls of Greek yoghurt and chopped parsley in summer.

SERVES 4

4 quails, spatchcocked (see Grilled
    Spiced Chicken with Mango
    Salsa, p. 90)

Salt

FOR THE MARINADE

4 tablespoons olive oil

Juice of 1 lemon

1 teaspoon cayenne pepper

1 teaspoon paprika

Spear the quails on wooden skewers to keep them flat and place in a shallow dish. Mix all the marinade ingredients and pour over the birds. Leave for at least an hour, and a lot longer if possible.

Pre-heat the grill thoroughly, then grill the quail, skin-side up, for about 7–8 minutes. Turn over and grill the bony side for a further 5 minutes, by which time they should be done to a turn. Brush them a couple of times with the marinade as they cook. Season with salt. Eat with your fingers and let the juices run down your chin.

Grilled Woodpigeon on Toasted Ciabatta

Woodpigeon are fairly common and reasonably priced and have no closed season, so you can enjoy them all year round. Their flesh is dark and moderately deep in flavour, though not overwhelmingly so. Assuming you have young birds, they should either be cooked very quickly or very slowly. In between and they tend to be tough. For roasting or grilling, they will need to be marinated if they are not to dry out.

Cooked this way they are finger-lickin' good, suitably messy and not for hoity-toity occasions. The toasted bread catches the juices, but you'll still need to use your fingers for the grilled woodpigeon. Tackle the birds first, wipe your chin with nice napkins, then sink your teeth into the bread and tomato. If you can't get woodpigeon, substitute quails.

SERVES 4

4 woodpigeon, or quails, spatchcocked
    (see Grilled Spiced Chicken with
    Mango Salsa, p. 90)

1 ciabatta loaf, split in half lengthwise

Olive oil

2 tomatoes, sliced

A pinch of sugar

Salt and freshly ground black pepper

A small bunch of watercress

FOR THE MARINADE

Juice of 1 lemon

4 tablespoons olive oil

1/2 teaspoon dried oregano

1/4 teaspoon cayenne pepper

A pinch of cinnamon

Spear the woodpigeons flat on wooden skewers. Mix all the marinade ingredients and pour over the woodpigeons, rubbing it in well. Leave for 1 hour or more. Make sure that at least the last half hour is at room temperature.

Grill the pigeons, breast side to the heat first, for 8 minutes, then turn over and give the other side a further 7–9 minutes. Quickly toast the split sides of the ciabatta and cut each piece in half. Drizzle over a little olive oil to moisten, lay the tomato slices on top and season with a pinch of sugar, salt and pepper, then lay a spatch-cocked pigeon on each piece of bread. Tuck a few sprigs of watercress around them and serve immediately.

Pigeon aux Pruneaux

This is a dark, rich game casserole, with a hint of sweetness given by the prunes. Adjust the cooking time to suit your birds. They remain tender when cooked very briefly, but any longer and they toughen up, before they soften once more. Some woodpigeon take longer to reach this stage than others.

Topping the list of ingredients here are two pig's trotters. If the thought of eating trotters makes you uneasy, don't worry. Their main purpose is to give the sauce a velvety unctuousness that is quite impossible to reproduce otherwise, so don't leave them out. I like the texture of the trotters themselves, but if you're not sure about them, remove from the casserole before serving.

SERVES 4

2 pig's trotters
25 g (1 oz) butter
1 tablespoon oil
4 woodpigeon
12 small pickling onions or shallots, peeled
1 carrot, diced
1 celery stick, diced
100 g (4 oz) streaky bacon, cut into strips
1 cinnamon stick
1 bay leaf
2 sprigs of thyme
1¹/₂ tablespoons flour
16 prunes
2 sprigs of parsley
300 ml (10 fl oz) red wine
Salt and freshly ground black pepper

Singe or shave any hairs off the pig's trotters. Place them in a pan and cover with water. Bring up to the boil, cover and simmer for 1 hour, skimming any scum from the cooking liquid. Reserve the liquid and trotters.

Melt the butter and oil in a flameproof casserole. Quickly brown the pigeons, then remove and reserve. Add the onions or shallots, carrot, celery and bacon to the pan with the cinnamon, bay leaf and thyme. Stir to coat with fat, then lower the heat, cover and sweat gently for 10 minutes.

Sprinkle with flour and stir. Return the pigeons to the pan, together with the pig's trotters, prunes, parsley, wine and 600 ml (1 pint) of the trotters' cooking liquid. Season lightly with salt and pepper. Bring to the boil, cover and simmer gently, turning the pigeons over occasionally, for 45–60 minutes, or longer if necessary, until the birds are tender.

Remove the trotters. Serve the pigeons with vegetables and a little of the gravy.

Casserole of Rabbit with White Wine and Mushrooms

Let me be honest and up-front about this. I'm not too keen on wild rabbit. I don't like the flavour much and it is tough. Washing, or marinating in vinegar, will dampen the flavour. Lazy casseroling will tenderize it. Even so, I'd rather have a domesticated rabbit any day. Domesticated rabbit bears more resemblance to chicken, though the flavour is detectably different. It is excellent in casseroles and stews, where it combines just as well with creamy white sauces as with darker tomato or wine-based sauces.

The French are very keen on rabbit. In the small village that I know well in France, many people raise their own rabbits for the table. I often used to see our neighbour out cutting swathes of grass from the verges to take home to feed her small livestock. In this recipe with distinctly French overtones, the jointed rabbit is bathed in a creamy sauce flavoured with mushrooms. I use shiitake mushrooms if I can get them, but ordinary button mushrooms will do fine.

SERVES 4

1 rabbit, cut into 10 pieces
225 g (8 oz) mushrooms, button, or better still, shiitake
16 pearl onions
Seasoned flour, for dusting
2 tablespoons oil
25 g (1 oz) butter
120 ml (4 fl oz) dry white wine
600 ml (1 pint) chicken stock

1 bay leaf
2 tablespoons chopped parsley
Salt and freshly ground black pepper
40 g (1 1/2 oz) *beurre manié* (half butter, half flour, mashed thoroughly together)
150 ml (5 fl oz) crème fraîche or double cream
A squeeze of lemon juice

Either get the butcher to joint the rabbit for you or cut all 4 legs into 2 pieces and the saddle in half. Quarter the button mushrooms or slice the shiitakes thickly. Top and tail the pearl onions, cover with boiling water and leave for 30 seconds, then drain and skin.

Toss the rabbit in seasoned flour. Heat half the oil with half the butter in a wide frying-pan and brown the rabbit in two batches. Transfer to a flame-proof casserole. Add a little more butter and oil to the pan and sauté the mushrooms over a high heat until browned. Scoop out into the casserole. Add the remaining oil and butter to the frying-pan and brown the pearl onions. Into the casserole with those, too.

Pour the wine into the frying-pan and bring up to the boil, scraping in the residues from frying. Boil until reduced by half. Pour over the rabbit then add the stock, bay leaf, half the parsley, salt and pepper. Bring up to the boil, half cover and simmer for 45 minutes or until the rabbit is tender. Scoop out the rabbit, mushrooms and onions and keep warm.

Pour the juices into a wide frying-pan and boil hard until reduced by half. Reduce the heat to a bare simmer and add the *beurre manié* in small knobs, stirring it in. Cook for a further 3–4 minutes without boiling. Stir in the crème fraîche or cream and a touch of lemon juice. Taste and adjust the seasoning. Pour over the rabbit and scatter with the remaining parsley.

Lapin à la Moutarde

Lapin à la moutarde is one of France's most popular ways to cook rabbit and there are many versions of the recipe. The one I use is based on a recipe I cut out of a French children's magazine (I still have a scrapbook filled with their recipes, which were always first rate) when I was about 10 years old. It works so well that I've never seen any reason to try other methods! The heat of the oven kills the heat of the mustard, so if you want a slight tingle, stir in a little more at the end.

SERVES 4
3 tablespoons Dijon mustard
2 tablespoons sunflower oil
Salt and freshly ground black pepper
1 rabbit, jointed, or 4 rabbit joints,
   weighing about 1 kg (2 lb) in total

1 large carrot, sliced
1 onion, sliced
50 ml (2 fl oz) dry white wine
150 ml (5 fl oz) double cream

Pre-heat the oven to 200°C/400°F/Gas Mark 6. Mix the mustard with the oil, salt and pepper and smear all over the rabbit joints. Make a bed of the carrot and onion in a roasting tin that's just large enough to take the rabbit joints in a snug single layer. Pour in 100 ml (4 fl oz) water, then lay the rabbit pieces on top.

Roast for 25–30 minutes, basting frequently with the pan juices, until the joints are cooked through. Test by piercing the thickest part of a thigh with a skewer. If the juices run clear, then they are ready. If they are still pinkish, pop them back into the oven for another 5–10 minutes, then test again.

Lift the rabbit joints onto a warm serving dish and keep hot. Pick out the vegetables and discard. Set the roasting tin on the hob and pour in the wine. Bring to the boil, stirring, and boil hard until reduced by about two-thirds. Now add the cream, stir well and bring back to the boil. Let it bubble for a few more minutes, then taste and adjust the seasonings. Pour over the rabbit and serve.

Rabbit with Prunes

Rabbit with Prunes is a delicious dish from the Gascony region of France. Eau-de-vie de prunes *is a superb local spirit, scented with plums, which intensifies the flavour of prunes, but brandy works well as a substitute.*

SERVES 4

450 g (1 lb) prunes (weighed with their stones)

50 ml (2 fl oz) *eau-de-vie de prunes* or brandy

175 g (6 oz) lardons or whole piece of smoked streaky bacon

2 tablespoons sunflower or groundnut oil

25 g (1 oz) unsalted butter

1 rabbit, cut into 8 pieces

4 shallots, chopped

1 heaped tablespoon flour

150 ml (5 fl oz) dry white wine

1 bouquet garni (1 bay leaf, 2 sprigs each of fresh thyme and parsley, tied together with string)

Salt and freshly ground black pepper

TO GARNISH
Parsley

Put the prunes to soak with the *eau-de-vie* and 85 ml (3 fl oz) water. Leave for 2 hours (or longer), turning occasionally. If using a whole piece of bacon, cut into thick batons about 1 cm (¹/2 in) wide and 2.5 cm (1 in) long.

Heat the oil with the butter over a fairly high heat and brown the rabbit pieces briskly in 2 batches. Transfer to a heatproof casserole. Cook the shallots and lardons or bacon in the same fat over a moderate heat, until tender and translucent. Spoon around the rabbit, and sprinkle over the flour. Pour the excess fat out of the frying-pan, then add the wine and bring to the boil, stirring and scraping up the residues from frying. Pour over the rabbit, and tuck the bouquet garni in amongst the meat. Season with salt and pepper. Cover and simmer gently over a low heat for 1 hour. Turn the pieces of rabbit occasionally so that they cook evenly.

Now add the prunes and their soaking liquid, and simmer for a further 30 minutes, covered, until the rabbit is very tender.

To serve, arrange the pieces of rabbit in a shallow dish and surround with the prunes. Spoon a little of the pan juices over the meat and prunes to moisten, then cover and keep warm. Skim the fat off the rest, taste and adjust the seasoning. Strain into a sauce boat or jug and serve with the rabbit and prunes, garnished with a few sprigs of parsley or a scattering of chopped parsley.

Rabbit and Celeriac Pie

The light meat of rabbit goes very well with celeriac, that ungainly knobbly root vegetable. Together they make a sensational filling for a pie. Either use the meat from a whole rabbit or the leg meat from two rabbits, saving the saddles to roast on their own.

SERVES 6

1 rabbit, jointed, or the hind meat of 2 rabbits
Seasoned flour, for dusting
2 tablespoons sunflower oil
25 g (1 oz) butter
100 g (4 oz) streaky bacon, cut into strips
1 onion, chopped
1 celery stick, diced
1 large carrot, diced
1 small celeriac, peeled, diced and turned in lemon juice
1 bouquet garni (1 bay leaf, 2 sprigs of parsley and 2 sprigs of thyme, tied together with string)

85 ml (3 fl oz) Noilly Prat
1 tablespoon flour
450 ml (15 fl oz) strong chicken or rabbit stock
Salt and freshly ground black pepper
Freshly grated nutmeg
150 ml (5 fl oz) double cream
A dash of lemon juice
225 g (8 oz) shortcrust pastry (see p. 344; use any leftovers in another recipe or freeze)
1 egg yolk, beaten with 1 tablespoon water

Strip all the meat from the bones and cut into 2.5 cm (1 in) cubes, more or less. Dust with flour and brown briskly in half the oil and butter in a frying-pan. Transfer to a saucepan.

Add the remaining oil and butter to the frying-pan and fry the bacon in the fat. Scoop out and add to the rabbit. Now pop in the onion, celery, carrot and celeriac, together with the bouquet garni. Turn to coat, then cover and sweat over a low heat for 15 minutes, stirring once or twice. Pour in the Noilly Prat, raise the heat and boil until it has almost evaporated. Sprinkle over the flour, stir well and gradually stir in the stock. Bring to the boil and pour over the rabbit. Season with salt, pepper and a little nutmeg. Simmer gently for 30 minutes until the rabbit is almost done and the liquid much reduced. Stir in the cream, and again let it bubble down until the sauce is fairly thick and unctuous. Taste and adjust the seasonings, adding a dash of lemon juice. (You could serve it just as it is now, never mind the pastry!)

Pre-heat the oven to 200°C/400°F/Gas Mark 6.

Spoon the rabbit and celeriac stew into a pie dish. I use a 30 cm (12 in) oval dish, but whatever the shape, the filling should come up to within 1 cm (1/2 in) of the rim. Roll out the pastry to form a lid for the pie, then cut off a long narrow ribbon of pastry all around the edge. Using the egg yolk and water wash, moisten the edges of the dish and lay the ribbon of pastry round the edges. Brush with more egg and water wash, then lay the lid over the top. Trim and crimp the edges neatly, pressing down gently to seal. Make a hole in the centre to allow the steam to escape, give the top of the pastry a brush with the egg wash and bake for 20–30 minutes until nicely browned. Serve steaming hot.

My Mother-in-law's Hare Casserole

When my mother-in-law came to stay one Christmas, she arrived bearing a container full of hare marinating in red wine. She proceeded to make the most superb hare stew. This is not her exact recipe but it replicates roughly what I saw as I watched her work. My only input was the left-over gravy from the turkey, which was thrown in to aid and abet the sauce!

SERVES 6

FOR THE MARINADE
2 glasses of red wine
1 carrot, sliced
1 onion, sliced
2 bay leaves
1 sprig of thyme
4 juniper berries, lightly crushed

FOR THE CASSEROLE
1 hare, jointed
1 onion, sliced
2 carrots, cut into pieces about 5 cm (2 in) long, and quartered lengthwise

2 tablespoons olive oil
25 g (1 oz) butter
Flour, for dusting
1 sprig of rosemary
1 sprig of thyme
1 bay leaf
6 juniper berries, crushed
1 tablespoon flour
450 ml (15 fl oz) good game stock or left-over thin gravy
Salt and freshly ground black pepper
1–2 tablespoons tomato ketchup
1 tablespoon redcurrant jelly

Mix the marinade ingredients and pour over the hare. Leave to marinate for at least 12 hours and up to 2 days, turning occasionally. Take the hare out of the marinade and dry thoroughly. Strain the marinade and reserve.

Fry the onion and carrots in half the oil and butter until browned and tender. Transfer to a casserole. If necessary, add a little more oil and butter to the pan. Dust the hare joints in flour and fry briskly until browned, in batches if necessary. Then add them to the casserole and tuck in the herbs and juniper berries with them. Sprinkle over the flour.

Pre-heat the oven to 150°C/300°F/Gas Mark 2. Pour the excess fat out of the pan and add the marinade. Bring up to the boil, scraping in all the frying residues, then pour over the hare. Bring the stock to the boil in the frying-pan and add that too. Finally, season and stir in the ketchup. Cover and transfer to the oven and cook gently for 3–4 hours, until the meat is so tender it is practically falling off the bone. Stir in the redcurrant jelly, then taste and adjust the seasoning. Serve with mashed potato and braised red cabbage.

Pan-fried Venison with Port and Orange Sauce

Farmed venison is available all year round and is a good meat to approach for those who are not old hands at cooking game. The taste is usually no more pronounced than that of beef. This recipe is a quick but elegant way to deal with plain venison chops. Dried sour cherries are now available from several of the smarter super-markets and delis and have a marvellous flavour. If you can't get any, you could substitute large raisins or even a handful of little currants. It won't be quite the same, but it will still taste fine.

I've used this recipe both for venison chops and for prime venison saddle steaks. Quantities will vary according to cut and variety of deer, so you'll have to use your head when it comes to buying. The butcher should be able to advise you if you are ordering in advance.

SERVES 4

50 g (2 oz) dried sour cherries
Juice of 1 orange
25 g (1 oz) butter
1 tablespoon oil
8 small venison chops, or 8 small saddle steaks (see above)

1 shallot, very finely chopped
150 ml (5 fl oz) port
150 ml (5 fl oz) venison, beef or chicken stock
2 tablespoons redcurrant jelly
1/2 teaspoon Dijon mustard
Salt and freshly ground black pepper

Soak the dried cherries in the orange juice for half an hour. Heat the butter and oil in a pan over a moderate heat. Fry the chops in the fat for about 5–8 minutes on each side until cooked almost to your liking, then set aside.

Add the shallot to the pan and cook gently, until tender. Drain the excess fat from the pan, then deglaze with the port, bringing it up to the boil and scraping in the residues from the pan. Let it bubble until reduced almost to nothing, then add the stock, orange juice and cherries. Boil until reduced by half. Now stir in the redcurrant jelly and mustard. Stir until the redcurrant jelly has dissolved into the sauce. Taste and adjust the seasoning, then spoon a little over and around the chops and serve the rest of the sauce alongside.

Venison and Mushroom Toad in the Hole

Venison sausages make a tremendous toad in the hole and it tastes even better when a few mushrooms are thrown in as well.

SERVES 4
8 venison sausages
Dripping or sunflower oil, for frying
6 flat-cap mushrooms
175 g (6 oz) flour

$^1/_4$ teaspoon salt
2 eggs, lightly beaten
175 ml (6 fl oz) milk
Freshly ground black pepper

Pre-heat the oven to 200°C/400°F/Gas Mark 6. Put the sausages into a 20 × 30 cm (8 × 12 in) roasting tin with a good knob of dripping or 1–2 tablespoons of oil and pop into the oven for 20–30 minutes, turning once or twice, until they are just cooked through. As soon as they are in the oven, wipe the mushrooms clean, quarter them and then add to the tin with the sausages.

While they are sizzling in the oven, make the batter. Sift the flour with the salt and make a well in the centre. Add the eggs and about half the milk. Gradually whisk into the flour, adding the rest of the milk and 175 ml (6 fl oz) water as you go, to make a smooth batter. Stir in a generous grinding of pepper.

When the sausages are just cooked, remove them from the tin, along with the mushrooms, and set aside. Raise the oven temperature to 220°C/425°F/Gas Mark 7 and pop the tin back in for 5 minutes. When hot, quickly remove the tin from the oven, give the batter a quick stir and pour it into the tin. Spoon the sausages and mushrooms into the batter and return it immediately to the oven. After 15 minutes, reduce the heat to 200°C/400°F/Gas Mark 6 again and cook for a further 20 minutes or so until the batter is puffed, crisp and brown.

Swedish Braised Venison

Shoulder of venison is astoundingly cheap. Demand is almost entirely for haunch or saddle, so suppliers are happy if they can sell other parts even at a relatively low price. This is a good recipe for cooking shoulder, which can be dry if roasted naked in the oven. It is slightly adapted from a recipe in Julia Drysdale's Classic Game Cookery.

SERVES 6–8
2.75 g (6 lb) shoulder of venison
50 g (2 oz) pork back fat, or streaky
    bacon, cut into thin strips
Salt and freshly ground black pepper
40 g (1$^1/_2$ oz) butter

300 ml (10 fl oz) beef or venison stock
300 ml (10 fl oz) crème fraîche or
    double cream mixed with soured
    cream
1 tablespoon redcurrant jelly
1 tablespoon arrowroot

Pre-heat the oven to 220°C/425°F/Gas Mark 7. Make small slits all over the venison and push in the strips of fat or bacon. Season with salt and pepper and place in a greased roasting tin. Dot with the butter and roast for 15 minutes. Reduce the heat to 170°C/325°F/Gas Mark 3. Mix the stock with the crème fraîche or cream mixture and pour over the meat. Cover and cook for a further 2 hours, basting frequently, until the meat is tender.

Transfer the venison to a serving dish and return it to the oven with the heat turned off and the door slightly ajar. Leave to relax for 15 minutes or so while you finish the sauce.

Skim the fat from the cooking juices as best as you can and strain the juices back into the roasting tin. Place on the hob, over a gentle heat, and stir in the redcurrant jelly. Mix the arrowroot to a paste with a little of the juices, then stir back into the tin. Simmer for a minute or so, stirring constantly, until smooth and thickened. Taste, adjust the seasoning and serve with the meat.

Venison, Chestnut and Fruit Stew

This is a big, rich, warming winter stew, tempered with spices, sweetened with apricots and prunes, and gilded with mealy chestnuts. A sumptuous feast.

Don't be tempted to substitute canned chestnuts for fresh. They are far too soggy and will collapse and disappear into the stew. Fresh ones may be a bore to peel, but they are worth every minute of tedium.

SERVES 6

100 g (4 oz) dried apricots	1 tablespoon flour
100 g (4 oz) pitted prunes	1 onion, sliced
50 ml (2 fl oz) brandy	2 tablespoons sunflower or vegetable
225 g (8 oz) fresh chestnuts	oil
1.25 kg (2 lb 8 oz) venison	1 cinnamon stick
1/2 tablespoon coriander seeds	2 strips dried orange peel
	Salt and freshly ground black pepper

Put the dried fruit to soak in the brandy. It won't cover them, but that doesn't matter. Leave for 1/2–1 hour, turning occasionally, so that they suck up the alcohol. Score a cross in the curved side of each chestnut then place in a pan, cover with water and bring up to the boil. Simmer for 1 minute and turn off the heat. No more than one or two at a time, take the chestnuts from the water and strip off the tough outer skin and the brown papery inner skin. As the chestnuts cool, this becomes harder work, so if necessary, bring the water back to the boil. Set the peeled chestnuts to one side.

Pre-heat the oven to 150°C/300°F/Gas Mark 2.

Cut the venison into 5 cm (2 in) square pieces, about 2.5 cm (1 in) thick. Dry-fry the coriander seeds in a heavy-based frying-pan over a high heat, until they start to pop. Tip into a bowl and when cool, crush with a pestle or the end of a rolling pin. Mix with the flour.

Cook the onion in the frying-pan, in the oil, until lightly browned and then scoop into a flame-proof casserole. Raise the heat and brown the venison pieces in three batches. Then transfer to the casserole and sprinkle the flour and spice mixture evenly over the meat. Add the cinnamon stick, the dried fruits, the orange peel and salt.

Tip the excess fat out of the frying-pan and pour in 900 ml (1½ pints) water. Bring to the boil, scraping in the meaty residues from frying. Pour over the contents of the casserole, cover and immediately transfer to the oven. Cook for 2 hours, then stir in the chestnuts. After another hour or so, the meat should be very tender and the sauce should have reduced and thickened up nicely. If necessary, however, uncover the casserole and cook for another 20 minutes or so to cook off some of the liquid. Taste, adjust the seasoning and serve with mashed potatoes or buttered noodles.

Oven-Roast Wild Boar Steaks with Potatoes and Garlic

In the UK, 'wild' boar is farmed, though not in any great quantity. The boar that I have cooked and eaten has tasted very good, but really not much more than a marginally emphasized replica of first-rate free-range traditional-breed pork. This is a particularly good, simple way of cooking steaks of wild boar, though I think that it could well be used for free-range pork if you can't find any wild boar.

SERVES 6

6 wild boar steaks
85 ml (3 fl oz) olive oil plus a little for frying
900 g (2 lb) potatoes, peeled and cut roughly into 2.5 cm (1 in) chunks

1 teaspoon thyme leaves
1 large sprig of rosemary, snapped in two
3 garlic cloves, crushed
Salt and freshly ground black pepper
150 ml (5 fl oz) dry white wine

Pre-heat the oven to 180°C/350°F/Gas Mark 4. Brown the steaks in a little olive oil over a high heat. Lay them, overlapping, in a roomy oven-proof dish and fill the gaps around them with potatoes. Sprinkle over the thyme leaves, tuck the sprigs of rosemary between the steaks and smear the garlic around the meat and potatoes. Season generously with salt and pepper and drizzle over the white wine. Now trickle 85 ml (3 fl oz) olive oil over the potatoes and cover the dish with foil.

Bake for 1–1½ hours until the meat and potatoes are both tender. Raise the heat to 230°C/450°F/Gas Mark 8, uncover the dish and return to the oven for a final 10–15 minutes to brown. Serve immediately.

Meat

BEEF

Korean Steak Tartare

The most delicious, Far Eastern version of steak tartare is the Korean Yuk Hwe,
flavoured with sesame oil, soy sauce, pine nuts and the sweetness of pear. Though I
love steak tartare, I like this Korean dish even better. Try to get a Japanese Nashi pear
for a measure of authenticity – you sometimes see them for sale in supermarkets and
smart greengrocers' – though the extra sweetness of a ripe western-style pear is very
appetizing in its place.

SERVES 2 AS A MAIN COURSE
   OR 4 AS A STARTER

225 g (8 oz) fillet of beef

1/2 tablespoon sugar

1 tablespoon light soy sauce

1 teaspoon sesame seeds

Freshly ground black pepper

4 teaspoons sesame oil

1/2 ripe but firm pear

Lemon juice (optional)

1 egg yolk

1 tablespoon pine nuts

To make it easier to cut, chill the beef in the freezer for 10–20 minutes until it's firm but
not actually frozen. Cut into slices, across the grain, about 3 mm (1/8 in) thick, then cut
into narrow strips about 3 mm (1/8 in) across and 2.5 cm (1 in) long.

As close as possible to the time you are to serve the beef, mix it with the sugar,
soy sauce, sesame seeds, pepper and finally the sesame oil. Core the pear and cut
into matchsticks. If not serving immediately, toss in a little lemon juice to prevent
browning. Arrange the meat in a neat round mound in the centre of a plate. Arrange
the pear pieces around it, then make a dip in the centre and carefully place the egg
yolk in it. Scatter with pine nuts. Mix the meat with the egg yolk and pear at the table.

Thai Beef Salad

I ate very little beef when I was in Thailand. The sight of butchers' stalls in markets,
open to the sun and awash with flies, was enough to put anyone off eating most meat
in fact. However, I pushed that to the back of my mind when it came to this salad.
Back here, where you can be sure of getting high-quality, tender steak, I think it tastes
even better than it did on its home patch.

Raw vegetables are added to contrast with the meat and the spicy dressing. I've
chosen tomato and cool cucumber, although others, such as sweet peppers or
carrots, could be used instead. The beef and the dressing can be prepared in
advance, but don't put the salad together until the very last minute. It makes a fairly
substantial first course for 6, but can also be served as a main course for 4.

SERVES 4–6
450–675 g (1–1 lb 8 oz) high-quality lean
   steak, such as fillet, rump or sirloin
Oil, for grilling or frying
3 tablespoons freshly squeezed lime
   juice
3 tablespoons Thai fish sauce (*nam pla*)
1 tablespoon sugar
4 shallots, thinly sliced
2 garlic cloves, crushed

2 small, thin red chillies, seeded and
   thinly sliced

TO SERVE
6–8 lettuce leaves
Chopped coriander
Chopped chives
$1/2$ cucumber, peeled and sliced 5 mm
   ($1/8$ in) thick
2 tomatoes, cut into eighths

The meat can either be grilled or roasted.

To grill, heat the grill until hot then brush the steak with oil and grill close to the heat until browned on the outside, but still rare inside.

To roast, pre-heat the oven to 240°C/450°F/Gas Mark 8. Heat a little oil in a flame-proof dish until it is very hot. Add the meat and brown it quickly over a fierce heat. Transfer to the oven and roast for 10–15 minutes.

Whichever method you use, err, if anything, on the side of undercooking rather than overcooking the beef as it will continue to cook a little in its own heat as it rests. Leave to cool for at least 5 minutes, then slice thinly.

Mix together the lime juice, fish sauce and sugar, stirring to dissolve the sugar. Add the shallots, garlic and chillies. Make a bed of lettuce on a serving dish and pile the beef in the centre. Spoon over the dressing and scatter with coriander and chives. Arrange the cucumber and tomatoes around the edge.

Steak Teriyaki

Japanese teriyaki sauce is dark, sweet and sticky and sets off a juicy steak beautifully. If you can get real sake and mirin (from oriental food stores) then the sauce will be especially good, though dry and sweet sherry stand in quite well.

SERVES 2
Sunflower or vegetable oil
2 sirloin steaks, about 2.5 cm (1 in)
   thick
2 tablespoons sake or dry sherry

2 tablespoons dark soy sauce
2 tablespoons mirin or sweet sherry, or
   sake plus 1 tablespoon sugar
1 teaspoon sugar

Cover the base of a heavy frying-pan with a very thin film of oil. Place over a high heat. When it is searingly hot, place the steaks in the pan and cook for 6 minutes, turning once.

After the first 4 minutes, having turned the steaks, spoon over the sake or dry sherry. Be warned, it will sizzle and smoke. Cover the pan tightly and cook for the final 2 minutes. Transfer the steaks to a warm plate and keep warm.

Add the remaining ingredients to the pan and stir and scrape all the residues into the liquid. Let it boil hard until reduced by half. Return the steaks to the pan, with any juices that have seeped out, and cook for 1 final minute, turning once.

Steak au Poivre

Retro Cuisine is the latest buzz. In other words, all those dishes that were the height of fashion in the 1970s are making a comeback – Beef Wellington, Coq au Vin, prawn cocktail and the like – far more exciting and appetizing than the renaissance of flared trousers. Let's hope it will be more of a success, too. One dish that has been severely neglected is steak au poivre (which actually dates from the early years of the twentieth century), a luxurious but quickly made dish for a special occasion. If you don't fancy all that cream, just eat the steaks with the pan juices poured over them. And, if you're not a meat-eater, you can use the same method for firm fish steaks.

SERVES 4
3 tablespoons black peppercorns, crushed
4 fillet or rump steaks, about 2.5 cm (1 in) thick
30 g (1 oz) clarified butter or 2 tablespoons sunflower oil
2 tablespoons brandy
100 ml (3$\frac{1}{2}$ fl oz) dry white wine
300 ml (10 fl oz) double cream
Salt

Spread the peppercorns out on a plate. Press the steaks firmly into them, so that each side is evenly coated. Heat the butter or oil in a frying-pan that is large enough to take all four steaks. Fry them over a moderate heat, until they are done to your liking. For a medium-rare steak, allow around 3–4 minutes on each side. Take the steaks out of the pan and keep them warm.

Skim off the fat in the pan, leaving only the juices. Add the brandy, warm through for a minute or so and then, if you have a gas hob, tilt the pan so that the juices ignite; if you have an electric hob, light the juices with a match at arm's length. Once the flames have died down add the wine and bring up to the boil, scraping in all the residue. Boil until reduced by half and then stir in the cream and boil down for another 3–4 minutes, until reduced to a sauce with a pleasing consistency. Season with salt and then serve with the steaks.

Pan-fried Strips of Beef in Wild Mushroom and Mustard Sauce

This is a rich and luxurious beef dish, perfect for a mid-week dinner party or a special treat. Serve it with parsley-speckled noodles to balance the creaminess of the sauce.

SERVES 4
15 g (¹/₂ oz) dried porcini
3 shallots, finely chopped
50 ml (2 fl oz) Noilly Prat or other dry
  vermouth
300 ml (10 fl oz) whipping cream
Salt and freshly ground black pepper
25 g (1 oz) butter

1 tablespoon sunflower oil
450 g (1 lb) rump or fillet steak, cut into
  strips 1 cm (¹/₂ in) thick, 5 cm (2 in)
  long, and 2.5 cm (1 in) wide
175 g (6 oz) button mushrooms, halved
  or quartered
2 tablespoons Moutarde de Meaux or
  other coarse-grained mustard

Soak the porcini in a little warm water for 20–30 minutes until softened, then chop roughly. Let the soaking water settle for 5 minutes, then carefully pour it off into a separate bowl, leaving the earthy grit behind. Reserve the liquid.

Put the shallots into a pan with the vermouth and boil until reduced to a damp mass. Stir in the cream, bring to the boil and simmer until reduced by a third. Season with salt and pepper.

Melt the butter with the oil in a wide frying-pan over a high heat and heat until foaming. Sauté the strips of beef for a few minutes, turning and tossing until lightly browned but no more. Scoop out and reserve.

Add the button mushrooms to the same pan and fry until tender, then scoop out and add to the meat. Pour off any excess fat and add the liquid from soaking the porcini mushrooms. Bring up to the boil, stirring in all the residues in the pan. Add the porcini and simmer for a couple of minutes until the liquid has mostly boiled off.

Return the beef and fresh mushrooms to the pan and pour over the cream sauce. Stir in the mustard. Bring to the boil and simmer for a minute or so to heat through. Taste, adjust the seasoning and serve.

Good Old Hamburgers

When they are made properly, with good minced beef – try asking your butcher to mince some chuck steak or even sirloin steak for you – home-made hamburgers are a great pleasure. I usually grill them, but you could tart them up no end by frying them, then deglazing the pan with a slug of wine, reducing and finishing with some cream and a little mustard to make a luxurious sauce.

Whether you grill or fry, test them for doneness by pressing them with the tip of your finger, in exactly the same way as you would with a steak. A rare burger or steak will be soft and spongy. Medium rare will feel a little firmer. Medium will offer some resistance and will feel just firm to the touch. If you must cook it well-done, which seems a shame as it won't be half as succulent and juicy, the burger or steak will feel solid. You can also use the less elegant method of testing, which is to cut into the steak or burger with a knife. Not professional, but more accurate for the inexperienced.

SERVES 4

675 g (1 lb 8 oz) lean minced beef

1/2 onion, grated or very finely chopped

1/2 tablespoon Worcestershire sauce

1 tablespoon very finely chopped parsley

Leaves from 2 sprigs of thyme, finely chopped

Salt and freshly ground black pepper

1 egg, lightly beaten (optional)

Oil, or a combination of oil and butter, for grilling or frying

TO SERVE

4 buns, split open and lightly toasted on the inside

Shredded lettuce leaves

Sliced tomato

Dill-pickled cucumbers, sliced

Tomato ketchup, mayonnaise, Tabasco, or your favourite relish

Mix the beef with the onion, Worcestershire sauce, parsley, thyme, and salt and pepper. Use your fingers to squelch it all together thoroughly. If the mixture seems rather crumbly, add a little beaten egg to hold it together. Divide into 4 and shape into nice round patties about 2 cm (3/4 in) thick, then grill or fry.

To grill, brush each burger with a little oil or oil and butter, and grill close to a thoroughly pre-heated grill until browned and crusty on the outside, but still moist and tender on the inside.

To fry, heat a little oil or oil and butter in a frying-pan and fry the burgers over a high heat until nicely browned outside and done to your taste on the inside.

Sandwich in the buns together with lettuce, tomato and pickled cucumber, salt and pepper, and whatever sauces or relishes you happen to like best.

Cha Bo

This recipe for Vietnamese spiced hamburgers with a hot, sour, sweet and salty dipping sauce is based on one I came across in an American book called The Foods of Vietnam *by Nicole Routhier. It turns plain hamburgers into something marvellously exotic. Cans of coconut milk, rice vinegar and fish sauce are all available in oriental supermarkets and in some ordinary supermarkets as well.*

SERVES 4

FOR THE *NUOC CHAM* (DIPPING SAUCE)

1 small red chilli, seeded and finely chopped

2 garlic cloves, chopped

2 tablespoons sugar

Juice of 1 lime

4 tablespoons rice vinegar or cider vinegar

4 tablespoons Thai fish sauce (*nam pla*)

FOR THE BURGERS

4 tablespoons shelled unsalted peanuts

450 g (1 lb) lean minced beef

3 shallots, very finely chopped

4 teaspoons Thai fish sauce (*nam pla*)

3 tablespoons coconut milk

1 teaspoon ground cumin

1 1/2 tablespoons finely chopped coriander

1 teaspoon sugar

Salt and freshly ground black pepper

A little oil, for brushing

To make the dipping sauce, pound the chilli with the garlic and sugar to a paste in a mortar. Work in the lime juice, then the vinegar, fish sauce and finally 3 tablespoons of water. Serve in small bowls.

Pre-heat the grill thoroughly. Grind the peanuts to a coarse powder and mix with all the remaining burger ingredients except the oil, kneading well with your fingers to form a cohesive mass. Divide into 4 portions, roll each one into a ball, then flatten to make a patty about 2 cm (3/4 in) thick. Brush with a little oil and cook under the grill for about 3–4 minutes on each side. Serve with the dipping sauce.

Beef Lindstrom

Beef Lindstrom is the Swedish answer to the hamburger, and a very good answer it is too. The bulk of the patty is made up of minced beef and mashed potato, with capers and finely diced beetroot dotted through them. They are often served with a fried egg on top, a delicious addition but not absolutely necessary.

On the whole I'm not too taken with pickled beetroot, or even ordinary bought cooked beetroot that has been saturated in vinegar. For this recipe, however, I make an exception. Since it is finely diced, the sharpness works quite well.

SERVES 4
450 g (1 lb) lean minced beef
8 oz (225 g) cooked peeled potato,
   mashed
1 egg yolk
Salt and freshly ground black pepper
85–150 ml (3–5 fl oz) milk
1 medium-sized cooked or pickled
   beetroot, finely diced

1/2 onion, grated
2 tablespoons capers
15 g (1/2 oz) butter and 1 tablespoon oil,
   or 2 tablespoons oil

TO SERVE
4 fried eggs (optional)

Using your hands, mix the beef thoroughly with the potato, egg yolk, salt and pepper and just enough milk to hold the mixture together without making it too sticky to shape. If you have a food processor, work the mixture in it to make it smoother. Mix in the beet-root, onion and capers. Divide into 4 portions and form each one into a hamburger shape, about 2 cm (3/4 in) thick. Fry in the butter and oil mixture or just oil until nicely browned on both sides. Serve as they are or, even better, with a fried egg on top.

My Mince

This is how I cook mince and I can think of no special name for it. It is good enough to eat in all sorts of ways, just as it is, spooned over baked potatoes, on pasta with lashings of Parmesan, or as the basis for My Cottage Pie, p. 127

SERVES 4–6

1 large onion, chopped

1 carrot, finely diced

2 tablespoons olive oil or sunflower oil

1–2 garlic cloves, crushed

675 g (1 lb 8 oz) best-quality, lean
    minced beef

400 g (14 oz) can chopped tomatoes

^{1}/$_2$ red pepper, grilled, skinned and
    chopped (optional)

3 tablespoons tomato ketchup

2 teaspoons Worcestershire sauce
    (optional)

^{1}/$_2$ teaspoon dried thyme

^{1}/$_2$ teaspoon ground cumin

Salt and freshly ground black pepper

Cook the onion and the carrot in the oil in a large, wide, heavy frying-pan over a medium heat until tender and lightly coloured. Add the garlic and stir for a few seconds, then increase the heat to high and add half the mince. Fry briskly, breaking up the lumps and turning the meat over, until it is lightly browned. Then scoop out onto a plate.

Add the remaining mince to the pan and fry in the same way. When it is done, return the first batch to the pan along with the chopped tomatoes, pepper (if using) and all the remaining ingredients. Add 300 ml (10 fl oz) of water. Bring to the boil and half cover. Simmer gently, stirring from time to time, for about an hour, adding more hot water as needed. By this time the meat should be tender and most of the liquid evaporated away to leave a delicious moist mush. Taste and adjust the seasoning. (I often add a splash more ketchup or Worcestershire sauce at this stage!)

My Cottage Pie

I use my standard method of cooking mince as the basis for my cottage pie. The result is absolutely delicious and we all tend to end up eating far too much of it.

SERVES 4–6

1 quantity My Mince (see My Mince,
    p. 126)

675 g (1 lb 8 oz) floury potatoes

65 g (2^1/$_2$ oz) butter

150–300 ml (5–10 fl oz) full cream milk

Salt and freshly ground black pepper

Pre-heat the oven to 200°C/400°F/Gas Mark 6. While the mince is cooking, make the mashed potatoes. Cook the potatoes by boiling them in their skins, baking them in the oven or microwaving them. Peel while still hot and mash thoroughly in a saucepan with 50 g (2 oz) of the butter. Season with salt and beat energetically over a low heat, gradually adding the milk, until the mash is light, fluffy and smooth. Taste and adjust the seasoning.

To assemble the pie, spoon the mince into a pie dish. Dot the mashed potato over the top and smooth down, then make patterns in the surface with a fork. Dot with the remaining butter and bake in the oven until the potato is patched with brown. Dish up immediately.

Meatloaf

Meatloaf is really pâté by another name, though not quite so fancy. But who cares when it tastes this good? It is lovely straight from the oven (make a tomato sauce to serve with it), though it tends to crumble when sliced. Cold left-overs are just as good and will slice more neatly. It's excellent with chutney and a salad, or in sandwiches.

SERVES 6–8
1 large onion, chopped
2 garlic cloves, chopped
15 g (¹/₂ oz) butter
1 tablespoon oil
25 g (1 oz) soft white breadcrumbs

675 g (1 lb 8 oz) minced beef
350 g (12 oz) best-quality sausagemeat
2 eggs, lightly beaten
2 tablespoons chopped parsley
1 teaspoon dried thyme
Salt and freshly ground black pepper

Pre-heat the oven to 180°C/350°F/Gas Mark 4. Fry the onion and garlic gently in the butter and oil until tender. Scrape into a mixing bowl. Add all the remaining ingredients and mix thoroughly. Quickly fry a small knob of the mixture to test the seasoning, then adjust, adding more salt, pepper, parsley or thyme as required. Pack the mixture into a buttered loaf tin or terrine, smoothing down the surface, then bang hard on the work-top to expel any trapped air bubbles.

Bake in the oven for 1–1¹/₂ hours until done. To test, pierce the centre with a skewer – the juices should run clear, rather than raw and bloody. Serve hot or cold.

Bobotie

Bobotie is a recipe of South African origin, credited to the kitchens of the slaves and labourers brought in by the Dutch from the Far East, though it is now a national dish. The Malays, as they were known (though they might well have come from other Far Eastern countries), brought their own culinary traditions with them, gradually adapting them to fit the local supplies of food. Bobotie is just one of a legacy of spiced dishes that they gave their new country.

It's a wonderful way to dress up minced beef (or lamb) and, unlike for so many minced meat dishes, you don't even have to fiddle around browning and cooking the meat before you put it together with all the other ingredients.

SERVES 4
1 medium onion, chopped
1 garlic clove, chopped
15 g (¹/₂ oz) butter or 1 tablespoon oil,
   plus a little extra for greasing
1 thick slice bread
150 ml (5 fl oz) milk
450 (1 lb) minced beef or lamb

1 tablespoon mild curry powder
¹/₂ tablespoon sugar
2 tablespoons lemon juice
25 g (1 oz) flaked almonds
75 g (3 oz) raisins
Salt and freshly ground black pepper
2 eggs

Pre-heat the oven to 180°C/350°F/Gas Mark 4. Fry the onion and garlic in the butter or oil until lightly browned. While they are cooking, remove the crust from the bread and soak the bread in the milk for 2–3 minutes. Squeeze the milk out of the bread and keep both separately.

Mix the fried onion and garlic with the minced beef or lamb, curry powder, sugar, lemon juice, almonds, raisins, salt and pepper and soaked bread, beating to mix evenly. Finally beat in one of the eggs. Then spoon into a greased pie dish and smooth down.

Beat the second egg with the reserved milk, salt and pepper and pour over the minced meat mixture. Bake for 55–60 minutes until the top is set and browned. Serve with rice and a fruit chutney.

Red Flannel Hash

An American classic – corned beef hash with cubes of beetroot. It is not elegant fare, but who cares when it tastes so wonderful? Pile it on to the plate and dig in – you won't be disappointed. If you want to go right over the top, add a fried egg per person, perched on top of the mound of hash.

SERVES 4–6

350 g (12 oz) can corned beef, diced

1 onion, finely chopped

450 g (1 lb) cooked potatoes, peeled and diced

275 g (10 oz) cooked beetroot, peeled and diced

Salt and freshly ground black pepper

50 g (2 oz) butter

1 tablespoon Worcestershire sauce

TO SERVE

Chopped fresh parsley

Mix together the corned beef, onion, potatoes, beetroot and a little salt and pepper. If you have the time, leave for a few hours or even overnight, covered, stirring occasionally. This is not essential, but it improves the flavour.

Melt the butter in a wide, heavy frying-pan and heat until it is foaming. Add the corned beef mixture and the Worcestershire sauce. Stir, then press down fairly firmly. Turn the heat down to medium-low and cook gently for about 15 minutes until a brown crust forms on the base. Stir and break up, so that some of the crust gets mixed in with the rest. Add about 4 tablespoons of hot water. Press down again and cook for a further 15 minutes or so, until a second crust has formed. Scoop out on to a dish, scatter with parsley and serve immediately.

Cuban Picadillo

From Cuba comes this unusual minced beef hash, cooked with tomatoes, raisins, capers and olives. It's an odd idea but a real winner for all that. Serve it over boiled rice (or sautéd potatoes, as they sometimes do in Cuba), along with slices of avocado, or guacamole (mashed avocados mixed with finely diced tomato, onion, garlic, a hint of chilli, lime juice and chopped fresh coriander). It also makes a very good filling for tortillas, or taco shells, along with a tomatoey salsa, avocado again and generous dollops of soured cream.

SERVES 4–6
1 onion, chopped
1 green pepper, seeded and finely
   chopped
2 tablespoons sunflower oil
4 garlic cloves, chopped
450 g (1 lb) minced beef
150 ml (5 fl oz) passata

12 green olives, stoned and roughly
   chopped
60 g (2 oz) raisins
1 tablespoon capers
150 ml (5 fl oz) dry white wine
1 teaspoon caster sugar
Salt and freshly ground black pepper

Fry the onion and green pepper gently in the oil until tender, without browning. Add the garlic and cook for about a minute more, then add the minced beef. Fry, breaking up the lumps, for about 5 minutes. Now add all the remaining ingredients, reduce the heat, cover and simmer for a further 25–30 minutes, stirring occasionally. By the time the hash is cooked, it should be reduced and thick but still quite wet. Taste and adjust the seasoning and then serve.

Mefarka

Broad beans and mince may not sound too enticing, but add spices, herbs, olive oil and lemon juice and a miracle happens. I found this recipe for mefarka *a few years ago in Claudia Roden's* New Book of Middle Eastern Food *(Penguin), and return to it time and again.*

SERVES 6
5 tablespoons light olive oil
450 g (1 lb) shelled broad beans
Salt and freshly ground black pepper
1/2 teaspoon dried thyme
750 g (1 lb 8 oz) lean minced beef
1/4 teaspoon freshly ground nutmeg
1/4 teaspoon ground cloves

1/2 level teaspoon cayenne
1/2 teaspoon cinnamon
3 eggs

TO SERVE
Juice of 1/2 lemon
Chopped fresh parsley or coriander

Mix 3 tablespoons of the oil with 120 ml (4 fl oz) water in a saucepan. Add the broad beans, sprinkle with salt and pepper, and add the thyme. Simmer gently until the beans are tender, adding a little extra water if necessary.

In the meantime, prepare the meat mixture. Heat the remaining 2 tablespoons of oil in a deep frying-pan or heavy, flameproof casserole. Add the minced beef when it is just warm – if the oil is too hot the meat will dry up. Stir, then add the spices, salt and pepper and just enough water to cover. Simmer until the meat is soft and moist and well-cooked, and has absorbed the water.

Add the meat mixture to the beans and stir well, crushing lightly with a fork. Break the eggs into the pan and stir. Cook, stirring constantly, until they are just set. Turn out on to a serving dish and allow to cool. Taste and adjust the seasoning. Serve cold, sprinkled with lemon juice, and parsley or coriander.

Old-fashioned Beef and Carrot Stew with Parsley Dumplings

This is a wonderful traditional stew and the dumplings flavoured with parsley add a special touch. You can make the stew the day before to let the flavours mingle, but the dumplings should be made on the day. Re-heat the stew thoroughly before serving.

SERVES 4–6
2 onions, sliced
50 g (2 oz) dripping or lard
900 g (2 lb) chuck or shin of beef, cut into 5 cm (2 in) cubes
Seasoned flour, for dusting the meat
900 g (2 lb) carrots, cut into 2.5 cm (1 in) lengths
1 bouquet garni (1 bay leaf, 2 sprigs parsley and 2 sprigs thyme, tied together with string)

Salt and freshly ground black pepper
750 ml (1 1/4 pints) beef stock, or 300 ml (1/2 pint) water and 450 ml (15 fl oz) stout or Guinness

FOR THE DUMPLINGS
100 g (4 oz) self-raising flour
1/2 teaspoon baking powder
1/4 teaspoon salt
50 g (2 oz) shredded suet
2 tablespoons chopped parsley

Pre-heat the oven to 170°C/325°F/Gas Mark 3. Fry the onions in half the dripping or lard in a wide frying-pan over a medium heat until lightly browned. Transfer to a casserole dish. Dust the meat with the seasoned flour and fry in batches over a high heat in the same fat as the onion, until browned all over. Add more fat as needed. As the meat is done, add it to the casserole. Tuck in the carrots and bouquet garni, season and sprinkle over a tablespoon of flour.

Put the stock or water and stout into the frying-pan and bring to the boil, stirring and scraping in the residues on the bottom of the pan. Pour over the meat and season. The liquid should cover the meat; if necessary, add a little more stock or water. Cover the casserole, transfer to the oven and cook for 2 hours until the meat is tender. There should be enough sauce to poach the dumplings but if it looks a bit dry, stir in some boiling water.

Meanwhile, get down to making the dumplings. Sift the flour with the baking powder and salt. Stir in the suet and parsley and add just enough water to make a slightly sticky dough. With floured hands, roll into small balls about the size of a quail's egg.

When the meat is nearly ready, dot the dumplings over the surface of the stew and return it to the oven, covered, for 30–40 minutes, or until the dumplings are puffed and tender and cooked through. Baste them once or twice with the stew's juices as they cook. Serve the stew and dumplings hot and steaming.

Beef, Guinness and Mushroom Stew

Guinness gives a dark, rich, savoury satisfaction to a beef stew while mushrooms underline the deep flavour – I usually use a few right at the beginning of the cooking time, then supplement the stew with freshly cooked mushrooms at the last moment. If you can't get shiitake mushrooms, replace them with large, meaty flat-caps.

SERVES 6
900 g (2 lb) shin of beef
Seasoned flour, for dusting
50 g (2 oz) butter
2 tablespoons sunflower oil
2 onions, roughly chopped
100 g (4 oz) button mushrooms
400 ml (14 fl oz) Guinness, Murphy's or any other stout

2 tablespoons tomato purée
1/2 tablespoon sugar
1 bouquet garni (1 bay leaf, 2 sprigs thyme, 2 sprigs parsley and 1 sprig rosemary, tied together with string)
Salt and freshly ground black pepper
225 g (8 oz) shiitake mushrooms

Pre-heat the oven to 170°C/325°F/Gas Mark 3. Trim the beef and cut into 2.5 cm (1 in) cubes. Toss lightly in seasoned flour. Heat a third of the butter and 1 tablespoon of the oil in a frying-pan and brown the meat briskly in batches, without overcrowding the pan. Transfer to a casserole. Add a little more butter and oil to the pan and fry the onions until lightly browned. Scoop into the casserole. Finally fry the button mushrooms and add those to the casserole too.

Pour the stout into the pan and bring to the boil, scraping in the brown residues from frying. Stir in 350 ml (12 fl oz) boiling water, the tomato purée and sugar, then pour into the casserole. Add the bouquet garni to the casserole with salt and pepper. Cover and transfer to the oven. Cook for 2–3 hours or until the meat is very tender. Check occasionally, and if necessary add a little more hot water.

Remove the stalks from the shiitake mushrooms and discard. Slice the caps thickly. Heat the remaining butter in a frying-pan and sauté the mushrooms, then stir into the casserole and return to the oven for 5 minutes. Discard the bouquet garni, adjust the seasoning and serve.

Carbonnades à la Flamande

Made with beer and plenty of onions, this stew may be rather less chic than Daube de Boeuf (see p.134), but it is just as welcome on a chilly evening. What I really like about it is the contrast between the crisp mustardy layer of bread on the top, and the tender meat and juices underneath.

If you make the stew in advance, don't put the bread on top until after you've begun to re-heat it on the day of serving.

SERVES 4–6
900 g (2 lb) shin of beef
About 2 tablespoons vegetable oil
2 onions, sliced
2 garlic cloves, chopped
3–4 tablespoons seasoned flour
300 ml (10 fl oz) brown ale or stout
1 tablespoon light muscovado sugar

1 bouquet garni (see p. 133)
Salt and freshly ground black pepper

FOR THE CRUST
40 g (1^1/$_2$ oz) butter, softened
1^1/$_2$ tablespoons Dijon mustard
6 slices French bread

Pre-heat the oven to 170°C/325°F/Gas Mark 3. Cut the beef into strips about 1 cm (^{1}/2 in) thick, 8 cm (3 in) long and 2.5 cm (1 in) wide. Heat 2 tablespoons of oil in a large frying-pan, add the onions and fry over a moderate heat until tender. Add the garlic and continue cooking for 2 minutes, then scoop the onion and garlic out of the pan and put them in the bottom of an oven-proof casserole.

Raise the heat under the frying-pan and add a little more oil if necessary. Toss the meat in the flour and brown in two batches. Transfer to the casserole.

Reduce the heat under the frying-pan and pour in the beer. Bring to the boil, stirring and scraping in all the residues. Stir in the sugar, then pour over the meat and onions. Add the bouquet garni and season with salt and pepper. Add enough water to just cover the beef. Cover and cook in the oven for 2^1/2–3 hours, stirring occasionally and adding a little more water if it begins to get dry.

Meanwhile, mash the butter with the mustard and spread it thickly on the bread slices. Place the bread, buttered side up, on top of the stew. Return to the oven and cook, uncovered, for a further 30 minutes, or until the bread is crisp and lightly browned on top. Serve immediately.

Daube de Bouef

This is France's most famous beef stew and it comes, perhaps not surprisingly, with many variations. When it is good it is wonderfully fragrant and aromatic. The name comes from the earthenware dish it is cooked in, a daubière, *with a fat pot-belly that narrows to a relatively small rim. Essential to its flavour are red wine, brandy and dried orange zest. Serve the stew with buttered and parsleyed noodles.*

SERVES 6–8

3 sprigs of thyme
1 bay leaf, snapped in two
2 sprigs of parsley
1 strip of dried orange zest
225 g (8 oz) unsmoked streaky bacon,
  in a single piece, or thick-cut,
  cubed
3 tablespoons olive oil
2 large onions, sliced
1.5 kg (3 lb) chuck or rump of beef, cut
  into 5 cm (2 in) squares, about
  2.5 cm (1 in) thick

3 large carrots, scraped and sliced
675 g (1 lb 8 oz) tomatoes, skinned,
  seeded and roughly chopped
1 tablespoon tomato purée (optional)
3 garlic cloves, crushed
Salt and freshly ground black pepper
50–100 g (2–4 oz) pork rinds, diced
600 ml (1 pint) fruity red wine
50 ml (2 fl oz) brandy

Pre-heat the oven to 150°C/300°F/Gas Mark 2. Tie together the herbs and orange zest with string to make a bouquet garni. Fry the bacon in the olive oil until lightly browned. Scoop out and spread over the base of an oven-proof casserole. Now fry the onions over a moderate heat in the same fat, until golden, and add to the casserole.

Dry the meat carefully, then brown in the fat over a high heat in three batches. Arrange on top of the onions. Add the bouquet garni, the carrots, tomatoes, tomato purée, if using, garlic, salt and pepper. Cover with the pork rinds.

Pour the excess fat out of the frying-pan and pour in the wine. Bring to the boil, scraping in the brown residues from frying. Pour over the contents of the casserole.

Add the brandy to the pan, warm quickly and set alight at arm's length either with a match, if you cook over an electric hob, or by using the gas flame, tilting the pan so that the warm brandy ignites. When the flames die down, pour the brandy into the casserole too. Add enough water to almost cover the contents.

Cover tightly and place in the oven. Cook gently for 3–4 hours, stirring once or twice, until the meat is marvellously tender. After 3 hours, check the state of the liquid. If it is a little watery, uncover the pan and let it reduce. When meat and sauce are ready, skim off what fat you can and serve.

VARIATIONS

Try stirring 225 g (8 oz) black olives, stoned, into the stew half an hour before it is done. Another nice variation is to make a *persillade*. Mix together 2 tablespoons chopped parsley and 1 garlic clove, very finely chopped, and sprinkle over the stew just before serving. You can use the olives and *persillade* together if you wish. Alternatively you can mix together 4 canned anchovy fillets, chopped, 1 tablespoon capers, chopped, 2 tablespoons chopped parsley and 1–2 garlic cloves, chopped. Either stir into the stew half an hour before it is cooked, so that the flavours mellow out into the sauce, or sprinkle over the stew just before serving for a sprightlier, brassier taste.

Stiffado

Though this Greek beef and onion stew is usually made with small onions, I like it best with shallots. Either way, it is wonderfully dark and savoury, the perfect dish for a cold winter's night.

SERVES 6–8
1.5 kg (3 lb) braising beef
1.5 kg (3 lb) small shallots or pickling onions
85–120 ml (3–4 fl oz) olive or sunflower oil
3 cloves garlic, peeled and chopped

150 ml (5 fl oz) red wine
3 tablespoons red wine vinegar
2 bay leaves
1 stick of cinnamon, snapped in two
3 tablespoons tomato purée
Salt and freshly ground black pepper

Cut the meat into large chunks of about 5–7.5 cm (2–3 in) wide. Slice tops and bottoms off the shallots or onions. Pour boiling water over them, stand for 1 minute, then squeeze them out of their skins. Drain well.

Heat half the oil in a large, wide frying-pan and brown the meat, in several batches. Transfer to a flameproof casserole. Brown the onions in the same fat, adding more oil as needed, and add the garlic 2–3 minutes before the onions are browned. Then add the onions and garlic to the casserole. Pour off excess fat in the frying-pan and add the wine and vinegar. Bring to the boil, scraping in all the brown residue on the base of the pan. Tip over the meat and onions.

Add the remaining ingredients and enough water to cover. Bring to the boil, stirring occasionally. Turn down the heat, cover and simmer gently for 2 hours until the meat is tender. Stir it every once in a while.

Uncover and raise the heat slightly. Let it bubble for a further 30 minutes, stirring occasionally. Skim off the fat on the surface. Taste and adjust seasonings. Serve immediately.

Steak and Kidney Pudding

There is nothing in the world to beat our own steak and kidney pud – at least when it is made properly. The very thought of that pale, steaming, fragrant crust enclosing the velvety darkness of melting pieces of steak and kidney swathed in rich gravy makes my mouth water.

I have tried short-circuiting the method, popping the filling ingredients straight into the crust and then steaming it for ever and a day (which is, I'm sure, the way that it was originally made), but the end result is always disappointingly thin and I could probably charge entry to the kitchen as a public sauna.

No, to make the ultimate, unctuous, devastating steak and kidney pudding, you must cook the filling before it goes into the pudding itself. In fact, this has several advantages besides mere deliciousness. The filling can be made a day in advance and the fat skimmed off when cold, and then the pudding will need no more than an hour and a half's steaming, leaving the crust lighter and less soggy. Incidentally, I think rump makes a marginally better pud, but there's not a lot in it. If you want to make a truly serious steak and kidney pud, then buy fresh suet from the butcher and chop it finely yourself.

SERVES 6

FOR THE FILLING
50 g (2 oz) butter
2–3 tablespoons sunflower oil
1 large onion, chopped
900 g (2 lb) rump or chuck steak, trimmed and cut into 2.5 cm (1 in) cubes
225–350 g (8–12 oz) ox or veal kidney, trimmed and sliced
1 1/2 tablespoons plain flour
600 ml (1 pint) beef or chicken stock, or 300 ml (10 fl oz) beef or chicken stock and 300 ml (10 fl oz) Guinness or stout

275 g (10 oz) flat-cap mushrooms, halved and sliced
1 bouquet garni (1 bayleaf, 2 sprigs of parsley and 2 sprigs of thyme tied together with string)
Salt and freshly ground black pepper

FOR THE SUET CRUST
350 g (12 oz) self-raising flour
1 teaspoon baking powder
1/2 teaspoon salt
175 g (6 oz) prepared suet

Heat 25 g (1 oz) of the butter and 1 tablespoon of oil in a wide frying-pan over a medium heat. Add the onion and fry until golden then set aside. Add half of the remaining butter and oil to the pan and turn the heat up high. Brown the meat in two batches (three if the pan is on the small side), then scoop out and reserve. Add the remaining butter and oil, if necessary, and quickly brown the kidney. Set aside. Pour any excess fat from the pan and sprinkle over the flour. Gradually pour in the stock, stirring constantly, then the Guinness if using, scraping in all the browned bits from the meat. Bring to the boil, still stirring.

If the frying-pan is big enough, return the meat, kidneys and onions to it, adding the mushrooms, bouquet garni, salt and pepper. Otherwise transfer them all to a flame-proof casserole. Either way, cover and simmer gently on the hob for 2–3 hours, stirring occasionally, or transfer to the oven, set to 150°C/300°F/Gas Mark 2, and cook for 2–3 hours until the meat is tender and the sauce reduced to a pleasing thickness. Then taste and adjust the seasoning. Cool and skim off any congealed fat.

To make the crust, sift the flour with the baking powder and salt. Mix in the suet and just enough cold water to make a firm dough. Roll out on a well floured board to make a large circle. Cut out a quarter and set aside for the lid. Drop the rest into a generously buttered 1.75 litre (3 pint) pudding basin, so that the centre sits on the base of the basin and the outer edges of the pastry overhang the rim of the bowl. Using your fingers, gently press the dough into the corners of the basin and round to line it completely, pinching the cut edges together.

Fill the crust with the steak and kidney stew, stopping about 2.5 cm (1 in) below the rim of the basin. Roll out the remaining pastry to form a lid for the pudding. Lay over the pudding and dampen the edges of the overhang. Flip them over on to the lid, and press together to seal neatly.

Take a large sheet of silver foil or greaseproof paper and make a double pleat down the centre. Lay over the pudding basin and tie in place securely with string. Leave the ends trailing and loop them over and under the string on the outside of the basin, then knot to form a string 'handle' to lift the pudding in and out of the pan.

Stand the pudding, on a small trivet if you have one or an upturned saucer, in a large saucepan, and pour enough boiling water around it to come about two-thirds of the way up the basin. Bring to the boil, then reduce to a simmer. Cover tightly (make a dome of silver foil if the lid won't fit) and leave it to simmer for 1½ hours. Check the water level regularly and top up with more boiling water as needed.

Serve the pudding straight from the basin: lift it out of the pan and remove the string and foil or paper. Wrap a clean white napkin or tea-towel around the basin and present the pudding proudly.

Rib Roast of Beef with English Mustard

Forerib is the best of all roasting joints. It is the grand roast beef of Old England, the joint that made, and still makes, foreigners and natives alike drool. Almost as essential as the grand joint itself are the sandwiches made from the left-overs, so it's important to invest in a generously proportioned piece of beef that will look impressive on the table and keep everyone well-fed for a couple of days.

Ask the butcher to prepare the joint for you, trimming it nicely, but without removing too much of the fat as this is what gives such a good flavour and protects the meat from drying out. To make carving easier, ask the butcher to chine the joint, i.e. loosen the chine or backbone so that it comes away easily once the joint is cooked.

The hot mustard forms a thin crust on the beef, but mellows in the heat of the oven, so serve a little more alongside.

SERVES 8
3.5 kg (8 lb) forerib of beef
1 generous tablespoon traditional hot
   English mustard
Salt and freshly ground black pepper

Pre-heat the oven to 220°C/425°F/Gas Mark 7. Weigh the joint and then calculate the cooking time, allowing 14 minutes per 500 g (13 minutes per lb) plus 15 minutes for rare meat, 18 minutes per 500 g (16 minutes per lb) plus 20 minutes for medium, 22–27 minutes per 500 g (20–24 minutes per lb) plus 25 minutes for well-done.

Place the joint in a roasting tin, fat-side up. Smear the mustard over the fat and season with salt and pepper. Roast for 30 minutes or so, then cover with foil to prevent burning. Check for doneness. Plunge a skewer into the heat of the meat and leave for 30 seconds. Pull it out and place the tip on the inside of your wrist. If it is cold, then the meat is not yet done. When it is warm, the meat is rare, when fairly hot it's medium, and when very hot it's well-done. When done, remove the foil, turn off the heat, open the door a crack, and leave the roast to relax in the oven for 30 minutes (or transfer to a warm place to relax if you are making Yorkshire pudding). Serve with Yorkshire pudding (see p. 342), Horseradish and Walnut Sauce (see p. 357) and a selection of vegetables, depending on what's in season.

Roast Fillet of Beef with Quick Tomato, Red Wine and Olive Sauce

This is the perfect dish for a mid-week dinner party. Fillet of beef is expensive but it cooks quickly with no waste. The meat is as tender as butter but has a tendency to be on the bland side, and that's where the sauce comes into play, pepping up the whole ensemble.

SERVES 4, GENEROUSLY
600–700 g (1 lb 4 oz–1 lb 8 oz) piece of
    finest beef fillet
1 garlic clove, halved
Salt and freshly ground black pepper
Olive oil
1 onion, sliced

FOR THE SAUCE
2 garlic cloves, crushed
500 g (1 lb 2 oz) fresh tomatoes,
    skinned, seeded and chopped,
    or 14 oz (400 g) can chopped
    tomatoes

110 ml (4 fl oz) red wine
1/2 teaspoon sugar
2 tablespoons tomato purée
1 teaspoon Worcestershire sauce
Salt and freshly ground black pepper
3 tablespoons chopped parsley
12 black or green olives, stoned and
    halved
2 tablespoons capers

Pre-heat the oven to 220°C/425°F/Gas Mark 7. Rub the beef all over with the cut sides of the halved clove of garlic and then season with salt and pepper. Oil a small roasting tin generously, spread out the onion in it and toss in the halved garlic, too. Place the fillet on top and drizzle over 2 tablespoons of olive oil. Roast for 20 minutes, until cooked medium-rare. Transfer the fillet to a warmed serving dish and keep it warm while you make the sauce.

Lift the onion and garlic halves out of the roasting tin with a slotted spoon, letting the oil and juices drip back into the tin. Place the tin over a moderate heat. Add all the sauce ingredients, except the parsley, olives and capers. Stir to mix and then turn up the heat and cook the sauce at a furious pace, stirring frequently to prevent it from catching, until well reduced, thick and not at all watery. Aim for about 5 minutes' cooking time, at most. Now stir in the parsley, olives and capers. Give them a few seconds to heat through and then taste and adjust the seasoning.

Slice the fillet and serve with the sauce.

Barbecued Fillet of Beef with Mustard Butter

A whole fillet of beef is just the right shape and size for barbecuing and it makes a glamorous centrepiece for a summer party. It's not cheap, but it will taste marvellous.

Since fillet is so lean, it has to be marinated for as long as possible to keep it moist in the dry heat of the barbie. It will take up far less space than, say, 10 pork chops, so you can fill in the gaps around the meat with vegetables that grill well – aubergine, courgettes and peppers, perhaps. If you start the vegetables off 5–10 minutes before the beef, you or a helper can peel and chop them as appropriate while the meat finishes cooking.

SERVES 8–10
1 fillet of beef, weighing about
   1.5–1.75 kg (3–4 lb)
4–5 garlic cloves, cut into thin slivers
Salt

FOR THE MARINADE
3 tablespoons sherry vinegar
150 ml (5 fl oz) olive oil
2 shallots, sliced

2 sprigs of thyme, bruised
1 sprig of rosemary, bruised
1 tablespoon coarsely crushed black
   pepper

FOR THE BUTTER
175 g (6 oz) butter, softened
4 tablespoons coarse-grained mustard
3 tablespoons chopped parsley
Freshly ground black pepper

Ask the butcher to prepare and tie the fillet with string at regular intervals so that it keeps its shape. Make slits in the meat and push in slivers of garlic. Settle the meat in a close-fitting plastic bag. Mix together all the marinade ingredients and pour over the meat. Knot the bag tightly, sit in a shallow dish (it's bound to leak slightly) and pop into the fridge. Leave to marinate for at least 8 hours, preferably 24 or better still 48 hours, turning occasionally.

To make the butter, mix together all the ingredients thoroughly. Put into a neat roll on a sheet of silver foil. Wrap up and chill until needed.

Remove the meat from the fridge at least half an hour before cooking. Drain, reserving the marinade. Barbecue the fillet over a high heat, turning to brown on all sides, then move to a slightly cooler spot on the barbecue (or raise the grill rack away from the charcoal) and cook for a further 18–25 minutes, basting frequently with the marinade and turning every 5 minutes or so. Season with salt and rest on a plate at the side of the barbecue for 10 minutes.

Slice the beef and serve each portion with a pat of mustard butter perched on top.

VEAL

Wiener Schnitzel

Wiener schnitzel is just a grand name for breaded veal escalopes. Proper wiener schnitzel are fried in lard. You could, if you prefer, use butter or even olive oil, but technically you'd be making something quite different. For such a delicate meat, you really do need fine breadcrumbs, not large lumpy ones.

When buying veal do look out for pink meat that has been raised in Britain. Then you can rest assured that it has not been cruelly crated.

SERVES 4
4 veal escalopes
Lard, for frying
Seasoned flour, for dusting
1 egg, lightly beaten

Fine breadcrumbs, to coat
Salt and freshly ground black pepper

TO SERVE
Lemon wedges

Snip the edges of the escalopes here and there to prevent them from curling in the pan when they are fried. Sandwich each one between two sheets of greaseproof paper and beat lightly with a rolling pin until they are slightly thinner and larger. Don't be too energetic or you'll end up with unsightly holes in the schnitzels.

Melt enough lard in a frying-pan to give a depth of about 1 cm ($^{1}/_{2}$ in). While it is heating, flour the escalopes on both sides, shaking off the excess, then dip them into egg, shake off the excess, and finally, coat each one evenly in breadcrumbs, pressing them into place. Fry until golden brown on both sides, turning once. This should only take 4–5 minutes. Drain briefly on kitchen paper, season with salt and pepper and serve immediately with lemon wedges.

Saltimbocca alla Romana

Saltimbocca means something like 'jump into the mouth', presumably because these little bundles of meat, ham and sage are so irresistibly good.

The rolls can be made in advance, but they should be cooked only at the last minute as they don't benefit from being re-heated. If you temporarily store the uncooked rolls in the fridge, bring them back to room temperature before they go into the pan.

SERVES 4
8 thin slices veal or turkey breast
  steaks
8 slices Parma ham

8 sage leaves
25 g (1 oz) butter
120 ml (4 fl oz) Marsala
Salt and freshly ground black pepper

Sandwich each slice of veal or turkey between two sheets of greaseproof paper and flatten them out using a rolling pin. A bit of bashing is fine, but not too much as it can make them holey. It is simpler to just roll them out like pastry.

Lay a piece of Parma ham on each slice of veal, trimming it to fit. Grind over a little pepper. Perch a sage leaf in the centre, flip the sides in over the sage leaf, then roll up neatly and skewer each one in place with a wooden cocktail stick.

Brown the rolls in the butter, then pour in the Marsala and season with salt and pepper. Cover and simmer for about 10 minutes, until cooked through. Serve immediately.

Escalope de Veau aux Fines Herbes

A snappy way to cook veal escalopes, with a creamy, luxurious sauce laden with fresh herbs.

SERVES 2
2 veal or turkey escalopes
Seasoned flour, for dusting
25 g (1 oz) butter
2 tablespoons vermouth
5 tablespoons crème fraîche or double cream

1 teaspoon finely chopped parsley
1 teaspoon finely chopped chives
1 teaspoon finely chopped chervil
Salt and freshly ground black pepper
A squeeze of lemon juice (optional)

Make a few snips round the edges of the escalopes to prevent them from curling up as they fry. Sandwich each one between two sheets of greaseproof paper and use a rolling pin to roll and beat them out lightly until they are about half their original thickness. Don't go overboard – you are not aiming for a web of meat but for tender, hole-free, escalopes of an even thickness. Dust with seasoned flour.

Melt the butter in a wide frying-pan over a medium-high heat. As soon as it is foaming, add the escalopes and fry for about 3–4 minutes on each side, until they are lightly browned and just cooked through. Transfer to a warm serving dish, cover and keep warm.

Pour off the excess fat, return the pan to the heat and add the vermouth. Bring to the boil, scraping in the brown residues stuck to the bottom of the pan, and boil until reduced to a scant tablespoonful. Stir in the crème fraîche or double cream and bring to the boil. Draw off the heat, stir in the herbs, salt and pepper and, if you used double cream, a squeeze of lemon juice. Taste and adjust the seasoning, then pour over the escalopes. Serve immediately.

Grilled Veal Chops with Deep-fried Sage Leaves

Simple though this may sound, the combination of tender, grilled chops and crisply deep-fried sage leaves is superb. It is an idea I came across some years ago at the Pont de la Tour restaurant in London, and it made a deep and lasting impression on me.

The sage leaves take only a couple of seconds to deep-fry. If you've never deep-fried herbs before, have a few extra leaves to hand so you can experiment with one or two first. There's nothing particularly tricky about it, but timing is crucial. The fried leaves should be translucent and crispish, but not burnt! They can be quite addictive, so once you get the knack, you may want to cook more than I suggest in this recipe.

SERVES 4

20–24 sage leaves
Oil, for frying
4 veal chops

2 tablespoons olive oil
1 tablespoon lemon juice
Salt and freshly ground black pepper

Wash and dry the sage leaves thoroughly. Heat a small pan of oil until a cube of bread dropped in fizzes gently. Drop in about a third of the sage leaves and, as soon as they stop sizzling, scoop them out and drain them on kitchen paper. Cook the rest in two more batches.

Brush the veal chops with a little oil then season with pepper. Grill them under a moderately hot grill, turning occasionally, until crusty and just cooked through. When they are almost done, warm the olive oil with the lemon juice in a small pan, taking care not to overheat it. Place the veal chops on plates, season with salt and spoon over the oil. Place the deep-fried sage leaves on top and serve at once.

Braised Veal Shanks

Veal shanks, like lamb shanks, are an underrated cut of meat. They are superb slowly braised until the meat is so tender that it falls off the bone. In this recipe, they sit on a bed of vegetables, sharpened with a few capers and scented with citrus zests and herbs.

SERVES 4–6

4 veal shanks
3 tablespoons olive oil
1 onion, chopped
1 large carrot, finely diced
1 celery stick, sliced
1 head of garlic, separated into cloves
**   and peeled but not chopped**
3 tablespoons capers

1 bouquet garni (2 strips dried orange
**   zest, 2 strips lemon zest, 3 sprigs**
**   thyme, 1 small sprig rosemary,**
**   3 sprigs parsley, tied together with**
**   string)**
300 ml (10 fl oz) dry white wine
Salt and freshly ground black pepper
A squeeze of lemon juice

Brown the veal shanks in the olive oil, then set aside. Fry the onion, carrot and celery in the oil until browned. Transfer to a heat-proof casserole. Pour boiling water over the garlic, leave for 1 minute, then drain and add to the vegetables. Scatter over the capers. Bed the bouquet garni down amongst the vegetables. Snuggle the veal shanks on top, pour over the white wine and season with salt and pepper.

Bring to the boil, then reduce the heat to as low as possible and cover tightly (if the lid is slightly loose, lay a sheet of foil over the pan first, then clamp the lid on). Leave to cook gently for about 2 hours, turning the meat every now and then, until it is meltingly tender. Put the meat onto a serving dish, skim what fat you can from the juices and taste. Sharpen if necessary with a dash or two of lemon juice and adjust the seasoning. Spoon the vegetables around the veal and moisten with a little of the sauce. Strain and serve the rest separately.

Osso Buco alla Milanese

Osso buco *refers directly to the piece of meat used for this stew. It comes from the shin, cut across into steaks with the bone sitting squat in the centre. Ask for the slices to be cut from the upper, thicker part of the shin, so there's plenty of meat on them.*

There is some debate about the proper way to make Osso buco alla Milanese. *Tomatoes are at the crux of the matter, though tomato-less versions are often given a different name. To me, they are what make the stew so good, invigorating what might otherwise be rather a mild dish. However, what really injects vitality into the stew is the final addition – the gremolata, an uncomplicated mixture of very finely chopped garlic, parsley and lemon zest. If you are not keen on raw garlic, then you can sprinkle over the gremolata five minutes or so before the stew is finished so that some of the rawness is lost in the heat, but it really isn't half as good.*

Osso buco is traditionally served with Risotto Milanese, see p. 291.

SERVES 4

4 slices shin of veal, 4–5 cm (1^{1}/2–2 in) thick, cut with the marrow bone
Seasoned flour, for dusting
50 g (2 oz) butter
1 garlic clove, quartered
150 ml (5 fl oz) dry white wine
350 g (12 oz) tomatoes, skinned, seeded and chopped
150 ml (5 fl oz) chicken, veal or vegetable stock
Salt and freshly ground black pepper

FOR THE GREMOLATA

Finely grated zest of 1 lemon
2–3 tablespoons chopped parsley
1–2 garlic cloves, chopped

Dust the veal with flour and fry in the butter in a wide frying-pan over a brisk heat until browned on both sides. Add the quartered garlic clove to the pan when the meat is half done, so that it has time to flavour the butter without burning. Scoop out and discard the garlic when the veal is browned.

Reduce the heat and add the wine to the pan. Let the *ossi buchi* simmer gently for 10 minutes. Next add the tomatoes and cook for another 10 minutes or so until they begin to collapse to a purée. Add enough stock to barely cover the meat and season with salt and pepper. Bring to a quiet simmer, cover tightly (use foil or a tin tray if there is no proper lid for your frying pan) and leave to simmer for 1½–2 hours or until the meat is very tender. Check every now and then, turning the meat once or twice and adding a little water if the liquid level seems to be dropping perilously low. By the end of the cooking time the sauce should be fairly thick. If it is on the watery side, uncover and let it boil down for another 10–15 minutes or so until it has thickened. Taste and adjust the seasoning.

Serve with a spoonful of the cooking liquid and a sprinkling of the gremolata scattered over each dish.

Ragout of Veal with Fennel and Shallots

Veal, fennel and lemon are happy companions and here they meet in a light ragout bound with a sauce of crème fraîche. Instead of using a purpose-made stock for the base of the sauce, the cooking water from the vegetables is boiled down to concentrate the flavour. This results in a lovely, pure-tasting sauce.

SERVES 4
12 small shallots
2 fennel bulbs
60 g (2 oz) butter
1 tablespoon sunflower oil
650 g (1 lb 6 oz) fillet, rump or loin of
   veal, cut into 2–3 cm (1–1¼ in)
   cubes

6 tablespoons crème fraîche
Finely grated zest of 1 lemon
Salt and freshly ground black pepper
A squeeze of lemon juice

Leave the shallots in their skins, merely topping and tailing them. Trim the fennel, saving a few of the feathery green fronds. Cut each bulb into six or eight wedges, depending on size. Blanch the shallots, in their skins, in a pan of boiling water, for 4 minutes. Scoop out and drain thoroughly and then slip off their skins. Blanch the fennel wedges in the same water until half cooked – about 5 minutes but this will depend on their size. Scoop out and drain thoroughly. Don't throw out the cooking water but let it boil down to concentrate the flavours, while you get on with the rest of the preparation.

Make sure that the shallots and fennel are dry. Heat half the butter, with the oil. Fry the shallots and the fennel over a brisk heat until patched with brown. Set aside. Add the remaining butter to the pan, dry the pieces of veal and then brown them in the butter. Pour off excess fat and return the vegetables to the pan, along with about 300 ml (10 fl oz) of their reduced cooking water. Simmer for 5 minutes, until the veal is just cooked, and then boil the sauce for a little longer to reduce the liquid to a few tablespoonfuls. Now add the crème fraîche and lemon zest, bring to the boil and simmer for a few final minutes, until it has reduced to a satisfying consistency. Season with salt, pepper and a squeeze or two of lemon juice.

Vitello Tonnato

Vitello tonnato, veal with a tuna fish mayonnaise, is an Italian dish that I love to make for large summer buffets. It comes as a welcome change from endless Coronation chicken and is every bit as good, quite apart from being rather more unusual. If you've not come across it before, it may sound a rather bizarre combination, but in fact it turns out to be a marriage made in heaven. You can use a large turkey breast joint instead of veal, although the meat tends to be rather drier and less interesting.

Cook the veal in advance and blend the mayonnaise ahead of time, but leave the final arranging on the plates until as late as possible. Ideally you should make your own mayonnaise, but actually it works just fine with high-quality, bought mayonnaise.

SERVES 8–10
1 carrot, diced
1 onion, chopped
2 celery sticks, chopped
1 bay leaf
1 sprig of thyme
1.5 kg (3 lb) joint of veal, rolled and tied
250 ml (8 fl oz) dry white wine
120 ml (4 fl oz) olive oil
Salt and freshly ground black pepper

FOR THE TUNA MAYONNAISE
450 ml (15 fl oz) mayonnaise
200 g (7 oz) canned tuna, drained
5 canned anchovy fillets, roughly chopped
1 teaspoon capers
A squeeze of lemon juice

TO DECORATE
A few sprigs of parsley
A few capers

Make a bed of the carrot, onion, celery, bay leaf and thyme in the bottom of a flame-proof casserole which will take the veal snugly. Lay the veal on top and pour over the wine and olive oil. Bring to a simmer, then reduce the heat, cover and cook gently for about 1$^1/_2$ hours or until tender. Turn the veal once or twice during the cooking time so that it cooks evenly. Cool in its own juices and when cold strain off the juices and discard the vegetables and herbs.

For the sauce, put a little of the mayonnaise into the bowl of the processor with the tuna, anchovy and capers and whizz until smooth. Mix in the rest of the mayonnaise and enough of the cooking juices from the veal to thin the sauce down to the consistency of double cream. Taste and adjust the seasoning, sharpening the sauce with a little lemon juice.

To serve, slice the veal thinly and arrange on a serving plate. At the last possible minute, spoon over the sauce and decorate with sprigs of parsley and a few capers.

Grilled Lamb Chops with Tomato, Olive and Rosemary Salsa

Serving a salsa, a fresh-tasting sauce made of finely chopped raw ingredients, with grilled lamb chops is a very modern way of upgrading them into something rather stylish. Though you can warm the salsa through gently, if you prefer, I rather like the combination of sizzling hot meat with a cool salsa. It also means less last-minute fiddling and one less pan to wash up!

SERVES 4
4 lamb chops
A little oil
Salt and freshly ground black pepper

FOR THE SALSA
225 g (8 oz) well-flavoured tomatoes, skinned, seeded and finely diced
5 pieces of sun-dried tomato, chopped
8 black olives, pitted and roughly chopped

1 shallot, finely chopped
1 garlic clove, crushed
1 teaspoon finely chopped rosemary leaves
A generous pinch of sugar
1/2 tablespoon balsamic or sherry vinegar
3 tablespoons olive oil
Salt and freshly ground black pepper

Make the salsa at least an hour before eating. Mix together all the ingredients except the salt. Cover loosely and leave at room temperature (or in the fridge if it is for more than 4 hours). Taste and adjust the seasoning, adding a little salt if needed. Either serve at room temperature or warm gently in a small pan.

Brush the chops lightly with oil and grill fairly close to the heat until crusty and brown, turning once. Season with salt and pepper and serve with the salsa.

Spiced Lamb Chops

This is one of my favourite ways to improve on a chop. The natural acidity of the yoghurt tenderizes the meat (after 48 hours it should just melt in the mouth) and the spices enhance the flavour of the meat without overwhelming it. The spice and yoghurt mixture verges on a tandoori marinade, though without any of the red colouring! Make the cooked chops part of an Indian meal with rice or naan bread and maybe some dhal, or plonk them straight into a more Western setting, by serving them with boiled new potatoes and spinach or broccoli.

SERVES 4

4 lamb loin chops

FOR THE SPICE MIXTURE

1 teaspoon cumin seeds

1 teaspoon coriander seeds

1 cm ($^1/_2$ in) piece fresh root ginger, chopped

1–2 red chillies, seeded and chopped

2 garlic cloves, chopped

1 small shallot, chopped

1 teaspoon salt

2 tablespoons roughly chopped coriander

$^1/_4$ teaspoon ground turmeric

1 tablespoon freshly squeezed lime juice

4 large tablespoons Greek yoghurt

Dry-fry the cumin and coriander seeds over a high heat in a small frying-pan. Once they begin to jump, tip them out, let them cool, then grind to a powder. Pound the ginger root, chillies, garlic and shallot in a mortar with the salt to form a paste. Gradually work in the coriander, then mix in the spices, turmeric, lime juice and finally the yoghurt. Smear the mixture thickly over the lamb chops and leave for as long as possible. It'll take some 3–4 hours to begin to work well, but they will get much better with time. One or two days, covered, in the fridge, is best.

Take the chops out of the fridge, if that's where they've been, at least half an hour before cooking so that they are at room temperature. Either grill the chops under a high heat until crusty and brown – about 4–5 minutes on each side – or heat a little oil in a non-stick frying-pan and fry until browned and just cooked to your liking. Again, 4 minutes per side should be adequate.

Grilled Lamb Chops in a Honey and Ginger Marinade

To me, lamb with honey sounds delicious – and indeed it is. Serve these chops with noodles tossed in a little sesame oil.

SERVES 4

4 lamb chops

Oil

FOR THE MARINADE

2 tablespoons honey

1 teaspoon finely grated fresh ginger

1 garlic clove, crushed

2 tablespoons soy sauce

1 fresh red chilli, seeded and finely chopped

3 fresh thyme sprigs, bruised

3 tablespoons sunflower oil

Mix all the marinade ingredients and pour over the lamb chops. Turn the chops so that they are nicely coated and then leave to marinate for at least an hour, turning occasionally.

Pre-heat the grill thoroughly, and line the grill pan with foil. Brush the rack with a little oil. Grill the chops for about 4–5 minutes on each side, until browned and crusty outside but still pink and juicy inside. Serve immediately.

Pan-fried Noisettes of Lamb with Red Wine and Shallot Sauce

Noisettes, neat little roundels of tender meat, are usually cut from the boned, skinned and rolled loin or rack of lamb. One of the pluses of noisettes of lamb is that they are quick to cook, and rather elegant into the bargain ... certainly more of a dinner party cut than, say, the common or garden chop. Here, they are cooked and then served up with a simple red wine sauce. They are particularly good served with plain accompaniments such as boiled or roasted new potatoes, peas, and glazed carrots or pearl onions.

SERVES 4
25 g (1 oz) butter
1 tablespoon oil
4 noisettes of lamb
4 shallots, sliced
1 large glass red wine

1 bouquet garni (1 sprig parsley,
 1 sprig thyme and 1 small sprig
 rosemary, tied together with string)
300 ml (10 fl oz) stock
1/2 tablespoon redcurrant jelly
Salt and freshly ground black pepper

Melt half the butter and the oil in a heavy frying-pan and fry the noisettes over a medium heat for about 5–6 minutes each side until just nicely browned and cooked medium rare. Season and keep warm.

Add the shallots to the pan and cook over a gentle heat, stirring occasionally, until meltingly tender. Don't rush this part – give them time to soften and develop a natural sweetness. Now add the wine and the bouquet garni, and boil down until almost no liquid remains, stirring and scraping in all the residues from frying. Next add the stock and the jelly and bring to the boil. Continue to boil, stirring in the jelly, until reduced by about two-thirds. To finish the sauce, dice the remaining butter and swirl in a few pieces at a time to enrich. Spoon over and around the noisettes. Serve immediately.

Grilled Lamb Steaks with Fresh Mango Chutney

One step on from a straight salsa, this chutney combines the depth of cooked spices and fruit with the freshness of uncooked mango. I love it with lamb but it goes well, too, with chicken or prawns.

SERVES 4
4 lamb leg steaks
Juice of 1/2 orange
1/2 teaspoon ground coriander
2 tablespoons oil
Salt and freshly ground black pepper

FOR THE CHUTNEY
1 orange
2 tablespoons white wine vinegar
4 tablespoons caster sugar

1 teaspoon cumin seeds, coarsely crushed
1 teaspoon coriander seeds, coarsely crushed
1/2 tablespoon black mustard seeds
1 medium-sized mango, peeled, stoned and finely diced
1 fresh red chilli, seeded and finely chopped

Marinate the lamb steaks with the orange juice, ground coriander, oil, salt and pepper for at least an hour.

For the chutney, slice the orange thinly, discarding the ends. Quarter the slices and put them in a pan, with the vinegar, sugar and spices. Add 300 ml (10 fl oz) of water. Bring to the boil, stirring once or twice, and then simmer for about 25 minutes, until the peel on the orange slices is translucent and most of the liquid has boiled away, leaving just a moist mixture.

Peel, stone and dice the mango finely, tipping any juice over the lamb steaks, and then stir the flesh into the orange, together with the chilli. Leave to cool and, if not using immediately, cover and store in the fridge for no longer than 24 hours.

Pre-heat the grill to hot. Grill the lamb steaks for about 4 minutes on each side, until just cooked through but still tender inside. Serve with the mango and orange chutney.

Moussaka

When it is made with care and high-quality ingredients, moussaka becomes one of the most delicious lamb dishes around. If you've been put off by tired, greasy restaurant slabs of moussaka, then I urge you to try your hand at home. It's not a dish to be rushed – the three elements take some time to prepare, but both sauces can quite happily be made a day in advance.

To cut down on the oil content, I bake the aubergine slices, brushed with just enough oil to keep them moist and add a little flavour (the traditional way is to fry them). You could do away with the oil on the aubergines altogether by steaming them, but I think you then lose out on too much flavour. As is often the case, compromise is the best option. Whichever way you cook them, do it on the day the moussaka is to be eaten.

Try to get proper Greek kephalotiri cheese if you can (most Greek food stores stock it), as its rich twang suits this production to a T. If you don't have the right-sized dish, use one that is slightly smaller, rather than larger, so that you still get a decent thickness.

SERVES 6

FOR THE MEAT SAUCE
1 large onion, chopped
2 garlic cloves, chopped
3 tablespoons olive oil
450 g (1 lb) minced lamb
1 generous glass dry white wine
2 tablespoons tomato purée
450 g (1 lb) tomatoes, skinned and
    roughly chopped
1 teaspoon sugar
1$^{1}/_{2}$ teaspoons ground cinnamon
1 tablespoon dried oregano
Salt and freshly ground black pepper
3 tablespoons chopped parsley

FOR THE WHITE SAUCE
55 g (2 oz) butter
55 g (2 oz) flour

570 ml (1 pint) milk
50 g (2 oz) grated kephalotiri cheese, or
    mixed Parmesan and Gruyère
Salt and freshly ground black pepper
1 egg
1 egg yolk

FOR THE AUBERGINES
3 large or 4 medium aubergines, sliced
    lengthways
Salt
Olive oil

FOR THE TOPPING
50 g (2 oz) kephalotiri cheese, or mixed
    Gruyère and Parmesan
A generous $^{1}/_{2}$ teaspoon ground
    cinnamon

To make the meat sauce, cook the onion and garlic gently in the olive oil until tender, without browning. Add the lamb and stir until it loses its raw look. Now add all the remaining meat sauce ingredients except the parsley and season with salt and pepper. Simmer for 20–30 minutes until thick. Stir in the parsley.

Next, make the white sauce. Melt the butter and stir in the flour. Keep stirring for about 1 minute. Draw the pan off the heat and add the milk gradually, stirring in well between sploshes. Once you've incorporated about one third of it, increase the amount you add each time. Return to a gentle heat and let it simmer for a good 10–15 minutes, stirring frequently, until it is fairly thick. Remove from the heat, stir in the cheese and salt and pepper. If not using immediately, spear a knob of butter on a fork and rub over the surface to prevent a skin forming. Re-heat the white sauce gently when needed. Just before using, beat the egg and yolk into the sauce.

Sprinkle the slices of aubergine with salt and leave for at least half an hour, preferably a full hour. Wipe clean and steam if you wish, or lay them on oiled baking sheets, brush quite generously with olive oil and bake in the oven at 190°C/375°F/Gas Mark 5 for about 20 minutes until tender and patched with brown.

Take a rectangular or square baking dish, about 30 × 20 cm (12 × 8 in) or 25 × 25 cm (10 × 10 in) and brush lightly with oil. Lay half the aubergine slices on the base, overlapping if necessary, then spread half the meat on top. Repeat these layers, then spoon over the white sauce, covering the meat entirely. Sprinkle over the grated cheese set aside for the topping and the cinnamon. Bake at 180°C/350°F/Gas Mark 4 for 50–60 minutes until nicely browned. Let it settle, out of the oven, for 5 minutes before cutting into squares and serving.

Sautéd Sweet Potatoes with Lamb and Mint

A lip-smacking, finger-licking good dish. With the bright colour of orange-fleshed sweet potatoes, it looks as pretty as it tastes.

SERVES 4

FOR THE MEATBALLS
450 g (1 lb) minced beef
1 onion, grated
2 garlic cloves, crushed
2 tablespoons chopped fresh mint
Finely grated zest of 1 lime
1 teaspoon crushed coriander seeds
Salt and freshly ground black pepper
A dash of lime juice

FOR THE SWEET POTATOES
Olive oil
1 large red onion, cut into 8 wedges
1 large orange-fleshed sweet potato, peeled and cut into 1.5 cm (^{1}/$_2$ in) cubes
1 fresh red chilli, seeded and shredded
Juice of ^{1}/$_2$ lime
Salt and freshly ground black pepper

TO SERVE
A handful of fresh coriander leaves
Lime wedges

Make the meatballs by mixing all the ingredients together, kneading thoroughly with your hands. Dampen your hands with cold water. Now break off walnut-sized pieces and roll into balls. Heat a little olive oil in a wide, heavy frying-pan and brown the meatballs all over. Lift out and drain on kitchen paper.

Now pour out all the fat and raise the heat under the frying-pan. Let it heat through for a couple of minutes, then add the onion wedges. Cook over a high heat, turning them once or twice, until they are browned on the cut sides. Take out and put with the meatballs. Add a little more oil to the pan and sauté the sweet potato cubes for a few minutes, until they begin to brown. Now return the meatballs and the onions to the pan, along with the chilli, lime juice, 300 ml (10 fl oz) of water, salt and pepper. Stir carefully and simmer, half-covered, for 10–15 minutes, until most of the water has evaporated. Taste and adjust the seasonings, scatter over the coriander and serve with the wedges of lime.

Seamus's Irish Stew

Like other traditional dishes which were born out of poverty, there are many different versions of Irish stew. Controversy reigns over whether there should be carrots in it or whether one should brown the meat first.

This version was made for me by an old friend, Seamus. When he first made Irish stew as a student, Seamus and his flatmate would get a cheap lamb bone from the butcher, with just a few scraps of meat on it. First thing in the morning, they would throw it into a large casserole with lots of potatoes, carrots and water. By lunch-time it was ready.

These days, he's moved up a little in the world and his Irish stew has become a touch more substantial. The important thing is that whatever cut of lamb you use, and in whatever quantity, it should be stewed on the bone. A 2 kg (4 lb 8 oz) shoulder is ideal, but 1.5–1.75 kg (3–4 lb) of scrag-end of neck, or neck chops, does the job well too. Cut the meat into large cubes or chops, as appropriate.

Seamus usually spices up his stew with a shake of Worcestershire sauce and I have known him to add, most unauthentically, a scant tablespoonful of lightly crushed coriander seeds. In the end, the important thing is that the stew cooks long enough for the potatoes to soften to such a degree that it takes barely any encouragement for them to melt down into the juices to thicken it.

SERVES 6
1.5–2 kg (3–4 lb 8 oz) lamb (see above)
Lard or butter
3 onions, peeled and thickly
    sliced
675 g (1 lb 8 oz) carrots, scraped and
    cut into thick chunks
900 g (2 lb) potatoes, peeled and halved
    if large

1 bay leaf
2 teaspoons Worcestershire sauce
Salt and freshly ground black pepper
Water or stock, to cover

TO SERVE
Chopped parsley

Trim a fair amount of the fat off the meat and reserve. Cut the meat up into large cubes or chops as appropriate. In a thick-bottomed pan, render down the fat over a low heat. Discard the solid bits and add extra lard or butter if necessary. Brown the meat in the fat, then set aside and brown the onions and carrots in the same fat. Drain off any excess fat. Return the meat to the pan with the potatoes, bay leaf, Worcestershire sauce, salt, pepper, and water or stock to cover. Simmer for 2–3 hours until the meat is tender and the potatoes are soft and melting. Skim off the fat, remove any very large bones and serve scattered with parsley.

Lancashire Hot Pot

Forget fancy dishes from the East and the Mediterranean; our own traditional, homely Lancashire hot pot makes a really great meal on a cold evening. It is cheap, quick to prepare, and lip-smackingly good. Once you've got it going in the oven, you don't need to bother about it for a couple of hours. No fussing or fiddling. I love it – there's that delicious crisp layer of potatoes on the top, covering tender lamb (or mutton if you can get it) and melting potatoes underneath that just beg to be mashed into the juices.

No doubt Lancastrians would debate the list of ingredients needed to make a genuine hot pot. I've read that mushrooms are added only in Bolton and, in times *past, oysters were frequently included as they were cheap and nutritious. I can think of better things to do with oysters these days, but mushrooms do add something special, and I always slip some in. You don't have to brown the meat, but it does improve the colour and flavour.*

SERVES 6

6 meaty loin chops, or 12 lamb cutlets
6 lambs' kidneys, halved
50 g (2 oz) dripping or butter, melted
1 kg (2 lb 4 oz) potatoes, peeled and thinly sliced
3 large onions, sliced

225 g (8 oz) flat-cap mushrooms, thickly sliced (optional)
Salt and freshly ground black pepper
300 ml (10 fl oz) lamb or chicken stock, or water

Pre-heat the oven to 220°C/425°F/Gas Mark 7. Brown the chops and the kidneys in half the dripping or butter over a high heat, to give them a little colour. Layer the potatoes, chops, kidneys, onions and mushrooms, if using, in a deep casserole, seasoning well between each layer. End with a layer of potatoes, neatly overlapping and covering the contents of the dish. Pour over the stock or water. There should be enough to come about half-way up the ingredients. If you seem to be running short, add a little more water. Brush the remaining dripping or butter over the top layer of potatoes, then season well.

Cover the casserole and place it in the oven. Give it 20–25 minutes to heat through, then reduce the oven temperature to 150°C/300°F/Gas Mark 2 and leave to cook for a further 2 hours. Finally, remove the lid, raise the oven temperature back to 220°C/425°F/Gas Mark 7 and cook for a final 20–30 minutes until the top layer of potatoes is browned.

Navarin Printanier

This is a perfect spring dish – warming enough to stave off those chilly winds that still blow, but bursting with the freshness and promise of the summer months. To be honest, to make the ultimate navarin printanier, you really have to have your own vegetable garden, so that you can harvest the tiny, young vegetables for it on the very day that you cook it. Failing that, choose the smallest carrots, turnips and potatoes you can find, so they can be cooked whole. If your turnips and potatoes are more than about 4 cm (1½ in) across, cut them in half. If you wish, the Navarin can be enriched at the last moment with a slug of double cream or crème fraîche.

SERVES 6

1.5 kg (3 lb) shoulder of lamb, trimmed
  and cubed
25 g (1 oz) butter
1 tablespoon sunflower oil
2 tablespoons flour
600 ml (1 pint) lamb, chicken or
  vegetable stock
1 tablespoon tomato purée
1 bouquet garni (1 bay leaf, 2 sprigs of
  parsley and 2 sprigs of thyme, tied
  together with string)

1 garlic clove, crushed
Salt and freshly ground black pepper
225 g (8 oz) small carrots, scrubbed
450 g (1 lb) small new potatoes,
  scrubbed
225 g (8 oz) small white and purple
  turnips, peeled and halved or
  quartered
350 g (12 oz) shelled peas

Brown the lamb in the butter and oil over a high heat, in several batches. Transfer to a flameproof casserole and pour off all except about 2 tablespoons of the fat from the pan. Add the flour and stir over a moderate heat until you have a light brown roux. Stir in the stock gradually as if making white sauce and then add the tomato purée. Bring to the boil, stirring continuously, then pour over the meat. Add the bouquet garni, garlic, salt and pepper. Cover and simmer gently for about 1 hour.

Now add the carrots, potatoes and turnips and continue cooking for 30 minutes, uncovered, before adding the peas. If necessary, add a little more water or stock if the liquid levels fall low – the aim is to get a creamy, but not over-thick sauce of about the consistency of single cream. Once the peas are in, continue cooking until all the vegetables are tender. Taste, adjust the seasoning and serve.

Spanish Lamb Stew

The lamb in the Extremadura region of south-west Spain is so good that it needs little seasoning to bring out the flavour. Back home in England I've found that sneaking a sprig of thyme in with the lamb as it cooks is no bad thing.

The stew is thickened with a pounded paste of fried onion, garlic and bread, added towards the end of the cooking time, which gives a rich thick sauce that just coats the lamb.

SERVES 4

900 g (2 lb) boned leg of lamb, trimmed
4 tablespoons olive oil
1/2 onion, chopped
4–5 cloves garlic, sliced
1 bay leaf

1 slice of stale bread, crust removed
1 teaspoon Spanish paprika (*pimentón*)
Pinch of chilli powder
120 ml (4 fl oz) red wine
Salt and freshly ground black pepper
1 sprig of fresh thyme (optional)

Cut the lamb into pieces about 5 × 7.5 cm (2 × 3 in). They can be bigger, in which case they'll be pinker in the middle, or smaller, in which case the meat will end up well-done all the way through. Trim off the excess fat and any gristle.

Heat the oil in a wide saucepan or deep frying-pan. Add the onion, garlic and bay leaf and fry gently until the onion is tender and golden. Discard the bay leaf. Scoop the onion and garlic out into a mortar (or small grinder) and pound to a paste. In the same oil (add a little more if you need to) fry the bread over a medium heat until nicely browned and crisp. Break the bread into the onion/garlic mixture, then pound it in, to form *el machado*, the pounded mixture that will thicken the sauce at the end of the cooking time. If you have a processor that can handle small quantities, onion, garlic and bread can all be whizzed up together.

Take the pan off the heat while you are busy pounding and stir the paprika and chilli powder into the oil, followed by the meat. Return to a gentle heat and pour in the wine. Season with salt and pepper, and add the thyme (if using). Cover tightly and cook over a very low heat, stirring occasionally, until the meat is tender – about 10–15 minutes. Stir in the *machado* and simmer for another 5 minutes or so, by which time the sauce should be thick and moist, but not runny. Adjust the seasoning and serve.

Persian Lamb and Rhubarb Stew

Partnering fruit and meat is common enough in the Middle East, but this recipe may come as a surprise, even so. I usually make it in the spring with forced rhubarb, but you could use ordinary rhubarb, bearing in mind that it will have more of a bite to it. If you use forced rhubarb and like a bracing hit of acidity, use the full 675 g (1 lb 8 oz) but if, like me, you like the sharpness more muted, or if you use ordinary rhubarb, then the smaller amount should be sufficient.

SERVES 4–6

675 g (1 lb 8 oz) boned shoulder or leg of lamb
50 g (2 oz) butter
1 tablespoon sunflower or vegetable oil
2 large onions, sliced
1 level teaspoon ground coriander
1 small bunch of parsley, chopped
3 tablespoons chopped mint
450–675 g (1 lb 8 oz) rhubarb, trimmed and cut into 2.5 cm (1 in) lengths
Salt and freshly ground black pepper

Cut the meat into 5 cm (2 in) cubes. Melt half the butter with the oil in a frying-pan and fry the onions until golden. Raise the heat, add half the meat and fry until browned. Scoop out with the onions then brown the remaining meat. Return the first batch to the pan with the coriander, or transfer everything to a heat-proof casserole. Add just enough water to cover and simmer, covered, for 1 hour. Season.

Fry the parsley and mint in the remaining butter, stirring constantly, for 5–10 minutes. Add them to the stew and continue simmering for a further 30 minutes, with the lid half off, stirring occasionally. Shortly before serving, add the rhubarb. Stir to mix and simmer for 2–4 minutes if it is forced rhubarb, 5–10 minutes if it is ordinary rhubarb. Taste and adjust the seasoning and serve immediately with rice.

Lamb (or Mutton) and Vegetable Couscous

A Moroccan dish, this, and a great way to feed a crowd of hungry people. Couscous is actually the 'grain' (technically a type of pasta, in fact), that is served to soak up the juices of the soupy stew. It is easy to buy these days, not only from specialist shops, but also from most supermarkets. Nearly all of the couscous sold in this country has already been cooked and dried, so just needs rehydrating. It's probably best to follow the instructions on your packet, but I'll tell you my method anyway. I measure out double the volume of hot water to couscous and pour it over the couscous. After 20–30 minutes it will all, or at least nearly all, have been absorbed. Any excess should be drained off.

As with the Tagine of Mutton or Lamb with Dried Fruit and Almonds, p. 158, in Morocco this dish is more likely to be made with mutton than lamb.

SERVES 8–10

1 kg (2 lb 4 oz) shoulder of lamb or mutton, cut into 5 cm (2 in) cubes
3 onions, cut into eighths
5 large sprigs of coriander, tied in a bunch
1/2 teaspoon turmeric
2 teaspoons freshly ground black pepper
1/2 tablespoon ground ginger
1/2 tablespoon ground cumin
1 teaspoon ground coriander
Salt
1 tablespoon olive oil
225 g (8 oz) chickpeas, soaked overnight and drained
450 g (1 lb) tomatoes, skinned, seeded and roughly chopped

450 g (1 lb) carrots, each cut into 3 pieces, then halved lengthways
450 g (1 lb) small to medium turnips, peeled and halved or quartered
450 g (1 lb) courgettes, cut into 4 cm (1 1/2 in) lengths
450 g (1 lb) piece pumpkin or winter squash, de-rinded, seeded and cut into 5 cm (2 in) chunks (optional)
450 g (1 lb) potatoes, peeled and cut into 4 cm (1 1/2 in) chunks
2 tablespoons chopped coriander

FOR THE COUSCOUS
900 g (2 lb) couscous
Butter

TO SERVE
Harissa or hot chilli sauce

Find a generous, accommodating pan to cook the stew in. Dump the lamb or mutton, two-thirds of the onion and the bunch of coriander straight into it, then sprinkle over the spices. Season with salt and then drizzle over the olive oil. Pour in 4 litres (7 pints) water. Bring to the boil (allow plenty of time for this), then add the chickpeas. Cover the pan and let the mixture simmer for about 1 hour (1½ hours for mutton).

Now add the remaining onion and all the vegetables and let it all simmer for a further 30 minutes or so, uncovered, until all the vegetables are tender. Taste and adjust the seasoning. Carefully strain off the juices into a serving dish.

Meanwhile, prepare the couscous according to the packet instructions. Dot with butter, pile into a dish, cover with foil and let it steam in a warm oven. Just before serving, pour a couple of ladlefuls of the cooking juices from the big pan over the couscous. Stir briefly and, when absorbed, pile the couscous onto a big plate. Make a well in the centre and put all the bits of meat into it. Arrange the vegetables as prettily as you can over the couscous and meat and take it quickly to the table. Serve the remaining juices alongside so that everyone can make their couscous as moist as they like. Serve with harissa or chilli sauce for those who want to pep the spices up a bit.

Tagine of Mutton or Lamb with Dried Fruit and Almonds

Moroccan tagines take their name from the beautiful wide dishes with conical lids that they are cooked in. They are very aromatic, often combining fruit with meat, and may be sweetened with honey.

This recipe is a delight. It is richly but not overwhelmingly spiced and finished with the crunch of fried almonds and sesame seeds. If you prefer, you can use prunes alone (450 g/1 lb), or apricots alone (350 g/12 oz) . Only bother with soaking the fruit if it is bone-dry. Most of what we buy these days is only semi-dehydrated, leaving it soft and moist enough to cook with (or eat) straight from the packet.

SERVES 5–6

1–1.25 kg (2 lb 4 oz–2 lb 8 oz) boned shoulder of mutton or lamb
50 g (2 oz) unsalted butter
2 tablespoons oil
¼ teaspoon powdered saffron
1 teaspoon freshly ground black pepper
Salt
1 teaspoon ground ginger
1 teaspoon ground cumin
½ tablespoon ground cinnamon
2 medium onions, grated or very finely chopped
275 g (8 oz) prunes
175 g (6 oz) dried apricots
1 tablespoon sesame seeds
1 cinnamon stick
2 long strips lemon zest
2–3 tablespoons honey
75 g (3 oz) blanched, halved almonds

Cut the mutton or lamb into 4 cm (1$\frac{1}{2}$ in) cubes, trimming off any gristle and excess fat. Melt 40 g (1$\frac{1}{2}$ oz) butter, mix it with the oil, saffron, pepper, salt, ginger, cumin and ground cinnamon and coat the lamb in the mixture.

Tip into a wide frying-pan or shallow casserole and cook over a moderate heat for about 3 minutes to toast the spices. Add the onions, and enough water to cover. Bring to the boil and simmer gently, covered but leaving a small gap for the steam to escape, for 1–2 hours or until the meat is tender.

If necessary, soak the prunes and apricots in water. The prunes can be pitted if you wish, but it's not really necessary. Dry-fry the sesame seeds in a small pan over a high heat until they turn a shade darker.

If it has been soaked, drain the dried fruit. Add to the meat, along with the cinnamon stick, lemon zest and honey. Simmer, uncovered, for a further 30 minutes or so until the sauce has reduced enough to coat the meat and fruit without leaving them swimming (you may even have to add a little water if yours seems to have evaporated too quickly). While it simmers, sauté the almonds in the remaining butter until they are lightly browned, then set aside and keep warm. Taste the tagine and adjust the seasonings. Finally, scatter with the almonds and sesame seeds before serving.

Braised Lamb Shanks with Flageolets and Rosemary

I could happily eat far more than my fair share of this stew. It is packed to the hilt with marvellous flavours. There's the lamb, of course, the shanks being especially nice mini joints for braising or stewing, but after that come the flageolet beans (if you can't get dried flageolets, you can substitute dried haricot beans), and the tomatoes and chilli. The final perk is a sprinkling of gremolata, finely chopped garlic, lemon zest and parsley, which will lift practically any lamb stew you care to mention. It's something worth considering as a finishing touch with a chicken stew, too, though its classic use is in the Italian osso buco alla Milanese *(see p. 144).*

SERVES 4

4 meaty lamb shanks, trimmed
2–3 tablespoons olive oil
1 large onion, chopped
1 large carrot, finely diced
1 celery stick, finely diced
3 garlic cloves, chopped
350 g (12 oz) dried flageolet beans, soaked overnight and drained
1 bouquet garni (1 bayleaf, 2 sprigs parsley, 2 sprigs thyme and 2 sprigs rosemary, tied together with string)

675 g (1 lb 8 oz) tomatoes, skinned, seeded and chopped
1 heaped tablespoon tomato purée
1 dried red chilli
$\frac{1}{2}$ tablespoon light muscovado sugar
Salt and freshly ground black pepper

FOR THE GREMOLATA
Finely grated zest of $\frac{1}{2}$ lemon
1–2 garlic cloves, finely chopped
2 tablespoons chopped parsley

Brown the lamb shanks in the oil in a wide frying-pan then transfer the meat to a casserole. Cook the onion, carrot and celery gently in the same pan, until tender and lightly patched with brown. Add the garlic and cook for a minute or so longer, then tip the vegetables into the casserole. Add the flageolets and the bouquet garni.

Tip the excess fat out of the frying-pan and pour in 900 ml (1½ pints) of water. Bring to the boil, stirring and scraping in the brown residues from frying. Pour over the casserole and season with pepper but no salt. Either simmer on top of the stove, or transfer to the oven, set to 170°C/325°F/Gas Mark 3, and cook for 1–1½ hours, or until the beans are meltingly tender (but not quite on the point of collapse). Stir in the tomatoes, tomato purée, chilli and sugar, and season with salt (the tomatoes and the salt prevent the beans from softening, which is why you didn't add them earlier – added now, they should prevent them disintegrating). Return to the hob or oven and continue cooking for a further 1–2 hours, stirring occasionally, until the meat is so tender it practically falls off the bone.

Remove the chilli. Take a couple of ladlefuls of the beans and juices and blend them in the food processor until smooth. Stir back into the casserole to transform the liquid into a creamy sauce. Taste and adjust the seasoning.

To make the gremolata, mix the lemon zest, garlic and parsley and chop them together very, very finely. Sprinkle over the casserole just before serving.

Gigot d'Agneau Boulangère

To be honest, this isn't exactly what the boulangère, *the baker's wife, would be cooking in France. She would use butter, where I've used olive oil. I just happen to love the taste of olive oil with lamb and slowly cooked potatoes and find it a welcome change from the heaviness of butter. She might well be roasting a shoulder rather than a leg, too, if she was sticking firmly with her classic repertoire. If you do substitute a shoulder, then it should be cooked at a slightly lower temperature for rather longer.*

SERVES 6
1 leg of lamb, weighing around 2 kg (4 lb 8 oz)
2–3 garlic cloves, cut into thin slivers
Fresh thyme leaves (or rosemary if you prefer)
Olive oil
Salt and freshly ground black pepper

FOR THE POTATOES
1 large onion, sliced
4 tablespoons olive oil
1.5 kg (3 lb) potatoes, peeled and finely sliced
3 garlic cloves, chopped
150 ml (5 fl oz) lamb or chicken stock

Pre-heat the oven to 200°C/400°F/Gas Mark 6. Using a small, sharp knife, make slits all over the leg of lamb and push in shards of garlic and thyme (or rosemary) leaves. Rub with a little olive oil and season with salt and pepper. Fry the onion in 1 tablespoon of the olive oil until tender. Blanch the sliced potatoes in boiling water for 3–5 minutes until half cooked, then drain thoroughly. Put the lamb in a large, oiled oven-proof dish and arrange half the potatoes and onions around it. Sprinkle over half the chopped garlic and season with salt and pepper. Add the remaining potatoes and sprinkle over the last of the garlic. Season with salt and pepper and pour on the stock. Drizzle over the remaining olive oil.

Roast in the oven for 17–20 minutes per 500 g (15–18 minutes per lb). Rest the joint for 15–20 minutes before serving.

Roast Leg of Lamb with Flageolets

Spring green flageolet beans are a classic French accompaniment to a roast leg of lamb, and with some justification. I buy them from Italian delis or good wholefood shops and some supermarkets now stock them. If you can't find any, then white haricots or cannellini beans are almost as good, especially since it is these that the French in Brittany would use, anyway, which means that you won't be losing out at all on authenticity!

SERVES 6–8

FOR THE FLAGEOLETS
450 g (1 lb) dried flageolet beans
1 onion, quartered
5 garlic cloves, peeled but whole
1 bouquet garni (1 bay leaf, 1 sprig thyme, 2 sprigs parsley and 1 large sprig rosemary, tied together with string)
Salt and freshly ground black pepper
2 tablespoons olive oil

FOR THE LAMB
1 leg of lamb weighing about 2.75 kg (6 lb)
2–3 garlic cloves, cut into long slivers
Leaves from 2 sprigs of rosemary
2–3 tablespoons olive oil
Salt and freshly ground black pepper
300 ml (10 fl oz) white wine

Soak the flageolets overnight in cold water, then drain and rinse. Place in a pan with the onion, garlic, bouquet garni and enough water to cover by about 5 cm (2 in). Bring to the boil and simmer until the beans are tender, about 1–1½ hours. Strain off most of the water that's left and reserve, leaving the beans in the pan. Fish out the bouquet garni and discard.

Liquidize about a quarter of the beans, along with as many of the garlic cloves as you can find, with enough of the cooking water to make a thin purée. Stir the purée back into the pan of beans and re-heat when the lamb is cooked, adding the olive oil, salt and pepper to taste and a little more of the water if needed.

Pre-heat the oven to 230°C/450°F/Gas Mark 8. Prepare the lamb, making slits all over the meat with a small-bladed knife, then pushing in slivers of garlic and rosemary leaves. Rub with olive oil, season well, and place in an oiled roasting tin. Pour the wine around it.

Calculate the roasting time by allowing 13 minutes per 500 g (12 minutes per lb) for rare meat, 18 minutes per 500 g (16 minutes per lb) for medium and 20–22 minutes per 500 g (18–20 minutes per lb) for well-done. Start the meat at 230°C/450°F/Gas Mark 8 and then reduce the heat to 200°C/400°F/Gas Mark 6 after 15 minutes. Baste frequently as it cooks, adding a little water if the juices begin to dry up. When done, turn off the heat, leave the door slightly ajar, and let the meat rest for 20–30 minutes before carving. Skim any fat from the juices and pour them into a small jug to serve as a thin gravy, or stir into the flageolets for extra flavour.

Grilled Butterflied Leg of Lamb

This is a stunning way of cooking lamb – the inside stays moist and tender while the outside becomes a deep crusty brown. Though it works well on an indoor grill, it really comes into its own in the summer months when it can be barbecued outdoors over charcoal; perfect for a party on a balmy July evening. The idea is to open the leg of lamb out flat, removing the bones so that it can be barbecued or grilled. First of all, you should know that there are three bones to negotiate and extract and that they run consecutively from the tip to the base, which is the best place to start the boning. Place the leg on a board with the thinner covering of flesh uppermost. Locate the first bone and slice along the length of it, cutting right down to the bone. Cut the meat away from the bone with short strokes, keeping the blade close to the bone and turning the leg as you work. Ease out the bone and then repeat with the 2 remaining bones. Open out the meat. Beat with a rolling pin or meat mallet to flatten, then make a couple of slashes through the thickest parts of the muscle.

Put the lamb to marinate the day before cooking if you can, so that it has plenty of time to soak up those eastern Mediterranean scents of lemon, olive oil and mint. It minimizes effort on the day of your party too, so that apart from cooking the meat, the only thing to do is to throw together the yoghurt and mint sauce that goes so well with the grilled meat.

SERVES 6–8
1 boned leg of lamb (see above)

FOR THE MARINADE
Juice of 2 lemons
1 onion, chopped
3 garlic cloves, sliced
150 ml (5 fl oz) olive oil
2 bay leaves, crumbled

3 tablespoons chopped fresh mint or
3 teaspoons dried mint
8 peppercorns, lightly crushed

FOR THE YOGHURT AND MINT SAUCE
300 ml (10 fl oz) Greek yoghurt
A handful of mint leaves, chopped
3 garlic cloves, crushed
Salt and freshly ground black pepper

Make a few deep slashes in the lamb at its thickest parts. Lie it flat in a shallow dish large enough to take it without folding over. Mix the marinade ingredients. Pour over the lamb. Cover, and leave in the fridge or a cool place for 8–24 hours, turning occasionally.

Pre-heat your grill to its highest temperature and arrange the grill rack so that you can get the meat very close to the heat. Remove the meat from the marinade, brushing off bits of onion and herbs. Strain the marinade, reserving the liquid for basting.

Grill the lamb, cut side up first, very close to the heat, for 5–7 minutes on each side to give a deep brown crust. Re-arrange the grill rack so that the lamb is 10–13 cm (4–5 in) from the heat, and give it a further 12–19 minutes on each side, depending on how well done you like it. Baste the meat with marinade every time you turn it. Keep an eye on it so that you don't allow it to overcook, and test it now and again by plunging a knife into the centre – I turn off the heat the moment the scarlet translucence of raw meat disappears, which gives the most perfect succulent pink lamb. Lift the meat onto a serving dish and leave it to relax in a warm oven (or by the side of the barbecue) for 15 minutes before carving.

Meanwhile, to make the yoghurt and mint sauce mix together all the ingredients, adjusting the seasoning to taste.

Serve the carved lamb with the meat juices and the yoghurt and mint sauce alongside it.

Roast Rack of Lamb with a Herb Crust

There is no more perfect joint for two than a tender little rack of lamb. It doesn't come cheap, but for a special occasion it is worth every penny. The meat, cooked on the bone, has an excellent sweet flavour. The cooked rack looks pretty and it hardly takes any time to prepare and roast.

This is my favourite way of cooking rack of lamb, with a crisp crust of buttery crumbs flavoured with lots of fresh herbs.

You can doll up the tips of the cutlets with cutlet frills (they're often sold with the rack, in which case, do remember to take them off before the meat goes into the oven, replacing them just before serving). If you buy your rack ready-prepared and they've over-zealously trimmed off every last scrap of fat, then be a little more generous with the butter in the crumbs as this will help to protect the meat from the fierce heat.

SERVES 2
1 rack of lamb
25 g (1 oz) stale fine breadcrumbs
20 g (a generous $^1/_2$ oz) unsalted butter, melted

1$^1/_2$–2 tablespoons chopped herbs such as a mixture of parsley, chervil, chives, marjoram, thyme, savory, etc.
1 garlic clove, crushed (optional)
Salt and freshly ground black pepper

Pre-heat the oven to 230°C/450°F/Gas Mark 8. If the rack hasn't already been pre-pared, carefully cut off the skin, leaving a thin layer of fat on the chops. Trim the tips of the cutlets, scraping away the scraps of meat and fat, exposing the top 4 cm (1¹/₂in). Mix the breadcrumbs with the butter, herbs, garlic (if using), salt and pepper in a bowl. Using your hands, keep turning the mixture over until the crumbs have soaked up all the butter evenly. Lay the rack of lamb, fat side upward, in a lightly oiled small oven-proof dish or roasting tin. Pat the crumb mixture firmly and thickly onto the fat side.

Roast the rack for about 20–30 minutes, depending on how well cooked you like your lamb (I usually opt for little more than 20 minutes since it seems a shame to over-cook such a choice morsel). If necessary, cover the crumbs loosely with foil towards the end of the cooking time to prevent them from burning. Let the meat rest for 5 min-utes, then to serve, simply cut down between the cutlets, dividing the rack in half. It's best to do this at the table, as some of the crumbs are bound to fall off in the process and your fellow diner gets to see how appetizing it looks first.

Roast Rack of Lamb with a Pecan, Lemon and Parsley Crust

The nuts in the crust toast in the oven's heat, making a sweet, rich, crisp contrast to the tender lamb. The same mixture can be used on thick pieces of fish fillet (cod, for example, if it is very fresh), which, again, can be roasted in a hot oven.

SERVES 4

2 racks of lamb, French trimmed (see method)

FOR THE CRUST
60 g (2 oz) shelled pecans
30 g (1 oz) fine, slightly stale white breadcrumbs

Finely grated zest of 1 lemon
2 tablespoons chopped fresh parsley
45 g (1¹/₂ oz) butter, melted
Salt and freshly ground black pepper

Prepare the racks of lamb, if necessary, as described in the recipe for Roast Rack of Lamb with a Herb Crust (see p. 163).

Pre-heat the oven to 230°C/450°F/Gas Mark 8. To make the crust, chop the pecans very finely in a food processor or by hand. Mix with all the remaining ingredi-ents, working in the butter with your hands until it is all evenly distributed.

Lay the racks of lamb, curved sides up, in a lightly oiled, ovenproof dish or roasting tin. Pat the crust mixture evenly and firmly on to the racks. Roast for 20–30 minutes, depending on how well cooked you like your lamb. I usually opt for around

23 minutes, for nice pink lamb. If necessary, cover the crust loosely with foil towards the end of the cooking time, to prevent it from burning.

Let the meat rest for 5 minutes in a warm place. Bring it to the table uncut since, unless your knife is supremely sharp and you are very deft, the crust is bound to crumble as you carve. To carve, slice down between the cutlets, dividing each rack in half.

Crown Roast of Lamb with Sage, Lemon and Chestnut Stuffing

A stuffed crown roast of lamb is one of the most glamorous joints you can place on the table. It is made of two racks of lamb and is usually roasted with a stuffing in the centre. You can, of course, use any stuffing you fancy, though ones with a hint of fruity sweetness, or herb-strewn stuffings, are particularly appropriate.

Though any butcher will prepare a crown roast for you, it's not at all difficult to construct for yourself, as long as you are armed with a sturdy needle, some thread and a thimble and two racks of lamb, chined. Scrape away the meat and fat from the tips of the bones, down to about 4 cm ($1^1/2$ in). Trim any remaining skin off the racks. Shape each rack into a semi-circle with the bones curving outwards, slitting the connecting tissue at the base of each rack if necessary. Place the racks together, then sew up each side with a trussing needle and thick thread or fine string. Stand them on a roasting tin and push into a cicular crown. Tie a piece of string around the middle to hold the crown in place. Protect the tips of the bones with twists of silver foil toprevent them from burning in the oven. Stuffing the central cavity helps the crown to hold its shape.

SERVES 6

2 chined best ends of neck of lamb, or a prepared crown

FOR THE STUFFING
$1/2$ onion, chopped
1 garlic clove, chopped
25 g (1 oz) butter
Finely grated zest of $1/2$ lemon

2–3 sage leaves, finely chopped
175 g (6 oz) cooked, skinned chestnuts, crumbled
1 tablespoon lemon juice
40 g ($1^1/2$ oz) fresh white breadcrumbs
1 tablespoon chopped parsley
1 egg, lightly beaten
Salt and freshly ground black pepper

Pre-heat the oven to 180°C/350°F/Gas Mark 4. If you haven't been able to buy a crown roast ready prepared, or have chosen to do it yourself, prepare the racks of lamb as described above.

To make the stuffing, cook the onion and garlic gently in the butter until tender but without browning. Mix with all the remaining ingredients, adding just enough egg to bind. Fill the centre of the crown with the stuffing then cover the stuffing with a piece of foil.

Roast the crown for about 1 hour, removing the foil over the stuffing after 40 minutes. Baste the joint from time to time as it cooks and when it is ready, turn off the heat, leave the door ajar and let the roast rest for 10 minutes. Before serving, remove the foil from the tips of the bones and replace it with cutlet frills, if you have them.

Côtes de Porc
Sauce Charcutière

Sauce charcutière is one of the great French sauces for pork; it takes its name from the wife of the charcutier, the pork butcher and traiteur found in every town throughout the country. It is a lovely way to jazz up plain grilled pork chops, though if you get a taste for it you may well want to dish it up with sausages and other pork products as well.

Some recipes for sauce charcutière *include tomato but others don't. I quite like it in there, but if you want to simplify matters, leave it out.*

SERVES 4
4 pork chops
A little oil
Salt and freshly ground black pepper

FOR THE SAUCE CHARCUTIÈRE
90 g (3^1/$_2$ oz) shallots, finely chopped
25 g (1 oz) butter or lard
1 tablespoon flour
50 ml (2 fl oz) dry white wine
50 ml (2 fl oz) white wine vinegar

450 ml (15 fl oz) pork or chicken stock
225 g (8 oz) tomatoes, skinned, seeded and roughly chopped (optional)
1 teaspoon sugar (optional)
4 cornichons or gherkins, chopped
1 heaped tablespoon Dijon or coarse-grained mustard
1 tablespoon chopped parsley
1 teaspoon chopped tarragon
^{1}/$_2$ tablespoon chopped chives

To make the sauce, sweat the shallots gently in the butter or lard until tender. Sprinkle over the flour and stir over a medium heat until the roux turns a nice hazelnut brown. Stir in the wine, then the vinegar and finally the stock. Let it simmer quietly for half an hour or so until about the thickness of single cream (or a little thicker if you prefer). Meanwhile, if using the tomatoes, put them into a small pan with the sugar and cook them down to a thick mush over a high heat. Sieve into the main sauce. Finally stir in all the remaining ingredients, then taste and adjust the seasoning. If you intend to re-heat the sauce, leave this last stage until the sauce is hot again or the re-heating process will damage the flavours of the mustard and herbs.

Meanwhile, brush the chops with oil and grill gently until cooked through, then season. Serve with the sauce.

Porc aux Pruneaux de Tours

The area around Tours in western France was once famed for its prunes, though now prune drying is history. Prunes, however, linger on in the local repertoire. The classier pâtisseries make wicked pruneaux fourrés, *stuffed with apricot and almond pastes* and glazed with apricot gel, then there's the unlikely sounding but absolutely delicious *matelote d'anguilles – prune and eel stew – and this dish of pork cooked with prunes, the local wine and lots of cream.*

When I was a child we spent every summer in this area and on highdays and holi-days my mother would often make us *porc aux pruneaux de Tours. Though it can be made with cheaper cuts of pork and is all too often drowned in a floury wine sauce, the best recipe and by far the easiest is this one, largely my mother's version though with a few more prunes (I love them!) and a little less cream. It is a fabulous dish for a dinner party, particularly mid-week when cooking and preparation time is at a pre-mium. If you remember, put the prunes to soak the night before, even if they are of the soft, no-soak, ready-to-eat variety.*

SERVES 6

24 prunes	Seasoned flour, for dusting
300 ml (10 fl oz) Vouvray or other dry white wine	1 level tablespoon redcurrant jelly
	300 ml (10 fl oz) whipping cream
2 pork fillets	A squeeze of lemon juice
50 g (2 oz) butter	Salt and freshly ground black pepper

Soak the prunes in the wine for as long as possible – at least an hour – but if you have time, leave them overnight. Slit open the prunes and remove their stones. Reserve the prunes and don't throw out the wine!

Slice each tenderloin thickly into 9 discs (that's 18 altogether). Heat the butter in a wide frying-pan until it is foaming, dust the pieces of pork with flour and fry over a moderate heat until just tender. If necessary, do this in two batches so as not to over-crowd the pan. Slices of fillet don't take very long – about 4 minutes on each side. Remove from the pan, arrange on a serving dish and keep warm.

Pour any excess fat from the pan, return to the heat and pour in the wine from soaking the prunes. Bring up to the boil, scraping in all the meaty residues. Stir in the redcurrant jelly, then boil hard over a high heat until reduced to a syrupy consistency.

Now stir in the cream and reduce the sauce until nicely thickened. When it is almost done, pop in the prunes to warm through. Finally add a splash of lemon juice to heighten the flavours and season with salt and pepper. Dot the prunes around the pork and pour over the sauce. Serve at once.

Pork with Cheese and Mustard Crust

The cheese and mustard topping on these pork chops bakes to a delicious brown in the heat of the oven, while the meat stays tender and moist.

SERVES 2
2 pork chops, about 2 cm (³/₄ in) thick
A little oil
Salt and freshly ground black pepper

FOR THE CRUST
25 g (1 oz) breadcrumbs
25 g (1 oz) grated Cheddar
1 tablespoon Dijon mustard
2 teaspoons oil

Pre-heat the oven to 170°C/325°F/Gas Mark 3. First, prepare the chops by trimming off excess fat. Next, make the crust by mixing all the ingredients thoroughly with your hands to form a thick paste. Brush the chops with oil and season with salt and pepper. Place them in an oven-proof dish and bake for 15 minutes. Whip out of the oven, turn them over and spread the top side thickly with the crust mixture. Return to the oven for 10–15 minutes until browned.

Japanese Pork with Ginger

This Japanese recipe for pork uses fresh ginger juice to spice up the marinade and sauce for a quickly fried dish of pork and vegetables. To extract the ginger juice, grate a large knob of ginger (no need to peel first) and then squeeze hard with your fingers. Mirin is a sweet cooking wine; sake or dry sherry and a little sugar makes an acceptable substitute.

SERVES 3–4
450 g (1 lb) tender, boneless, lean pork
2 tablespoons vegetable oil
110 g (4 oz) beansprouts
1 large carrot, cut into fine
 matchsticks

FOR THE MARINADE
3 tablespoons sake or dry sherry
1¹/₂ tablespoons mirin, or 2¹/₂
 tablespoons sake or dry sherry,
 mixed with 1 teaspoon caster sugar
3 tablespoons dark soy sauce
1 tablespoon fresh ginger juice

Slice the pork as thinly as you can (chilling it in the freezer for 30 minutes will make slicing easier). Mix all the marinade ingredients and pour over the pork. Turn to coat nicely and leave for 30 minutes. Drain off the marinade and reserve.

Heat the oil in a wide frying-pan over a high heat. Add half the pork and sauté for about a minute, until all but cooked through. Scoop out and repeat with the remaining pork. Quickly return the first batch to the pan, along with the marinade. Bring to the boil, stirring so that the meat is evenly coated. Scoop the meat out on to a plate and keep warm. Throw the beansprouts and carrots into the juices left in the pan and stir for 1–2 minutes, to heat through. Serve with the pork.

Meatballs in Tomato Sauce with Goats' Cheese

My whole family love these meatballs, sizzling in tomato sauce and finished with browned goats' cheese.

Adding bread soaked in a little milk makes tender, delicate meatballs that melt in the mouth. Sometimes I will use basil instead of the oregano, or even coriander. Kecap manis is Indonesian sweet soy sauce, sold now in some larger supermarkets. If you can't get it, substitute dark soy sauce and a pinch of light muscovado sugar.

SERVES 4

FOR THE MEATBALLS
25 g (1 oz) fresh or slightly stale breadcrumbs
Milk
340 g (12 oz) minced pork or lamb
1 tablespoon chopped fresh oregano or marjoram
2 tablespoons chopped fresh parsley
2 teaspoons *kecap manis*
Salt and freshly ground black pepper
Olive oil, for frying

FOR THE TOMATO SAUCE
1 onion, chopped
2 garlic cloves, chopped
2 tablespoons olive oil
2 × 400 g (14 oz) cans chopped tomatoes
1 tablespoon tomato purée
1–2 tablespoons sugar
Salt and freshly ground black pepper
8–10 fresh basil leaves, shredded
100 g (3$^{1}/_{2}$ oz) goats' cheese, diced

Pre-heat the oven to 200°C/400°F/Gas Mark 6. Soak the breadcrumbs in milk for 10 minutes, then squeeze dry. Mix with the pork, herbs, *kecap manis*, salt and pepper. Roll into walnut-sized balls. Pour enough oil into a heavy frying-pan to cover the base. Heat the oil and then fry the balls in it over a medium heat, until nicely browned and cooked through. Drain briefly on kitchen paper.

To make the tomato sauce, fry the onion and garlic gently in the olive oil. Add all the remaining ingredients, except the basil and goats' cheese, and cook hard until reduced to a very thick sauce. Stir in the basil.

Place the meatballs in a shallow ovenproof serving dish and spoon over the sauce. Scatter the goats' cheese over the top (don't worry that it doesn't cover completely: it's not meant to!). Bake for about 30 minutes, until sizzling and bubbling. Serve hot, with good bread and a green salad.

Thai-style Fried Noodles with Pork

I find a big plateful of noodles totally irresistible and always end up eating more than my fair share. This recipe is based on the Thai noodle dishes that sustained me royally and cheaply when I travelled round the country. All the effort goes into the preparation of the ingredients; the cooking time is only a matter of a few minutes. For this dish, I like to use the tiny, slender, fiery red Thai chillies – a singleton will give a fairly mild heat, while two will liven things up rather more. In Thailand, the table would be set with extra bowls of condiments – one of sugar, a bowl of fish sauce with chopped chillies in it (a bottle of Tabasco or other chilli sauce is an easy option for those who crave violent heat), and another bowl with rice vinegar and probably more chillies in it! Assemble and prepare all the ingredients before you start cooking – this is what takes the time.

SERVES 4

280 g (10 oz) Thai *sen lek* noodles or medium Chinese egg noodles
3 tablespoons sunflower oil
4 garlic cloves, chopped
2.5 cm (1 in) piece of fresh ginger, finely chopped
1–2 small fresh Thai chillies, seeded and thinly sliced
280 g (10 oz) minced pork
4 tomatoes, seeded and cut into strips
3 eggs, lightly beaten
Juice of 1 lime

2 tablespoons Thai fish sauce (*nam pla*)
^{1}/2 tablespoon caster sugar
4 tablespoons chopped roasted peanuts
6 spring onions, sliced
75 g (2^1/2 oz) beansprouts
Salt and freshly ground black pepper

TO SERVE
3 tablespoons roughly chopped fresh coriander
Lime wedges

Soak and drain the noodles, or cook them according to the packet instructions.

Heat a large wok over a high heat, until it begins to smoke. Add the oil, warm through for a few seconds and then add the garlic, ginger and chillies. Give them a couple of stirs and then add the pork. Stir-fry for about 2 minutes, breaking up the lumps, and then add the tomatoes and eggs. Fry for a couple of seconds, add the noodles and toss and stir, scraping up egg and bits from the sides of the wok.

Now in go the lime juice, fish sauce and sugar. Mix well and then quickly add the peanuts. Stir-fry for a few seconds and then add the spring onions and beansprouts. Give the whole lot another couple of quick turns and tosses to heat it all through. Draw off the heat. Taste, adjust the seasonings and sprinkle with coriander. Serve with wedges of lime to squeeze over.

Hunter's Stew

Hunter's stew or bigos *is almost the national Polish dish – well, it's certainly one of the best known and best loved. It's a tremendous, filling, hearty 'stew' of sauerkraut and pork, flavoured with mushrooms and wine. Though it tastes great when it is first made, those in the know will prefer it re-heated the next day, or even the day after, allowing time for the flavours to mellow and mature. Do store it carefully in the fridge, however, and re-heat it thoroughly each time, adding a little extra stock and/or butter to lubricate it.*

This recipe for bigos *(and there are many variations on the theme) came from the Magical Buska restaurant in north London.*

SERVES 8–10

25 g (1 oz) dried porcini

1.25 kg (2 lb 8 oz) sauerkraut

675 g (1 lb 8 oz) white cabbage

100–225 g (4–8 oz) smoked streaky
   bacon, diced

25 g (1 oz) butter or oil

1 large onion, chopped

225–450 g (8 oz–1 lb) boneless pork
   chops, cubed

225–450 g (8 oz–1 lb) smoked boiling
   sausage, or garlic sausage, sliced

8 prunes, pitted and chopped

300 ml (10 fl oz) stock or water

300 ml (10 fl oz) red wine

1 bay leaf

1 tablespoon sugar

Salt and freshly ground black pepper

Cover the porcini with hot water and soak for half an hour. Pick out the mushrooms and chop. Then strain and reserve the soaking liquid. Rinse the sauerkraut in cold water. Shred the cabbage finely, discarding the tough stalks. Put the sauerkraut into a large pan with the cabbage and add 300 ml (10 fl oz) water and some pepper. Simmer for 40 minutes.

Meanwhile, cook the bacon in a large frying-pan, adding a little of the butter or oil if needed, until lightly browned. Scoop out and reserve. Fry the onion in the fat, adding the remaining butter or oil, until tender and translucent but not browned. Now add the cubed pork and cook gently until lightly coloured. Add the soaked mushrooms and their soaking liquid, bacon, onion, cooked meat and all the remaining ingredients to the sauerkraut and cabbage. Cook gently, covered, simmering quietly for 40 minutes. Taste and adjust the seasonings, then serve.

Gumbo Ya Ya

Louisiana gumbo is a big soupy stew, but what a stew it is! There are as many recipes for this classic of Cajun cuisine as there are cooks who cook it, and probably more. A few things are common to most versions of gumbo (but not all). First the roux, cooked slowly and patiently until it darkens to a deep almost mahogany brown – not just a thickener, but a powerful contributor of flavour. Then there's the 'holy trinity' or, in other words, onions, peppers and celery, all chopped finely. And finally, there's okra, or sometimes file *(powdered sassafras)*. Okra and file both give gumbo its special silky smoothness, but it is only okra that provides flavour as well.

In Louisiana, gumbo may be served as a first or main course. Either way, it is spooned over a mound of hot rice piled up in individual bowls.

SERVES 6–8
120 ml (4 fl oz) sunflower oil
1 large chicken, cut into 8 pieces
65 g (2¹/₂ oz) plain flour
450 g (1 lb) garlic sausage or other smoked cooked pork sausage, skinned and cut into 1 cm (¹/₂ in) slices
100 g (4 oz) cooked ham, diced
400 g (14 oz) okra, topped, tailed and halved
2 onions, chopped
2 green peppers, seeded and chopped
2 stalks celery, chopped
2 cloves garlic, peeled and chopped
2 tablespoons finely chopped fresh parsley
1 teaspoon each cayenne pepper and black pepper
1 bouquet garni (1 bay leaf, 2 sprigs parsley and 2 sprigs thyme, tied together with string)
Salt

In the largest, heaviest flameproof saucepan or casserole you have, heat the oil over a high heat. Brown the chicken pieces evenly in the oil. Set aside. Keep the heat high, and stir the flour into the oil until evenly mixed. Turn the heat down to medium-low and keep stirring with a metal spoon, scraping the brown bits off the base of the pan, until the mixture turns a dark nut brown. (Allow a good 15 minutes or more.)

Then add the sausage, ham, vegetables, garlic and half the parsley. Stir for a minute. Stir in about 150 ml (5 fl oz) water, then add the chicken pieces, both cayenne and black pepper, the bouquet garni and salt. Gradually add another 1.75 litres (3 pints) of water. Bring to the boil, then simmer for 1 hour, stirring occasionally. Taste and adjust seasonings. Remove the bundle of herbs. Sprinkle with remaining parsley and serve.

Austrian Pork with Pears and Potatoes

This is a heavenly simple dish that requires only a few minutes of preparation time. The real work happens in the oven, untended by human hand, as the pork, potatoes and pears cook gently together to a melting tenderness. It's not grand cuisine, but it does make a perfect (and very cheap) family supper, and I bet there won't be any left-overs.

SERVES 4

450 g (1 lb) belly of pork, cut into 5 cm (2 in) cubes

450 g (1 lb) potatoes, peeled and thickly sliced

450 g (1 lb) pears, cored and quartered

1 stick cinnamon

2 teaspoons caraway seeds

1/2 tablespoon sugar

Salt and freshly ground black pepper

600 ml (1 pint) meat or chicken stock

Pre-heat the oven to 190°C/375°F/Gas Mark 5. Mix the pork, potatoes and pears together in a lightly greased roasting tin. Tuck the cinnamon down amongst the pork cubes. Sprinkle with the caraway seeds, sugar, salt and pepper. Pour over the stock. Cover with foil and bake for 2 hours.

Once cooked, serve immediately with green vegetables.

Chocolate-Chilli Glazed Pork

Before you throw up your hands in horror at the title, read the rest of this paragraph. This recipe was invented by that truly original chef, Paul Gayler, for his book Great Value Gourmet (Meals and Menus for £1) *published by Weidenfeld & Nicolson. It sounded so weird that I had to try it. It's fabulous, as it turns out. Everyone in my house pooh-poohed the idea as I was cooking (I suffered a lot of jokes about puddings and pigs) but the ribbing (get it?) stopped once it was cooked. In fact, an appreciative silence descended and, within a remarkably short time, the dish was empty. Be bold and give it a try. You'll be amazed.*

SERVES 4

675 g (1 lb 7 oz) pork belly, cut into 3 cm (1 1/4 in) strips

Salt and freshly ground black pepper

4 fresh red chillies, seeded

2 tablespoons clear honey, warmed

50 g (2 oz) plain chocolate, melted

Pre-heat the oven to 200°C/400°F/Gas Mark 6. Season the pork, lay it on a rack in a roasting tin, and then roast it in the hot oven for 30–35 minutes, until golden brown.

Meanwhile, in a liquidizer, blend the chillies and the honey. Add the melted chocolate and process again to mix.

Remove the pork from the oven and drain off the fat. Brush the meat generously all over with the chocolate glaze and return to the oven for 10 minutes. Serve on a bed of crisp vegetables, stir-fried with a little ginger.

Chinese Honey-roast Pork

Chinese honey-roast pork or char siu *has to be one of my all-time favourite ways of cooking pork. It is the stuff you see hanging up in the windows of Chinese restaurants, and this recipe, from Yan-Kit So's* Classic Food of China *(Macmillan), is a marvellous home version. The best cuts of pork to use are best chump end, neck end and shoulder blade. Serve it thinly sliced with rice and maybe some stir-fried greens fragrant with ginger and garlic.*

Most supermarkets now sell hoisin sauce and yellow bean sauce. For the red beancurd you'll have to head for an oriental food store. You could leave it out, but the flavour wouldn't be so superb. If possible, use an ordinary oven and not a fan oven, to prevent the meat from drying out.

SERVES 4–6
1–1.25 kg (2 lb 4 oz–2 lb 8 oz) pork (see above for cuts), boned and rinded but with the fat left on
About 3 tablespoons clear honey

FOR THE MARINADE
1 teaspoon salt
8 tablespoons sugar
2 tablespoons hoisin sauce
2 tablespoons ground yellow bean sauce
1 tablespoon mashed red beancurd cheese
1 teaspoon very finely chopped garlic
4 tablespoons light soy sauce
1 tablespoon Shaoxing wine or medium dry sherry

Cut the pork into three strips. Make 3 diagonal cuts in opposite directions on each strip, cutting three-quarters through the thickness. Mix all the marinade ingredients then pour over the pork. Turn the pieces so that they are all thoroughly coated. Leave for 4–8 hours, turning the pieces frequently.

Pre-heat the oven to 180°C/350°F/Gas Mark 4. Place the pork, fat side up, on a wire cake rack in the top of the oven, over a roasting tin containing 1 cm (1/2in) water. Roast for about 50 minutes. Half-way through the roasting time, brush the pork with marinade and turn it over. After 50 minutes, test that the pork is cooked through. If the fat does not yet have a caramelized, almost burnt colour (mine is usually way off at this stage), turn the pieces fat-side up and roast at the highest possible temperature for a final 5–10 minutes.

Take the meat out of the oven, still on its rack, and brush all over with honey, making sure it gets right down into the crevices. Let any excess honey drip off through the rack.

Pour the remaining marinade into a pan and boil hard for 1 minute, then pour into saucers for use as a dipping sauce. Transfer the pork to a serving plate and carve into slices. Serve immediately. Left-overs can be served cold, or re-heated in the oven.

Roast Fillet of Pork with Peaches

Since fillet is long and lean, it benefits from fast roasting at a high temperature. Here it is lightly spiced, but what makes this dish is the accompanying baked peaches. Use firm, all-but-ripe peaches that won't collapse in the heat of the oven.

SERVES 6

1/4 teaspoon ground coriander
1/4 teaspoon ground cinnamon
1/4 teaspoon freshly ground black
   pepper
2 pork fillets

2 tablespoons oil
3 tablespoons honey
3 peaches, halved and pitted (but not
   skinned)
Salt

Pre-heat the oven to 220°C/425°F/Gas Mark 7. Mix the coriander, cinnamon and pepper. Oil a roasting tin or oven-proof dish which is just large enough to take the fillets and later on the peach halves. Lay the pork in the dish and sprinkle over the mixed spices. Spoon over the oil. Bake in the oven for 20 minutes. Meanwhile, put the honey and 2 tablespoons of water in a small pan and warm very gently, stirring, until the honey has dissolved.

After the first 20 minutes, place peach halves, cut side up, around the pork. Pour the honey mixture over the fillet and peaches and season the pork with salt. Cook for a further 20 minutes, basting occasionally. Turn off the oven, prop the door slightly ajar and leave to rest for 5 minutes. Slice the fillets and serve with the peaches and pan juices.

Roast Pork, Florentine Style

One of the joys of Tuscan food is its proud simplicity, secure in the knowledge that its basic ingredients are of superb quality. Nowhere is this more obvious than in arista alla Fiorentina – *roast pork, Florentine style. There's nothing particularly unusual about the cooking method – the meat is just roasted gently in the oven – for the recipe relies absolutely on the meat itself, and the pigs around Florence are obviously happy, well fed, free-ranging creatures. I don't think there is really much point in trying it unless you take the trouble to buy high quality, free-range pork: that is more than half the battle won. The only 'tricks' are, first, roasting the meat on the bone, which gives extra flavour and richness, and ample quantities of finely chopped rosemary and garlic, pushed right into the flesh.*

Ask the butcher for a loin of free-range pork on the bone (also known as a rack of pork), cut from the thicker end of the loin, so that there is plenty of meat relative to bone. Ask him to trim off most of the fat and skin leaving just a thin layer of fat over the meat. Make sure that he gives you the back fat and skin, which you can wrap around game birds as they roast to keep them moist, or cut into small squares and add to a stew to give a velvety texture to the sauce.

SERVES 4–6
1 loin of pork on the bone, weighing 1.25–2 kg (3–4 lb)
3 tablespoons finely chopped fresh rosemary leaves
2 garlic cloves, finely chopped

Coarse salt and freshly ground black pepper
1 glass white wine (nothing too sharp and acidic)
2 tablespoons extra virgin olive oil

If time is on your side, prepare the joint the day before you want to cook and eat it, so that the scent of the garlic and rosemary has time to make its mark on the meat. Mix the rosemary with the garlic. Make holes in the pork with the blade of a narrow knife, then stuff a little of the rosemary and garlic mixture as deeply as you can into each one. Season the outside of the pork generously with salt and pepper. If you are preparing this a day in advance, cover the joint loosely and transfer to the fridge. Bring back to room temperature before roasting.

Pre-heat the oven to 170°C/325°F/Gas Mark 3.

Pour the wine into a roasting tin just large enough to take the pork. Place the pork in it, bones downwards so that they form a support for the meat itself. Rub the skin with the extra virgin olive oil. Roast for 2 hours, basting occasionally with its own juices. Add a few good splashes of water to the pan each time you baste, so that the juices do not dry out and burn.

To check that it is cooked, plunge a skewer into the centre (not too near the bone) and pull out – if the juices run clear, then it is ready. Leave the pork to rest in a warm place (you can simply turn the oven off and leave the door ajar) for about 20 minutes.

Before you can carve the meat you need to remove it, in one piece, from the bones. To do this, place the rack of pork so the rib bones stand upright. Use a sharp knife and cut down close to the ribs, sliding the knife underneath the meat, until you reach the long, solid chine bone at their base. Swivel the blade of the knife upwards and guide it over the chine bone and down the other side, to release the meat. Lift the meat off and cut into slices about 2.5 cm (1 in) thick. Arrange on a plate, cover and keep warm. Quickly put the roasting tin over the heat and bring to the boil, scraping in all the residues on the base and adding a little more water if they taste too strong – you won't end up with a huge amount of pan juices, but just enough to moisten each slice of meat. Pour into a jug, and serve with the meat.

Roast Loin of Pork with Apple, Ginger and Orange Stuffing

This is a smaller roast for a family meal, boned and rolled so that it is as easy as pie to carve. It's not an onerous task to bone and roll the loin at home and scoring the skin for crackling is great fun, but if you want to save time, ask your butcher to prepare it for you.

The best way to stuff the loin depends rather on which end of the animal it comes from, but whether you smear it over the flap or push it into the pocket, this stuffing is perfect for pork. The apple and orange provide the fruitiness that goes so well with it and the ginger adds a high note without dominating.

I like to serve roast pork with French Canadian Roast Apple Sauce on p. 358. But if you want to extend the pan juices to moisten the meat, the easiest way is to boil them up with a generous slug of cider and a pinch of sugar (or two) to soften the acidity.

SERVES 6

1 boned loin of pork, weighing about
   1.25–1.5 kg (3 lb–3 lb 8 oz)
Salt
1 big glass cider (optional)
A pinch of sugar (optional)

FOR THE STUFFING
1 small onion, finely chopped
1 small eating apple, cored and finely
   chopped

1–2 spheres preserved stem ginger,
   finely chopped
Finely grated zest and juice of
   1/2 orange
2 tablespoons chopped parsley
50 g (2 oz) fresh white breadcrumbs
1 egg, lightly beaten
Salt and freshly ground black pepper

Pre-heat the oven to 190°C/375°F/Gas Mark 5. If you've bought the joint ready boned and rolled, snip off the strings and unroll the pork carefully. If you've bought a whole boned piece, score the skin for crackling. If the joint comes from the upper fillet end, make a pocket for the stuffing by cutting into the thickest part of the meat. If it comes from the rump end, there may not be enough flesh to cut a pocket. A straight flap will be more successful. Slice the meat horizontally through the centre, open it out like a book, then spread with the stuffing and roll up.

Mix the stuffing ingredients, adding just enough egg to bind, and push into the pocket or spread over the cut sides of the meat. Only add enough to stay in place when the meat is rolled and tied or it will ooze out in an unsightly way. Far better to save the excess to make little stuffing balls. Roll up the meat and tie it firmly in place with string, making sure that the skin which will become the crackling is back on top of the joint. Weigh the joint and calculate the cooking time, allowing 33 minutes per 500 g (30 minutes per lb) plus 30 minutes. Set the rolled joint on a rack over a roasting tin. Dry the skin thoroughly, then rub plenty of fine salt into it. Roast in the oven.

Roll any left-over stuffing into walnut-sized balls and pop them into the roasting tin about half an hour before the joint is done so that they have time to brown and cook through. Check occasionally and remove when they seem nicely browned.

Test the meat to see if it is done; the juices should run clear when a skewer is inserted. Transfer to a serving plate and let it relax in a warm place for 15–20 minutes while you make a simple gravy, if you want to.

Spoon any excess fat out of the roasting tin then place it over the hob and add the cider and a pinch of sugar. Bring to the boil, stirring and scraping in the meaty residues. Let it bubble for a few minutes before tasting and adjusting the seasonings, adding a little more sugar if it is on the sharp side. Strain and serve alongside the meat and crackling.

Peking Star Anise Pork

The smell as this cooks is heavenly. It's almost worth cooking for that alone. As it happens, the finished product is every bit as good: subtly scented pork, to be served cold with a little of the cooking juices. It is an ideal dish for a cold summer lunch, or even a Christmas-time buffet, since it can be made a day or two in advance. Try serving it with a watercress salad or with peppery rocket: not very authentic but very good. Left-overs make great sandwiches.

The pork rind gives a gelatinous, smooth quality to the liquid and improves the flavour but it's still very good with a rindless joint, though the juices are less likely to gel.

SERVES 4–6

1 kg (2 lb 4 oz) boned pork shoulder or
    leg
2 teaspoons Szechuan peppercorns or
    black peppercorns
1 cm ($1/2$ in) piece of fresh ginger,
    sliced
5 star anise

1 cinnamon stick
4 spring onions, roughly chopped
120 g ($4^1/2$ oz) demerara sugar
60 ml (4 tablespoons) dry sherry
100 ml ($3^1/2$ fl oz) dark soy sauce
1 litre ($1^3/4$ pints) chicken or pork
    stock or water

Bring a large pan of water to the boil and lower the pork into it. Bring back to the boil and blanch for 3 minutes. Drain thoroughly and cut off the rind. Cut the rind into postage-stamp sized pieces. Place the pork in a pan that will take it neatly, along with the pieces of rind. Dry-fry the peppercorns in a heavy frying-pan, until they give off a heady scent. Tip into the pan. Tuck the ginger, star anise, cinnamon stick and spring onions around the pork. Add the sugar, sherry and soy sauce. Pour in the stock or water. Bring up to the boil and then reduce the heat, cover the pan and leave to simmer very gently for $2^1/2$ hours, until the pork is heart-rendingly tender. Turn the meat every now and then, so that it cooks evenly.

Lift the cooked pork into a bowl. Return the pan to a high heat and boil hard, until the liquid has reduced by about half. Strain the liquid over the meat and leave to cool. Cover and store in the fridge overnight or longer, turning the meat once in a while.

Serve the pork thinly sliced, with a little of the juices, roughly chopped if they've set.

Crown Roast of Pork with Spiced Prune and Apricot Stuffing

This is one of the most impressive joints you can serve, but do give your butcher ample notice as the pork will have to be cut from the carcass in a way that is slightly different from the norm (the rib bones are cut longer than usual). Allow plenty of time for cooking, too. Mine took a full 4½ hours!

The joint produces a fair amount of its own juices, but if you want to extend them just deglaze the pan (as in the Roast Loin of Pork with Apple, Ginger and Orange Stuffing, see p. 178) with wine, stock or even cider. You can't fit a huge amount of stuffing inside the crown, so, if you wish, double the quantity and bake the extra alongside the joint for the final 40 minutes.

**SERVES 8 GREEDY PEOPLE OR
10 MORE ABSTEMIOUS ONES**
1 prepared crown roast of pork
  weighing about 3–3.5 kg (7–8 lb)

FOR THE STUFFING
6 prunes
6 dried apricots
1 onion, chopped

25 g (1 oz) butter
1½ teaspoons black mustard seeds
1 teaspoon coriander seeds, coarsely
  crushed
1 level teaspoon aniseeds
225 g (8 oz) pork sausagemeat
75 g (3 oz) soft brown breadcrumbs
Salt and freshly ground black pepper

Pre-heat the oven to 230°C/450°F/Gas Mark 8. To make the stuffing, soak the prunes and apricots until soft, if necessary, then dry and chop them. Soften the onion in the butter until tender, then add the spices. Sauté until the mustard seeds begin to jump. Draw off the heat and mix with the dried fruit, sausagemeat, breadcrumbs, salt and pepper.

Weigh a roasting tin (you'll see why in a minute). Now grease and stand the crown roast in it. Fill the central cavity with the stuffing, doming it up in the centre and gently pushing the meat into a nice circular crown. Weigh in the tin, then deduct the weight of the tin to get the weight of the stuffed crown. Calculate the roasting time by allowing 33 minutes per 500 g (30 minutes per lb) and 20 minutes extra. Protect the tips of the bones with twists of silver foil. After it has had 1½–2 hours in the oven you will also need to protect the stuffing from burning with a circle of foil.

Roast the crown at the pre-heated oven temperature for the first 15 minutes, then reduce it to 180°C/350°F/Gas Mark 4 for the remainder of the cooking time. Test to make sure the meat is cooked, then turn off the oven, open the door and leave the roast to relax for 25–30 minutes before carving.

Cut each side of each of the rib bones to divide the crown into chops. Spoon the stuffing from the inside and serve with the pork.

Boiled Smoked Bacon Knuckle with Savoy Cabbage

A modern way of cooking a traditional Irish favourite. Instead of the cabbage being boiled to death with the bacon, the two just come together at the last minute. It's a remarkably economical dish too, though you'll have to go to an old-fashioned butcher for the bacon knuckle. Serve with boiled potatoes (main-crop not new) and soda bread. Save the second lot of cooking water for making split pea or lentil soup.

SERVES 4

1 smoked bacon knuckle
1 onion, halved
1 carrot, quartered
2 garlic cloves
1 bay leaf

50 g (2 oz) butter
1/2 Savoy cabbage, thickly shredded
3 juniper berries, crushed
A few shakes of balsamic or sherry
  vinegar
Freshly ground black pepper

Cover the knuckle with water and bring up to the boil. Simmer for 5 minutes, then drain. Cover with clean water and add the onion, carrot, garlic and the bay leaf. Bring to the boil and simmer until the meat is tender – about 1 hour – skimming off any scum as it cooks. When cooked, leave the meat to cool in the broth. This can all be done up to a day ahead.

Skin the knuckle, then strip the meat off in biggish chunks and strain the broth. Measure 300 ml (10 fl oz) of it into a pan large enough to take the cabbage and add 15 g (1/2 oz) of the butter. Bring to the boil, cram in the cabbage and the juniper berries, then bring back to the boil and let it simmer for about 2 minutes. Add the meat to the pan and simmer for a final 3–5 minutes until the cabbage is tender but not smelly. Draw off the heat. Stir in the remaining butter, the vinegar and plenty of pepper and serve immediately.

Lentilles aux Lardons et Saucisson à l'Ail

This is my kind of food. I love this sort of filling, solid, comforting fodder that is the mainstay of the French brasserie in the winter months. Here, the lentils are simmered slowly with a piece of bacon and a garlic sausage, absorbing their flavours. The salt of the meats and the wine slow down the cooking process, so that the lentils take longer to cook than they would normally. It's worth the wait.

SERVES 4, HEARTILY
300 g (11 oz) Puy lentils or other small,
   green lentils, rinsed
150 g (5 oz) meaty streaky bacon, in a
   single chunk, with rind
45 g (1^1/$_2$oz) butter
1 onion, chopped
2 garlic cloves, chopped
1 garlic sausage or rich pork boiling
   sausage

1 generous wine glass (200 ml/7 fl oz)
   red wine
1 bouquet garni (1 bay leaf, 2 sprigs
   thyme and 1 sprig parsley, tied
   together with string)
2 tablespoons chopped fresh parsley
Salt and freshly ground black pepper

TO SERVE
French mustard

Rinse and drain the lentils. Carefully cut the rind off the bacon in a single piece and reserve it. Melt 30 g (1 oz) of the butter in a large saucepan and fry the onion in it gently, until translucent. Add the garlic and the lentils and stir them about in the butter for a minute or so. Push the chunk of bacon, its rind and the sausage (pricked here and there with a fork and cut in half, if necessary) down into the lentils. Pour in the red wine and let it simmer for about 3 minutes. Add the bouquet garni, pepper and enough water to cover by about 3 cm (1 in). Bring to the boil, reduce the heat, half-cover and leave to simmer for 50–60 minutes, or until the lentils and bacon are tender.

Discard the bacon rind. Lift out the bacon and sausage and keep them warm. Drain off most of the cooking liquid, leaving just enough to keep the lentils moist. Stir in the remaining butter and the chopped parsley. Taste and adjust the seasonings – you may not need more salt. Spoon the lentils into a serving dish. Slice the bacon and sausage and arrange them on top and serve with lots of French mustard.

Maple Beans with Smoked Ham Knuckle

Based on a recipe from the Ontario Maple Syrup Producers' booklet of maple syrup recipes, this is an unusual take on slow-cooked beans, sweetened with the syrup, salted with the juices of the ham and spiced up with Tabasco sauce. The fruity apple slices bring all the elements of the dish together, so don't be tempted to leave them out.

SERVES 6
500 g (1 lb 2oz) dried cannellini beans,
   soaked overnight
1 large onion, chopped
4 garlic cloves, sliced
2 fresh thyme sprigs
1 large fresh rosemary sprig
1 bay leaf
4 strips of lemon zest

1 ham knuckle, soaked overnight
150 ml (5 fl oz) maple syrup
1–1^1/$_2$ tablespoons Tabasco or other
   chilli sauce
1 tablespoon Dijon mustard
Salt and freshly ground black pepper

FOR THE TOPPING
3–4 eating apples, cored and cut into 8
30 g (1 oz) butter, softened

Drain the beans, put them into a pan and cover them with fresh water. Bring to the boil and boil hard for 10 minutes. Reduce the heat and simmer until properly tender – about 45–60 minutes. Drain, reserving the cooking water. Pre-heat the oven to 150°C/300°F/Gas Mark 2.

Put half the beans, together with half the onion and garlic into a large, ovenproof casserole. Tie the herbs together with a piece of string and tuck them in, too. Bury two of the strips of lemon zest in the beans. Lay the ham knuckle on top and then cover with the remaining beans, onions, garlic and lemon zest. Mix the syrup, Tabasco or chilli sauce and mustard and pour over. Season with salt and pepper and then pour over enough of the reserved cooking water to barely cover. Cover the casserole tightly and bake for 3 hours.

Arrange the apple pieces decoratively over the beans; you may not need them all. If there is rather too much liquid left in the dish, just scoop a little out so that the apples can perch more comfortably. Dot with butter and return to the oven for a final hour until the apples are tender. Serve piping hot.

Ham with Sauce Robert

Sauce Robert is a white wine sauce with a hint of mustard that goes particularly well with ham. Sometimes it is made with vinegar as well as wine to sharpen it up. I prefer it without, but you can if you wish replace 25 ml (1 fl oz) of the wine with white wine vinegar for a tarter flavour. The sauce can be made in advance and kept in the fridge for a day or two.

When ham is to be served hot like this, you will need the best cooked ham possible, cut thick to give substance. If no one near you sells good ham, cut freshly as you like it, then partner the sauce with thin gammon steaks, or pork chops. It also goes well with poached eggs, or grilled pork and herb sausages.

The sauce dates back a good 400 years ... but who, you may wonder, was Robert? The invention of the sauce is often credited to a cook called Robert Vinot who plied his trade towards the end of the sixteenth century. Larousse Gastronomique *tells us that this is wrong. Rabelais mentioned 'Robert, the inventor of sauce Robert' in 1552, years before M. Vinot came on the scene. Who Rabelais's Robert was remains a mystery, though he was obviously a fine cook.*

SERVES 4
15 g (¹/₂ oz) butter
1 tablespoon sunflower oil
4 thick slices of cooked ham

FOR THE SAUCE
1 large onion, finely chopped

25 g (1 oz) butter
1 tablespoon flour
200 ml (7 fl oz) dry white wine
300 ml (10 fl oz) pork or chicken stock
1 tablespoon Dijon mustard
1 teaspoon sugar
Salt and freshly ground black pepper

First make the sauce. Cook the onion slowly in the butter in a fairly large pan until golden – a good 10 minutes or more. Sprinkle with the flour and stir until hazelnut brown. Gradually stir in the wine as if making a white sauce. Then stir in the stock. Bring to the boil and simmer, stirring occasionally, until the sauce has reduced by about one third. (If you are making the sauce in advance, stop at this point and re-heat it when needed.) Mix a tablespoon or two of the sauce into the mustard, then stir back into the sauce with the sugar, salt and pepper to taste. Keep warm.

Heat the butter and oil in a wide frying-pan and fry the ham briefly to heat through and brown lightly. Serve the hot ham with the sauce.

Glazed Gammon

A large joint of glazed gammon looks pretty impressive and, as long as you allow plenty of time, it is very easy to cook. It will need to be soaked first, then boiled (well, simmered really) and then gets a final spell in the oven to gloss the glaze.

SERVES 8–10
1 gammon joint, weighing around
    2.75 kg (6 lb)
1 onion
1 carrot
1 bay leaf
A few sprigs of parsley

FOR THE GLAZE
2 tablespoons Dijon or English mustard
2 tablespoons demerara sugar
Whole cloves, to decorate

Soak the gammon joint overnight in cold water then drain well. If you don't have time to do this you can accelerate the process by putting the joint into a pan of cold water, bringing it to the boil and letting it simmer for 5 minutes. Then throw out the water, which will take a fair amount of salt with it.

Put the soaked or blanched joint into a large pan with the onion, carrot, bay leaf and parsley. Cover with cold water and bring slowly to the boil. Cover and simmer lazily for 2 hours, topping up the water level regularly with more hot water. Leave the joint to cool for half an hour in its cooking liquid if you plan to serve it hot, or longer at your convenience if you wish to serve it cold, as this lets the meat absorb more of the liquid, keeping it moist.

Lift the joint out of the liquid onto a board and wipe it dry. Carefully peel the skin: start by making a couple of cuts just through the skin itself, not the fat underneath, so that you can get a hold of it, then pull it off, without removing the fat. Taste the stock. If it isn't too salty, save it for making soup – it's especially good for a dried pea soup.

Pre-heat the oven to 220°C/425°F/Gas Mark 7.

Transfer the joint to a roasting tin. Smear the fat with the mustard, then press the sugar firmly and evenly all over it. Using the tip of a sharp knife, score the fat with par-allel lines, first in one direction, then at an angle, to form diamonds. Finally, press a clove into the centre of each diamond. Roast the joint for about 25 minutes until nicely browned and glazed.

If you are serving the joint hot, let it rest for 20 minutes before carving. Otherwise leave it to cool slowly in its own time.

Jambon Persillé

On the whole I'm not keen on bits and bobs set in aspic, but Jambon Persillé is a glorious exception. It makes a stunning centrepiece for a buffet, but should be made at least a day in advance (it keeps for several days in the fridge). A classic Jambon Persillé does not need gelatine. A calf's foot is simmered with the meat to gel the liquid, as well as giving extra flavour. However, I find my method simpler.

SERVES 8
1.75 kg (4 lb) gammon joint, soaked
    overnight and drained
1 large onion, quartered
1 leek, cut into 5 cm (2 in) lengths
1 celery stick, cut into 4
1 large carrot, thickly sliced
1 bouquet garni (1 bayleaf, 2 sprigs
    parsley and 2 sprigs thyme, tied
    together with string)

6 black peppercorns
300 ml (10 fl oz) dry white wine
300 ml (10 fl oz) chicken or veal stock
2 sachets powdered gelatine
25 g (1 oz) chopped parsley

Place the gammon in a pan and cover with water. Bring to the boil and simmer for 10 minutes. Drain and rinse under cold water. Rinse the pan, and return the gammon to it. Add the vegetables, bouquet garni, peppercorns, wine, stock and enough water to cover. Bring to the boil and skim, then simmer for 2–3 hours until the gammon is very tender. Frequently skim off any scum and fat as it simmers. If necessary, top up with boiling water so that the meat is always covered.

Remove the meat and boil the liquid hard to concentrate the flavour. Taste frequently and remove from the heat before it becomes too salty. Strain through a sieve lined with muslin or kitchen paper. Measure out 900 ml (1½ pints). If you don't have quite enough, top up with stock or water. Place 6 tablespoons of the cooking liquid into a small pan and sprinkle over the gelatine. Leave for 4–5 minutes then heat very gently, stirring, until completely dissolved. Mix in another 6 tablespoons of the warm liquid one at a time then tip the mixture back into the liquid, stirring well. Leave to cook, then transfer it to the fridge until it begins to thicken.

Using two forks, tear the meat into pieces around 2.5 cm (1 in) thick and mix with the chopped parsley. Spread a third of the meat and parsley mixture in a single layer in a 2 litre (3½ pint) bowl and pour over enough of the stock to barely cover it. Chill until just set. Repeat twice more, first re-heating the stock until it's almost liquid, then adding just enough to cover the meat. Pour over all the remaining stock the last time round. Cover and chill for at least 5 hours or overnight.

To turn out, loosen the edges with a sharp knife, then invert the Jambon Persillé onto a serving dish and shake gently until it slips out. If it clings stubbornly, dip into hot water for a few seconds, then try again.

Sausages Cooked in Red Wine

A straightforward upgrading for good butcher's sausages. Serve piping hot with plenty of mashed potato and mustard.

SERVES 4
8 good-quality meaty sausages
25 g (1 oz) butter

1 bay leaf
150 ml (5 fl oz) red wine
Salt and freshly ground black pepper

Pre-heat the oven to 190°C/375°F/Gas Mark 5. Prick the sausages all over, then fry briskly in the butter to brown them. Transfer to an oven-proof dish which is only just big enough to take them all in a single layer. Tuck the bay leaf down amongst them. Pour the wine into the frying-pan in which the sausages were browned, bring to the boil, stirring, and pour over the sausages. Season with salt and pepper, then cover with foil and bake for 20–30 minutes.

Sausage and Apple Pie

This is the kind of homely, countryish dish that I love. It tastes best hot or warm from the oven, though I suspect that any cold left-overs won't be hanging around for long.

SERVES 6–8
450 g (1 lb) puff pastry
450 g (1 lb) good quality pork
**   sausagemeat**
3–4 sage leaves, chopped

Salt and freshly ground black pepper
A little freshly ground nutmeg
2 large eating apples, peeled, cored
**   and sliced**
1 egg yolk

Roll out half the pastry and use to line a 21–23 cm (8½–9 in) round pie plate. Using your hands, spread out the sausagemeat over the base. Scatter the sage leaves over it and season lightly with salt, pepper and nutmeg. Now cover with the apple slices and sprinkle again with salt, pepper and nutmeg. Roll out the remaining pastry to form a lid. Beat the egg yolk lightly with 1 tablespoon of cold water. Brush the edges of the pie pastry with this egg wash and lay the lid on top. Press the edges together to seal and trim off any excess pastry, then make a hole in the centre of the lid so the steam can escape. Chill in the fridge for 30 minutes.

Put a baking tray in the oven and pre-heat the oven to 220°C/425°F/Gas Mark 7.

Brush the pastry with the egg wash and pop it into the oven on top of the baking tray so that the base gets an instant blast of heat. After 15 minutes, reduce the heat to 180°C/350°F/Gas Mark 4 and cook for a further 30–40 minutes. Test with a skewer to make sure that the apple is tender.

Leek and Black Pudding Tart

I find large pieces of black pudding too cloying to enjoy, but cut into smaller pieces and mixed with other things, the flavour is what you notice rather than the texture. I love the combination of black pudding and lots of leeks in this savoury tart.

SERVES 6–8

350 g (12 oz) shortcrust pastry (see p. 342)

FOR THE FILLING

25 g (1 oz) butter

750 g (1 lb 8 oz) leeks, trimmed and thinly sliced

150 ml (5 fl oz) single cream or half cream

2 eggs

2 tablespoons finely chopped fresh parsley

2 sprigs of fresh marjoram, chopped, or 1/4 teaspoon dried

50 g (2 oz) Gruyère cheese, finely grated

Salt and freshly ground black pepper

225 g (8 oz) black pudding, skinned and cut into chunks

Line a 25 cm (10 in) tart tin with the pastry. Let it rest for 30 minutes in the fridge. Meanwhile place a baking sheet in the oven, and heat to 200°C/400°F/Gas Mark 6. Prick the pastry base, then line the tart tin with foil or greaseproof paper and weigh down with baking beans. Bake for 10 minutes. Remove the beans and paper and return to the oven to dry out for a further 5 minutes.

Melt the butter in a pan and add the leeks. Cover and cook over a moderate heat for 10–15 minutes until tender, stirring occasionally. Draw off the heat and beat in the cream, and then the eggs, parsley, marjoram and half the Gruyère. Season to taste.

Scatter the black pudding over the base of the tart and spoon the leek mixture evenly over the top. Sprinkle on the remaining cheese, and bake at 190°C/375°F/Gas Mark 5 for 30–35 minutes until just set, and golden brown. Serve hot or cold.

Spiced Chinese Spare Ribs

I'm a big fan of sticky, grilled spare ribs. You can't possibly eat them tidily and neatly and half the fun would be lost if you tried. The only refinement to introduce to the table is plentiful fingerbowls. I prefer to grill the ribs in groups of 3 or 4 – easier to handle than large sheets, but not as fiddly as individual ribs – and I always blanch them first to ensure that the meat stays meltingly tender. Although they are nicest grilled (particularly over an outdoor barbecue, in which case I'd suggest you double the quantities as there's nothing like fresh air to sharpen the appetite), they can also be roasted in the oven if it makes life easier.

SERVES 4 AS A FIRST COURSE
1.5 kg (3 lb) pork spare ribs

FOR THE MARINADE
1 heaped teaspoon Szechuan peppercorns or black peppercorns

7 tablespoons hoisin sauce
1 1/2 tablespoons clear honey
3 garlic cloves, crushed
2 tablespoons rice wine or dry sherry
1 tablespoon Chinese black vinegar or red wine vinegar

Divide the sheets of spare ribs into clumps of 3 or 4 ribs, for easy handling. Blanch them in boiling water for 15 minutes.

Dry-fry the peppercorns (either sort) over a high heat until they start to smell aromatic. Cool and grind them to a powder. Mix with the remaining marinade ingredients and slather thickly over the spare ribs. Set aside for at least 1 hour and preferably 3–4 hours or even overnight (in the fridge).

To grill the ribs, pre-heat the grill (or barbecue) thoroughly. Grill them fairly slowly, about 15 cm (6 in) away from the heat, turning frequently, until they are crisp and catching at the edges. This should take a good 15 minutes, so if necessary move the ribs further away from the heat so that they don't get burnt to a crisp.

If you prefer, you can cook them in an oven pre-heated to 220°C/425°F/Gas Mark 7. Place the ribs on a wire rack over a roasting tin and roast for 20–25 minutes until crisp and slightly frazzled.

Jerked Pork Fillet with Fresh Pineapple Chutney

The key ingredient in Jamaican jerked pork, apart from the pork itself, is the allspice berries, toasted to bring out the full aroma. The fresh pineapple chutney is not an authentic Jamaican accompaniment, but it does add an appropriate balancing note of sweetness. The fillet can be either barbecued, which gives a lovely smoky flavour, or grilled.

SERVES 6
2 pork fillets, weighing about 675 g (1 lb 8 oz) in all
A little sunflower or vegetable oil
Salt and freshly ground black pepper

FOR THE SPICE PASTE
2 heaped tablespoons allspice berries

1 teaspoon cinnamon
1/2 teaspoon grated nutmeg
4 spring onions, chopped
1/2 Scotch Bonnet chilli or 1 red chilli, seeded and roughly chopped
1 bay leaf, chopped
1 tablespoon dark rum

FOR THE PINEAPPLE CHUTNEY
1 ripe pineapple, peeled, cored and
   finely diced
Juice of 1 lime
1 cm (¹/₂ in) piece fresh root ginger,
   grated

4 spring onions, sliced
¹/₂ Scotch Bonnet chilli or 1 red chilli,
   seeded and finely chopped
2 tablespoons chopped coriander

To make the paste, dry-fry the allspice berries in a small heavy pan over a high heat until they give off a delicious scent. Grind or pound to a powder with the other dry spices. Either pound or process with the spring onions, chilli, bay leaf, rum, salt and pepper to make a paste. Rub this over the pork fillets and leave for an hour at room temperature (or longer in the fridge, in which case they should be brought back to room temperature before cooking).

To make the chutney, just mix all the ingredients, cover and leave for an hour before using. Taste and adjust the seasonings.

Brush the fillets with oil and barbecue or grill at a high heat until lightly browned, then move to a medium heat (or turn down the grill) and continue cooking for 15–20 minutes until cooked through. Rest for 5 minutes on a plate by the side of the barbecue, or in a warm place, before slicing. Serve with the fresh pineapple chutney.

Sautéd Calf's Liver with Balsamic Vinegar and Sage

The Italians love lightly sautéd calf's liver with sage, and so do I. It takes only minutes to rustle up and is the kind of supper dish I really appreciate when I've had a hard day. A real treat.

Be sure to add the vinegar after the pan is off the heat. Over-heating balsamic vinegar destroys much of its aroma, leaving it flat and dull. Though you can cook lamb's liver this way, it's really a recipe to save for the marvellous, tender sweetness of more expensive calf's liver.

SERVES 2

2 slices calf's liver cut 1 cm (^{1}/$_2$ in) thick and weighing 225–350 g (8–12 oz) in total
Salt and freshly ground black pepper

3 tablespoons olive oil
50 g (2 oz) shallots, thinly sliced
3 large or 6 small sage leaves
1 tablespoon balsamic vinegar

Season the calf's liver with salt and pepper. Heat the olive oil in a wide frying-pan over a medium heat. Add the shallots and fry gently until golden and tender. Raise the heat and add the calf's liver to the pan. Cook for about 1 minute on the first side, by which time it should be nicely browned (if not, crank the heat up a bit more), then turn over, add the sage to the pan and cook the other side for 1–3 minutes depending on how well done you like your liver and bearing in mind that to overcook calf's liver is well nigh a mortal sin and a terrible waste of money.

Transfer the calf's liver to a warmed serving dish. Remove the pan from the heat, pour the vinegar into it and stir. Pour over the liver and serve. Very nice with mashed potato, flavoured with olive oil and Parmesan.

Fegato alla Veneziana

Liver and onions! Not the British version, but the Italian one, where the onions are cooked down slowly to a melting sweetness to form a bed for quickly fried, tender calf's liver. A blissful combination. If it makes life easier, the onions can be cooked up to a day in advance, then re-heated while you fry the liver.

SERVES 2 GENEROUSLY
350 g (12 oz) calf's liver, or lamb's liver
2 tablespoons olive oil
25 g (1 oz) butter
2 onions, thinly sliced

1¹/₂ tablespoons chopped parsley
Salt and freshly ground black pepper
¹/₂ tablespoon balsamic or sherry
**   vinegar, or red wine vinegar**

Cut the liver into pieces about 2.5 cm (1 in) square. Set aside for the moment. Heat half the olive oil and half the butter in a wide saucepan. Add the onions and 1 tablespoon of parsley, stir, then cover and cook slowly for 30 minutes, stirring once or twice. Remove the lid, raise the heat and continue cooking until golden – another 10 minutes or so. Season with salt and pepper and scoop out onto a serving dish. Keep warm, if necessary.

When the onions are nearly done, heat the remaining oil and butter in a separate pan. Sauté the calf's liver over a high heat for 1–2 minutes. Draw off the heat, drizzle over the vinegar and season with salt and pepper. Stir, then spoon onto the onions. Scatter with the remaining parsley and serve.

Sweetbreads with Gooseberry Sauce

First of all, let me put paid to one myth. The term sweetbread is not a euphemism for testicles. In anatomical terms, sweetbreads are the thymus glands, well removed from the reproductive organs. I find their delicate flavour and smooth texture immensely appealing. Lamb's sweetbreads are what you are most likely to come across. Few butchers carry fresh ones as a regular day-to-day line (although frozen aren't at all bad). Most, however, are happy to buy fresh ones in if you give a day's notice.

Soak the sweetbreads in cold water for 2 hours – this dissolves any blood and gunk. Drain and put them into a pan with enough cold water to cover. Bring to the boil and simmer for 5 minutes. Drain and trim the sweetbreads, removing the skin, fat and ducts. Sandwich the sweetbreads between two plates, set a weight on top (a couple of cans of something or other will do), then leave in the fridge for at least an hour to firm up.

Tart, green gooseberries make a pretty summer sauce for breaded sweetbreads. Both sweetbreads and sauce can be prepared in advance. All you need to do at the last minute is fry the sweetbreads and gently re-heat the sauce.

SERVES 4

FOR THE SAUCE
225 g (8 oz) gooseberries
A knob of butter
1 tablespoon sugar
Salt and freshly ground black pepper
1 tablespoon chopped chives

FOR THE SWEETBREADS
450 g (1 lb) prepared and cooked lamb's
**   sweetbreads**
1 egg, beaten
Breadcrumbs, for coating
Oil, for frying

First, make the gooseberry sauce. Don't bother to top and tail the gooseberries, just put them straight into the pan with the butter, sugar and 3 tablespoons of water. Cover and cook over a gentle heat for a few minutes until the juices begin to run. Uncover and cook until all the gooseberries have collapsed. Push through a sieve and season to taste with a little salt and plenty of pepper. Set aside until needed.

Slice the larger pieces of sweetbread in half lengthwise. Dip first in the beaten egg and then coat in breadcrumbs. Fry gently in oil until nicely browned. Season with a little salt. Meanwhile, re-heat the sauce, stir in the chives and serve with the sweetbreads.

Kidneys Turbigo Ma Façon

The proper recipe for kidneys turbigo *demands a* demi-glace *sauce, which is the kind of thing that may well be readily to hand in the kitchens of a French restaurant but takes far too long to make to be of any great use to the domestic cook. This then is kidneys* turbigo *made my way, with nothing more* recherché *than a tomato and white wine sauce. It is a hearty dish of kidneys, mushrooms and chipolata sausages. Lovely with sautéd potatoes or rice.*

SERVES 4–6
15 g (¹/₂ oz) butter
1 tablespoon sunflower oil
6 lambs' kidneys, split in half
8 chipolatas
225 g (8 oz) button mushrooms
1 garlic clove, crushed
400 g (14 oz) can chopped tomatoes
1 teaspoon sugar

1 small glass of dry white wine
1 bouquet garni (1 bay leaf, 1 sprig thyme and 1 small sprig rosemary, tied together with string)
Salt and freshly ground black pepper

TO SERVE
Finely chopped parsley

Melt the butter with the oil in a frying-pan over a medium heat. Fry the kidneys fairly swiftly until just cooked (don't overdo them, though, as they are going to have to sit around for a while). Scoop out of the pan and set aside. Now fry the chipolatas and set them aside with the kidneys. Next, fry the mushrooms over a keen heat until tender and scoop out.

Add the garlic to the pan and swish around for a few seconds. Tip in the tomatoes with their juice, then add the sugar, wine and bouquet garni. Season with salt and pepper and bring to the boil. Simmer for about 15 minutes until the sauce is well reduced with not a trace of wateriness. Taste and adjust the seasoning. Return the kidneys, chipolatas and mushrooms to the pan and let them simmer for a couple of minutes to heat through. Sprinkle with parsley and serve immediately.

Rognons à la Moutarde

These are Rolls-Royce kidneys, napped in cream and speckled with grains of mustard, a veritable feast for anyone who is partial to inner organs. Serve with plain buttered noodles and maybe some mangetout or spinach on the side and you can be tucking in in less than half an hour.

Though kidneys with a mustard sauce is a particularly fine combination, this method is widely adaptable to other meats (sliced chicken breast, perhaps). You will have to adjust the frying times to suit, of course, but the final additions of wine, cream and mustard are standard.

SERVES 4
12 lambs' kidneys
1 shallot, finely chopped
25 g (1 oz) butter
1 tablespoon sunflower oil
150 ml (5 fl oz) white wine

4 tablespoons crème fraîche or
  double cream
2 tablespoons coarse-grained or
  Dijon mustard
Salt and freshly ground black pepper
A little chopped chervil or parsley

Cut the kidneys in half. Sauté the shallot gently in the butter and oil in a wide frying-pan until tender. Raise the heat and add the kidneys. Fry briskly for about 3 minutes. Pour off the excess fat, then tip in the white wine. Bring to the boil and simmer, stirring once or twice, until the wine has almost boiled away. Now stir in the crème fraîche or cream, the mustard and a little salt and pepper. Leave to bubble steadily for a minute or so to reduce the cream slightly, then taste and adjust the seasoning. Stir in the chervil or parsley and serve immediately.

Kidney and Mushroom Parcels

In this recipe, the kidneys are baked, but protected from the drying heat of the oven with a moist stuffing and a wrapping of puff pastry. The golden brown parcels of kidney look neat and pretty on the plate and can be made in advance (though not too long in advance or the pastry will be sodden), so that they are ready to pop into the oven when needed.

SERVES 2 AS A MAIN COURSE
  OR 4 AS A STARTER
1/2 onion, finely chopped
1 garlic clove, finely chopped
1 tablespoon olive oil or 15 g (1/2 oz)
  butter
100g (4 oz) mushrooms, finely chopped

1 tablespoon finely chopped parsley
A dash of lemon juice
Salt and freshly ground black pepper
4 lambs' kidneys
225 g (8 oz) puff pastry
1 egg, beaten

Fry the onion and garlic gently in the olive oil or butter without browning until tender. Add the mushrooms, parsley, lemon juice, salt and pepper. Continue cooking, stirring constantly, until virtually all the liquid has evaporated and the mixture is thick, dark and moist. Taste and adjust the seasonings, then leave to cool.

Pre-heat the oven to 230°C/450°F/Gas Mark 8.

Split the kidneys in half. Sandwich the halves back together with a thick layer of the mushroom mixture in between. Season with salt and pepper.

Roll out the pastry very thinly and divide into four. Wrap each kidney in a quarter of the puff pastry and lay on a baking sheet, neatly tucking the joins underneath. Rest in the fridge for 15 minutes. Brush with beaten egg, then bake in the oven for 10 minutes until puffed and golden. Turn the heat down to 190°C/375°F/Gas Mark 5 and cook for a further 15 minutes. Serve immediately.

Hearts Braised with Red Wine and Rosemary

This is a rich stew of hearts and carrots in red wine. Use either pigs' or lambs' hearts – lambs' hearts have a slightly more refined flavour but there's not a massive difference as there is, say, between calf's and pig's liver.

SERVES 4–6

4 pigs' hearts or 5 lambs' hearts
About 2 tablespoons olive oil
2 onions, thinly sliced
3 garlic cloves, chopped
450 g (1 lb) carrots, thickly sliced
1 bouquet garni (1 bay leaf, 2 sprigs rosemary and 2 sprigs parsley, tied together with string)

450 ml (15 fl oz) red wine
2 tablespoons red wine vinegar
300 ml (10 fl oz) hot water or light stock
Salt and freshly ground black pepper

TO SERVE
Finely grated zest of 1 lemon
1 tablespoon finely chopped parsley

Pre-heat the oven to 180°C/350°F/Gas Mark 4. Trim the hearts, snipping away fat and tubes with kitchen scissors. Rinse thoroughly, but leave whole. Heat 2 tablespoons of oil in a frying-pan and brown the hearts. Place in a casserole. Fry the onions in the same oil, adding a little more if needed, until lightly browned. Add the garlic and cook gently for another couple of minutes. Spoon into the casserole and tuck in the carrots. Add the bouquet garni to the casserole.

Pour the wine into the frying-pan and bring to the boil, scraping in the brown gloop from the bottom of the pan. Pour over the hearts and add the vinegar and hot water or stock. Season well. Cover, transfer to the oven and cook for 2–2¹/₂ hours, or until the hearts are tender. Mix together the lemon zest and chopped parsley.

To serve, lift out and slice the hearts. Arrange in a dish with the carrots and onions and pour over the sauce. Sprinkle with the lemon and parsley.

Oxtail Stew

Oxtail makes a brilliant, sticky stew but all too often it is forgotten and ignored. A shame, as it is far more economical than cubes of expensive beef. Don't think of the heavy weight of the bones as wasteful, either. They are what yield up that special velvety texture which is the hallmark of an oxtail stew.

The seasonings for this oxtail stew are similar to those used in a French daube, an aromatic collection of orange zest, spices, herbs and a generous slurp of red wine. The stew positively benefits from being cooked in advance and re-heated thoroughly 24 hours later. Lift congealed fat off the surface first.

SERVES 4–6

2 oxtails weighing about 1.5 kg (3 lb) in total, jointed
Seasoned flour, for dusting
3 tablespoons olive oil
2 onions, sliced
3 garlic cloves, sliced
450 g (1 lb) carrots, peeled and thickly sliced
4 wide strips orange zest, dried or fresh
5 cm (2 in) cinnamon stick
3 cloves
1/2 bottle red wine
2 sprigs thyme
2 bay leaves
1 sprig rosemary
Salt and freshly ground black pepper

Coat the oxtail in seasoned flour and brown in the oil in a flame-proof casserole over a high heat. Lift out the oxtail and set aside. Reduce the heat and add the onions and garlic, and extra oil if needed. Fry gently, without browning, until the onions are tender.

Return the oxtail to the pan with all the remaining ingredients and enough water to cover. Bring to the boil, skim the scum from the surface, then cover and simmer for 3 hours. Uncover and continue simmering for a further 1–2 hours, stirring occasionally, until the meat falls easily from the bone and the sauce has thickened. Alternatively, the stew can be cooked in the oven, set to 150°C/300°F/Gas Mark 2. Adjust the heat so that it simmers happily.

Skim the fat from the surface, then taste and adjust the seasoning. Serve with potatoes or noodles.

Tongue with Raisin and Almond Sauce

Tongue is easy to cook, though it does require a few hours' steady simmering. This can be done up to 24 hours in advance (once skinned, let it cool, then keep covered with foil in the fridge), so that all you need do on the day is re-heat it and make the sauce. If you haven't got a full complement of eight to feed, don't dismiss the idea out of hand. Left-over tongue is good cold, especially in sandwiches with a fruity chutney, or made into a gratin.

This sauce is a Germanic one, sweet and sharp, just the thing to bring out the full flavour of the tongue. It does no harm to make it an hour or two in advance and re-heat it.

SERVES 8

1 whole cured ox tongue
1 celery stick, quartered
1 carrot, quartered
1 onion, quartered
1 bouquet garni (1 bayleaf, 2 sprigs of parsley and 2 sprigs of thyme, tied together with string)
6 peppercorns

FOR THE SAUCE
25 g (1 oz) butter
2 level tablespoons flour

300 ml (10 fl oz) red wine
300 ml (10 fl oz) light chicken or ham stock
5 tablespoons red wine vinegar
50 g (2 oz) caster sugar
75 g (3 oz) raisins, soaked and drained
50 g (2 oz) currants, soaked and drained
Zest of 1/2 lemon, shredded
1 cinnamon stick
50 g (2 oz) slivered almonds
Salt and freshly ground black pepper

Put the tongue into a large pan and tuck the vegetables around it with the bouquet garni and peppercorns. Add enough water to cover, bring to the boil and simmer for 3–4 hours. Test with a skewer to see if it is tender. Take the tongue out of the pan, trim off the skin (which will look rather revolting by now) and any odd bits of bone and gristle at the thicker end. If not serving immediately, cool and wrap loosely in foil.

To re-heat the tongue, pop into a pan of boiling water and leave to simmer for another 30 minutes or so. Drain, slice and serve hot with the sauce.

To make the sauce, melt the butter and stir in the flour. Cook over a gentle heat, stirring, until the roux is light brown with a nutty smell. Gradually mix in the wine and then the stock and vinegar. Add the sugar and stir to dissolve. Add all the remaining ingredients, bring to the boil and simmer for 20 minutes until reduced to a good consistency. Taste and adjust the seasoning. Re-heat when needed and serve with the tongue.

Black Pudding with Apple and Mashed Potatoes

This is not so much a recipe as an idea. The French often serve black pudding with fried apple slices, mashed potato and, of course, lots of French mustard, which is milder than our own. You could grill the black pudding if you wish or replace the mash with, perhaps, hot lentils or fashionable polenta. The caramelized apple slices, though, are a stroke of genius and I wouldn't change them for the world.

SERVES 4

FOR THE POTATOES
900 g (2 lb) potatoes
50–75 g (2–3 oz) butter
Salt
A little full cream milk

FOR THE BLACK PUDDING
25 g (1 oz) butter
1 tablespoon sunflower or vegetable
oil
12 slices black pudding
2 eating apples, cored and cut into
eighths

TO SERVE
A little chopped parsley

Make the mashed potatoes in the usual way; boil the potatoes in their skins (or better still, bake them if you have the time). Peel and mash in the pan while still warm. Beat in the butter and salt. Place the pan over a medium heat and start to add milk, trickling it down the side of the pan and beating it in energetically with a big spoon. Keep going until the potatoes are light and fluffy and about as thick as you like them. I prefer my mash fairly soft and verging on sloppy, but you may well prefer something a little sturdier. Taste and adjust the seasoning. Re-heat when needed and spoon into a serving dish.

Shortly before sitting down to eat, heat half the butter and half the oil in a frying-pan over a high heat until the foaming subsides. Fry the black pudding slices on both sides. Transfer to a dish lined with kitchen paper. Add the remaining butter and oil to the pan and fry the apple slices briskly, until browned. Drain briefly on kitchen paper, then arrange the apple and black pudding over the mashed potatoes. Sprinkle with a little chopped parsley and serve.

Meat-free

VEGETARIAN

Gnocchi with Sage

This has to be my favourite sage recipe of all time. Gnocchi alla Romana are made with semolina, not potato, and are verging on the addictive. They are enriched with Parmesan and then drenched in sage-scented butter and more Parmesan. A wicked and wonderful main course, best served with simple accompaniments – a tomato and olive salad, perhaps, and/or a rocket-laden green salad.

SERVES 4

FOR THE GNOCCHI
570 ml (1 pint) milk
175 g (6 oz) semolina
60 g (2 oz) freshly grated Parmesan
2 eggs, beaten
Salt and freshly ground black pepper

FOR THE SAGE BUTTER
60 g (2 oz) butter
8 fresh sage leaves
2 garlic cloves, chopped
45 g (1^1/$_2$ oz) freshly grated Parmesan
Freshly ground black pepper

Bring the milk to the boil and pour in the semolina in a steady stream. Stir constantly with a wooden spoon, until the mixture is so thick that you can stand the spoon up in it. Draw off the heat and beat in the Parmesan and then the eggs and salt and plenty of pepper. Spread the mixture out in a shallow buttered dish to form a layer about 5 mm (1/4 in) thick. Leave to cool.

Pre-heat the oven to 200°C/400°F/Gas Mark 6. Cut the cooled semolina mixture into diamonds, with sides around 4 cm (1^1/2 in) long. Arrange in overlapping rows in an ovenproof dish. Melt the butter over a low heat and add the sage and garlic. Let it infuse gently for about 5 minutes and then pour over the gnocchi. Sprinkle with Parmesan and pepper and bake for about 20–30 minutes, until browned and sizzling.

Serve up and warn greedy guts to hold back for a few minutes. I've burnt my tongue many a time on this, so eager have I been to dig in.

Rocket, Saffron and Fresh Tomato Risotto

A beautiful risotto, with its fresh reds and greens and soft yellow, creamy sauce. It tastes lovely, too, with the barely cooked tomato and rocket balancing the richness of the rice.

SERVES 4–6

1.2 litres (2 pints) vegetable or chicken
   stock
A generous pinch of saffron strands
1 bouquet garni (1 bay leaf, 1 sprig
   thyme and 1 sprig rosemary, tied
   together with string)
3 shallots, finely chopped
3 garlic cloves, finely chopped
85 g (3 oz) butter

300 g (10 oz) risotto rice, e.g. arborio,
   carnaroli or vialone nano
675 g (1 lb 7 oz) fresh tomatoes,
   skinned, seeded and diced
Salt and freshly ground black pepper
1 good glass (about 200 ml/7 fl oz) dry
   white wine
60 g (2 oz) rocket, roughly shredded
60 g (2 oz) freshly grated Parmesan,
   plus extra to serve

Bring the stock to the boil and then reduce the heat to very low, so that it stays hot but doesn't boil away. Put the saffron in a small bowl and spoon in 2 tablespoons of the hot stock. Set aside until needed.

Cook the shallots and garlic gently in half the butter in a wide, deep pan, without letting it brown. When they are translucent, add the rice and the bouquet garni to the pan and stir for about a minute, until the rice becomes translucent. Add one-third of the tomatoes, salt and pepper and the glass of wine. Simmer, stirring constantly, until the liquid has all been absorbed. Add a generous ladleful of the hot stock. Stir again until the liquid has all been absorbed. Continue in this way until the rice is just tender but still has a slight resistance and is moistened with a creamy sauce. Now stir in the saffron and continue stirring for about a minute. Stir in the rocket and remaining tomatoes, stir again and then draw off the heat. Stir in the remaining butter and the Parmesan. Taste and adjust the seasoning and serve immediately.

Beetroot Gratin

This gratin brings out the very best in beetroot, with its mild hint of horseradish, smooth sauce and crisp crumbs. Serve it with ham, gammon or lamb, or maybe just on its own.

SERVES 4

FOR THE SAUCE
30 g (1 oz) butter
30 g (1 oz) plain flour
300 ml (10 fl oz) milk
4 tablespoons crème fraîche
1½ tablespoons creamed horseradish
Lemon juice
Salt and freshly ground black pepper

FOR THE BEETROOT
4 medium-sized beetroot, weighing
   about 650 g (1 lb 6 oz) in total, boiled
   whole until tender, peeled and
   sliced
4 tablespoons fine, stale breadcrumbs
1 tablespoon freshly grated Parmesan
20 g (3/4 oz) butter

Pre-heat the oven to 200°C/400°F/Gas Mark 6. To make the sauce, melt the butter in a pan and stir in the flour. Stir over a low heat for a minute. Draw off the heat and gradually stir in the milk. Bring back to the boil, stirring constantly, and then leave to simmer for 5 minutes, until fairly thick. Stir in the crème fraîche and the horseradish, followed by a squeeze or two of lemon juice. Season to taste with salt and pepper.

Arrange one-third of the beetroot in a layer in a 30 cm (12 in), lightly greased gratin dish. Spoon over about one-quarter of the sauce. Repeat the layers twice more, using up all the sauce on the last one. Mix the breadcrumbs and Parmesan together and scatter them evenly over the top. Dot with butter. Bake for 25–30 minutes, until golden brown. Serve immediately, or at least while still warm.

Parsnip, Carrot and Cauliflower Korma

This is a mild but warmly spiced curry, thickened with yoghurt and ground almonds. I usually make it with a mixture of parsnip, carrot and cauliflower, three different flavours and textures. Of course, you can adapt it to practically whatever vegetables you have to hand, as long as you add those that take less time to cook 5 or 10 minutes or so after the slow-cooking root vegetables.

Serve with rice, of course, and several relishes: mango chutney, sour lime pickles, and the Indian Raw Onion Chutney on p. 365.

SERVES 4
275 g (10 oz) parsnips
350 g (12 oz) carrots
1 medium onion, finely chopped
4 tablespoons sunflower oil
1 tablespoon ground cumin
2 teaspoons ground coriander
1 teaspoon ground cinnamon
1 teaspoon turmeric
2 cloves of garlic, peeled and very
   finely chopped
2.5 cm (1 in) piece fresh ginger, peeled
   and very finely chopped

1 fresh green chilli, seeded and very
   finely chopped
300 ml (10 fl oz) Greek-style yoghurt
40 g (1¹/₂ oz) ground almonds
Salt
275 g (10 oz) small cauliflower florets

TO GARNISH
Finely chopped fresh coriander or
   parsley

Peel the parsnips and carrots if necessary, and cut in 1 cm (¹/₂ in) slices. If they are large then cube them.

In a saucepan large enough to take all the ingredients fry the onion in the oil until golden brown. Stir in all the dry spices and when well mixed add the garlic, ginger and chilli. Stir gently for 1 minute. Stir in the yoghurt, a tablespoonful at a time, and then add the almonds. Cook, stirring, for 2 more minutes.

Stir in 300 ml (10 fl oz) of water and some salt, then add the parsnips, carrots and cauliflower. Cover and simmer gently for 20–25 minutes until the vegetables are almost done, stirring occasionally. Uncover and simmer for a final 5 minutes or so. Taste and adjust the seasonings. Sprinkle with coriander or parsley before serving.

Baked Mushrooms with Broad Bean Purée

What is so enjoyable about this combination is the contrast of the rich mealiness of the purée against the smoothness of the baked mushrooms. If it makes life easier, the mushrooms can be grilled instead. The purée is made with Italian Mascarpone cheese – so outrageously calorie-laden that I'd advise you not to scan the label too closely. Still, once in a while …

SERVES 4 AS A MAIN COURSE

FOR THE BROAD BEAN PURÉE
450 g (1 lb) shelled broad beans
100 g (4 oz) Mascarpone cheese
Squeeze of lemon juice
Salt and freshly ground black pepper
Leaves of 2 sprigs of fresh winter
  savory or fresh thyme

FOR THE MUSHROOMS
4 large flat cap mushrooms
Olive oil for brushing

TO SERVE
Cayenne pepper

Drop the broad beans into a pan of boiling water. Simmer for 2 minutes, then drain and run the beans under the cold tap. Using a sharp knife, slit the tough outer skin and squeeze out the tender beanlets inside. Discard the skins.

Simmer the skinned beans in salted water until tender – a matter of a couple of minutes. Drain well. Process or liquidize with the Mascarpone and a squeeze of lemon juice. Season with salt and pepper and stir in the savory or thyme. Spoon into a saucepan, ready to be warmed through when needed.

Pre-heat the oven to 190°C/375°F/Gas Mark 5. Brush the mushrooms with olive oil. Place on a baking sheet, and bake for 20–30 minutes until tender. When they are almost done, re-heat the broad bean purée. Taste and adjust the seasonings. Place mushrooms on a dish, and spoon purée on top of them. Dust lightly with cayenne, and serve.

Courgettes Stuffed with Sweetcorn

I came across this recipe in a book called The Cuisines of Mexico *(Harper & Row) by the American food writer, Diana Kennedy, who probably knows more about Mexican cooking than any other non-Mexican. I tried it out, substituting Lancashire cheese for Mexican* queso fresco, *because it seemed like it would be a good way to use up large courgettes which might otherwise be a touch on the dull side. And so it is … turning them into a really stunning dish, far better than you might expect from the simple list of ingredients.*

If you serve the stuffed courgettes as a main course, make a slightly chillied tomato sauce to accompany it (fry a chopped, seeded chilli or even two, with the onion in the Basic Tomato Sauce on p. 353).

SERVES 6 AS A FIRST COURSE, 4 AS A MAIN COURSE

6 plump courgettes, about 750 g (1 lb 8 oz) in weight
Salt and freshly ground black pepper
275 g (10 oz) sweetcorn kernels, thawed if frozen
2 eggs
2 tablespoons milk
175 g (8 oz) Lancashire cheese, crumbled
25 g (1 oz) butter

Cut the courgettes in half lengthwise. Using an apple corer or a sharp-edged teaspoon, scoop out enough of the inner flesh to give a canoe-shaped courgette container, with walls about 1 cm (1/2 in) thick. Either save the pulp for another dish, perhaps a soup, or throw it away. Sprinkle the insides of the courgettes lightly with salt and turn upside-down on a wire rack to drain.

Put the corn, eggs, milk and a little salt in a food processor and blend to a knobbly purée. Stir in 100 g (4 oz) of the crumbled cheese and season generously with pepper.

Pre-heat the oven to 180°C/350°F/Gas Mark 5. Wipe the courgettes dry and set in an oiled ovenproof dish. Fill with the corn mixture. Sprinkle over the remaining cheese and dot with butter. Cover with foil and bake for 30 minutes. Uncover and bake for a further 15–20 minutes until the courgettes are tender and the top lightly browned. Serve hot.

Summer Vegetable Terrine

Spinach works well as a wrapping for terrines of all kinds, but is particularly appropriate for this light, fresh summer terrine of fennel, asparagus and courgettes set in a jellied tomato sauce. Allow plenty of time for making it – the layers have to be built up and left to set individually. Be patient. It's worth it in the end.

SERVES 8 AS A FIRST COURSE
175 g (6 oz) thin asparagus
1 large fennel bulb
175 g (6 oz) small courgettes
1 onion, chopped
3 cloves garlic, peeled and chopped
1 1/2 tablespoons olive oil
1 litre (1 3/4 pints) passata or liquidized
    canned tomatoes

175 ml (6 fl oz) dry white wine
1 teaspoon dried oregano
Salt and freshly ground black pepper
12 large fresh basil leaves, roughly
    torn up
2 sachets powdered gelatine
340 g (12 oz) fresh large-leafed spinach

Trim the asparagus. Slice off the base and stalks of the fennel and cut into thin wedges. Halve or quarter the courgettes lengthwise. Steam or simmer the asparagus, fennel and courgettes separately until tender. Drain, cool and cover until needed.

Fry the onion and garlic gently in the olive oil until tender. Add the passata or liquidized tomatoes, wine, oregano, salt and pepper and simmer for 10 minutes. Add the basil then liquidize and sieve. Adjust seasonings. Sprinkle the gelatine evenly over 6 tablespoons of hot water in a small saucepan and leave for 3 minutes. Warm gently, without boiling, stirring until the gelatine has dissolved. Draw off the heat and stir in 3 tablespoons of the warm tomato sauce. If any lumps form return to the heat for a few seconds. Mix into the remaining sauce.

Trim the stalks from the spinach, and drop into a large saucepan of boiling water. Bring back to the boil, drain and spread out on kitchen paper to dry. Line a 1.75 litre (3 pint) long loaf tin with clingfilm and brush with oil. Line with spinach leaves, letting them flap over the top. Spoon in a quarter of the sauce, arrange the fennel on top. Chill, loosely covered, until just set. Repeat the layers using asparagus, then courgettes, chilling each time to let the sauce set, then cover with the remaining sauce. Flip over the trailing spinach leaves to cover, and chill until set. To serve, turn out, peel off the clingfilm, and slice thickly with a sharp knife.

Baked Onions with Goats' Cheese

These baked onions, sweet and tender, filled with goats' cheese and olives, could be served as a side dish to a simple main course, but they are good enough to stand on their own as a first course, or as part of a buffet. They can be eaten hot or cold. I think that they are marginally better hot, but I wouldn't argue the cause too vehemently.

SERVES 4
4 largish onions
100 g (4 oz) young fresh goats' cheese
1 egg
8 black olives, pitted and chopped

1/2 teaspoon fresh thyme leaves or
    1/4 teaspoon dried
2 tablespoons chopped fresh parsley
Salt and freshly ground black pepper
2 tablespoons olive oil

Peel the onions and cook whole in salted boiling water for 15 minutes. Drain and run under the cold tap. Carefully ease out the centre of the onions, leaving a sturdy shell. Sit the onion shells in an oiled heatproof dish.

Pre-heat the oven to 200°C/400°F/Gas Mark 6. Chop the onion hearts finely, mix with the goats' cheese, and all the remaining ingredients except the oil. Fill the onion shells with the mixture. Drizzle over the olive oil, and bake for 30 minutes. Eat hot or cold.

Tomato and Pepper Summer Pudding

Made in much the same way as a sweet summer pudding, this savoury version filled with tomatoes and peppers is a perfect dish for a lazy summer lunch. The 'pudding' has to be made at least 12 hours, preferably 24 hours, in advance. It looks pretty too, a glowing red mound decorated with fresh green herbs.

**SERVES 4 AS A MAIN COURSE,
6–8 AS A FIRST COURSE**

FOR THE FILLING
2 onions, chopped
2 cloves garlic, peeled and chopped
1 red pepper, seeded and cut into
    strips
1 green pepper, seeded and cut into
    strips
3 tablespoons olive oil
2 × 400 g (14 oz) cans tomatoes or 1 kg
    (2 lb) fresh tomatoes, skinned and
    roughly chopped

2 tablespoons tomato purée
3 sprigs of fresh thyme or 1 teaspoon
    dried
1 tablespoon red wine vinegar
2 teaspoons salt
Salt and freshly ground black pepper

FOR THE PUDDING
6–10 thin slices slightly stale white
    bread, crusts removed

TO GARNISH
Fresh herbs (parsley and basil)

Make the filling first. Cook the onions, garlic and peppers gently in the oil until tender. Add all the remaining ingredients and simmer until fairly thick. Taste and adjust seasoning. Remove the thyme sprigs.

Line a 900 ml–1.2 litre (1½–2 pint) pudding basin with the bread, trimming it so that it fits in snugly with no gaps but no overlaps either. Fill with the tomato and pepper mixture and cover with bread trimmed to fit. Lay a plate or large saucer on top and weigh down with cans or metal weights. Leave overnight in the fridge.

Just before serving remove weight and plate, and cover the pudding with a shallow serving dish. Invert, give it a firm shake and the pudding should slip nicely out onto the plate. Garnish with the fresh herbs and serve.

Aubergine Baked with Pesto and Mozzarella

This dish of aubergine layered with mozzarella and pesto and baked in the oven makes a good main course or a rich side dish, accompanying plainly barbecued meat. It tastes best if you whizz up your own pesto, but you can always use bought pesto.

SERVES 6–8

2 large aubergines, sliced about 1 cm (¹/₂ in) thick
Salt
Olive oil

FOR THE TOMATO SAUCE
675 g (1 lb 8 oz) ripest red tomatoes
2 garlic cloves, chopped
2 tablespoons olive oil

Fresh thyme sprig
Salt and freshly ground black pepper
Sugar (optional)

TO FINISH
5–6 tablespoons Pesto (see p. 361)
2 × 140 g (5 oz) mozzarella cheeses, diced
60 g (2 oz) Parmesan, freshly grated
Freshly ground black pepper

Pre-heat the oven to 190°C/375°F/Gas Mark 5. Lay the slices of aubergine out and sprinkle with salt. Leave for half an hour or so to degorge their juices.

Wipe the aubergine slices clean and lay on oiled baking sheets. Brush lightly with olive oil. Bake in the oven for about 20 minutes, until golden brown and tender.

Meanwhile, make the tomato sauce. Cover the tomatoes with boiling water, leave for a minute and then drain and skin. Seed and chop roughly. Put the garlic and olive oil into a frying-pan and heat over a moderate heat, until the garlic begins to sizzle and colour. Now add the tomatoes and thyme, and boil fiercely for 5–10 minutes, until the tomatoes have collapsed and the sauce is fairly thick. Season to taste with salt, pepper and a little sugar if it is on the sharp side. Discard the thyme stalk.

Down to the final stage. Oil a 30 cm (12 in) gratin dish and make a bed of about one-third of the aubergine slices in it. Smear with half the pesto, add a thin coat of tomato sauce and then scatter with half the diced mozzarella. Season with pepper. Repeat the layers once more. Now finish with the last of the aubergine, and cover with the last of the tomato sauce. Sprinkle with Parmesan and drizzle over a little oil. Bake for 30–40 minutes, until browned and bubbling. Serve hot or warm.

Grilled Aubergine and Red Pepper Tart with Goats' Cheese

A very trendy type of quiche, if that is still possible, and very, very good, even if it isn't. Grilling the vegetables imbues this tart with an unusual smoky flavour, while Greek yoghurt is rich enough to give a silky-soft texture to the filling.

SERVES 6–8

340 g (12 oz) shortcrust pastry
(see p. 344)

FOR THE FILLING
3 large garlic cloves
1 large aubergine
2 large red peppers
240 ml (8¹/₂ fl oz) Greek yoghurt

2 egg yolks
1 egg
Salt and freshly ground black pepper
85 g (3 oz) goats' cheese, rinded and
thinly sliced
1 teaspoon finely chopped fresh
rosemary leaves

Line a 28 cm (11¹/₂ in) tart tin with the pastry and prick it all over with a fork. Rest it in the fridge for at least half an hour. Pre-heat the oven to 190°C/375°F/Gas Mark 5.

Line the pastry case with greaseproof paper or foil, weigh the paper or foil down with baking beans and bake blind for 10 minutes. Remove the beans and paper or foil and return the pastry case to the oven for 5–10 minutes, to dry out without browning. Leave the pastry case to cool and turn the oven down to 180°C/350°F/Gas Mark 4.

Pre-heat the grill to hot. Thread the unpeeled cloves of garlic on to a skewer, to prevent them from falling through the bars. Grill the garlic, the whole aubergine and whole red peppers close to the heat, turning occasionally, until all are thoroughly charred. The garlic will be ready first and should feel soft to the touch. Remove from the skewer, leave to cool for a few minutes and then peel. The aubergine, too, will feel soft and squishy when it's ready. Drop into a plastic bag and leave until cool enough to handle. Then strip off the skin, cut the flesh up roughly and leave it to drain in a colander. Drop the peppers into a plastic bag and leave until cool enough to handle. Strip off the skins and cut the flesh into strips.

Press the aubergine gently, to expel excess moisture, and then drop into a food processor, with the peeled garlic and a couple of spoonfuls of the yoghurt. Whizz until smooth and then add the remaining yoghurt, egg yolks and egg and salt and pepper. Process again briefly, to mix. Spread half the mixture on the base of the pastry case. Cover with the strips of red pepper and then smooth over the rest of the aubergine mixture. Arrange the cheese on top and scatter with rosemary. Bake for 25–30 minutes, until just set. Serve warm or cold.

Pear, Stilton and Walnut Strudel

A savoury twist on a fruity pudding. Adding Stilton, salt and pepper to this strudel turns it into a substantial main course for a vegetarian meal.

Try to get large sheets of filo pastry – the exact dimensions vary considerably but they should be around 45 × 20 cm (18 × 12 in).

SERVES 6–8

FOR THE FILLING

700 g (1 lb 8 oz) ripe pears, peeled, cored and diced

Juice of $1/2$ lemon

140 g (5 oz) Stilton, de-rinded and crumbled

75 g ($2^1/2$ oz) walnuts, toasted and roughly chopped

Salt and freshly ground black pepper

FOR THE STRUDEL

6 sheets of filo pastry

90 g (3 oz) butter, melted and cooled until tepid

2 tablespoons dry breadcrumbs or semolina

1–2 tablespoons poppy seeds

TO SERVE

A bunch of watercress

Pre-heat the oven to 190°C/375°F/Gas Mark 5. As you prepare the pears for the filling, turn them in the lemon juice in a large bowl, to prevent them from browning. Add all the remaining filling ingredients, and mix lightly.

To prevent the filo pastry from drying out, cover it with a sheet of greaseproof paper and cover that with a tea-towel wrung out in cold water. Lay a large sheet of greaseproof paper on the work surface. Take the first sheet of filo and lay it out flat in front of you on the greaseproof paper. Brush with melted butter. Take the next sheet and lay it out flat, overlapping the first along one of the long edges by about 7.5 cm (3 in). Brush with butter. Lay the third sheet exactly over the first and then brush it with butter, the fourth over the second and so on until all the pastry is used up. You should end up with a large rectangle, about 45 × 52 cm (18 × 21 in).

Sprinkle the dry breadcrumbs or semolina over the half of the filo pastry nearest you, in a band that runs parallel to the central overlap, leaving a 5 cm (2 in) border around the edges. Pile the filling evenly over the breadcrumbs or semolina. Flip the bare edge nearest to you over the filling. Roll up the pastry round the filling, using the greaseproof paper to help you and making sure that the sides stay neatly tucked in. Carefully lift on to a greased baking tray and curve round gently to fit. Brush the top with the remaining butter and sprinkle with poppy seeds.

Bake for 40–50 minutes, until browned and crisp. Poke a skewer into the centre of the strudel, to make sure the pear is tender. Loosen with a knife and then slide carefully on to a serving dish. Serve hot, with the watercress tucked in around it.

Asparagus and Gruyère Quiche

This is a quiche to make at the height of the asparagus season when you've feasted your fill of plainly cooked asparagus – a good way of stretching a small quantity.

SERVES 6–8
350 g (12 oz) shortcrust pastry
  (see p. 344)

FOR THE FILLING
305 g (12 oz) asparagus
100 g (4 oz) Gruyère cheese
3 shallots or 1 small onion, chopped
15 g (1/2 oz) butter

3 eggs
150 ml (5 fl oz) milk
85 ml (3 fl oz) double cream
1 tablespoon chopped fresh chervil or
  fresh parsley
Salt and freshly ground black pepper

Pre-heat the oven to 200°C/400°F/Gas Mark 6. Line a 23 cm (9 in) tart tin with the pastry. Leave it to rest in the fridge for 30 minutes. Prick the base with a fork and line with greaseproof paper or foil and weigh down with baking beans. Bake for 10 minutes. Remove paper or foil and beans and return to the oven for 5 minutes to dry out. Leave to cool.

Trim the asparagus, breaking off the tough ends (save these and the cooking water for making soup). Cut into 2 cm (3/4 in) lengths, keeping the tips separate. Pour 4 cm (1 1/2 in) of water into a large saucepan, add salt, and bring to the boil. Add the stem pieces and simmer for 5 minutes. Add tips and simmer gently for 2–3 minutes, until almost *al dente*, but still firm. Drain. If prepared in advance, cool and cover.

Dice 75 g (3 oz) of the Gruyère and grate the remaining 25 g (1 oz). Fry the shallots or onion gently in the butter until tender, without browning. Scatter the asparagus, diced Gruyère and shallots over the base of the pastry case.

Whisk the eggs lightly, then whisk in the milk, cream, chervil or parsley and salt and pepper. Pour over the asparagus and Gruyère. Scatter the remaining Gruyère over the top. Bake at 180°C/350°F/Gas Mark 4 for 25–30 minutes, until just set in the centre and nicely browned. Serve hot, warm or cold.

Pea, Ricotta and Herb Quiche

This is an enchantingly pretty, country-ish quiche, with a puffed yeast dough crust, filled with herb-flecked ricotta and peas. I think that the yeast pastry is what makes it extra special, but if you are pushed for time, line the tart tin with shortcrust pastry (see p. 342) and bake blind before filling. Use a mixture of at least three sweet, fresh herbs, such as parsley, chives, chervil, basil or marjoram. Thyme, lovage or salad burnet are good too, but use in comparatively small quantities as they are strongly flavoured. Like most quiches, this one tastes nicest when served warm.

SERVES 6–8

FOR THE PASTRY
200 g (7 oz) strong white bread flour
Salt
1/2 packet easybake or easyblend
   dried yeast
1 egg
3 tablespoons olive oil

FOR THE FILLING
225 g (8 oz) ricotta

2 eggs
200 ml (7 fl oz) milk
4 tablespoons freshly grated Parmesan
   cheese
4 spring onions, thinly sliced
3 tablespoons chopped mixed sweet
   fresh herbs (e.g. parsley, chives,
   chervil, basil, marjoram, oregano,
   thyme, lovage, salad burnet)
Salt and freshly ground black pepper
350 g (12 oz) cooked peas

To make the pastry, sift the flour with the salt. Stir in the yeast. Make a well in the centre and break in the egg. Add the oil. Gradually work into the flour, adding enough water to form a soft dough. (Use a food processor for maximum speed and ease.) Gather the dough up into a ball, knead for 5–10 minutes until smooth and elastic, set in a clean bowl, cover and leave to rise in a warm place until it has doubled in bulk.

While it rises, prepare the filling. Beat the ricotta with the eggs, and gradually mix in the milk. Stir in 3 tablespoons of the Parmesan, and all the spring onions, herbs, salt and pepper.

Place an upturned metal baking sheet in the oven, and heat to 190°C/375°F/Gas Mark 5. Punch down the dough and knead again briefly. Using the heel of your hand, press the dough into an oiled 25 cm (10 in) tart tin, easing the dough to cover the base and come up around the sides. The dough should be thickest around the sides, rising up a little above the rim of the tin.

Scatter the peas evenly over the dough. Stir the ricotta custard and pour over the peas. Sprinkle the remaining tablespoon of Parmesan over the surface. Set on the hot baking sheet in the oven (which gives the base of the tart an instant blast of heat) and bake for 30–35 minutes until barely set and golden. Serve hot, warm or cold.

Frittata con Ricotta e Basilico

A mild, ricotta 'omelette', flavoured with Parmesan and basil and served with a brassy, uncooked tomato sauce.

SERVES 4

FOR THE SAUCE
500 g (1 lb 2 oz) best, ripest tomatoes,
   skinned, seeded and finely diced
1–2 tablespoons balsamic vinegar
1/2 red onion, very finely diced
4 tablespoons olive oil
1–2 garlic cloves, crushed
Salt, freshly ground black pepper
   and sugar

FOR THE FRITTATA
350 g (12 oz) ricotta
6 eggs
5 tablespoons freshly grated Parmesan
A small handful of fresh basil leaves,
   roughly torn up
2 tablespoons finely chopped fresh
   parsley
Salt and freshly ground black pepper
1 tablespoon olive oil

Make the sauce first. Mix all the ingredients, cover and leave for at least an hour before using. Taste and adjust the seasoning, adding a pinch of sugar if needed.

Beat the ricotta with the eggs and then beat in the Parmesan, basil, parsley, salt and a generous dose of black pepper.

Heat the oil in a 25 cm (10 in) frying-pan over a moderate heat. Add the ricotta mixture. Fry until the eggs are just set underneath and the omelette comes away freely from the base of the pan. As it cooks, push the set egg up with a spatula, so that the runny mixture can trickle down to the bottom. When the frittata is just set, run the spatula or a knife around the edge to loosen it and then invert it on to a plate. Return the pan to the heat, and slide the frittata back into it, uncooked side down. Give it a minute or two to colour and then slide the whole thing out on to a serving plate. Cut into wedges and serve piping hot, with the cool tomato sauce.

Cauliflower and Tomato Crumble

This recipe transforms cauliflower into a more substantial offering, with a savoury crumble topping that browns appetizingly in the heat of the oven. For a wetter dish, moisten the cauliflower in a béchamel sauce or tomato sauce before covering with the crumble mixture. Serve as a main or first course.

SERVES 4–6
1 head of cauliflower, broken into florets
4 tomatoes, sliced
1 teaspoon fresh thyme leaves or
   1/2 teaspoon dried
Salt and freshly ground black pepper
25 g (1 oz) butter

FOR THE CRUMBLE
100 g (4 oz) plain flour
50 g (2 oz) rolled oats
50 g (2 oz) Cheddar cheese, grated
Salt and freshly ground black pepper
100 g (4 oz) butter

Cook the cauliflower in salted, boiling water, or steam, until almost tender. Pack tightly in a lightly buttered, heatproof dish. Cover with tomato slices. Sprinkle with thyme leaves, salt and pepper, then dot with the butter.

Pre-heat the oven to 200°C/400°F/Gas Mark 6.

To make the crumble, mix the flour, oats, grated cheese, salt and pepper together in a bowl. Melt the butter and stir enough of it into the mixture with a palette knife to make a crumbly mixture. Cool slightly then scatter over the vegetables in a thick layer. Bake for about 30 minutes until the crumble is golden brown and crisp. Serve immediately.

Pisto

Julian and Robert Diment-Castillo's mother is Spanish and runs three of the best tapas bars in London. Every summer the family heads off to their home near Valencia, bringing back ample supplies of local olive oil when they return. Julian has always been a keen cook, though when I first met him, when he and his brother were both studying at Bristol University, he was restricted by the lack of funds typical of students everywhere. He loves making Spanish food and this dish is one that he turns to often. It's quick and easy to prepare and, what's more, tastes delicious. The traditional way of eating it is to place the dish in the middle of the table and let everyone dig in, using plenty of good bread to mop the dish clean.

**SERVES 4 AS A FIRST COURSE,
2 AS A MAIN COURSE**
3 tablespoons olive oil
1 onion, roughly chopped
**2 cloves garlic, peeled and
chopped**
**1 red pepper, seeded and cut roughly
into 2.5 cm (1 in) squares**
**1 green pepper, seeded and cut
roughly into 2.5 cm (1 in) squares**

**1 yellow pepper (or a second red one),
seeded and cut roughly into
2.5 cm (1 in) squares**
400 g (14 oz) can tomatoes
**1/2 teaspoon dried mixed herbs or
1 tablespoon chopped fresh parsley**
Salt and freshly ground black pepper
1 egg per person

Pre-heat the oven to 190°C/375°F/Gas Mark 5.

Warm the oil in a frying-pan and add the onion and garlic. Cook gently for about 3 minutes. Add the peppers and continue cooking over a gentle heat until the peppers are tender, without letting them brown. Add the tomatoes, herbs, salt and pepper. Simmer for about 15 minutes, breaking up the tomatoes with a spoon, until the peppers are bathed in a thick tomato sauce.

Quickly pour the mixture into an ovenproof dish and carefully break the eggs on top of it. Bake for about 10 minutes until the egg whites are just set. Serve immediately with lots of good bread to mop up the juices.

Cabbage, Onion and Dolcelatte Tian

A tian is a French gratin dish with sloping sides so that you get the maximum possible expanse of delicious, crusty, brown top. The word has also come to mean what is cooked in the dish.

SERVES 6
2 large onions, thinly sliced
1 clove garlic, peeled and chopped
2 tablespoons olive oil
1 small Savoy cabbage
3 eggs, beaten

150 ml (5 fl oz) milk
100 g (4 oz) dolcelatte cheese,
  crumbled
2 tablespoons chopped fresh parsley
Salt and freshly ground black pepper

Fry the onions and garlic in the oil until tender, without browning. Whilst they are cooking, shred the cabbage finely, discarding damaged outer leaves and the tough inner core. Bring a large saucepan of water to the boil, and drop in the cabbage. Bring back to the boil and simmer for 2 minutes. Drain and run under the cold tap. Drain again, press to expel excess moisture, then pat dry on kitchen paper.

Pre-heat the oven to 160°C/325°F/Gas Mark 3. Mix the cabbage with the onion and garlic. Beat the eggs lightly into the milk and pour into the vegetables, adding the dolcelatte, parsley and salt and pepper. Mix well. Spoon into an oiled 30 cm (12 in) gratin dish, or other ovenproof dish to make a layer about 2.5 cm (1 in) thick.

Bake for 40–50 minutes until set and browned on top. Eat hot or warm.

Broad Bean and Goats' Cheese Omelette

This has to be one of the all-time top-league omelettes. A blissful mixture of flavours and, once you've skinned and cooked the beans, very little work.

SERVES 1
75 g (3 oz) shelled broad beans
3 eggs
1 teaspoon finely chopped fresh dill

Salt and freshly ground black pepper
Butter for frying
25–40 g (1–1 1/2 oz) firm goats' cheese,
  diced

Skip this first part if you are in a hurry or if the beans are very small and tender, but if you have a bit of spare time, it will give you the best possible omelette imaginable. Drop the broad beans into a pan of boiling water. Simmer for 1 minute, then drain and run beans under the cold tap. Using a sharp knife, slit the tough outer skin and squeeze out the tender beanlets inside. Discard the skins.

Simmer the skinned or unskinned beans in salted water until tender – a matter of a couple of minutes for skinned beans, a little longer for unskinned. Drain well.

Beat the eggs, and add the dill, salt and pepper. Melt a knob of butter in a frying-pan and, when it is foaming, pour in the eegs. Scatter the beans over the eggs. Cook, as you would any omelette, scraping in the edges so that the liquid egg can run underneath, until the omelette is set but still moist on the surface. Quickly scatter the goats' cheese over the omelette, roll up, and tip on to a plate. Eat immediately.

Indian Spiced Squash

In theory, this exotically buttery spiced mash of pumpkin or squash should be enough to feed four, but I'll admit to greedily downing more than my quarter share on several occasions. It is hopelessly more-ish.

This recipe is one exception to the rule that pumpkin and squash should not be cooked in water. The liquid becomes an integral part of the spiced purée, so no flavour is lost. If there still seems to be a copious lake of liquid when the pumpkin is done, boil hard for a few minutes to reduce.

Star anise is a spice with a superb aniseed flavour, much used in oriental cooking and now very fashionable in smart restaurants. Buy it from good delicatessens or oriental food stores.

SERVES 4
1–1.25 kg (2–2lb 8 oz) wedge of
   pumpkin or orange winter squash
   (e.g. butternut)
1/2 star anise
1/4 teaspoon turmeric
1 bay leaf
1 teaspoon sugar
Salt
50 g (2 oz) lightly salted butter
2 tablespoons oil
1 small onion, chopped

1/2 tablespoon cumin seeds, coarsely
   crushed
1/2 tablespoon coriander seeds,
   coarsely crushed
2 cloves garlic, peeled and chopped
2.5 cm (1 in) piece fresh ginger, peeled
   and grated
1–2 green chillies, seeded and chopped

TO SERVE
Handful of fresh coriander leaves

Peel the pumpkin, discard the seeds, and cut into 2.5 cm (1 in) chunks. Place in a saucepan with the star anise, turmeric, bay leaf, sugar and salt. Add 150 ml (5 fl oz) water, bring to the boil, then cover and simmer gently, stirring occasionally until the pumpkin is very tender – about 20 minutes. Do not drain.

Just before serving, re-heat the pumpkin. Heat the butter with the oil in a small saucepan over a fairly high heat. Add the onion, and fry until golden. Raise the heat and add the crushed cumin and coriander seeds, frizzle for about 20 seconds, then add the garlic, ginger and chilli and cook for about a minute more. Transfer the pumpkin to a warm serving dish, mashing it slightly as you do so, and pour over the sizzling butter. Stir lightly to streak the butter into the pumpkin, then scatter with coriander leaves and serve.

Butternut Squash with Lemon Grass

A recipe inspired by Vietnamese cooking but made with sweet, orange butternut squash and chunks of red onion. Serve it with rice or naan bread.

SERVES 6

2 medium-sized butternut squash, weighing about 1.5 kg (3 lb) in total

2 red onions

75 g (2¹/₂ oz) caster sugar

3 tablespoons sunflower or vegetable oil

5 garlic cloves, sliced

1.5 cm (³/₄ in) piece of fresh ginger, finely chopped

45 g (1¹/₂ oz) prepared, finely chopped lemon grass

Salt and cayenne pepper or freshly ground black pepper

3 tablespoons Thai fish sauce (*nam pla*)

TO SERVE

4 spring onions, finely chopped

Lime wedges

Cut the butternut squash into rings about 2.5 cm (1 in) thick, then cut off the rind and remove the seeds. Cut the flesh into cubes. Cut each onion into eight wedges, slicing from stalk to root so that the wedges stay more or less together. Put 60 g (2 oz) of the sugar into a small pan with 3 tablespoons of water. Stir over a moderate heat until the sugar has completely dissolved. Stop stirring, raise the heat and boil hard until the syrup cooks to a rich, hazelnut-brown caramel. At arm's length, pour in 4 table-spoons of water. Swirl the pan to mix in and then stir. If it is lumpy, warm gently, stirring, to melt the lumps.

Heat the oil over a high heat and add the onion wedges. Fry briskly until well browned on both the cut sides. Lift the onion out and reserve. Now add the butternut squash and a pinch of salt. Fry until the squash is patched with brown. Add the garlic and ginger and continue cooking for a minute or so. Add the lemon grass and a scant ¹/₄ teaspoon of cayenne pepper or black pepper. Fry for a minute and then return the onion to the pan, along with the fish sauce, remaining sugar and 1 tablespoon of the caramel mixture. Stir and then add another 300 ml (10 fl oz) of water. Half cover and leave to simmer gently for about 30 minutes, until the butternut squash and onion are tender. Sprinkle over the spring onions and serve with the lime wedges.

Spiced Turnips and Chickpeas

This is adapted from a Moroccan recipe for a tagine of lamb, turnips and chickpeas. I've jettisoned the lamb but kept the original blend of aromatic spices and the honey sweetener. It is still substantial enough to work as a main course, served over a bed of couscous or rice.

SERVES 4

175 g (6 oz) dried chickpeas, soaked
    overnight
750 g (1 lb 8 oz) medium-sized turnips,
    peeled and cut into 1 cm (¹/2 in)
    cubes
25 g (1 oz) unsalted butter
1 tablespooon sunflower oil
1 onion, coarsely grated

1 teaspoon ground cinnamon
1 teaspoon ground ginger
1 teaspoon ground cumin
¹/2 tablespoon ground coriander
1 tablespoon honey
2 tablespoons chopped fresh coriander
Salt and freshly ground black pepper

Drain the chickpeas and cook in unsalted water until almost but not quite tender. Drain, reserving the cooking water. Blanch the turnips for 2 minutes in boiling water, then drain.

Melt the butter and oil in a wide saucepan and add the chickpeas, onions, turnips, spices and enough of the water from cooking the chickpeas to just cover. Cover and simmer for 15 minutes. Uncover and stir in the honey, half the chopped coriander, salt and plenty of pepper. Simmer, uncovered, for a further 10–15 minutes until the liquid is reduced to a thick sauce. Sprinkle with the remaining coriander and serve.

Stuffed Parsnips with Sunflower Seeds

Brutally big end-of-season parsnips can seem daunting, but they are just what you need for this recipe. The toughened core goes out, leaving a neat hole to fill up – just begging for a well-flavoured stuffing like the one below. Though the stuffed parsnips could be served as a side dish, I prefer to feature them as a main course, adding a home-made tomato sauce (see p. 353) to bolster them up into prominence.

SERVES 4

750 g (1 lb 8 oz) large parsnips
1 onion, chopped
1–2 cloves garlic, peeled and chopped
1¹/2 tablespoons finely chopped fresh
    parsley
50 g (2 oz) butter or 4 tablespoons
    sunflower oil

100 g (4 oz) breadcrumbs, white or
    brown
15 g (¹/2 oz) sunflower seeds
¹/2 tablespoon fresh thyme leaves
    or chopped fresh rosemary or
    ¹/2 teaspoon dried
Finely grated zest and juice of
    ¹/2 lemon

Peel the parsnips and trim off the tops. Chop the lower thinner parts finely (where the parsnip thins down to less than 4 cm (1¹/2 in) across). Slice the wider parts into 2.5 cm (1 in) thick rings. Using an apple corer or a small sharp knife, cut out the woody core. Blanch the rings in boiling salted water for 5 minutes. Drain well and arrange in a single layer in a greased shallow ovenproof dish.

Fry the onion, garlic and chopped parsnips slowly in 40 g (1½ oz) of the butter or 3 tablespoons of the oil until tender. Mix in all of the remaining ingredients. Taste and adjust the seasoning.

Pre-heat the oven to 200°C/400°F/Gas Mark 6. Fill the holes in the parsnip rings with the stuffing, mounding it up over the individual rings. Dot with the remaining butter, or drizzle over the remaining oil. Bake for 25–30 minutes until golden brown. Serve.

Root Vegetable Pie

This sturdy root vegetable pie wrapped in puff pastry makes a magnificent main course without breaking the bank. It's one of those recipes that somehow seems to exceed the sum of its parts, tasting ten times better than you might expect. As long as you drain the vegetables thoroughly, the pie can be constructed a couple of hours in advance, and whipped into the oven an hour or so before you plan to eat.

SERVES 4–6

450 g (1 lb) carrots, peeled and sliced
450 g (1 lb) potatoes, peeled and sliced
225 g (8 oz) turnips, peeled and sliced
50 g (2 oz) butter, plus extra for greasing tin
450 g (1 lb) puff pastry, thawed if frozen

Flour for rolling out
2 tablespoons finely chopped fresh parsley
2 teaspoons caraway seeds
Salt and freshly ground black pepper
1 egg, beaten

Bring a large pan of lightly salted water to the boil. Cook the carrot slices for about 6 minutes, then scoop out and drain. Repeat with potatoes and turnips, keeping each vegetable separate.

Butter a loose-bottomed cake tin, 5 cm (2 in) deep by 20 cm (8 in) in diameter. Roll out two-thirds of the pastry on a lightly floured board to give a rough circle, about 33 cm (13 in) in diameter. Loosely fold in half and then in quarters, then lift into the tin with the centre tip of the pastry at the centre of the tin. Carefully unfold, then lift the edges and gently push the pastry down to line the sides of the tin using a small knob of pastry rolled into a ball to ease it right into the corner.

Make separate layers of potatoes, carrots, and turnips, sprinkling parsley, caraway seeds, salt and pepper between layers and dotting with butter as you go. Roll out the remaining pastry, and lay over the pie. Trim off the excess and press the edges of the pastry together firmly. Make a hole in the centre, then let the pie rest for 30 minutes in the fridge. Pre-heat the oven to 220°C/425°F/Gas Mark 7.

Brush the top of the pie with beaten egg and bake for 10 minutes until golden brown. Then reduce the heat to 180°C/350°F/Gas Mark 4 and cook for a further 50–60 minutes. Test with a skewer to check that the vegetables are cooked and tender. Unmould carefully and serve hot or warm.

Braised Oriental Radish with Black Beans

Braised gently with salted black beans, chillies and other oriental flavourings, oriental radish, or mooli, takes on a distinctly new character. Hot and spicy, this will make you appreciate the radish in a totally new way.

SERVES 4

450 g (1 lb) mooli (white radish), peeled

2 tablespoons sunflower or vegetable oil

4 spring onions, chopped

1 cm (¹/₂ in) piece fresh ginger, peeled and finely chopped

2 cloves garlic, peeled and finely chopped

1 green chilli, seeded and finely chopped

1 tablespoon Chinese salted black beans, rinsed

2 tablespoons dark soy sauce

1 tablespoon rice vinegar or white wine vinegar

2 teaspoons sugar

¹/₂ star anise

300 ml (10 fl oz) chicken or vegetable stock

Slice the radish into 5 mm (¹/₄ in) thick discs, then quarter the discs.

Heat the oil in a wok or deep frying-pan until it smokes. Quickly add the spring onions, ginger, garlic and chilli and stir-fry for a few seconds. Add the radish and black beans and stir-fry for about 1 minute. Add all the remaining ingredients. Bring to the boil, stirring, then cover and simmer for 20–30 minutes until the radish is almost tender. Uncover and boil for a few minutes until the sauce is reduced. Serve.

Dry Spiced Cauliflower

One of the best curries I had in India was, surprisingly, in the dingy restaurant in Delhi's small national airport. It was a dry cauliflower curry, scooped up with chapattis. I was about to ask the man how it was made, but our flight was called and we had to rush off. This is the best approximation to that curry that I've come up with yet.

SERVES 2 AS A MAIN COURSE, 3–4 AS A SIDE DISH

450 g (1 lb) cauliflower

2 tablespoons sunflower or vegetable oil

1 cm (¹/₂ in) piece fresh ginger, peeled and finely chopped

2 cloves garlic, peeled and chopped

¹/₄ teaspoon chilli powder or cayenne pepper

1 teaspoon ground turmeric

1¹/₂ teaspoons ground cumin

Salt

225 g (8 oz) tomatoes, skinned, seeded and chopped

1 teaspoon lemon juice

TO GARNISH

¹/₂ teaspoon garam masala (optional)

Break or cut the cauliflower into florets no larger than 2.5 cm (1 in) long and wide.

Heat the oil in a frying-pan over a medium heat. Add the ginger and garlic and fry for about 30 seconds. Now add the chilli or cayenne pepper, turmeric and cumin. Stir and then add the cauliflower and salt. Turn gently so that the cauliflower is coated in spices, then add 4 tablespoons water. Turn the heat down low, and cover the pan tightly. Cook for 5 minutes.

Now add the tomatoes and lemon juice, stir to mix, and cover again. Cook for a further 5 minutes or so until the cauliflower is tender, stirring once. By the end of the cooking time, the vegetables should have absorbed virtually all the liquid. Sprinkle with garam masala, if using, and serve.

Mallorcan Vegetable and Bread Stew

There are many different versions of sopas Mallorquinas. *This is based on one I ate in Palma on my first trip to Mallorca. It is a sturdy peasant bread and vegetable stew, not elegant fare, but from the school of thrifty Mediterranean cooking that lets nothing go to waste. 'Sopas' does not mean soup. It is the name given to the thin dried slices of left-over bread used to soak up the juices of the vegetable broth. The final dish is thick and substantial, not at all soupy. It tastes good made with water but even better with stock.*

SERVES 4
150 g (5 oz) thin slices good bread
450 g (1 lb) Swiss chard
50 ml (2 fl oz) olive oil
4 cloves garlic, peeled and chopped
2 leeks, thinly sliced
450 g (1 lb) tomatoes, skinned and chopped

1 tablespoon chopped fresh marjoram or 1 teaspoon dried
1 tablespoon chopped fresh parsley
Salt and freshly ground black pepper
300 ml (10 fl oz) water or stock

TO SERVE
Extra virgin olive oil

If you have the time, leave the bread out on an uncovered tray for several days until it is dried. Otherwise, spread the bread out on baking trays and bake in a very low oven (120°C/250°F/Gas Mark 1/2) until dry and brittle.

Cut the green parts off the Swiss chard and shred thinly. Save the ribs for another dish. Heat the olive oil in a wide deep frying-pan and add the garlic and leeks. Cook gently until tender, without browning. Add the tomatoes, marjoram and parsley and simmer until thickened. Add the shredded chard leaves, salt and pepper, water or stock and simmer until the chard is tender. Taste and adjust the seasonings.

Break up the slices of bread and place in a warmed bowl large enough to take the vegetable stew as well. When the stew is done, pour over the bread. Stir and let it stand for a few minutes so that the bread can soak up the juices, then trickle over a little extra olive oil and serve.

Vegetables

Saffron and Garlic Mash

These mashed potaotes are traditionally buttery but they are togged up with two other stylish ingredients – garlic and golden saffron. Don't be too taken aback by the quantity of garlic: cooked this way, the garlic mellows and softens to something very subtle. Surprisingly, the mere pinch of saffron gives far more definition.

SERVES 4–6
10 garlic cloves, peeled but whole
1 kg (2 lb 4 oz) floury potatoes
300 ml (10 fl oz) milk

A good pinch of saffron strands
60 g (2 oz) butter
Salt

Put the garlic into a small pan, cover with water and bring up to the boil. Drain. Boil the potatoes in their skins, with the blanched garlic. While the potatoes are cooking, bring the milk to the boil, draw off the heat and sprinkle the saffron strands over it. Drain and peel the potatoes and return them to the pan, along with the garlic and the butter. Mash thoroughly with a potato masher while still hot. Beat over a low heat, gradually adding the saffron milk a splash or two at a time. Season with salt. Taste and adjust the seasoning and serve.

Himmel und Erde

Himmel und Erde means heaven and earth, though the connotations here are not particularly spiritual. It refers to the two main ingredients: apples from up above (i.e. trees) and potatoes from the earth. The Germans are particularly strong on combinations of fruit with savoury ingredients, and this is a favourite of mine.

SERVES 4 GENEROUSLY
1 kg (2 lb) floury potatoes
450 g (1 lb) cooking apples

Salt and freshly ground black pepper
Sugar to season
Generous knob of butter

Peel the potatoes and cut into chunks. Put in a pan with just enough lightly salted water to cover them. Bring to the boil and simmer until almost cooked. Meanwhile, peel, core and roughly chop the apples.

Pour off about two thirds of the water the potatoes are cooking in, then add the apples and simmer gently until they have collapsed and the potatoes are melting. Mash together, and season with salt, pepper and a little sugar. Stir in the butter, then tip into a serving dish and serve.

Creole Potatoes

Papas chorreadas, or Creole potatoes, is a dish I first tasted in Colombia. Before the Spanish conquest the Colombian Indians used to bury a special kind of potato in bags in the ground, leaving them until they were semi-rotted and imbued with a strange, cheesey flavour. This great delicacy was dished up to the Spaniards who enjoyed the taste but baulked at the theory. Modern-day papas chorreadas is the conquistadors' version of that ancient dish.

SERVES 6–8
1 generous pinch saffron threads
1 kg (2 lb) red-skinned potatoes
   (e.g. Desirée)
4 spring onions, cut into 5 cm (2 in)
   pieces and shredded
Salt

FOR THE SAUCE
2 tablespoons sunflower oil
1 onion, finely chopped

1 clove garlic, peeled and crushed
1 teaspoon dried thyme
$1/2$ teaspoon cumin seeds
225 g (8 oz) tomatoes, skinned, seeded
   and chopped
1 bay leaf
Salt and freshly ground black pepper
150 g (5 oz) mature Cheddar cheese,
   grated
85 ml (3 fl oz) double cream

Pour a few tablespoons of boiling water over the saffron threads and leave for 10 minutes, stirring occasionally. Place the potatoes in a saucepan with the spring onions, salt and enough water to just cover. Add the saffron and its water to the saucepan together with some salt. Bring to the boil, then cover and simmer until the potatoes are tender. Drain and arrange on a serving dish. Keep warm if necessary.

While the potatoes are cooking make the sauce. Heat the oil in a frying-pan and fry the onion until lightly browned. Add the garlic, thyme and cumin seeds and fry for 1 minute. Then add the chopped tomatoes, bay leaf, salt and pepper. Cook over a vigorous heat until the tomatoes have broken down to form a thick sauce. Add the cheese and cream and stir until the cheese has melted smoothly into the sauce. Pour over the potatoes and serve immediately.

Baked New Potatoes with Anchovy and Parsley

There's no law to say that new potatoes should only be boiled or steamed. Baking them slowly in the oven gives them a luxurious buttery texture. The anchovy fillets dissolve into the pan juices, without giving an overtly fishy flavour, so the potatoes are good with any main course, fish, meat or vegetable.

SERVES 4–6

1 kg (2 lb) new potatoes

40 g (1¹/₂ oz) butter

3 tablespoons olive oil

3 anchovy fillets, chopped

**2 cloves garlic, peeled and crushed
    with a little salt**

2 tablespoons chopped fresh parsley

2 tablespoons lemon juice

Salt and freshly ground black pepper

Pre-heat the oven to 200°C/400°F/Gas Mark 6.

Scrub the potatoes, removing as much skin as you can. Halve or quarter larger ones. Pat dry on kitchen paper. In a flameproof roasting tin, heat the butter with the oil. Add the anchovy fillets and cook for a minute or so, mashing the fillets into the oil with a fork. Add the potatoes and fry for 4 minutes until they are beginning to colour. Stir in the garlic and parsley, and pour in 150 ml (5 fl oz) water at arm's length (it's bound to spit back at you). Add the lemon juice, a little salt and plenty of pepper.

Move the tin to the oven and bake the potatoes for 25–30 minutes, stirring and basting every 10 minutes or so, until browned and meltingly tender. Spoon the potatoes into a warm dish and pour the richly flavoured juices in the pan over them. Serve.

Stoved Potatoes with Garlic and Coriander

Slowly cooked in olive oil, stoved potatoes are meltingly tender. The whole cloves of garlic not only give flavour, but soften and mellow to a mild sweetness. This is a lovely way to cook both new and old potatoes.

SERVES 3–4

**450 g (1 lb) new potatoes or waxier
    main-crop potatoes (e.g. Cara)**

1 head of garlic

Salt and freshly ground black pepper

3 tablespoons olive oil

TO SERVE

2 tablespoons chopped fresh coriander

If the new potatoes are very small, leave them as they are. With medium-sized ones, cut in half or quarters. The aim is to get all the chunks about the same size so that they cook evenly. If using main-crop potatoes peel and cut into 2.5–4 cm (1–1¹/₂ in) chunks. Separate all the cloves of garlic and peel, but leave whole.

Put the potatoes and garlic into a heavy frying-pan in a single layer. Don't try to force them in too tightly, because you have to be able to turn them. If you've got a few bits too many, then leave them out. Season with salt and pepper, then add 6 tablespoons of water. Drizzle over the olive oil.

Cook, covered, over a low heat for 40 minutes, shaking the pan and stirring occasionally, until potatoes and garlic are very tender and patched with brown. By then the water should have been absorbed. If not, uncover the pan and boil it off. Once they are done, sprinkle over the coriander and serve.

Hot Potato Salad

The Gironde is the wide stretch of water that runs from the Atlantic ocean down almost as far as Bordeaux, fed by the Dordogne and the Garonne. It gives its name to the area of land bordering on it. Here you will find the vineyards of many of the great wine-growing châteaux of Bordeaux. The fertile soil is also perfect for growing other produce – the potatoes of Eysines, a few miles from Bordeaux, are highly rated by the locals.

The curious thing about this method of cooking potatoes is that they end up with a distinct taste of artichokes. Be that as it may, it is a very easy way to cook pommes de terres Girondines, *a most delicious dish with its hint of garlic, and the mild sharpness of vinegar sizzled in at the end.*

SERVES 4
750 g (1 lb 12 oz) potatoes
Salt and freshly ground black pepper
100 g (4 oz) smoked streaky bacon, diced
2 cloves garlic, peeled and halved
2 tablespoons chopped fresh parsley
2 tablespoons white wine vinegar

Peel the potatoes and rinse in cold water. Slice thinly. Find a heavy frying-pan or wide pan, into which the potatoes will just fit neatly. Press the potatoes into the pan, add enough water to half cover, and season lightly with salt. Cover and cook over a fairly high heat, for 12 minutes or so, until the potatoes are just cooked.

Meanwhile, fry the bacon slowly so that it begins to release its own fat. Once there's a thin layer of fat on the base of the pan, add the cloves of garlic. Continue to cook over a gentle heat, until the bacon has given up all its fat and is beginning to brown. Draw off the heat and wait until the potatoes are done.

Once the potatoes are cooked drain off any excess water, and return to the heat. Re-heat the bacon in its fat, until it begins to smoke. Fish out the garlic and discard. Pour bacon and fat evenly over the cooked potatoes, still in their pan, and add the parsley, pepper and vinegar. Stir gently to mix, and serve.

Carrot and Tarragon Purée

Puréed carrots take on the most remarkable, almost fluorescent, orange colour. The taste isn't at all bad either and a hint of tarragon points up the flavour neatly. Serve the purée as a side dish with roast chicken or feathered game, or with plainly cooked fish.

SERVES 4
450 g (1 lb) carrots, peeled and sliced
100 g (4 oz) floury potatoes, peeled and cut into chunks
1/2 teaspoon sugar
1/2 tablespoon lemon juice
1 teaspoon chopped fresh tarragon or 1/2 teaspoon dried
Salt and freshly ground black pepper
25 g (1 oz) butter

TO SERVE
Chopped fresh parsley

Put the carrots, potatoes, sugar, lemon juice, tarragon and salt in a pan. Add enough water to cover, bring to the boil and simmer until the vegetables are very tender. Drain, reserving the cooking liquid. Place the vegetables in a food processor with 2 tablespoons of the cooking water. Whizz to a smooth purée, adding more cooking water if necessary. Taste and adjust the seasonings. Cool if not serving straight away.

To re-heat the purée, place in a pan with the butter and stir over a moderate heat until piping hot. Pile into a serving bowl and scatter with parsley.

Parsnip Purée

If parsnips are very small and tender, you may not even need to scrape them before cooking. Once the girth increases they will probably need to be peeled at some stage, before or after cooking. Only with enormous parsnips should you bother to remove the core – more easily done when the parsnip is partially cooked. Parsnips are low in calories, but they do benefit from some kind of lubrication. Boiled or steamed, they are vastly improved by a generous knob of butter melting over them as they are served. Parsnips make irresistible chips (see Saratoga Chips, p. 226) and are wonderful roasted around the joint (in both cases, boiled first until half-cooked).

It's not worth giving quantities here. If you can mash potatoes, then you can mash parsnips. The balance of parsnip to potato is very much an individual taste. The potato gives a smoother texture and softens the potentially insistent taste of the parsnip. I usually use roughly half potatoes and half parsnips, but for a stronger sweeter flavour increase the parsnips as you like.

Parsnips	**Freshly grated nutmeg or ground**
Potatoes	**cinnamon**
Butter	**Salt and freshly ground black pepper**
Milk or single cream	

Peel and chop the potatoes and parsnips roughly. Cook in boiling salted water. Drain thoroughly, and return to the pan. Add a large knob of butter, and start mashing over a low heat. Gradually mash in enough milk or cream to give a creamy purée. Season with nutmeg or cinnamon, and plenty of salt and pepper. Serve.

Fried Parsnips with Walnuts

This is a damn-the-calories way with parsnips. The parsnips are sautéd in butter with walnuts, then finished with sugar and a dash of vinegar to balance. Great with roast game or with hot ham.

SERVES 4
450 g (1 lb) small parsnips
15 g (¹/₂ oz) light muscovado sugar
¹/₄ teaspoon cinnamon
40 g (1¹/₂ oz) butter
25 g (1 oz) walnuts, chopped

1 tablespoon white wine vinegar
Salt and freshly ground black pepper

TO GARNISH
Chopped fresh parsley

Peel the parsnips and cook in lightly salted boiling water until almost tender. Drain well, cut each one in half, and then cut the thicker part into quarters lengthwise. Mix the sugar with the cinnamon.

Melt the butter in a wide pan and add the parsnips and walnuts. Fry gently, stirring and turning, until the parsnips are lightly patched with brown. Scatter with sugar and cinnamon, stir to distribute evenly, then drizzle over the vinegar and salt and pepper. Cook for a final minute and serve, scattered with parsley.

Saratoga Chips

Or in other words, parsnip chips. The only difference between making potato chips and parsnip chips is that the parsnips should be parboiled before they are deep-fried. The real difference lies in the taste.

SERVES 4
1 kg (2 lb) parsnips, peeled

Oil for deep-frying
Salt

Cut the parsnips into 5 cm (2 in) lengths. Quarter the larger ends and remove the woody core. Parboil the parsnip pieces until half-cooked. Drain thoroughly and pat dry on kitchen paper. Deep-fry until golden brown. Drain briefly on kitchen paper and sprinkle with salt. Serve.

Sautéd Turnips with Cumin and Lemon

The French have a serious appreciation for turnips. They cook them lovingly, choosing petite specimens when possible for a more delicate flavour, but they also know how to show their portly and hefty elders at their best. In England we tend to go for the big boys and boil them hard. Big and overboiled and nothing more is not very fair on poor old turnips. They deserve better, which does not necessarily mean elaborate.

This is a snappy way to give turnips a lift out of the ordinary. Parboiled turnips are quickly fried with cumin and finished with lemon and coriander leaf. Who said turnips were boring?

SERVES 4
450 g (1 lb) turnips
2 tablespoons olive oil
1 teaspoon cumin seeds, crushed
Finely grated zest of $^1/_2$ lemon

$^1/_2$ tablespoon lemon juice
Salt and freshly ground black pepper

TO SERVE
1 tablespoon chopped fresh coriander

If the turnips are on the large side, peel and cut into 2 cm ($^3/_4$ in) cubes. If they are small spring turnips, just trim and quarter. Drop into a pan of lightly salted boiling water and simmer for 5 minutes until almost, but not quite, cooked. Drain and run under the cold tap. Drain thoroughly and pat dry on kitchen paper.

Heat the oil in a wide frying-pan. Add the cumin seeds and stir for about 30 seconds. Add the turnips and fry until nicely browned. Stir in the lemon zest and juice, plenty of pepper and a little salt. Turn into a serving dish, scatter with the coriander and serve.

Ginger-glazed Turnips

I'm not taken with ginger wine as a drink, but it is a great cooking ingredient. In this recipe it gives the turnips a subtle gingery glaze. If you have very small turnips leave them whole. The same method can be used very successfully for carrots.

SERVES 4
450 g (1 lb) medium-sized turnips,
    peeled and cut into 1 cm ($^1/_2$ in)
    cubes
40 g (1 $^1/_2$ oz) butter

2 tablespoons ginger wine
Squeeze of lemon juice
1 tablespoon caster sugar
Salt and freshly ground black pepper

Cook the turnip cubes in salted boiling water for 2–3 minutes or until almost tender. Drain and run under the cold tap. Drain thoroughly.

Melt the butter in a frying-pan and add the turnips. Fry for a minute or so. Add the remaining ingredients and stir over a medium heat until the turnip cubes are glazed with a rich syrup. Serve immediately.

Celeriac Purée

Probably my all-time favourite celeriac dish is a straight celeriac purée, one of autumn and winter's highlights. Serve it in place of potato mash – it is lovely with game and a blissful partner for rich, meaty winter stews. It isn't at all bad with fish, either. Celeriac purée is so easy to make that it needs no real recipe – the method alone will suffice.

Mash roughly equal quantities of cooked celeriac and potato together, over a moderate heat, with a generous knob of butter (or two) and hot milk or, for a really luxurious version, milk and cream, beating vigorously until fluffy and light. Season with salt, pepper and lots of freshly grated nutmeg.

Roast Celeriac

These caramel-brown wedges of celeriac, baked slowly in the oven, are quite irresistible. They would make a marvellous accompaniment to a dish of roast game, though I found myself eating them all on their own, just because they were there and too good to ignore. They can be cooked in advance and re-heated, when needed, in the oven. There is no need to fiddle around with acidulated water as you're peeling as the wedges of celeriac will brown as they cook.

SERVES 4
1 medium–large celeriac
Sunflower oil
A knob of butter

Salt and freshly ground black pepper
75 ml (5 tablespoons) Marsala or
    Madeira

Pre-heat the oven to 180°C/350°F/Gas Mark 4. Cut the celeriac into eight wedges and then trim off the skin as neatly and economically as you can. Toss the wedges in just enough oil to coat. Smear butter thickly around an ovenproof dish, just large enough to take the celeriac wedges lying down flat (well, flattish, anyway). Lay the celeriac in the dish, season with salt and pepper and pour over the Marsala or Madeira. Roast for about an hour, turning the wedges and basting every now and then, until they are richly browned all over and very tender. You may find that you have to add a table-spoon or two of water towards the end, to prevent the celeriac from burning.

Celeriac Gratin

Celeriac makes a first-rate gratin, rather in the mould of a gratin dauphinois. A scattering of Parmesan accentuates its particular flavour, as does a small measure of mustard. This goes very well with fish, being neither too strong nor yet too insipid, but it is excellent, too, with roast chicken – a great combination, in fact, for a family Sunday lunch.

SERVES 6–8
2 medium-sized celeriac, peeled and
    thinly sliced
Lemon juice or white wine vinegar
300 ml (10 fl oz) single cream

1 tablespoon plain flour
1 tablespoon Dijon mustard
Salt and freshly ground black pepper
45 g (1^1/$_2$ oz) butter
2 tablespoons freshly grated Parmesan

Pre-heat the oven to 180°C/350°F/Gas Mark 4. Drop the slices of celeriac into water acidulated with lemon juice or vinegar as you work and then drain and blanch them in acidulated boiling water for 2 minutes. Drain and run under the cold tap. Drain thoroughly.

    Butter a 25–30 cm (10–12 in) gratin dish. Mix a spoonful of the cream into the flour, to give a smooth paste, and then gradually work in the rest. Stir in the mustard and season with salt and pepper. Spread about one-third of the celeriac in the dish, dot with a little butter and pour over one-third of the cream mixture. Repeat twice more, until the celeriac, butter and cream are all used up. Sprinkle the Parmesan over the top. Bake for about an hour, until the celeriac is completely tender and the top browned. Serve hot.

Beetroot Purée

This is so pretty! Beetroot makes the most beautiful deep pink purée that tastes every bit as good as it looks. I first made it to go with roast pheasant, but it would sit happily alongside any main course that can take its rich earthy taste.

SERVES 4

225–275 g (8–10 oz) cooked, peeled beetroot
225 g (8 oz) floury potatoes, peeled and cooked

85 ml (3 fl oz) soured cream
1 tablespoon chopped fresh dill or 1 teaspoon dried
Salt and freshly ground black pepper
25 g (1 oz) butter

Chop the beetroot and potato roughly. Put them in a food processor together with the soured cream, dill, salt and pepper and whizz until smooth. Taste and adjust the seasoning. Re-heat gently with the butter when needed.

Beetroot and Apple Mash

This mash turns out the most sensational, unbelievable colour and tastes wonderful too. Serve with browned, sizzling sausages.

SERVES 4

2 medium-sized beetroot, weighing about 325 g (12 oz) in total
600 g (1 lb 4 oz) floury potatoes
1 large cooking apple, peeled, cored and diced

60 g (2 oz) butter
Milk
2 tablespoons chopped fresh parsley

Cook the beetroot whole, until tender. When cool enough to handle, peel and grate them.

Peel the potatoes and cut them into large chunks. Put them into a pan with salt and enough water to cover by about 2 cm (3/4 in). Bring to the boil and leave to simmer, uncovered, for 5 minutes. Add the apple and continue cooking until both apple and potatoes are very tender.

Drain off the water carefully. Mash the potatoes and apple with the butter. Over a low heat, beat in enough milk to give a soft, light mash. Stir in the beetroot and the parsley and then season well and give it all a final stir. Serve immediately.

Instead of mash, try Beetroot with Apple. Cut 2 medium-sized cooked beetroot into small cubes. Fry 2 dessert apples, cored and cut into slices, in 1 tablespoon oil and add 25 g (1 oz) butter. Once golden, remove to a serving plate. Sauté the beetroot cubes and pile them into the centre of the apples. Quickly add 2 tablespoons lemon juice and 1/2 teaspoon creamed horseradish to the pan and stir, scraping in fat and juices. Pour over the beetroot. Season the whole lot, scatter with chopped fresh parsley or chives and serve.

Jerusalem Artichokes with Bacon, Paprika and Breadcrumbs

One thing is certain about Jerusalem artichokes. They have nothing whatsoever to do with Jerusalem, nor for that matter with artichokes proper. They come, in fact, from North America where they have long been a staple of native Indian tribes. When the Frenchman, Samuel de Champlain, first came across these Indian tubers at Cape Cod in 1605, he described them as having 'the taste of artichokes' (I think there is a passing resemblance in flavour, but others disagree) and from that likeness they acquired the second part of their name.

The 'Jerusalem' part of this vegetable's name is harder to explain. There are two hypotheses that I've come across – the one I like best is that botanists realized that the tubers were related to the sunflower, girasole in Italian. In England, girasole was soon corrupted into 'Jerusalem'.

If you have the choice, pick out Jerusalem artichokes that are as smooth as possible, which will make them easier to peel. I usually just scrub the artichokes, then steam or boil in acidulated water in their jackets until tender (or half-cooked depending on the recipe). I leave the peeling until they are done, at which point the skins will pull off easily. This is not so practical when you want to serve them straight from the pan, embellished with no more than a knob of butter, in which case you'd better peel them before cooking. Their high iron content makes them prone to greying when exposed to the air, so drop them into acidulated water as you peel.

The salt of the bacon and the crispness of the breadcrumbs used in this recipe set off the tender, sweet Jerusalem artichokes perfectly. I usually keep this as a separate course all on its own. Pancetta is an Italian form of bacon, with a particularly good flavour for cooking. It is available from Italian delicatessens, but if you can't get it use streaky bacon instead. Vegetarians shouldn't ignore this recipe altogether – sliced mushrooms make a good substitute for the bacon.

SERVES 4
750 g (1 lb 8 oz) Jerusalem artichokes
Juice of 1/2 lemon (optional)
Salt
2 teaspoons paprika

1 tablespoon olive or sunflower oil
100 g (4 oz) thickly sliced pancetta or
streaky bacon, diced
3 tablespoons fine dry breadcrumbs

Either peel the Jerusalem artichokes before cooking them or vice versa. Steam or simmer them in lightly salted water acidulated with the lemon juice until just cooked but not soft and mushy. Sprinkle the peeled artichokes evenly with a little salt and all the paprika, rolling them around so that they are fairly evenly coated.

Heat the oil in a medium-sized frying-pan. Add the pancetta or bacon and fry over a high heat until crisp and brown. Scoop out with a slotted spoon, letting as much fat as possible drain back into the pan. Drain the pancetta or bacon on kitchen paper.

Add the breadcrumbs to the pan and fry until golden brown. Scoop the breadcrumbs out of the pan, add the hot artichokes and, if necessary, a tiny bit of extra oil. Fry over a high heat for a couple of minutes, turning carefully, until piping hot. Tip into a warm serving dish and scatter with the breadcrumbs and pancetta or bacon.

Stoved Jerusalem Artichokes

This was my mother's favourite way of cooking Jerusalem artichokes, and is one of mine too. I've adapted the recipe slightly from the one she gives in her Vegetable Book *(Michael Joseph), by adding lemon zest to the finely chopped garlic and parsley to make an Italian gremolata, one of the best, simple ways to give a lift to practically any savoury dish.*

SERVES 4
1 kg (2 lb 4 oz) Jerusalem artichokes
Juice of 1/2 lemon
1 tablespoon olive oil
25 g (1 oz) butter

2 tablespoons chopped fresh parsley
1 large clove garlic, peeled and
chopped
Finely grated zest of 1/2 lemon
Salt and freshly ground black pepper

If you are going to save the trimmings for soup, or flavouring a vegetable stock, scrub the artichokes thoroughly. Peel and cut them into halves or quarters if they are large – the pieces should be about the size of a quail's egg or slightly larger, give or take the odd corner. Drop the artichokes into water acidulated with the lemon juice as you work, to prevent browning.

Drain and dry the artichokes. Heat the oil and the butter in a wide frying-pan over a low to moderate heat, until foaming. Tip the artichokes into the fat in a single layer. If you have too many and they are hopelessly heaped up, you'll need to use a second pan, or cook them in batches.

Cover and cook for 10 minutes or so, occasionally shaking the pan gently. Check after 5 minutes and turn them over carefully. After 10 minutes, remove the cover. The artichokes should be beginning to brown. Cook for a further 10 minutes until they are tender, turning occasionally, so that they colour evenly.

While they cook, chop the parsley, garlic and lemon zest together very finely to make a gremolata. When cooked, season the Jerusalem artichokes with salt and pepper and sprinkle over the gremolata.

Baked Onions with Sun-dried Tomatoes and Rosemary

Choose firm, unblemished onions, of a medium to moderately large size for this dish, but not great big heffalumps. Don't bother peeling them before you begin cooking. The skin comes off very easily after they have been boiled and gives the outer layer a good colour. The sun-dried tomatoes add a welcome sprightly flavour, a fine contrast to the onions.

SERVES 4–6
4 onions, unpeeled
6 pieces sun-dried tomato, cut into strips
1 large sprig of fresh rosemary, snapped in two, or 1 teaspoon dried

2 cloves garlic, peeled and chopped
1 tablespoon chopped fresh parsley
Salt and freshly ground black pepper
1 tablespoon white wine vinegar
6 tablespoons olive oil

Pre-heat the oven to 150°C/300°F/Gas Mark 3.

Place the onions in a pan and cover with water. Bring to the boil and simmer for 12 minutes. Drain, peel and quarter. Arrange the quarters in a single layer in a lightly oiled gratin dish and mix in the strips of sun-dried tomato. Tuck the rosemary amongst them, then sprinkle over the garlic, parsley, salt and pepper. Drizzle over the vinegar and then the olive oil. Cover loosely with foil, and bake for 50 minutes. Remove the foil, and baste the onions with their juices. Continue cooking, uncovered, for a further 20 minutes. Serve hot, warm or cold.

Caramelized Shallots

Shallots are really a type of onion, but they are a very particular type with their own characteristics that mark them out from the commoner round onion. They grow in tight clusters, joined together loosely at the root. Inevitably, this affects their shape. They may be up to 7.5 cm (3 in) long, though they are usually a little shorter, but they are squeezed into a slimmer and more elongated form than bulbous onions. The value of the shallot in culinary terms lies predominantly in the flavour – very oniony but with only the mildest hint of tear-inducing pungency. This makes them just perfect for salads or any other raw use. I far prefer small rings of shallot to hefty hoops of onion, scattered over a tomato salad.

There's some value in their size too. Being small, they are handy for one- or two-person cooking, when you might not want to delve into a full-sized onion. The French, quite rightly, appreciate the shallot far more than we do, using it abundantly in cooking. Every year I return from France with big bunches of different types of shallot to hang up in my kitchen. This is more of a relish than a real vegetable side dish. It is relatively quick to make (and won't keep for more than a few days), and is served hot. It is a lovely accompaniment to roast beef, steak or game, or boiled gammon.

SERVES 4
275 g (10 oz) shallots
50 g (2 oz) butter

1 tablespoon caster sugar
Salt and freshly ground black pepper

Peel the shallots. If a few are far larger than the rest, take off another layer or two of skin – underneath you will find that they separate into two distinct cloves.

Melt the butter in a heavy saucepan, large enough to take the shallots in a single layer. Fry them for about 5 minutes until patched with brown. Sprinkle with sugar and stir for a minute or so, then add enough water just to cover. Season, stir and bring to a simmer.

Simmer, stirring occasionally, adding more water if needed, until the shallots are very tender and there is only the thinnest layer of syrupy liquid left in the pan. This takes around an hour, but can be done in advance. The cooked shallots keep in the fridge for at least 2 days, and can be re-heated when needed.

VARIATION

To make maple-glazed shallots, replace the caster sugar with 1$^1/_2$ tablespoons maple syrup and add 1 tablespoon lemon juice. Simmer until the shallots are very tender and there is only a thin layer of syrupy liquid left in the pan.

Creamed Leeks with Orange

This cross between a vegetable side dish and a sauce was something I originally came up with to serve with roast pork, and very good partners they were too. However, the creamed leeks are so delicious that I've since served them with all manner of main courses, fish, fowl and vegetable.

SERVES 4–6
5 large leeks, trimmed
40 g (1$^1/_2$ oz) butter
Juice of 1 orange
Salt and freshly ground black pepper

40 g (1$^1/_2$ oz) plain flour
300 ml (10 fl oz) milk
Finely grated zest of 1 orange
Squeeze of lemon juice

Cut the leeks into 4–5 cm (1^1/2–2 in) lengths, then shred finely. Melt the butter in a wide pan and add the leeks. Stir to mix, then add the orange juice and a little salt and pepper. Cover and simmer gently together for 10 minutes or so, stirring occasionally, until the leeks are just tender. Uncover and boil off most of the watery juices until all that remains is a few tablespoons of buttery liquid.

Now sprinkle with the flour and stir to mix evenly. Gradually add the milk, stirring, and then the orange zest. Bring to a simmer and cook for 3–5 minutes until very thick and creamy. If absolutely necessary add a little more milk. Season with salt and pepper and stir in the lemon juice. Taste and adjust the seasoning. If not using immediately, spear a small knob of butter on the tip of a knife and rub over the surface to prevent a skin forming. Serve with roast pork, chicken, or fish.

Stir-fried Celery with Ginger and Coriander

This is a lively, fresh way of cooking celery with ginger, coriander and orange juice.

SERVES 4

2 tablespoons vegetable or sunflower
    oil
2.5 cm (1 in) piece of fresh ginger,
    peeled and finely chopped
6 stalks celery, thinly sliced

1 teaspoon coriander seeds, coarsely
    crushed
Juice of $1/2$ large orange
Salt and freshly ground black pepper
1 tablespoon chopped fresh
    coriander

Heat the oil in a large wok over a high heat. Add the ginger and stir for a few seconds. Now add the celery and stir-fry for about 2 minutes. Add the crushed coriander seeds and continue to stir-fry for about another 3 minutes until the celery is browned. Reduce the heat, add the orange juice, salt and pepper. Toss, then cover and simmer for 4 minutes or so, until the liquid is absorbed. Finally stir in the chopped coriander and serve.

Celery with Chestnuts

Celery and chestnuts have a natural affinity. I'd rather have this combination than Brussels sprouts and chestnuts any day. Peeling the chestnuts is a bore, but a fairly brief one – don't be tempted to settle for canned chestnuts which are a poor substitute.

SERVES 4

15 chestnuts
1 small head of celery, sliced
Chicken, duck, beef or vegetable stock
1 bouquet garni (1 bayleaf, 2 sprigs
    parsley and 2 sprigs thyme, tied
    together with string)

40 g (1$1/2$ oz) butter
Salt and freshly ground black pepper

With a sharp knife score a deep 'x' through the tough skin of each chestnut. Put them in a saucepan with enough water to cover generously. Bring to the boil and simmer for 2 minutes. One or two at a time, take the chestnuts out of the saucepan and peel off outer and inner skin. Discard any chestnuts that are discoloured. Rinse out the pan and return the chestnuts to it with enough fresh water or stock to cover. Simmer until tender, then drain and break into large pieces.

Place the celery in a pan in just enough stock to cover. Add the bouquet garni and simmer until barely tender. Drain, and discard the bouquet garni. Rinse the saucepan and return the celery to it with the chestnuts, butter, salt and pepper. Stir over a moderate heat for a few minutes until chestnuts and celery are thoroughly heated through and impregnated with butter. Serve.

Butter-fried Fennel and Onions with Vinegar and Thyme

Florence fennel is a marvellous vegetable with a unique aniseed taste. Or at least, I think it is a marvellous vegetable, but I can understand why some people may dislike it. It announces its presence in no uncertain way, particularly when eaten raw. That's what I like about it. No namby-pamby background recluse, Florence fennel tastes strong and refreshing in a salad. Heat, though, induces a remarkable change, tempering the assertive flavour down to a mellow but distinctive sweetness when cooked. How you use fennel will depend on how much you like it. It's not cheap to buy so choose your fennel carefully to minimize waste, and remind yourself that a little stretches a long way. Size is of no great importance: big fat bulbs are usually just as juicy and tender as more slender ones. The condition of the vegetable is what counts here. Look for firm, white orbs, with no soft or browning patches. The tufts of feathery green fronds should still be bright and fresh. If the fennel is in good condition when it enters your kitchen, it will keep for up to four days (or even a little longer).

Both my cousin, Lucy, and my aunt, Mary, are wonderful cooks, and I owe this dish entirely to them. Lucy came across the original recipe, which included no fennel at all, in The Green's Cook Book *by Deborah Madison (Bantam Press) which is one of the most inspiring of vegetarian cookery books. She and her mother adapted it between them, introducing the fennel. The whole ensemble doesn't take long to cook, but once done can be kept warm in the oven, covered, for up to 20 minutes or so.*

SERVES 4
1 large or 2 small fennel bulbs
2 medium red onions
50 g (2 oz) butter
2¹/₂ tablespoons sherry vinegar or red wine vinegar

Leaves of 3 sprigs of fresh thyme, roughly chopped
Salt and freshly ground black pepper

Trim the stalks off the fennel, halve lengthwise, and cut into slices 5 mm (¹/₄ in) thick, erring on the thin side. Halve the onions and cut into 5 mm (¹/₄ in) slices.

Melt the butter in a wide, heavy frying-pan. Add the fennel and cook gently for 5 minutes. Raise the heat to high, add the onions and sauté briskly, flipping and stirring them frequently. After 4–5 minutes they will be lightly browned, sweet and still a little crunchy. If you prefer them softer, cook for a couple of minutes longer. Now add the vinegar and sizzle until it is virtually all evaporated. Stir in the thyme leaves, salt and pepper and serve.

Grilled Ceps

I've not specified quantities here. Being precise seems a bit pointless – who can say how many you'll find if you pick your own, and who can say how many you'll be able to afford if you splash out on bought ceps, always phenomenally pricy? Use your imagination, and this outline as a guide, and you are unlikely to go wrong.

What makes wild mushrooms so special is their full, earthy flavour, which puts the traditional cultivated mushrooms firmly in the shade. Ceps, also known as penny buns for their plump, round heads, are the best of all boletus mushrooms – those distinguished by their spongy gills.

Large ceps at least 7.5 cm (3 in) across **Sunflower or groundnut oil**
Cloves garlic, cut into thin slivers **Salt and freshly ground black pepper**

Clean the ceps with a cloth, scraping off any leaves and other gunge with a knife. Cut out any wormy bits. Slice off the stems and save for some other dish. With the tip of a sharp knife, make slits in the caps, and push slivers of garlic down into them. Quite how many depends on the size of the caps and your fondness for garlic, but don't be too stingy. Brush with oil, season with salt and pepper and grill gently, smooth side upwards at first, turning the spongy side up later, until tender. Allow a good 15–20 minutes, so that both the mushrooms and the garlic are cooked right through.

Ceps with Garlic and Parsley

Wild mushrooms with garlic and parsley is a really delicious combination. Again, I haven't specified quantities, so you can vary the amounts depending on how many mushrooms you have and how much garlic you like.

Small–medium ceps less than 7.5 cm **Finely chopped parsley**
   (3 in) across **Finely chopped garlic**
A few cloves garlic, cut into slivers **A handful of fresh breadcrumbs**
Goose fat, or 1/2 butter and **Salt and freshly ground black pepper**
   1/2 sunflower or groundnut oil

Clean the ceps as described in Grilled Ceps, above. Leave the caps whole; make 2 or 3 slits in each one and push in a sliver of garlic. Slice the stems thickly. Keep the caps and stems separate. Melt a generous amount of fat in two separate pans and put the caps in one, the stems in the other. Cook gently, stirring and turning every now and then, for a good 20 minutes or so, until they begin to colour.

Throw a small handful of chopped parsley and garlic in with the stems, and carry on cooking for 3–4 minutes. Now add just enough breadcrumbs to each pan to sop up a good deal of the fat, and then season with salt and pepper. Stir for 2 minutes or so, then serve piping hot.

Tomates à la Crème

Fried tomatoes with a touch of indulgence. With their rich cream sauce, they make a marvellous accompaniment to plainly cooked meat. You could also serve them as a first course on slices of toast or, better still, fried bread.

SERVES 4
500 g (1 lb 2 oz) medium-sized tomatoes
Sunflower oil

150 ml (5 fl oz) crème fraîche
Chopped fresh parsley
Salt and freshly ground black pepper

Cut the tomatoes in half horizontally (that is, through the middle, rather than from stalk to stem end). Oil a heavy-based frying-pan lightly and set it over a high heat. Leave until searingly hot. Lay the tomatoes in it, cut-sides down, and cook for 30–60 seconds until browned underneath. Turn the other way up and reduce the heat. Cook for another minute or so and then spoon in the cream, parsley, salt and pepper. Simmer for a further 3–4 minutes, until the cream is reduced to a rich sauce. Taste and adjust the seasonings and serve.

Tomatoes with Tarragon Butter and Capers

Adapted from one of Elizabeth David's recipes (from her Spices, Salts and Aromatics in the English Kitchen, *a book that is often ignored in the shadow of her French and Italian works), this is a sublime and beautiful dish of whole plum tomatoes, cooked gently in butter and finished with lots of tarragon and a sprinkling of capers. Though it is meant as a side dish (excellent with red meats), it is really too good to play second fiddle. I serve the tomatoes as a course on their own, with thick slices of sturdy bread to mop up the juices.*

SERVES 4

FOR THE TARRAGON BUTTER
85 g (3 oz) butter, softened
1 1/2 tablespoons very finely chopped
fresh tarragon
A dash of lemon or lime juice
Freshly ground black pepper

FOR THE TOMATOES
30 g (1 oz) butter
500 g (1 lb 2 oz) firm plum tomatoes
Salt and sugar
1–2 tablespoons small capers

To make the tarragon butter, mash the butter and tarragon together well and season with pepper and a dash of lemon or lime juice. Wrap in foil and chill in the fridge. You won't need all the tarragon butter for this recipe but it keeps quite well, and can be used on vegetables or fish.

Keep the tomatoes whole. Melt the ordinary butter in a frying-pan. Add the tomatoes and season with salt and a pinch or two of sugar. Cook over a very low heat for about 10 minutes, turning the tomatoes once or twice, very gently.

When they are soft (but not collapsing) and the juice is running a little, add a tablespoon of the tarragon butter and the capers. Turn up the heat for a few seconds, to melt the butter. Spoon the pan juices over the tomatoes and then serve them quickly, before they lose their shape and turn to sauce.

Ratatouille

Like the little girl with the curl, when it's good, ratatouille is very, very good, but when it's bad, it's awful. There are different theories about how to make the perfect ratatouille. Some people insist on cooking all the vegetables separately, combining them only for the last few minutes. True, they keep their individual shapes better that way, but I prefer the other more standard approach. I always cook them together, adding them in stages, so that the flavours all intermingle. I think the key to making a good ratatouille is slow lazy burbling on top of the stove (the stew that is, not you or me). Never rush the cooking process. Allow plenty of time for the dish to mellow to a Provençal richness.

There's no point trying to make ratatouille in a smaller quantity than this. It keeps well in the fridge for a couple of days, and, in fact, tastes even better cold than hot.

SERVES 6–8
1 large aubergine
450 g (1 lb) courgettes
1/2 tablespoon salt
1 green pepper
1 red pepper
400 g (14 oz) can tomatoes or 450 g (1 lb) fresh tomatoes, skinned
1 large onion, chopped
2 cloves garlic, peeled and chopped
4 tablespoons olive oil

1 tablespoon tomato purée
1/2 teaspoon sugar
Salt and freshly ground black pepper
1/2 teaspoon coriander seeds, crushed

TO GARNISH
2 tablespoons chopped fresh basil or fresh parsley
A little more extra virgin olive oil (optional)

Cut the aubergine into 2.5 cm (1 in) chunks. Cut the courgettes into slices about 1 cm (1/2 in) thick. Put both into a colander and sprinkle with the salt. Leave for 30 minutes to drain, then rinse and pat dry on kitchen paper. Halve the peppers and remove stalk, seeds and white inner membrane. Cut into 1 cm (1/2 in) wide strips. If using canned tomatoes, chop roughly in their can with a sharp knife. If using fresh tomatoes, chop roughly.

In a wide frying-pan, or saucepan, cook the onion and garlic gently in the oil until tender, without browning. Add the aubergine and peppers, stir, then cover and cook for 10 minutes, stirring once or twice. Now add the courgettes, tomatoes, tomato purée, sugar, salt and pepper. Bring to the boil, then lower the heat and simmer gently, uncovered, for about 30 minutes, stirring occasionally to prevent burning. Stir in the crushed coriander seeds and continue cooking for another 10 minutes or so, until all traces of wateriness have gone and the ratatouille is thick and rich. Taste and adjust the seasonings, adding a little more sugar if it is on the sharp side. Serve hot or cold sprinkled with the basil or parsley and maybe a drizzle of extra virgin olive oil.

Sautéd Peppers with Balsamic Vinegar

A quick, easy way to cook peppers, bringing out their sweetness to the full. The sautéd peppers can be served hot or cold, as a side dish, hors d'oeuvre or even on hot pasta.

SERVES 4

3 tablespoons olive oil
1 large red onion, sliced
1 red pepper, seeded and cut into 1 cm (1/2 in) wide strips
1 green pepper, seeded and cut into 1 cm (1/2 in) wide strips

1 clove garlic, peeled and finely chopped
1/2 teaspoon ground coriander
1/2 tablespoon balsamic vinegar
Salt and freshly ground black pepper

Heat the oil over a moderate heat in a wide frying-pan. Add the onion and fry over a gentle heat, stirring occasionally, for 10 minutes. Raise the heat and add the peppers and sauté briskly until tender and patched with brown. Add the garlic and coriander and continue to fry for a further 2 minutes. Tip into a dish and season with balsamic vinegar, salt and pepper. Serve.

Peas with Ham

The traditional British way of cooking peas with sprigs of fresh mint is one of the best. Some people add a pinch of sugar too, but it's quite unnecessary with newly picked garden peas or frozen peas. It does help shop-bought fresh peas regain some of their natural sweetness. Pea pods shouldn't be wasted. Chopped up, they make a good soup (sieve it to remove the tough strings). This Spanish way of cooking peas highlights their natural sweetness with the saltiness of cured jamón serrano, the superb dried mountain ham. If you don't have a Spanish supplier near you, Parma ham makes a good substitute. Normally, I wouldn't cook frozen peas for such a long time, but in this recipe they need time to absorb the flavour of the ham.

SERVES 4

1 kg (2 lb) peas in their pods or 450 g (1 lb) thawed, frozen peas

1 carrot, peeled and very finely chopped

1 onion, finely chopped

2 tablespoons olive oil

50–75 g (2–3 oz) piece Spanish *jamón serrano* or other dried raw ham

TO GARNISH
Sweet paprika

Shell the fresh peas, if using. In a saucepan large enough to hold the peas in a layer no more than 2.5 cm (1 in) thick, sauté the carrot and onion in the oil until the onion is golden brown. Add the ham, and stir for a further 30 seconds or so, then add the peas. Stir, then cover tightly and cook slowly for 30–40 minutes, until the peas are tender. (If using frozen peas reduce the cooking time by 10 minutes.) Stir occasionally, to make sure that they don't catch on the base. Dust with paprika before serving.

French Beans with Cumin and Almonds

Who would have thought that adding a spoonful of cumin and a few almonds to a panful of French beans would turn them into something so exotic? Well, it does, though they're not so over-the-top exotic as to clash with an otherwise straightforward meal.

SERVES 4

450 g (1 lb) French beans, topped and tailed

2 tablespoons olive or sunflower oil or 25 g (1 oz) butter

15 g (1/2 oz) flaked almonds

1 small onion, chopped

1 teaspoon ground cumin

Salt and freshly ground black pepper

Cut the beans into 2.5–4 cm (1–1 1/2 in) lengths.

Heat the oil or butter in a wide frying-pan. Fry the almonds briskly until golden brown. Scoop out and drain on kitchen paper. Reduce the heat under the pan and fry the onions until tender, without browning. Add the beans, cumin and salt and pepper and fry for 3 minutes. Add 2 tablespoons of water, then cover and cook for 5 minutes or so until the beans are tender and most of the liquid has been absorbed. Return the almonds to the pan, stir for a few seconds to re-heat, and serve.

Curried Beans à la Crème

This curried cream sauce is much the same as the one I use for chard (see p. 254),
but the final dishes taste quite different. Instead of the dark savouriness of the chard,
it is the sweet snap of French beans that picks up the mild fragrance of curry.

SERVES 4
450 g (1 lb) French beans, topped and
    tailed
25 g (1 oz) butter

1 teaspoon mild curry powder
120 ml (4 fl oz) whipping cream
Salt and freshly ground black pepper
Dash of lemon juice

Cut the beans in half. Blanch in boiling salted water for 3–4 minutes. Drain thoroughly.

    Melt the butter in a wide frying-pan. When it is foaming, add the beans and fry
for 1 minute. Sprinkle over the curry powder and mix in, then fry for a further minute.
Add the cream and a little salt and pepper and simmer until the cream has reduced
to a thick sauce. Draw off the heat and add a squeeze of lemon juice to highlight the
flavours. Taste and adjust the seasoning and serve.

Sichuan Green Beans

This recipe is remarkable. Until I came across it, it had never occurred to me to deep-
fry green beans. In fact, it is an excellent way of cooking them, even if you don't go
on to finish them with all the aromatics. However, I'd urge you to try the full treatment.
Dried shrimps and Sichuan pepper can be found in Chinese food shops.

SERVES 4 AS A FIRST COURSE
2 tablespoons dried shrimps
Sunflower or vegetable oil for
    deep-frying
1/2 kg (1 lb) French beans, topped and
    tailed
2 cloves garlic, peeled and thinly
    sliced
1/2 teaspoon Sichuan or black
    peppercorns, coarsely crushed

2.5 cm (1 in) piece of fresh ginger,
    peeled and cut into matchsticks
1/2 teaspoon salt
1 tablespoon sugar
1 tablespoon dark soy sauce
2 teaspoons rice vinegar or white wine
    vinegar
1 tablespoon sesame oil

Cover the shrimps generously with boiling water and soak for 20 minutes. Drain
and reserve the liquid. Chop the shrimps finely. Heat a panful of oil to 190°C/375°F
and deep-fry the beans for 5 minutes, until tender and patched with brown. Drain on
kitchen paper.

    In a wok, or large high-sided frying-pan, heat 1 tablespoon of oil until it smokes.
Add the garlic, pepper and ginger and stir-fry for a few seconds. Then add the
shrimps and stir-fry for 30 seconds. Add the salt, sugar, soy sauce and 5 tablespoons
of the shrimp water.

Finally add the green beans. Toss in the sauce to coat well, then cover and, keeping the heat high, cook until virtually all the liquid has been absorbed. Check after 1 minute – the sauce should have caramelized and the beans should be several shades darker, even verging on black. Toss and, if necessary, cover again for a further 30 seconds or so to finish cooking. Remove from the heat and mix with the vinegar and sesame oil. Serve hot or, better still, cold.

Bean and Potato Ratatouille

This isn't a ratatouille in the real sense of the word, but the cooking method is similar, even if French beans and potatoes do replace the aubergines, courgettes and peppers. In fact, the dill gives it more of an eastern Mediterranean flavour. Like ratatouille, it can be served hot or cold, as a side dish, first course or even a main course, perhaps with a few eggs poached in it when it is nearly done.

SERVES 4–6
1 onion, chopped
2 cloves garlic, peeled and chopped
4 tablespoons extra virgin olive
    oil
275 g (10 oz) new potatoes or waxy
    salad potatoes, halved or quartered
    if large
750 g (1 lb 8 oz) fresh tomatoes,
    skinned, seeded and chopped, or
    1¹/2 × 400 g (14 oz) cans chopped
    tomatoes

1 tablespoon tomato purée
¹/2 tablespoon sugar
Salt and freshly ground black pepper
350 g (12 oz) French beans, topped and
    tailed and cut in half
2 tablespoons chopped fresh parsley
1¹/2 tablespoons chopped fresh dill or
    ¹/2 tablespoon dried

Cook the onion and garlic gently in 3 tablespoons of the oil in a large saucepan until tender, without browning. Add the potatoes, stir, then cover and cook for a further 5 minutes. Add the tomatoes, tomato purée, sugar, salt and pepper. Bring to the boil and simmer, uncovered, until the potatoes are half-cooked.

Put in the beans, 1 tablespoon of the parsley and all the dill. Simmer for a further 10–15 minutes, stirring occasionally, until the vegetables are all tender and the sauce is thick. If the sauce still looks a bit watery, turn up the heat and boil hard for a few minutes to reduce. Taste and adjust the seasonings. Serve hot or cold and, just before serving, sprinkle with the remaining parsley and drizzle the last tablespoon of olive oil over the 'ratatouille'.

Lentil Purée with Roast Carrots, Red Onions and Mint

The smooth, earthy lentil purée, enriched with butter and a slug of cream, makes a brilliant backdrop for the sweetness of roast carrots and onions, finished with a breath of fresh mint. A good dish for vegetarians – and any obdurate carnivores can be soothed with a grilled or fried sausage on the side.

SERVES 4

FOR THE ROAST VEGETABLES
2 red onions, cut into 8 wedges each, slicing from stalk to root end
600 g (1 lb 4 oz) carrots, halved (or quartered, if large) lengthways
3 tablespoons olive oil
Coarse salt and freshly ground black pepper
2 teaspoons balsamic vinegar
1¹/₂ tablespoons chopped fresh mint

FOR THE LENTILS
220 g (8 oz) green or brown lentils
2 shallots, peeled and halved

1 large carrot, quartered
2 garlic cloves
1 bouquet garni (1 bay leaf, 2 sprigs thyme, 1 sprig rosemary and 1 sprig parsley, tied together with string)
Salt and freshly ground black pepper
30 g (1 oz) butter
2 tablespoons double cream

TO GARNISH
Fresh mint sprigs

Pre-heat the oven to 190°C/375°F/Gas Mark 5. Put the onions and carrots in a shallow ovenproof dish, large enough to take them in a single, snug layer. Spoon over the oil and then turn the vegetables, so that they are coated in oil. Add 2 tablespoons of water and season with salt and a little pepper. Roast for 1–1¹/₄ hours, basting from time to time, until the carrots and onions are tender and patched with brown. Drizzle over the vinegar and then stir in the mint. Taste and adjust the seasoning.

While the vegetables are cooking, put the lentils in a pan with the shallots, quartered carrot, garlic, the bouquet garni and 1.2 litres (2 pints) of water. Do not add any salt. Bring to the boil and simmer gently for about 45 minutes, until the lentils are very, very tender. Reserve a tablespoon of cooked lentils. Discard the herbs, and tip the rest of the contents of the pan into a food processor. Season with salt and pepper, add the butter, and process until smooth. Stir in the cream. Taste and adjust the seasoning.

Serve in shallow dishes, ladling some lentil purée into each dish, topping with carrots, onions and their juices and then scattering a few of the reserved lentils over and around the whole lot. Garnish with sprigs of mint.

Flageolets Maitre d'Hôtel

Flageolets are a small, elegant, pale green type of haricot bean. They bear the freshest, subtlest flavour of all dried pulses and are very highly prized in France. Tinned flageolets make an excellent storecupboard stand-by for feeding unexpected guests, when you need a comforting treat, or just in case you get snowed in. Dried flageolets also keep well, stored in an airtight container and, like all dried pulses, they work out cheaper than the tinned ones.

This recipe is just a fancy name for flageolets dressed with butter, parsley and lemon. It's a lovely combination that brings a touch of class to, say, a few grilled lamb chops. Use the same maitre d'hôtel butter to upgrade canned flageolets.

SERVES 6
300 g (10 oz) dried flageolet beans, soaked overnight and drained
4 fresh parsley sprigs
1 fresh thyme sprig
2 garlic cloves, halved
Salt and freshly ground black pepper

FOR THE MAITRE D'HÔTEL BUTTER
75 g ($2^1/_2$ oz) butter
3 tablespoons finely chopped fresh parsley
$^1/_2$ tablespoon finely grated lemon zest
A generous dash of lemon juice

Put the flageolets into a pan with the parsley and thyme sprigs tied together with a piece of string, and the garlic. Add enough water to cover by about 5 cm (2 in). Do not add any salt. Bring to the boil, half-cover and simmer for 1–2 hours, or until very tender but not collapsing.

Drain the beans, reserving some of the cooking water, and discard the bundle of herbs and the garlic. If not using immediately, tip the beans into a bowl, add a little of their cooking water to moisten them, leave to cool and cover with cling film.

While the beans cook, mash the butter with the chopped parsley, lemon zest and lemon juice. Pile into a bowl and chill until needed.

Shortly before serving, put the beans into a wide shallow pan (a frying-pan is fine for this) and place over a moderate heat, with 2 tablespoons of their cooking water. Season with salt and pepper. Let them re-heat for a few minutes, tilting and shaking the pan so that they are evenly heated through. Dot the butter on to the beans in small pieces. Keep swirling and tilting and shaking the pan so that the butter melts into the beans appetizingly. Taste and adjust the seasoning and serve immediately.

Flageolet Beans in Tomato and Cream Sauce

This recipe is so very, very good. The cooked beans are re-heated in a rich tomato and cream sauce flavoured with rosemary, a combination that's hard to beat.

SERVES 8

340 g (12 oz) dried flageolet beans,
    soaked overnight and drained
1 bay leaf
2 fresh parsley sprigs
1 fresh rosemary sprig
5 garlic cloves, unpeeled

FOR THE SAUCE
1/2 onion, chopped
1 tablespoon butter

400 g (14 oz) can of tomatoes or
    500 g (1 lb 2 oz) fresh tomatoes,
    skinned and chopped
1 tablespoon tomato purée
1 large fresh rosemary sprig
1/2 teaspoon sugar
Salt and freshly ground black pepper
150 ml (5 fl oz) double cream

Cook the flageolets in fresh water with the herbs tied in a bundle with string, and the garlic, until tender. Drain and pick out the garlic and herbs. Reserve the garlic but discard the herbs.

To make the sauce, cook the onion gently in the butter. Add the tomatoes, tomato purée, rosemary, sugar, salt and pepper. Simmer for 10 minutes. Discard the rosemary.

Squeeze the reserved garlic cloves out of their skins and add to the sauce. Liquidize and sieve, or pass through the fine blade of a *mouli-légumes* (vegetable mill). Return to the pan and stir in the cream and the flageolets. Simmer gently for a few minutes, to heat through. Taste and adjust the seasoning and serve immediately.

Barbecued Corn-on-the-Cob with Olive and Lemon Butter

Barbecued fresh sweetcorn on the cob, streaked with brown, juicy and tender, has a superb, sweet smoky taste, emphasized by the saltiness of olives in the flavoured butter as it melts over the hot kernels. Soaking the corn plumps up the kernels, ensuring that they don't dry out over the hot charcoal. This is my version of bar-becued corn. Alternatively, you could cook them the way Norfolk organic gardener and broadcaster Bob Flowerdew prefers: left in the husk. This method produces a less smoky, more purely sweetcorn flavour. If you choose to leave the husks on, they will still need to be soaked in water for a good 30 minutes. Shake off excess water, then grill over a moderate heat for about 15 minutes, turning frequently.

SERVES 6
6 heads of corn-on-the-cob
Sunflower oil

FOR THE BUTTER
50 g (2 oz) black olives, pitted

100 g (4 oz) unsalted butter, softened
Finely grated zest of 1/2 lemon
1–2 tablespoons lemon juice
1 small clove garlic, peeled and
    crushed

Either place all the ingredients for the butter in a food processor and whizz until smooth, or chop the olives very, very finely and mash with the butter and remaining ingredients. Taste and add extra lemon juice if needed. Pile into a bowl, cover loosely and chill.

Strip the husks and silky threads off the corn. Immerse in a bucket of lightly salted water and leave to soak for at least 30 minutes and up to 3 hours. Just before barbecuing pat dry, brush with oil, then cook over a moderate heat, turning, until patched with brown on all sides. Eat the hot corn with the chilled butter.

My Version of Succotash

Succotash was originally a native American Indian dish of sweetcorn and lima beans thickened with sunflower seed flour. It now appears in almost every general American cookbook. Recipes vary considerably, so I've taken the liberty of doing a bit more tweaking and adapting for myself. Finding lima beans in Britain is not easy (though butter beans bear a close resemblance), so I use green flageolet beans or haricot beans instead. A squeeze or two of lemon juice added right at the end heightens the flavours neatly without making it obviously lemony. And to make it look a little less pallid, as well as adding a touch more taste, I sprinkle chopped parsley on top.

SERVES 6–8
450 g (1 lb) frozen sweetcorn kernels or
    4 heads of corn-on-the-cob
50 g (2 oz) butter
8 spring onions, cut into 2.5 cm (1 in)
    lengths
Salt and freshly ground black pepper

400 g (14 oz) cooked flageolet or
    haricot beans
150 ml (5 fl oz) double cream
Squeeze of lemon juice

TO GARNISH
Chopped fresh parsley

If using fresh sweetcorn, cut the kernels off the cob straight into a saucepan. Scrape down the cob, still over the pan, to extract juices. Put frozen sweetcorn straight into the pan. Add the butter, spring onions, salt and pepper and 4 tablespoons of water. Cover and cook over a low heat for 15 minutes, stirring occasionally. Add the flageolets, or haricots, and cream and simmer, uncovered, for 5 minutes or until the cream has reduced to a thick sauce. Taste and adjust the seasoning, adding a squeeze of lemon juice to bring up the flavour. Sprinkle with a little chopped parsley and serve hot and steaming.

Buttered Baked Marrow with Aromatics

My favourite way of cooking marrow, without a doubt. When marrow is baked with butter, herbs and spices, but absolutely no added water, its light flavour is preserved at full strength. Vary the herbs and spices as you will (though this seems a particularly appealing combination), but don't tamper with the method!

SERVES 4–6
1 kg (2 lb) marrow
50 g (2 oz) butter
1/2 teaspoon dried oregano

1 teaspoon coriander seeds, crushed
1 tablespoon caster sugar
Salt and freshly ground black pepper

Pre-heat the oven to 170°C/325°F/Gas Mark 3.

Peel the marrow, halve and scoop out the seeds, then cut into 2.5 cm (1 in) chunks. Use about a third of the butter to grease an ovenproof dish that will take the marrow in a tight, single layer.

Spread out the marrow chunks in the dish, sprinkle with oregano, coriander, sugar, salt and pepper, and then dot with the remaining butter. Cover the dish with foil, and bake for 35 minutes. Remove the foil, turn the marrow in its own juices, and return to the oven for a final 10–15 minutes until just cooked.

Sautéd Squash with Parmesan

The sweet mealiness of butternut squash fried in butter is enhanced by the saltiness of the Parmesan. This can be served as a side dish, but it's good enough to eat on its own.

SERVES 4
1 medium-sized butternut squash or about 675 g (1 lb 8 oz) chunk of kabocha, onion or other winter squash, seeded and peeled
30 g (1 oz) butter
2 tablespoons olive oil

2 tablespoons finely chopped fresh parsley
Salt and freshly ground black pepper

TO SERVE
45 g (1 1/2 oz) Parmesan cheese, finely shaved

Cut the squash into 1.5 cm (1/2 in) cubes. Heat the butter with the oil in a heavy, wide frying-pan. Add the cubes of squash in a single layer. If there are too many to fit comfortably, take the excess out and save for some other dish or discard: you want the squash to fry and not stew in its own juices in an overcrowded pan. Sauté over a moderate heat until evenly browned and tender. Season with salt and pepper. Draw off the heat, stir in the parsley and tip into a serving dish. Scatter over the Parmesan and serve immediately.

Fish-fragrant Aubergine

No fish at all in this Chinese recipe, despite the name. The aubergine is cooked with the flavourings that are often used with fish – hence fish-fragrant. Fish or no fish, it's a marvellous way to cook aubergine, spiced and melting and quite irresistible. Be warned, though, when the chilli hits the hot oil, the fumes are forceful enough to make you cough and splutter.

Sichuan pepper is not a true pepper at all, but it does have a tingly, numbing heat and a marvellous incense-like aroma. Some larger supermarkets and good delicatessens and all oriental food shops stock it. It's well worth hunting out, though black pepper can stand in at a pinch in this recipe.

SERVES 3–4

1 very large aubergine or 2 small ones	1 cm (1/2 in) piece of fresh ginger, peeled and finely chopped
1 teaspoon salt	1 tablespoon soy sauce
2 dried red chillies	1 teaspoon sugar
Sunflower or vegetable oil for deep-frying	Large pinch of freshly ground Sichuan or black pepper
3 spring onions, sliced	1 tablespoon rice vinegar or white wine vinegar
2 cloves garlic, peeled and finely chopped	1 teaspoon sesame oil

Cut the aubergine into slices about 2.5 cm (1 in) thick. Cut each slice into diamond-shaped chunks. Spread out in a colander and sprinkle with the salt. Leave to drain for 30 minutes. Rinse under the cold tap, drain and pat dry on kitchen paper. Soak the chillies in warm water for 15 minutes, then cut each one into 3 pieces, discarding the seeds.

Heat enough oil in a wok to deep-fry the aubergine chunks. When it's just smoking add the aubergine and deep-fry for 3–4 minutes, until golden brown. Scoop out and drain on kitchen paper. Pour off all but 1 tablespoon of the oil. Re-heat and add the chilli, spring onions, garlic and ginger. Stir-fry for 30 seconds. Add the aubergine and toss. Now add all the remaining ingredients except the sesame oil. Stir-fry for a further 1–2 minutes. Stir in the sesame oil and serve.

Okra in Tomato Sauce

When buying okra, choose pods that are on the small side (large ones can be stringy) without brown patches, or at least with as few as possible. They are quite nice eaten raw if small and tender (in which case you may want to scrub them gently under the cold tap to remove the light fuzz) but far better cooked.

They can be boiled or steamed whole until just tender – a scant 10 minutes – but it's not the best way to cook them. I prefer them fried gently in butter or oil, sliced or whole. They benefit from the addition of garlic or a few spices, and once cooked a squeeze of lemon or lime juice heightens their flavour.

This Greek-Cypriot way of cooking okra in a tomato sauce is one I particularly like. In Cyprus it may be served as a main course on 'fasting days'. Though it is good hot, I think it is even better cold, with an extra drizzle of olive oil trickled over just before serving.

SERVES 4
450 g (1 lb) okra
3 tablespoons olive oil
1 large onion, chopped
2 cloves garlic, finely chopped

200 g (7 oz) canned chopped tomatoes
1 tablespoon tomato purée
1 bayleaf
4 tablespoons chopped parsley
Salt and freshly ground black pepper

Trim the stalk end off the okra cone without cutting right into the okra. Fry quickly in the oil in a large saucepan, until lightly browned. Spoon into a saucepan.

Fry the onion and garlic in the same oil until tender but without browning. Add the chopped tomatoes and tomato purée, bayleaf and 4 tablespoons water. Bring to the boil and simmer for 10 minutes. Add plenty of pepper and a pinch of salt. Pour over the okra, then add just enough hot water to cover. Stir in half the parsley. Simmer for 30 minutes, until the sauce is thick. Taste and adjust the seasonings.

Serve hot or cold, sprinkled with the remaining parsley.

Colcannon

On the road from Dublin to the west coast of Ireland, not far from Mullingar in County Westmeath, is Mother Hubbard's Diner, a celebrated truckers' stop, where the food is good and wholesome, the surroundings are spruce and clean and the atmosphere cheerful and welcoming. At Mother Hubbard's they grow their own cabbages in the vegetable patch alongside the diner, together with herbs and rhubarb for making pies. Trish Doyle, who runs the diner, cooked colcannon for me, the traditional Irish dish of mashed potato and cabbage. It used to be served at Hallowe'en, with lucky charms buried deep inside the steaming, pale green mound. Whoever found the ring would be married within the year, while the coin promised a great fortune.

SERVES 6

450 g (1 lb) trimmed green cabbage or
   curly kale
300 ml (10 fl oz) full cream milk or
   better still, single cream

50 g (2 oz) butter
2 large onions or 2 large leeks or
   8 spring onions, chopped
450 g (1 lb) floury potatoes
Salt and freshly ground black pepper

Boil the cabbage in salted water for 20–30 minutes until very tender. Squeeze dry, then chop roughly. Put the milk, or cream, and butter into a saucepan with the onions, leeks or spring onions and simmer for 20 minutes.

Boil the potatoes in their skins. Drain thoroughly, peel and mash. Process or liquidize the milk/cream and onions/leeks/spring onion mixture with the cabbage until fairly smooth. Beat into the mashed potato. Taste, season and re-heat gently if necessary.

Slow-cooked Cabbage with Lemon

Stewed very slowly for an hour or more in its own juices with a generous knob of butter, dull white cabbage takes on a whole new persona. It softens down to a nutty, mellow flavour. When I was in Ireland, I nervously tried this one out on a hungry truck-driver in Mother Hubbard's Diner (see Colcannon recipe above). 'Scrumptious,' he said as he polished off his helping, and that about sums it up.

SERVES 4–6

1 kg (2 lb) white cabbage
1 lemon

75 g (3 oz) lightly salted butter
2 teaspoons sugar
Salt and freshly ground black pepper

Slice the cabbage into strips about 1 cm (1/2 in) wide, discarding the tough core. Pare the zest from the lemon in wide strips, and squeeze out the juice. Melt the butter in a saucepan large enough to take all the cabbage. Add cabbage, lemon zest, sugar, salt and pepper. Turn to mix, then cover tightly and cook over a low heat for 1 hour, stirring occasionally, until the cabbage is meltingly tender and all the liquid it has exuded has been reabsorbed or evaporated. If it still seems a little watery after an hour, remove the lid and let it burble quietly for another 5–10 minutes. Now add the lemon juice, cover and cook for a few minutes longer. Taste, adjust the seasonings and serve.

Stir-fried Sweet-and-sour Red Cabbage

The classic way to cook red cabbage is long and slow, with sweet and sour additions – a cooking apple, raisins, sugar or honey, vinegar or red wine, and orange juice. It's a marvellous dish, but I've not given a recipe for it as there are so many around that you will have no difficulty finding one if you don't already have your own version. Instead, I've suggested stir-frying which is much quicker. Stir-frying is one of the best methods to cook so many vegetables, and I find myself stir-frying all manner of things, often with not a hint of a Chinese flavour.

Don't be tempted to skip the salting of the cabbage. It draws out some of the water content, which means that it will cook much more quickly, without stewing in its own juices.

SERVES 4–5

1/2 head of red cabbage
1 teaspoon salt
2 tablespoons sherry vinegar or red wine vinegar
1 tablespoon caster sugar

1 1/2 tablespoons sunflower oil
15 g (1/2 oz) pine kernels
25 g (1 oz) raisins
Freshly ground black pepper

Cut the tough central stalk out of the cabbage, then shred finely. Spread out in a colander, and sprinkle with the salt. Turn, then leave to drain for 30 minutes. Rinse under the cold tap and pat dry with kitchen paper. Mix the vinegar with 1 tablespoon of water and the sugar.

Heat the oil in a wok, or a large frying-pan, until very hot. Keep the heat high throughout. Add the cabbage, and stir and toss for 3 minutes. Add the pine kernels and continue to stir-fry for 2 minutes. Stir in the vinegar mixture, and pour into the cabbage. Add the raisins and plenty of pepper. Stir-fry for 1–2 minutes longer until the liquid has evaporated, and serve.

Chard in a Curried Cream Sauce

Usually, I cook the mid-ribs and leaves of chard together, adding the leaves a few minutes after the ribs and sweating them both in butter or oil. However, before they get into the pan, they need to be separated. I find that the easiest way is to pile 3 or 4 leaves up, and slice out the mid-ribs with a sharp knife. For a more perfect separation cut them individually with a knife or scissors. Pull any tough strings from the ribs as you cut them into suitable lengths.

This is a luxuriously rich way of presenting chard. Hopeless if you are watching the cholesterol, superb when you throw dietary cares to the wind.

SERVES 4
**750 g–1 kg (1 1/2–2 lb) Swiss or ruby
  chard**
50 g (2 oz) butter

1 teaspoon mild curry powder
175 ml (6 fl oz) double cream
Salt and freshly ground black pepper
Squeeze of lemon juice

Separate the leaves from the thick ribs of the chard. Shred the leaves roughly. Slice ribs into 1 cm (1/2 in) wide strips (across the stalk, not lengthways). Melt the butter in a wide frying-pan and add the ribs. Stir to coat in butter, then cover and cook over a low heat, for 10–15 minutes, stirring occasionally. Add the leaves and the curry powder, stir then cover again and cook for a further 5–10 minutes until all are tender. When the chard is done, pour over the cream and stir to mix. Simmer, uncovered, for a few minutes until thickened, season with salt and pepper and a squeeze of lemon juice and serve.

Broccoli with Chilli and Parmesan

When my mother wrote her Vegetable Book *in the late 1970s, fresh plump green heads of broccoli calabrese (i.e. broccoli from Calabria where it was developed) were relative newcomers in shops and supermarkets. It was sold as calabrese to distinguish it from purple-sprouting broccoli which was far more widely known. Broccoli calabrese made a huge impact, soon ousting its older spindlier brother from a position of supremacy. For people of my generation and younger, broccoli invariably means the thick-stemmed newcomer, the name calabrese has been dropped, and purple-sprouting broccoli is now the more unusual of the two.*

This is a quick way to dress up cooked broccoli with a dash of fire. Spiked with chilli and garlic, with melting slivers of Parmesan on top, it's a nifty way to transform this vegetable into something special.

SERVES 4
750 g (1 lb 8 oz) broccoli
Salt
3 tablespoons olive oil
1/4–1/2 teaspoon chilli flakes

2–3 cloves garlic, peeled and finely
   chopped
15 g (1/2 oz) Parmesan cheese, cut into
   paper-thin slivers

Separate the broccoli florets from the stalks. Slice the stalks about 1 cm (1/2 in) thick. Drop the stalks into a pan of lightly salted boiling water. Simmer for 2 minutes, then add the florets and cook for a further 2–3 minutes until almost but not quite done. Drain, run under the cold tap to refresh then leave to drain completely and pat dry on kitchen paper.

Heat the oil in a wide frying-pan, and add the chilli and garlic. Cook over a low heat for about 1 minute, then add the broccoli. Raise the heat a little and stir and fry for 4–5 minutes until the broccoli is piping hot. Tip into a serving dish and scatter over the Parmesan. Serve at once.

Smothered Broccoli with White Wine

Forget al dente *for the moment – in this recipe the broccoli is cooked long and slow until meltingly tender, bringing out the full sweetness of the vegetable. It is so good that it should be savoured on its own as a first course, though it would make a good partner too, to a meaty main course.*

SERVES 4–6 AS A FIRST
   COURSE OR SIDE DISH
750 g (1 lb 8 oz) broccoli
2 dried red chillies
5 tablespoons olive oil
6 cloves garlic, peeled
6 pieces of sun-dried tomato, cut into
   thin strips, or 10 black olives,
   halved and pitted

Salt and freshly ground black pepper
250 ml (8 fl oz) dry white wine

TO SERVE
40 g (1 1/2 oz) Parmesan cheese, sliced
   into paper-thin shavings

Cut off the tough, woody ends of the broccoli stems. Leave thinner stems up to 1 cm (1/2 in) whole, cut thicker ones in half or quarters along their length. Cut each piece in half. Break chillies into pieces and shake out the seeds. Cover the base of a wide, deep, heavy frying-pan, or saucepan, with a thin layer of olive oil. Cover with a thick layer of the broccoli. Scatter over half the garlic, the sun-dried tomatoes or olives, the chilli, salt and pepper, and half the remaining olive oil. Repeat the layers. Pour over the wine. Cover and cook over a very gentle heat for 40 minutes to 1 hour until the liquid has almost evaporated, removing the lid towards the end of cooking if necessary. Spoon into a serving dish, and scatter with shavings of Parmesan. Serve immediately.

Chilli-crumbed Cauliflower

I have mixed feelings about cauliflower as a vegetable. Boiled, particularly over-boiled, it is often singularly dull and it looks anaemic. Even perfectly cooked cauliflower needs a helping hand, something to inject a little vigour into its palid sould. Crisp-fried breadcrumbs with a hint of garlic and chilli are a quick and tasty way to liven up a dish of plain cooked cauliflower. A nice contrast, too, with the smoothness of the pale vegetable.

SERVES 4–6
1 head of cauliflower, broken into
    florets
4 tablespoons olive oil
2 cloves garlic, peeled and finely
    chopped

1 green chilli, seeded and finely
    chopped
25 g (1 oz) fine white breadcrumbs
2 tablespoons chopped fresh parsley

Cook the cauliflower in salted boiling water, or steam. Drain well and arrange in a serving dish. Keep warm if necessary.

    While the cauliflower is cooking heat the oil over a moderate heat and add the garlic, chilli and breadcrumbs. Fry until the crumbs are golden brown. Stir in the parsley, then immediately pour over the cauliflower and serve.

Fried Brussels Sprouts

… or Brussels sprouts in disguise. They are certainly not recognizable cooked like this, not visually and possibly not tastewise, either. If you have a deep-rooted passion for sprouts then this may be no great recommendation. Personally, I find them much more interesting cooked this way than practically any other. Shredding the sprouts is a mite boring, but it won't take that long, and the speediness with which they cook makes up amply for lost time.

SERVES 4
450 g (1 lb) Brussels sprouts
2 tablespoons olive oil
2 cloves garlic, peeled and finely
    chopped

Salt and freshly ground black pepper

TO SERVE
1 tablespoon chopped fresh parsley

Shred the Brussels sprouts finely. Heat the oil in a wide frying-pan and add the garlic and sprouts. Sauté over a moderate heat until the sprouts are lightly patched with brown. Season with salt and pepper. Sprinkle with parsley and serve.

Brussels Sprouts with Bacon, Almonds and Cream

As far as I'm concerned, this is a recipe with CHRISTMAS LUNCH written large across it. It's about as decadent as you can get with a pound and a half of Brussels sprouts and just the thing to dish up with the roast turkey. Mind you, it tastes so good that it would be a shame to eat it only once a year.

SERVES 6

750 g (1 lb 8 oz) small Brussels sprouts
15 g (1/2 oz) butter
1 tablespoon oil
100 g (4 oz) piece of smoked back bacon or thick-cut bacon, diced

15 g (1/2 oz) flaked almonds
175 ml (6 fl oz) double cream
Finely grated zest of 1/2 lemon
Salt and freshly ground black pepper
Dash of lemon juice

Trim the sprouts, and drop into a saucepan of boiling salted water. Simmer until almost but not quite cooked, then drain thoroughly and pat dry with kitchen paper.

Heat the butter and oil in a wide frying-pan. Add the bacon and almonds and sauté until lightly browned. Add the sprouts and cook for 2–3 minutes, stirring. Draw off the heat, cool for a few seconds, then add the double cream and lemon zest. Return to the heat and let the cream bubble, stirring frequently, for about 4 minutes until reduced to a rich sauce. Off the heat, season with salt, pepper and a dash of lemon juice. Serve immediately.

Spinach with Seville Orange and Breadcrumbs

The spicy sourness of Seville oranges adds a wonderful zest to spinach, but sadly their season is short. There is a year-round alternative, though it is not quite the same. When the marmalade-making season is over, substitute the juice of 1/2 lemon mixed with the juice of 1/2 ordinary orange for the Seville orange juice, and serve with wedges of orange.

SERVES 4

1 kg (2 lb) fresh spinach
40 g (1 1/2 oz) butter
1 tablespoon sunflower oil
15 g (1/2 oz) fine dry breadcrumbs
Juice of 1 Seville orange

1 teaspoon ground cinnamon
Salt and freshly ground black pepper

TO SERVE
4 wedges of Seville orange

Wash the spinach thoroughly and discard any thick tough stems or damaged leaves. Shake off excess water, and pack the spinach into a large pan. Cover and cook over a gentle heat for 5 minutes. Stir, and cover again. Turn the heat up slightly, and cook for another 5–10 minutes, stirring occasionally until the spinach is just cooked. Drain well.

Heat 15 g (¹/₂ oz) of butter and the oil in a small frying-pan, and fry the breadcrumbs until golden brown. Drain on kitchen paper. Just before serving, re-heat the spinach with the remaining butter, Seville orange juice, cinnamon, salt and pepper, stirring as it heats up. Taste and adjust the seasonings. At the same time, re-heat the breadcrumbs.

Tip the spinach into a serving dish, and scatter the crumbs over the top. Serve with the orange wedges.

Spinaci alla Genovese

This dish of spinach (or sometimes chard) cooked with pine nuts and raisins is popular in Genoa but resurfaces in Catalonia and the Balearics. It is a surprisingly good combination and an easy way to dress up plain spinach.

SERVES 4

650 g (1 lb 6 oz) fresh spinach leaves
3 tablespoons olive oil
3 anchovy fillets, finely chopped
**2 tablespoons finely chopped fresh
    parsley**

60 g (2 oz) raisins or currants
60 g (2 oz) pine nuts
Salt and freshly ground black pepper
Freshly grated nutmeg

Pick over the spinach and discard any damaged leaves or tough, thick stalks. Rinse thoroughly in several changes of water and then drain but do not dry. Cram into a pan, cover and cook over a moderate heat, stirring once or twice, until the spinach has collapsed. Drain thoroughly, squeezing out any excess moisture, and then chop roughly.

Warm the oil in a saucepan over a moderate heat and add the chopped anchovies and the parsley. Stir for a minute or two and then add the spinach, raisins or currants, pine nuts, salt, pepper and nutmeg. Mix and cook gently for 5 minutes or so, half-covered. Serve piping hot.

Braised Lettuce with Mushroom and Bacon

Lettuce is only for salads … or is it? Not necessarily. Tightly furled dense Little Gem lettuces or hearts of other salads survive cooking extremely well, softening down but

*not dissolving away. Braised with mushrooms and bacon, they make a delicious side
dish to any main course.*

SERVES 4

4 Little Gem lettuces

**100 g (4 oz) unsmoked back bacon, in
one piece or thick cut**

25 g (1 oz) butter

1 onion, chopped

**225 g (8 oz) button mushrooms,
quartered**

1 sprig of fresh thyme

1 tablespoon chopped fresh parsley

1 teaspoon sugar

Salt and freshly ground black pepper

Remove and discard any damaged outer leaves of the lettuces. Then cut the whole
lettuces in half lengthwise and rinse well. Drain thoroughly. Dice the bacon into 5 mm
(¹/₄ in) cubes.

Melt the butter in a saucepan large enough to take all the lettuce halves in a tight
single layer. Add the bacon, onion, mushrooms, thyme and parsley, give them a quick
stir, and then snuggle in the lettuces. Sprinkle with sugar, salt and pepper. Cover
tightly and cook over a very gentle heat for 15 minutes, occasionally turning and
basting the lettuces. Remove the lid and simmer for a further 5 minutes, until the
lettuces are tender.

If there is still an ocean of liquid in the pan, scoop out the lettuces, bacon and
mushrooms on to a serving dish, keep them warm and boil the pan juices hard until
reduced by a third or so. Pour over the lettuces and serve.

Roast Chicory with
Balsamic Vinegar

*Here, a modicum of balsamic vinegar goes in at the start of the cooking time, so that
the chicory can absorb some of its flavour, then, when the chicory is tender, a little
more is added to restore the scent that has been sacrificed to heat. The end result is
a lovely, sweet, scented dish of tender chicory which goes beautifully with hot ham or
gammon.*

SERVES 4

4 chicory heads

30 g (1 oz) butter

3 tablespoons balsamic vinegar

2 tablespoons caster sugar

Salt and freshly ground black pepper

Pre-heat the oven to 200°C/400°F/Gas Mark 6. Trim the base of the chicory heads
and remove the outer layer of leaves, if they are damaged or bruised. Smear half the
butter over a shallow ovenproof dish that will just take the chicory snugly, without too
much room to spare. Drizzle over half the balsamic vinegar, scatter with sugar and
add 2 tablespoons of water. Season with salt and pepper and then dot with the
remaining butter. Cover with foil.

Roast for 20 minutes. Remove the foil, and turn the chicory. Return to the oven for another 20–30 minutes, depending on the size of the chicory heads, turning them once or twice and basting them with their own juices. When the chicory is very tender, take it out of the oven and drizzle over the remaining vinegar. Turn to mix it in and serve.

Fried Radicchio

Though we tend to think of it as just another decorative leaf for salads, radicchio, like chicory, can be cooked very successfully. The drawback is that its dark cherry-pink colour fades to brown, but the taste makes up for that.

SERVES 4–6
2 heads of radicchio
2 tablespoons olive oil
50 g (2 oz) pancetta or streaky bacon, diced
1 clove garlic, peeled and finely chopped
Salt and freshly ground black pepper

Separate out the leaves of the radicchio and wash well. Drain as thoroughly as you can, then cut roughly into strips about 2.5 cm (1 in) wide. Wrap in a clean tea towel until ready to cook.

Heat the oil in a frying-pan large enough to squash all the radicchio into. Fry the pancetta or bacon in the oil for a few seconds until it is opaque, then add the garlic and continue cooking until garlic and bacon begin to colour. Quickly add all the radicchio, salt and pepper, then slam on a lid (or a large plate) and turn down the heat slightly. Cook for about 10 minutes, stirring occasionally, until the radicchio has wilted. Taste and adjust the seasonings and serve immediately.

Salads

Green Leaf Salad with Walnuts

Whether you use a singleton or a mixture of salad leaves, the rules of salad making are straightforward, though often sadly neglected. The first thing to do is to wash them, rinsing and swishing the leaves around carefully in a large bowl of water to avoid bruising. On a hot day leave them in the water for an hour or two to crisp up. Then drain and dry them, ready for use. Make sure that they are dry before you use them – a damp salad is a damp squib. If necessary, pat the leaves dry, lightly and lovingly, in a clean tea towel or kitchen paper, or whizz them briefly in a salad spinner.

Always make salad dressings with the best quality oils and vinegars that you can afford. A dressing should not be so sharp that your mouth puckers when you taste it. Never toss the salad until it is on the table and ready to serve. Leaves doused in vinaigrette droop and darken with brutal speed. And finally, don't overdo the dressing – a light coating is all that is required.

Even supermarkets now sell the rarer nut oils, and a jolly good thing too. A vinaigrette made with nut oil and a scattering of matching toasted nuts gives a simple salad a major lift. Walnuts and walnut oil are excellent, but you might also try toasted hazelnuts or pine kernels with hazelnut oil.

SERVES 4
25 g (1 oz) walnut pieces
Selection of salad leaves (e.g. cos, frisée, radicchio, batavia, lollo rosso)

FOR THE DRESSING
1 tablespoon red wine vinegar

$^{1}/_{2}$–1 clove garlic, peeled and crushed (optional)
Salt and freshly ground black pepper
Pinch of sugar
3 tablespoons walnut oil and 2 tablespoons sunflower or groundnut oil

Pre-heat the oven to 200–230°C/400–450°F/Gas Mark 6–8.

Spread the walnut pieces out on a baking sheet and cook for 5–10 minutes, shaking the tray occasionally, until the walnuts are patched with dark brown. Tip into a wire sieve and shake to dislodge any papery flakes of skin. Cool.

Wash and dry the salad leaves. Store in a knotted plastic bag in the bottom of the fridge until needed. Either put all the dressing ingredients in a screwtop jar and shake well to mix, or whisk the vinegar with the garlic, if using, salt, pepper and sugar and then gradually whisk in the oil. Taste and adjust the seasonings.

Just before serving shake the dressing, and pour about half of it (save the rest for another salad) into a salad bowl. Cross salad servers in the bowl, and arrange the leaves on top. Scatter with the walnuts and toss at the table.

Wilted Salad with Goats' Cheese and Sun-dried Tomatoes

Grilled goats' cheese served with salad has become a standard first course in chic cafés and brasseries. This salad goes one step further, by grilling the entire salad to produce a sensational combination of warm and cool, melting cheese and buttery crisp pine nuts, bitter and sweet leaves.

SERVES 4

FOR THE DRESSING
2 tablespoons olive oil
1/2 tablespoon balsamic, sherry or red
   wine vinegar
Salt and freshly ground black pepper

FOR THE SALAD
1/2 head of radicchio, leaves separated
   and roughly torn up

1 handful of rocket leaves
8 leaves cos or Webb's lettuce, roughly
   torn up
100 g (4 oz) goats' cheese, rind
   removed, diced
6 pieces of sun-dried tomato, cut into
   thin strips
15 g (1/2 oz) pine kernels, lightly
   toasted

First make the dressing. Whisk the oil into the vinegar a spoonful at a time. Season with salt and pepper.

Mix the salad leaves. Just before serving, toss the salad leaves in a bowl with the dressing so that they are evenly coated. Spread them out in a 30 cm (12 in) gratin dish and scatter over the cheese, tomatoes and pine kernels. Whizz under a pre-heated grill for 3–4 minutes, until the salad leaves are wilting and the goats' cheese is beginning to soften. Serve immediately.

Caesar Salad

There are many recipes for this most famous of salads, invented in the 1920s by Caesar Cardini at his restaurant in Tijuana, Mexico. The original didn't include anchovies, but they often creep in none the less. The final preparation (which I've simplified a little) can be done discreetly in the kitchen, or more dramatically at the dinner table. If you choose to perform publicly, make sure you have a very large bowl, so that you don't shower your audience with lettuce.

SERVES 6
2 cos lettuces
3 slices stale white bread, crusts
   removed, cut into 1 cm (1/2 in) cubes
3 cloves garlic
160 ml (5 fl oz) extra virgin olive oil
2 eggs

1/2 can anchovy fillets, finely chopped,
   or 1/2 teaspoon Worcestershire
   sauce
Juice of 1 lemon
Salt and freshly ground black pepper
25 g (1 oz) freshly grated Parmesan
   cheese

Wash and dry the lettuce well. Store in a fridge in a plastic bag until needed. Fry the cubes of bread with the garlic in 5 tablespoons of the olive oil, until golden and crisp. Drain the croûtons on kitchen paper. Put the eggs into a pan, cover with water, and bring to the boil. Boil for 1 minute, then drain and run under the cold tap. At the last minute, Tear the lettuce up into manageable pieces and place in a large salad bowl. Pour over 6 tablespoons of olive oil and toss to coat each leaf. Add anchovies or Worcestershire sauce, croûtons, lemon juice, pepper and a little salt. Toss. Finally break in the eggs, taking care not to get specks of shell into the salad, and scatter with the Parmesan. Toss or turn again to mix evenly. You can now serve the salad.

Chicory, Watercress and Orange Salad

I always think of this as a Christmas salad, though there's no good reason not to make it at any time of the year. It's just that it goes particularly well with cold ham and turkey.

SERVES 6–8

FOR THE DRESSING
1 tablespoon sherry vinegar or red
   wine vinegar
Pinch of sugar
Salt and freshly ground black pepper
5 tablespoons extra virgin olive oil or
   3 tablespoons walnut oil and
   2 tablespoons sunflower oil

FOR THE SALAD
2 bunches of watercress
3 heads of chicory, sliced into rounds
2 oranges, peeled and cut into chunks
40 g (1 1/2 oz) walnut pieces

Either put all the dressing ingredients in a screwtop jar and shake well to mix, or whisk the vinegar with the sugar, salt and pepper and then gradually whisk in the oil(s). Taste and adjust seasonings and pour into a salad bowl, and cross salad servers in the bowl over the dressing.

    Wash and pick over the watercress and remove any damaged leaves. Tear into small pieces. Place in the bowl over the servers. Scatter chicory, orange and walnuts over the top. Toss at the table.

Cucumber Salad

This is a salad of heavenly simplicity, much nicer than chucking the slices of cucumber straight into a mixed salad. I like to eat it as a first course with canned tuna mixed with mayonnaise and capers or, for a real treat, with smoked salmon and brown bread and butter. Left-overs will keep for a day or so in the fridge and are lovely in sandwiches.

SERVES 4–6
1 large cucumber, peeled and thinly
  sliced
1/2 tablespoon salt
3 tablespoons white wine vinegar or
  tarragon vinegar

1 teaspoon sugar
Freshly ground black pepper
1 tablespoon chopped fresh chives

Put the sliced cucumber into a colander and sprinkle with the salt. Leave to drain for 30 minutes, then squeeze out the excess moisture with your hands. Mix with the vinegar and sugar and leave until almost ready to serve. Drain off most of the liquid, then arrange on a plate. Season with pepper and sprinkle with chives.

Cucumber, Caper and Horseradish Salad

A finely diced, cool salad to serve with summer fish – grilled or poached – or on its own as a first course with bread, or as part of a buffet. The left-overs are very nice piled on to steaming hot, baked potatoes.

SERVES 6
1 cucumber, peeled, seeded and finely
  diced
1/2 tablespoon salt
1 1/2 tablespoons creamed horseradish
3 tablespoons capers, roughly chopped
  if large

1 shallot, very finely chopped
2 tablespoons finely chopped fresh
  parsley
250 g (9 oz) Greek yoghurt
1/4 teaspoon sugar
Salt and freshly ground black pepper
Lemon juice

Spread the cucumber out in a colander and sprinkle with the salt. Leave to drain for 30 minutes, then squeeze out the excess moisture with your hands.

Mix with all the remaining ingredients except the seasoning. Taste and adjust the balance of flavours, adding a little salt, if needed, freshly ground pepper and a dash of lemon juice. Pile into a pretty bowl and serve at room temperature.

Fennel Salad

This salad is so simple that I'm not giving quantities. As a rough guide, one fennel bulb should be enough to feed three to four people depending on its size. It may not look like a huge amount, but raw fennel has a strong taste. As a first course this salad goes very well with thinly sliced bresaola or air-dried ham – such as Parma ham or jamón serrano – and good bread.

Fennel bulb(s)
Lemon juice
Olive oil
Salt and freshly ground black pepper

TO GARNISH
Chopped fresh parsley

Trim the fennel, removing tough stalks and the base, but reserving the green feathery fronds. Quarter, then slice each quarter very, very thinly. Arrange slices in a serving dish, squeeze over lemon juice, then a generous drizzle of olive oil. Season with salt and pepper. Chop the reserved fronds roughly and scatter over the top, along with a little chopped parsley.

Panzanella with Sun-dried Tomatoes and Rocket

Panzanella is an Italian salad, made with bread and tomatoes or, sometimes, celery and carrots. This is my version of the original, made with rocket and sun-dried tomatoes. It is essential that you use high quality, sturdy bread for this salad. Sliced white will definitely not do.

SERVES 6

2 thick slices of stale sour-dough bread or other good-quality, country-style bread, weighing about 200 g/(7 oz), crusts removed, cut into 1 cm ($1/2$ in) cubes

12 sun-dried tomatoes in olive oil, drained and cut into ribbons

$1/2$ red onion, finely chopped

450 g (1 lb) tomatoes, skinned, seeded and diced

$1/2$ teaspoon dried oregano

1 tablespoon red wine vinegar

4 tablespoons olive oil

60 g (2 oz) rocket, roughly torn up

Salt and freshly ground black pepper

Put the bread into a large salad bowl and sprinkle with water – enough to soften it a little, so that it doesn't absorb too much of the dressing, but not so much that it drowns and disintegrates. Leave for 10 minutes.

Now add all the remaining ingredients, except the rocket and seasoning. Turn to mix evenly and then leave for about $1/2$–1 hour.

Shortly before serving, add the rocket. Turn with your hands to mix evenly and then taste and add a little salt and lots of freshly ground pepper. Serve immediately.

Carrot and Mint Salad

If you grow your own carrots, use the slender thinnings to make this salad of fried carrots with mint. If you are not so lucky, then look out in shops for 'baby' carrots (actually fully mature carrots of a special miniature variety) and the little round extra

sweet Paris carrots, more highly priced than the usual varieties, but worth splashing out on from time to time. Failing that, get the smallest carrots you can and cut them into suitably sized pieces.

As the carrots fry slowly in the olive oil, they caramelize on the outside to an intense earthy sweetness. Dressed with lemon juice and plenty of mint, they make an excellent hors d'oeuvre.

SERVES 4

450 g (1 lb) baby carrots or small
    carrots
3 tablespoons olive oil

Juice of 1/2 lemon
2 tablespoons chopped fresh mint
Salt and freshly ground black
    pepper

If you are using baby carrots, just trim off the tops and any tails. If using small carrots, top and tail, then quarter lengthwise, and cut each piece in half.

Heat the oil in a wide, heavy frying-pan and add the carrots. Fry slowly, shaking and turning every now and then, until the carrots are patched with brown and tender. This should take about 20 minutes. Tip into a bowl and mix with the lemon juice, mint, salt and pepper. Leave to cool and serve at room temperature.

Beetroot and Orange Salad

A lot of people hate beetroot. Or at least, they think they do, but they've probably never tasted it as it should be. Beetroot is actually one of the best of all vegetables, with a sweet, earthy, unique flavour. I love it, and it infuriates me that it gets such a rotten deal in this country. What contorted reasoning has convinced commerce that swamping beetroot in a lake of malt vinegar is a good thing? No wonder so many people shove it to the side of their plate in disgust.

I won't buy ready-cooked beetroot. It upsets me too much. Besides, fresh beet-root is easy enough to cook. It just takes a bit of time, but the result is ample reward. I've made several beetroot converts in my time, and I'm hoping for more.

Peel a couple of oranges right down to the flesh. Slice with a sharp knife, and arrange on a plate. Spoon over a little vinaigrette. Dice beetroot, toss in my Basic Vinaigrette (p. 359) and pile in the centre of the orange slices. Sprinkle with chopped parsley and serve.

French Bean and Bacon Salad

Once a year I teach a children's cookery holiday, and on the last day the children and I have to prepare a meal for 70 people between us. We use whatever vegetables we have to hand to make huge bowls of salad. I gave one group of boys a box of French beans and some bacon, a few vague instructions, and this was what they came up with, though in rather larger quantity. The garlic and Worcestershire sauce were their additions, and are what really make the salad.

SERVES 4

FOR THE DRESSING
1 clove garlic, peeled and crushed
1/2 tablespoon white wine vinegar
1 teaspoon Worcestershire sauce
3 tablespoons olive oil
Salt and freshly ground black pepper

FOR THE SALAD
450 g (1 lb) French beans
4 rashers streaky bacon
2 tablespoons chopped fresh parsley

To make the dressing, whisk the crushed garlic with the vinegar and Worcestershire sauce. Gradually beat in the olive oil, and add salt and pepper to taste.

Top and tail the beans and cut into 2.5–4 cm (1–1½ in) lengths. Drop into a pan of boiling salted water and simmer for about 3 minutes or until just tender but retaining a slight crunch. Drain thoroughly and mix with enough of the dressing to coat well. Grill the rashers of bacon until browned then cut into small strips. Toss with the green beans and the parsley. Taste and adjust the seasoning, adding a little extra Worcestershire sauce if necessary. Serve.

Broad Bean, Red Pepper and Courgette Salad

This is a gloriously summery salad for when the first broad beans are ready to be harvested. It looks pretty and light-hearted – red and green dotted with black olives.

SERVES 4–6

FOR THE DRESSING
1 tablespoon balsamic or sherry
  vinegar or red wine vinegar or
  1½ tablespoons lemon juice
Salt and freshly ground black pepper
4–6 tablespoons extra virgin olive oil
1/2 tablespooon chopped fresh tarragon
  or 1 tablespoon mixed finely
  chopped fresh parsley and fresh
  chervil

FOR THE SALAD
1 red pepper
350 g (12 oz) shelled broad beans
450 g (1 lb) small courgettes
10 black olives, pitted and halved

First make the dressing. Whisk the vinegar or lemon juice with salt and pepper, and gradually whisk in the oil a tablespoon at a time. Add the herbs. Taste and adjust seasonings.

Quarter the red pepper, and remove the seeds and white membrane. Grill, skin-side up, under a hot grill, until the skin is blackened and blistered. Drop into a plastic bag, knot the ends and leave until cool enough to handle. Strip off the skin and cut the flesh into strips. Turn in a little of the dressing to keep moist. Cook the broad beans in salted boiling water, drain, then run under the cold tap. Slip the inner beans out of the coarse grey skins if you have time, then toss the beans in a little of the dressing.

Steam or boil the courgettes until just *al dente*. Drain thoroughly and slice. Mix courgettes, beans, red pepper and olives, adding just enough of the dressing to coat. Leave to cool. Cover and let them sit at room temperature for at least 30 minutes, and up to 2 hours. Taste and adjust the seasoning and serve.

Grilled Courgette and Pepper Salad with Feta and Mint

The smoky taste of grilled courgettes is very good in salads. Add grilled red peppers and salty Greek feta cheese and you have a salad that is substantial enough to form the main course of a light lunch or can be stretched further to serve as a first course. The courgettes and peppers can be grilled and dressed up to 24 hours in advance, but don't add the feta until you are ready to eat.

SERVES 4–6
450 g (1 lb) small to medium
   courgettes
Salt and freshly ground black pepper
5 tablespoons extra virgin olive oil
2 tablespoons lemon juice
1–2 cloves garlic, peeled and crushed
   (optional)

2 red peppers
2–3 tablespoons roughly chopped fresh
   mint

TO SERVE
100 g (4 oz) feta cheese, crumbled

Split the courgettes in half lengthwise. Spread out in a colander, and sprinkle lightly with salt. Leave for 30 minutes to 1 hour to drain. Rinse, and pat dry on kitchen paper. Brush with a little of the olive oil, then grill, turning, until browned and tender. While they are grilling, mix the remaining olive oil with the lemon juice and garlic, if using, and season with pepper and a little salt. Taste and adjust seasoning. As soon as the courgettes are cooked, cut into 2.5 cm (1 in) lengths and toss in the dressing.

Grill and skin the peppers as for Broad Bean, Red Pepper and Courgette Salad, p. 270. Cut into strips. Add to the courgettes, with the mint. Stir, then leave to cool completely.

To serve, spoon into a dish and scatter with feta cheese.

Grilled Pepper Salad

Grilled peppers have the most wonderful, voluptuous texture and a heavenly smoky sweetness. They make one of the best of all salads, served perhaps as an antipasto, alongside a plate of salamis and cured hams and with plenty of good bread to mop up the juices.

Choose as many peppers – green, red and yellow – as you need (one will serve 2–3 people) and grill and skin them as for Broad Bean, Red Pepper and Courgette Salad, p. 268.

Once skinned, cut the peppers into strips and place in a dish with any juice they have given out. Drizzle over some olive oil, add a little crushed garlic if you wish, then season with salt and freshly ground black pepper. Leave to cool and scatter over a little chopped fresh parsley, or roughly torn up basil leaves.

Anchovy fillets, halved lengthways, or pitted black olives, roughly sliced, or strips of sundried tomato preserved in olive oil are all good additions, their saltiness high-lighting the sweetness of the grilled peppers. A teaspoon or so of balsamic vinegar adds a mellow hint of sharpness.

Grilled Aubergine Salad

A favourite salad of mine – a dark gleaming mass of aubergines, smoky and rich with a garlicky hiss. Grilled aubergine slices, simply salted, then brushed with oil and seasoned before grilling, are good hot too.

SERVES 6
2 large aubergines
Salt

FOR THE DRESSING
1 1/2 tablespoons white or red wine
    vinegar
1–2 cloves garlic, peeled and crushed

Salt and freshly ground black pepper
7 tablespoons extra virgin olive oil

TO SERVE
2–3 tablespoons chopped mixed
    herbs – fresh parsley, fresh basil
    and/or fresh chives

Slice the aubergines into 1 cm (1/2 in) thick discs. Sprinkle lightly with salt and leave for 30 minutes to 1 hour. Wipe dry. To make the dressing, mix the vinegar with the garlic, pepper and a little salt. Whisk in the olive oil a tablespoon at a time. Toss the aubergine with half the dressing. Grill, close to the heat, until browned on both sides. Toss with enough of the remaining dressing to moisten, then leave to cool. Toss with the chopped herbs and serve.

Moroccan Salad

Cumin is the spice that I associate most strongly with Morocco. It goes into all manner of dishes, hot and cold, lending its warm aromatic scent. It is added to salads as well as cooked dishes, and it is what makes this salad of diced tomato and grilled green pepper so special.

SERVES 4–6
2 large green peppers
450 g (1 lb) ripe tomatoes, skinned,
  seeded and chopped

FOR THE DRESSING
1 tablespoon lemon juice
3 tablespoons extra virgin olive oil

1 large clove garlic, peeled and
  crushed
1/2 teaspoon ground cumin
2 tablespoons finely chopped fresh
  parsley or a mixture of parsley and
  fresh coriander
Salt and freshly ground black pepper

Grill and skin the peppers as for Broad Bean, Red Pepper and Courgette Salad, p. 268. Cut them into small pieces. Mix with the tomatoes and any juice given out by the peppers.

To make the dressing mix all the ingredients. Toss with the tomatoes and peppers. Serve at room temperature.

Salade Cauchoise

This salad from the Pays de Caux in northern France sets the crispness of celery against the softness of potatoes, with strips of ham in a creamy dressing. I sometimes replace the crème fraîche with fromage frais – not authentic but still French and still very good.

SERVES 6
750 g (1 lb 8 oz) waxy salad potatoes or
  new potatoes
6 stalks celery
100 g (4 oz) cooked ham

FOR THE DRESSING
4 teaspoons cider vinegar
1 1/2 tablespoons chopped fresh chervil
  or fresh parsley

1 1/2 tablespoons chopped fresh chives
Salt and freshly ground black pepper
8 tablespoons crème fraîche or
  fromage frais

TO GARNISH
A few sprigs of fresh chervil or fresh
  parsley

To make the dressing stir the vinegar, herbs, salt and pepper into the crème fraîche or fromage frais. Taste and adjust seasoning. Scrub the potatoes and steam until tender. While still warm, cut into cubes and toss in half the dressing. Leave to cool. I think it is a waste of time to try to remove odd pieces of skin, but if you are feeling pernickety strip them off before cutting up the cooked potatoes.

Slice the celery, and cut the ham into strips. Mix with the potatoes and enough extra dressing to coat without overwhelming. Spoon into a serving dish and arrange sprigs of chervil or parsley on top.

Spaghetti Squash Salad

Vegetable spaghetti, or spaghetti squash, is the most extraordinary vegetable. It looks like a Billy Bunter of a marrow, but it's not until you dig a fork into the cooked flesh that it reveals its bizarre nature. Suddenly the apparently firm pale green interior falls into long slender strands, just like spaghetti. This spaghetti, however, is juicy and slightly crisp. The taste itself is not remarkable, though it is pleasantly fresh. For that reason, it needs generous seasoning and flavouring. The cooked squash can simply be dressed with butter, garlic and freshly grated Parmesan, or it can be given the full treatment with any well-flavoured sauce that you might serve with pasta. One medium squash will feed two generously, or four as a first course or side dish.

Most of the time I treat spaghetti squash just like spaghetti, but once in a while I get a creative turn and come up with something a little different. This salad is one example, and probably the best so far. The cooked spaghetti squash is forked into threads, mixed with tomatoes, spring onions, olives and a sesame seed dressing. Light and fresh tasting, it is lovely for a summer lunch or supper party.

SERVES 6

FOR THE SALAD
1 medium-sized spaghetti squash
225 g (8 oz) cherry tomatoes or firm
    salad tomatoes
6 spring onions, chopped
12 black olives, pitted and roughly
    chopped
8 large fresh basil leaves, roughly
    torn up

FOR THE DRESSING
1 tablespoon sesame seeds
2 tablespoons lemon juice
5 tablespoons olive oil
Salt and freshly ground black pepper

To cook the squash for a salad, cut it into chunks and boil for 20 minutes or so, until tender. Scrape the flesh into a sieve or colander and drain well before using. Make the dressing while the squash cooks. Dry-fry the sesame seeds in a small heavy saucepan over a high heat until they turn a shade darker. Grind to a pasty powder. Mix with the lemon juice and gradually whisk in the olive oil, salt and plenty of pepper. Pour over the hot spaghetti squash and toss. Leave to cool.

Shortly before serving, quarter the cherry tomatoes, or seed and dice whole tomatoes. Mix the spaghetti squash with the tomatoes and all the remaining ingredients. Taste and adjust the seasonings. Serve.

Fattoush

In 1664 John Evelyn listed 35 plants in his salad calendar. Besides lettuces, there were nasturtiums, radish leaves, a handful of herbs, shallots and onion. Rocket, sorrel and purslane had their place in the scheme as well. These three were raised in British gardens for centuries, and then all fell out of favour and disappeared. Why, one wonders, when they grow so easily and have such distinctive and welcome flavours? There is no good reason for the whims of fashion, but at least fashion is bringing them back again. Creeping in first came rocket, then sorrel and lastly, more slowly and cautiously, purslane.

Purslane is the most outlandish of the trio with fleshy green leaves which vary deeply in flavour according to size and variety. It grows wild in many areas of the Mediterranean. Fattoush is a Middle Eastern salad and purslane is the essential ingredient. It makes a huge difference to the flavour, though to be honest I've always enjoyed it without as well.

SERVES 6–8

1 cucumber, diced
Salt and freshly ground black pepper
1 pitta bread
Juice of 1 lemon
4 tomatoes, seeded and diced
6 spring onions or 1 medium red onion, chopped
Leaves of 1 small bunch of purslane, chopped if large
4 tablespoons chopped fresh parsley
2 tablespoons chopped fresh mint
2 tablespoons chopped fresh coriander
2 cloves garlic, peeled and crushed
6–7 tablespoons olive oil

Spread the cucumber dice out in a colander and sprinkle lightly with salt. Leave for 30 minutes to drain. Rinse and dry on kitchen paper.

Split open the pitta bread and toast with the opened side to the heat, until browned and crisp. Break up into small pieces and place in a salad bowl. Sprinkle with about a third of the lemon juice. Now add all the remaining ingredients including the cucumber. Turn with your hands to mix. Taste and adjust the seasoning, adding more lemon juice if needed.

Warm Chorizo (or Bacon) and Frisée Salad

When fried to a sizzling brown, spicy Spanish chorizo sausage gives off a fairly copious amount of fat. Add garlic and a generous splash of vinegar and you can create a sensational dressing for a substantial salad. I serve this both as a main course and as a starter but, either way, friends always clear their plates and beg for more.

If you can't get chorizo, buy a slab of bacon and use that instead.

**SERVES 6 AS A FIRST COURSE,
4 AS A MAIN COURSE**
225–275 g (8–10 oz) chorizo sausage or
  slab bacon
Generous bowlful of frisée or dandelion
  leaves or a mixture of robust leaves

3 tablespoons extra virgin olive oil
1–2 cloves garlic, peeled and chopped
1 tablespoon red wine vinegar
Salt and freshly ground black pepper
6 spring onions, sliced

Skin the chorizo, if using, and cut into slices about 5 mm (¼ in) thick. If using bacon, cut into batons, about 2.5 cm (1 in) long by a generous 5 mm (¼ in) thick and wide. Pick over and wash the salad leaves, and dry thoroughly. Place in a large salad bowl.

Heat the oil in a wide frying-pan over a generous heat, and add the chorizo or bacon. Fry for about 1 minute and then add the garlic. Fry until the chorizo (or bacon) is browned.

Draw off the heat, and let it stand for about 15 seconds or so, then add the vinegar, stir and quickly pour over the salad. Add salt and pepper, toss and finally scatter with spring onions. Serve immediately.

Turkish White Bean Salad

Though you could make a quick version of this salad with tinned haricot or cannellini beans, the texture of home-cooked ones is usually better, as long as you don't over-boil them to a mush. The proportions of beans to other ingredients can be varied at will, though the beans should always predominate.

SERVES 6
175 g (6 oz) haricot beans, soaked in
  water overnight and drained
Juice of ½ lemon
6 tablespoons olive oil
Salt and freshly ground black pepper
1 red onion, chopped

1 large tomato, skinned, seeded and
  diced
2 tablespoons finely chopped fresh
  parsley

TO GARNISH
8 black olives
2 hard-boiled eggs, quartered

Put the beans into a pan with water to cover generously. Bring to the boil, boil hard for 10 minutes. Reduce the heat and simmer until very tender – probably 40 minutes to 1 hour, but this depends on their age, so try one every 5 minutes or so towards the end of the cooking time. Drain well and mix immediately with about two-thirds of the lemon juice and olive oil, and season with salt and pepper. Leave to cool.

Sprinkle the onion lightly with salt in a bowl and leave for 10 minutes. Rub the salt in well, and then rinse. Drain thoroughly. Mix with the beans, tomato and parsley and the rest of the lemon juice and olive oil as required. Spoon into a serving dish and garnish with the olives and eggs.

Tuna and Frisée Salad with Grilled Red Pepper Dressing

This salad was inspired by a Catalan dish called Xato, though I've simplified and twiddled with it so much that it can lay no claims to being the original. Nonetheless, it tastes very good with its smoky dressing made from grilled peppers, chillies, garlic and tomato. A word of warning, however – don't toss the salad until after everyone has seen it. The thick dressing may taste good, but it makes the salad look a little bit grungy.

For this recipe, you will need thick-fleshed chillies as they have to be grilled and skinned. Fresno and Jalapeno chillies are ideal and luckily they are readily available. The conical fresh green chillies that are sold in most supermarkets, usually imported from Kenya, with broad shoulders tapering quickly to a point, will be either Fresno or Jalapeno.

SERVES 4

FOR THE DRESSING
1 red pepper
1 Fresno or Jalapeno green chilli
3 cloves garlic
225 g (8 oz) tomatoes
1 tablespoon red wine vinegar
1 teaspoon sugar

Salt
6 tablespoons extra virgin olive oil

FOR THE SALAD
1/2 a head of frisée lettuce
200 g (7 oz) can tuna, drained and flaked
2 hard-boiled eggs, quartered
4 anchovy fillets, halved lengthwise

To make the dressing, grill the red pepper and chilli close to the heat, turning occasionally, until skins are blackened and blistered. Drop into a plastic bag, knot the ends and leave until cool enough to handle. Meanwhile, thread the garlic cloves onto a skewer and grill close to the heat until charred and softened. Grill the tomatoes until soft.

Skin the pepper, chilli and tomatoes. Peel the garlic. Liquidize or process the pepper, chilli, tomato and garlic with the vinegar, sugar and a little salt. Keep the motor running and gradually trickle in the olive oil. Taste and adjust the seasoning.

Pour the dressing into a salad bowl. Wash and dry the frisée lettuce, then tear into manageable pieces. Arrange over the dressing and scatter with the tuna. Arrange eggs and anchovy fillets on top. Toss at the table.

Swiss Sausage Salad

There's a sausage salad on the menu of every inn in Switzerland, and I've developed a great liking for the mixture of thinly sliced sausage, cheese and gherkins, dressed with a runny cross between mayonnaise and a vinaigrette. Sometimes Wurstsalat comes garniert – amplified with heaps of shredded carrot, beetroot, cucumber, wedges of tomato and other small salads, all around the edge of the plate.

SERVES 4 AS A STARTER OR 2 HUNGRY PEOPLE AS A MAIN COURSE

FOR THE SALAD
½ onion, sliced
100 g (4 oz) cabbage, finely shredded
Salt
4 saveloys or cervelas weighing about 225 g (8 oz) in total
100 g (4 oz) Gruyère or Emmenthal cheese, sliced

3 large gherkins, finely chopped
2 tablespoons chopped fresh chives
4–6 lettuce leaves, depending on size

FOR THE DRESSING
1½ tablespoons white wine vinegar
1 tablespoon Dijon mustard
1½ tablespoons mayonnaise
Salt and freshly ground black pepper
6 tablespoons sunflower or olive oil

Mix the onion with the cabbage in a bowl. Sprinkle with salt, turn to coat thoroughly and leave for 1 hour, turning occasionally. Rinse and drain well, squeezing with your hands to expel the excess moisture.

Make the dressing by stirring together the vinegar, mustard, mayonnaise, salt and pepper, then gradually beating in the oil. Taste and adjust the seasoning.

Skin the sausage and cut into slices about 3 mm (⅛ in) thick, then cut each slice in half if small or into 5 mm (¼ in) wide strips if of larger girth. Cut the sliced cheese into 5 mm (¼ in) wide strips about 4 cm (1½ in) long. Mix with the sausage, cabbage and onions, gherkins and chives. Just before serving, toss with enough of the dressing to coat nicely. Arrange the lettuce leaves on one large plate and pile the *Wurstsalat* on top.

Pasta, Rice and Grains

Penne with Rocket and Tomato Sauce

This pasta dish is based on one I ate years ago in the medieval town of Orvieto, in Umbria. On several occasions we lunched in a restaurant deep under the town, in the cellars that were once part of a Medici palace. This dish of pasta, dressed with a simple tomato sauce (all the better for being made with the juicy, sun-ripened tomatoes of July – here, canned tomatoes are the best substitute) and a handful of roughly torn-up rocket, featured high on the menu.

The heat of the sauce and the pasta will wilt the rocket a little, releasing and modifying the taste. The tomato sauce can be made in advance and re-heated when needed.

SERVES 3–4

FOR THE TOMATO SAUCE
1 onion, finely chopped
2 garlic cloves, finely chopped
1 large fresh thyme sprig
2 tablespoons olive oil
14 oz (400 g) can of chopped tomatoes
1 tablespoon tomato purée
2 tablespoons chopped fresh parsley

100 ml (4 fl oz) red wine
1 teaspoon sugar
Salt and freshly ground black pepper

FOR THE PASTA
340 g (12 oz) penne
Salt
A generous handful of rocket
Olive oil

To make the sauce, cook the onion, garlic and thyme gently in the olive oil, in a wide pan, without browning, until tender. Add all the remaining ingredients and cook hard over a high heat until reduced to a thick sauce. Taste and adjust the seasoning.

Bring a large pan of lightly salted water to the boil. Drop the penne into the water and cook until *al dente*. Meanwhile, tear up or chop (I don't think it makes much difference either way) the rocket roughly and then re-heat the tomato sauce. Drain the penne, pile into a serving dish, toss with a quick slug of olive oil and pour over the sauce. Scatter the rocket over the top and serve immediately.

Pasta alla Norma

Vincenzo Bellini, composer of the opera Norma, *was a native of Catania, Sicily. In his home town this dish of pasta with aubergine and tomato has been rechristened in his honour. Ricotta salata, salted ricotta is as hard as fresh ricotta is soft. It's made by extracting the curds at a high temperature and then salting and drying them slowly.*

SERVES 4
1 large aubergine
Salt
2–3 cloves garlic, peeled and chopped
Olive oil for frying
750 g (1 lb 8 oz) ripe tomatoes, skinned,
    seeded and chopped
Salt and freshly ground black pepper
400–450 g (14–16 oz) spaghetti

3 tablespoons grated *ricotta salata* or
    Pecorino or Parmesan cheese
Handful of fresh basil leaves, roughly
    torn up

TO SERVE
Extra grated ricotta salata or Pecorino
    or Parmesan cheese

Slice the aubergine into 1 cm (1/2 in) discs and cut into 1 cm (1/2 in) wide strips. Spread out in a colander and sprinkle with salt. Leave to drain for an hour, then rinse and pat dry.

Fry the garlic gently in 4 tablespoons olive oil until beginning to colour. Add the tomatoes, salt and pepper and simmer for 15 minutes or so to make a thick tomato sauce. Re-heat when needed.

Bring a large pan of salted water to the boil and add the spaghetti. Boil until *al dente*. While the spaghetti is cooking, heat a generous layer of olive oil in a wide frying-pan, and fry the aubergine until browned, in 2 batches if necessary. Drain on kitchen paper.

Drain the spaghetti and tip into a large serving bowl. Add the hot tomato sauce, the ricotta salata or Pecorino or Parmesan, and the basil. Toss quickly. Top with the fried aubergine and serve with extra cheese to hand round.

Spaghetti alla Puttanesca

This is amongst the most vivid of Italian pasta sauces, full of vim and vigour and salty, sharp and spicy notes, which is presumably how it got its name: puttana *is the Italian for prostitute. It is said to come from the old, picturesque but shabby Trastevere district of Rome, which is home to a number of fine unpretentious restaurants and a fair number of ladies of the night. This version of the recipe comes from Nick Howell, master of the last thriving pilchard works in this country. From him I discovered that it is salted pilchards, rather than anchovies, which should really flavour the sauce.*

SERVES 3–4
400 g (14 oz) dried spaghetti
4 tablespoons olive oil
500 g (1 lb 2 oz) tomatoes, skinned,
    seeded and roughly chopped, or a
    400 g (14 oz) can of plum tomatoes,
    roughly chopped
60 g (2 oz) butter
1 fresh red chilli, seeded and finely
    chopped

4 salted pilchard fillets, chopped,
    or 8 canned anchovy fillets,
    chopped
2 garlic cloves, chopped
100 g (4 oz) large black olives, stoned
    and sliced
1 tablespoon capers
2 tablespoons chopped fresh parsley
Salt

Bring a large pan of salted water to the boil and add the spaghetti.

While it is cooking, heat 1 tablespooon of oil in a frying-pan and add the tomatoes. If using fresh ones, cook down hard for about 6 minutes. Canned ones will probably need only 4 minutes; stir and crush them up as they cook. Set aside until needed.

In a separate large frying-pan, heat the remaining oil with the butter, chilli, pilchards or anchovies and garlic and fry over a moderate heat for about 1–2 minutes, mashing down the pilchards or anchovies with a fork until they dissolve, more or less. Add the tomato sauce, the olives and the capers and cook over a high heat for a further 2–3 minutes, stirring frequently to prevent the sauce catching on the bottom of the pan.

Drain the spaghetti, and tip it into the frying-pan of sauce. Add the parsley and stir for about a minute, so that the sauce coats the strands of spaghetti as they absorb all those piquant flavours. Serve immediately, from the pan!

Pasta with Wild Mushrooms

Alastair Lomax helps run Taste of the Wild, suppliers of wild mushrooms. He came into the business via his passion for wild mushrooms. These days, he is so busy that he hardly ever has time to head off on his own mushroom hunts, but he does make time to cook them for his friends and colleagues. He will rustle up a mean dish of pasta with wild mushrooms and cream at a moment's notice, and I was lucky enough to visit the company just as he was donning his apron. This recipe is one of the easiest ways to use wild mushrooms well, and ideal for using up a mixed basketful of fungi, though it is best of all made with plentiful, copious, generous quantities of cep. If you have only a poor little haul of wild mushrooms, stretch them further by mixing them with cultivated mushrooms – shiitake are particularly good but flat caps will do a more than decent job.

When Alastair cooked this for me, he used a mixture of pieds de mouton, saffron milk-caps, trompettes de la mort *and* ceps. *He says that the dried porcini are not absolutely necessary but they do give an extra lift against the blandness of pasta.*

In Italy, it is often considered a bit of a faux pas *to sprinkle Parmesan over wild mushroom pasta, but I like it and, luckily, so does Alastair!*

SERVES 4
8 g (1/4 oz) dried mushrooms
400 g (14 oz) tagliatelle
30 g (1 oz) butter
1 tablespoon olive oil
1 red onion, chopped
2–3 garlic cloves, chopped
At least 110–220 g (4–8 oz) wild
   mushrooms, cleaned, trimmed and
   thickly sliced where necessary

Salt and freshly ground black pepper
100 ml (3 1/2 fl oz) dry white wine
300 ml (10 fl oz) double cream
3 tablespoons chopped fresh parsley

TO SERVE
Freshly grated Parmesan cheese
   (optional)

Soak the dried mushrooms in hot water for half an hour.

Pick out and roughly chop the mushrooms. Leave the soaking water to settle. Put a large pan of salted water on to heat up for the pasta. Start on the sauce while you are waiting for the water to come to the boil. Once it is boiling, throw the pasta in to cook according to packet instructions. When *al dente*, drain well. The theory is that this moment should coincide, more or less, with the final turn of the sauce.

Alastair uses a wok to make his sauce in, which works very well, but a roomy frying-pan is a rather more standard implement for this kind of thing. Either way, heat the butter with the oil and add the onion and garlic. Cook gently until they are just tender. Add the soaked dried mushrooms, fry for a few seconds and then add the fresh wild mushrooms. Fry until tender and until most of the liquid thrown out by the mushrooms has evaporated. Now season with salt and pepper and then add the soaking liquid, taking care to stop short of the earthy grit at the bottom of the bowl. Next pour in the white wine. Simmer for a few minutes, until the liquid is reduced by about two-thirds. Stir in the cream and boil down for another 3–4 minutes, until reduced by about half. Stir in the chopped parsley.

Tip the drained pasta into a large serving bowl. Spoon the mushroom sauce over it and serve, with Parmesan for those who want it.

Pasta with Asparagus and Horseradish

A simple dish with lively flavours, that can be conjured up quickly. Horseradish may not sound like the ideal companion for delicate asparagus but used in moderation, as it is here, it marries surprisingly well. For a richer dish, add 150 ml (5 fl oz) of double cream to the asparagus when re-heating.

SERVES 4
450 g (1 lb) asparagus
Salt
450 g (1 lb) fusilli or other pasta shapes
50 g (2 oz) butter

1 tablespoon creamed horseradish
Squeeze of lemon juice

TO GARNISH
2 tablespoons chopped fresh chives

Trim the asparagus, breaking off the tough ends (save these and cooking water for making soup). Cut into 2 cm (3/4 in) lengths, keeping the tips separate. Pour 4 cm (1½ in) of water into a large saucepan, add salt, and bring to the boil. Add the stem pieces and simmer gently for 5 minutes. Add the tips and simmer gently for 3–4 minutes, until just tender. Drain. If prepared in advance, cool and cover.

Bring a large pan of salted water to a gentle, rolling boil, tip in the pasta and cook until *al dente*. A few minutes before the pasta is done, melt the butter in a frying-pan.

Add the asparagus and stir to re-heat thoroughly, without actually frying. Add the horseradish and lemon juice and stir.

Drain the pasta well, and tip into a hot serving dish. Spoon the asparagus mixture over the pasta, toss, scatter with chopped chives and serve.

Pasta with Savoy Cabbage and Shallots

The mixture of cabbage, caraway seeds and pasta may sound somewhat unpromising, but in practice it works brilliantly to produce an unusual but delicious pasta dish. No cheese with this one, please.

SERVES 2
25 g (1 oz) butter
2 shallots, sliced
2 cloves garlic, peeled and sliced
1 teaspoon caraway seeds

6 leaves Savoy cabbage, shredded
Salt and freshly ground black pepper
Paprika
225 g (8 oz) tagliatelle

Melt the butter in a medium-sized saucepan. Add the shallots, garlic and caraway seeds. Cover and cook over a low heat for 5 minutes, stirring once or twice to prevent catching. Add the Savoy cabbage, salt, pepper and a shake of paprika. Cover again, and cook for a further 5 minutes, stirring occasionally, until the cabbage has wilted.

Bring a large pan of salted water to the boil. Drop in the tagliatelle, and bring back to the boil. Simmer until *al dente*. Drain and toss with the cabbage and shallot mixture and all the buttery juices. Serve immediately.

Pasta with Three Cheeses

A simple pasta dish but one that always pleases and is very quick to cook. The sweetness of the fried onion balances the cheesiness of all those cheeses. For some reason, I have particularly taken to orechiette, 'ear-shaped' pasta, recently. I enjoy the feel of its curves against my tongue but any pasta shape will do fine in its place.

SERVES 4
400–500 g (14–18 oz) orechiette or
 other pasta shapes
2 onions, sliced
5 tablespoons olive oil
140 g (5 oz) mozzarella cheese, diced

100 g (4 oz) dolcelatte cheese, diced
60 g (2 oz) Parmesan cheese, freshly
 grated
Salt and freshly ground black pepper

TO SERVE
2 tablespoons chopped fresh parsley

Tip the *orechiette* into salted, boiling water and cook until *al dente*.

Meanwhile, fry the onions in 3 tablespoons of the olive oil, until nicely browned. Set aside, with their oil. Re-heat as soon as the pasta is cooked. Drain the pasta and, while it's still piping hot, tip it into a bowl and toss with the cheeses, fried onions, pepper and a little bit of salt. Sprinkle with parsley and serve.

Fusilli with Smoked Trout, Rocket and Basil

This dish takes just minutes to make – the rocket, basil and smoked fish cooking instantly in the heat of the pasta.

SERVES 4

1 handful of rocket leaves
400 g (14 oz) fusilli or other pasta
  shapes
6 tablespoons olive oil
Juice of 1/2 lemon

2 cloves garlic, peeled and crushed
Salt and freshly ground black pepper
12 large fresh basil leaves, shredded
175 g (6 oz) sliced smoked trout, cut
  into short thin strips

If the rocket leaves are fairly large, tear them up roughly. If they are tiny, 5 cm (2 in) or so in length, tear or snip them in half.

Cook the fusilli in a large pan of lightly salted water until just *al dente*. Drain well and return to the pan, set over a low heat. Toss in the olive oil, lemon juice, garlic, a little salt and plenty of pepper. Stir for a couple of seconds, then add the rocket and basil and toss again to mix evenly. Draw off the heat and finally toss in the trout. Serve immediately.

Pasta with Broccoli, Ham and Gruyère

In the south of Italy, pasta and broccoli are cooked in the same pan, so that the pasta absorbs the flavour of the vegetable. It's a good method, even if the broccoli does end up a little battered in the process. I like to add two rather more northerly ingredients to this dish – ham and Gruyère – for extra oomph.

SERVES 4

450 g (1 lb) broccoli
450 g (1 lb) tagliatelle, fresh or dried
1 small onion, chopped
50 g (2 oz) butter

3 thick slices cooked ham, cut into
  strips
Salt and freshly ground black pepper
Ground nutmeg
100 g (4 oz) Gruyère cheese, grated

Separate the broccoli into small florets and slice the stems thinly.

Bring a large saucepan of lightly salted water to the boil. If using fresh pasta add the broccoli and 15 g (½ oz) butter, and simmer for 3 minutes. Add the tagliatelle, and bring back to the boil. Simmer until the pasta is just *al dente*. Drain thoroughly and return to the pan. (For dried pasta add the tagliatelle to the saucepan at the same time as the broccoli and butter.)

Meanwhile, fry the onion in 25 g (1 oz) butter until tender, without browning. Add the ham and cook for a further 1–2 minutes. Turn the heat down low and keep warm. Once the pasta is drained and back in its pan, mix in the onion and ham and remaining butter, salt, pepper and nutmeg to taste. Quickly pile into a hot serving dish, and sprinkle with half the Gruyère. Serve immediately, with the remaining Gruyère for those who want it.

Tagliatelle with Broad Beans and Pancetta

This marvellous pasta dish was one of the best things I ate in Sicily, though it is surprisingly simple. If you use fresh tagliatelle, which only take a few minutes to cook, start warming the oil before you put the pasta in the boiling water.

SERVES 4 GENEROUSLY

- 1 lb (450 g) broad beans (shelled weight), thawed if frozen
- 1 lb (450 g) tagliatelle
- Salt and freshly ground black pepper
- 5 tablespoons olive oil
- 2 cloves garlic, sliced
- 6 oz (175 g) pancetta or streaky bacon, rinded and cut into thin strips
- 1½ oz (40 g) Parmesan cheese, freshly grated
- 2 tablespoons chopped fresh parsley

First prepare the broad beans. If they have been frozen, just let them thaw, then, using a small sharp knife, slit the outer skins and squeeze out the bright green inner beans. With fresh broad beans, blanch for 1 minute in boiling water, drain and cool quickly in cold running water. Remove the skins as for frozen beans, then cook in fresh water until barely done. Drain well.

Bring a big pot of salted water to the boil and add the tagliatelle. Boil until *al dente* in the usual way.

As soon as the pasta is in the pot, put the olive oil and garlic into a wide frying-pan over a moderate heat. Cook until the garlic is beginning to brown, then scoop it out. Immediately add the pancetta or bacon and broad beans. Fry gently over a low heat, stirring from time to time, until the tagliatelle are ready (it's fine if the beans go slightly fuzzy at the edges, just as long as they don't burn!). Drain the tagliatelle and tip into a warmed serving bowl. Immediately pour over the contents of the frying-pan. Add the Parmesan, parsley, salt and pepper to taste, and toss. Serve straight away.

RICE

Risi e Bisi

Risi e bisi, or rice and peas, is a Venetian dish. Though the peas and rice are cooked together in one large pot, it's not a risotto. In fact, it requires much less effort, as there is no need to stir constantly as it cooks. The result is soupier, and lacks the creaminess of a risotto, but it is, nonetheless, quite delicious.

SERVES 4
450 g (1 lb) peas in their pods or 225 g (8 oz) shelled peas, fresh or frozen
1.2 litres (2 pints) chicken stock
50 g (2 oz) butter
2 tablespoons olive oil
50 g (2 oz) pancetta or cured raw ham (e.g. Parma ham), chopped
1 onion, chopped

4 tablespoons chopped fresh parsley
200 g (7 oz) risotto rice, e.g. Arborio
Salt and freshly ground black pepper
3 tablespoons freshly grated Parmesan cheese

TO SERVE
Extra freshly grated Parmesan cheese

Shell the peas if using peas in their pods. Put the stock in a saucepan and bring gently to the boil. Meanwhile, heat half the butter and all the oil in a large saucepan. Add the pancetta or ham, onion, and parsley. Cook over a gentle heat until the onions are tender, without browning. Add the peas, and stir for a few minutes.

Now add the hot stock and bring back to the boil. Pour in the rice in a steady stream, then season with salt and pepper. Simmer for about 15–20 minutes until the rice is just tender. Draw off the heat and stir in the remaining butter and the Parmesan cheese.

Serve in deep bowls, passing round extra Parmesan for those who want it.

Saffron and Tomato Rice

Not a risotto, nor a paella or a pilaf for that matter, this is a simpler affair altogether, since it is baked in the oven and requires little attention, rather than the occasional stir. I love it on its own but it is really meant as an accompaniment, best served with fairly plain food: perhaps some prawns, sizzling hot from the barbecue, or grilled lamb chops and a green salad, or lightly cooked courgettes or spinach. It can be made with ordinary long-grain rice, though I prefer the taste and texture of risotto rice. Either way, the rice re-heats fairly well, if necessary, as long as you sprinkle over a couple of extra tablespoons of water or stock before you put it into the oven.

SERVES 6–8

1 red onion, chopped

2 tablespoons olive oil

3 garlic cloves, chopped

310 g (11 oz) risotto rice, e.g. Arborio or
  Carnaroli

A good pinch of saffron strands

2 tablespoons sun-dried tomato purée
  or ordinary tomato purée

1 teaspoon sugar

2 tablespoons chopped fresh parsley

520 ml (18 fl oz) vegetable or chicken
  stock or water

Salt and freshly ground black pepper

Pre-heat the oven to 150°C/300°F/Gas Mark 2. Fry the onion in the oil in a roasting tin, or flameproof and ovenproof shallow dish, until beginning to colour. Add the garlic and fry for another 2 minutes. Add the rice and stir for 1 minute. Now add the saffron strands and all the rest of the ingredients and bring to the boil, stirring to mix. Cover with foil and bake for 30 minutes, stirring once as it cooks, until the rice is tender and the liquid has all been absorbed.

Pine Nut and Saffron Pilaf

A lovely, golden pilaf perfumed with saffron and dotted with buttery pine nuts. Serve as a side dish to grilled fish or chicken, or even on its own, in which case the garlicky yoghurt becomes a key player.

SERVES 4–6

A generous pinch saffron threads

600 ml (1 generous pint) hot chicken or
  vegetable stock

1 large onion, chopped

1 clove garlic, chopped

85 g (3 oz) butter

250 g (9 oz) Basmati rice, rinsed and
  thoroughly drained

1 bay leaf

4 green cardamom pods

Salt and freshly ground black pepper

85 g (3 oz) pine nuts

3 tablespoons chopped parsley

TO SERVE (OPTIONAL)

200 g (8 oz) Greek yoghurt

3 cloves garlic, crushed

Pre-heat the oven to around 150°C/300°F/Gas Mark 2. To make the pilaf, put the saffron into a small bowl and spoon over 2 tablespoons hot stock. Leave to steep until needed. Fry the onion and garlic gently in 30 g (1 oz) of the butter in a heavy-based saucepan, without browning, until tender. Add the rice, bay leaf and cardamom pods and stir for about 30 seconds. Pour in the remaining stock and season with salt and pepper. Bring up to a lazy simmer, cover tightly, reduce heat as low as possible and leave to cook, undisturbed, for 10 minutes.

Meanwhile, mix the yoghurt with the crushed garlic if using. Sauté the pine nuts in half the remaining butter until lightly browned. Check the rice – by now it should be just nicely cooked and all the liquid should have been absorbed. If not, uncover and let it boil off for a few minutes. Stir in the parsley and saffron. Turn the rice into a shallow dish, spoon over the pine nuts and dot with the last of the butter. Cover with foil and pop into a warm oven to steam and keep warm – it can stay there happily for half an hour or so. Serve with the garlicky yoghurt.

Squash Risotto

I've made this risotto with several different types of squash, all of them good, but the sweet dumpling (also known as little apple) squash has come out top of the league. It has a pretty cream-coloured skin streaked with green, and a firm texture and sweet taste. Try it if you find it.

The final addition of cheese is optional. With a sweet dumpling, I found it unnecessary, but with other less sugary squashes it adds a final lift. Taste the risotto before you add it and see what you think.

SERVES 4–6

1 × 750 g (1 lb 8 oz) winter squash or a
    wedge of pumpkin
1 onion, chopped
75 g (3 oz) butter
1.2 litres (2 pints) chicken or vegetable
    stock
4 fresh sage leaves, torn up
350 g (12 oz) Arborio rice
2 medium-sized tomatoes, skinned,
    seeded and chopped

1 large glass dry white wine
Salt and freshly ground black pepper
2 tablespoons chopped fresh parsley
2 1/2 tablespoons freshly grated
    Parmesan cheese (optional)

TO SERVE

Extra freshly grated Parmesan cheese
    (optional)

Cut the squash into 1 cm (1/2 in) cubes, discarding skin and seeds. In a heavy-based saucepan, large enough to take all the ingredients with room to spare, cook the onion in half the butter until tender, without browning. Meanwhile, bring the stock to the boil in a separate pan. Turn the heat down as low as possible to keep hot, without actually boiling.

Add the sage and pumpkin to the onion and stir for about a minute, before adding the rice. Continue stirring for another minute. Now add the tomatoes, wine, salt and pepper, and simmer, stirring, until the wine has evaporated. Add a couple of ladlefuls of the hot stock. Simmer, stirring, until the liquid has evaporated. Repeat until the rice is tender but still *al dente*. Stir in the remaining butter, parsley, Parmesan (if using) and more pepper and salt if needed. Let it sit for a minute or so, then serve with more Parmesan to hand round if you like.

VARIATIONS

For a squash and aubergine risotto follow the recipe for Squash Risotto (above) but replace 250 g (8 oz) of the squash with 1 large aubergine, cut into 1 cm (1/2 in) cubes, without peeling. Add the aubergine at the same time as the squash.

You can also make a delicious risotto using courgette. Follow the recipe for Squash Risotto, on p. 287, using 450–750 g (1 lb–1 lb 8 oz) diced courgettes, and dry white wine. Thyme, marjoram, or rosemary all go well with courgettes, and can be substituted for the sage. If you have courgette flowers, too, stir those in, cut into strips, when the risotto is almost done.

Mushroom Risotto

This mushroom risotto made with dried wild mushrooms and cultivated mushrooms is as good as any, and better than most. If you happen to have a small cache of fresh wild mushrooms, but not enough to flavour a risotto in their own right, make this one and then serve the wild mushrooms, sautéd briefly in butter, as a garnish on top.

SERVES 4–6

30 g (1 oz) dried porcini mushrooms (or more if you are feeling generous)

5 tablespoons sweet sherry, Marsala or Madeira

1.2 litres (2 pints) vegetable or chicken stock

1 onion, finely chopped

2 garlic cloves, finely chopped

85 g (3 oz) butter

450 g (1 lb) open-cap flat mushrooms, or other cultivated mushrooms, e.g. shiitake or chestnut mushrooms, trimmed and sliced thickly

300 g (10 oz) risotto rice, e.g. Arborio, Carnaroli or Vialone Nano

4 tablespoons chopped fresh parsley

Salt and freshly ground black pepper

1 small glass (150 ml/5 fl oz) dry white wine

60 g (2 oz) Parmesan cheese, freshly grated, plus extra to serve

Soak the dried porcini in the alcohol for at least an hour, until softened.

Put the stock into a pan, bring gently to the boil and then turn the heat down to a mere thread, to keep the stock hot.

Cook the onion and garlic gently in half the butter in a wide, deep pan, without letting it burn. Meanwhile, pick out the porcini and chop them finely. Leave what little remains of the soaking liquid to settle. Add the soaked porcini and the fresh mushrooms to the pan and cook for a further 5 minutes or so, until the water thrown off by the mushrooms has evaporated. Stir in the rice and half the parsley and season lightly with salt and pepper. Stir for about a minute. Pour in the white wine and the soaking liquid, taking care to stop short of the gritty sediment left in the bowl. Stir the risotto until the liquid is all absorbed and then add a generous ladleful of the hot stock. Continue in this way, stirring until one batch of liquid has gone and then adding another, until the rice is just tender and bathed in a rich creamy sauce.

Draw off the heat and stir in the grated Parmesan and the remaining butter and parsley. Taste and adjust the seasoning and serve immediately, with extra Parmesan to hand round separately.

Shrimp and Broad Bean Pilau

This is an incredibly delicious pilau, packed with broad beans and shrimps and delicately spiced. It is best, naturally, made with fresh broad beans, though it is not bad made with frozen ones either. To make it really special, blanch and skin the beans before adding them to the rice.

SERVES 4

FOR THE RAITA
1/4 cucumber
Salt
300 ml (10 fl oz) Greek-style yoghurt

FOR THE PILAU
1 large onion, chopped
2 cloves garlic, peeled and chopped
2 tablespoons sunflower oil
1 teaspoon turmeric

1 teaspoon cumin seeds, bruised with a pestle or the end of a rolling-pin
1 teaspoon fennel seeds, bruised
225 g (8 oz) Basmati or long-grained rice, rinsed
Salt and freshly ground black pepper
275–450 g (10 oz–1 lb) shelled broad beans, thawed if frozen
225 g (8 oz) shelled cooked shrimps
2 tablespoons chopped fresh coriander

First make the raita. Grate the cucumber coarsely without peeling it. Spread it out in a colander and sprinkle with salt. Leave for 30 minutes to 1 hour. Squeeze out excess moisture and then dry on kitchen paper. Mix into the yoghurt and set aside.

In a large saucepan cook the onion and garlic for the pilau gently in the oil for a couple of minutes. Add the spices and continue cooking until the onion is tender. Stir in the rice and cook for 1 minute longer. Add 600 ml (1 pint) water, salt and pepper and bring to the boil. If you are using fresh whole broad beans add these now. Reduce to a simmer, cover tightly and leave to cook for 10 minutes.

Add the shrimps and thawed frozen beans, if using. Stir, then cover again and cook for 5–10 minutes until the rice is tender and all the liquid has been absorbed. If necessary add a little more hot water as the pilau cooks. Stir in the coriander, then taste and adjust the seasoning. Serve with the cool raita.

Arroz de Mariscos

Though this is similar to a seafood paella, it isn't the same by any means. It turns out fairly soupy, or at least it should, with the rice soaking in a rich tomato broth, and mussels, clams and prawns nestled on top. And where a paella is fragrant with saffron, arroz de mariscos is characteristically Portuguese with a good dose of fresh coriander.

SERVES 4–6
450 g (1 lb) mussels
450 g (1 lb) small clams
4 tablespoons olive oil
1 onion, chopped
2 cloves garlic, chopped
350 g (12 oz) tomatoes, skinned,
   seeded and chopped
1 tablespoon tomato purée
1 bay leaf
1 sprig of fresh parsley
1 dried red chilli
350 g (12 oz) long grain rice
Salt and freshly ground black pepper
450 g (1 lb) raw prawns in their shells
2 tablespoons chopped fresh coriander

Scrub the mussels well, scraping off the beards and barnacles. Rinse thoroughly in several changes of water and discard any that stay open when tapped sharply against a work surface. Rinse the clams thoroughly in several changes of water. Pour a 2.5 cm (1 in) depth of water into a large pan and bring to the boil. Add the mussels, cover and shake over a high heat until opened. Discard any that steadfastly refuse to open. Repeat with the clams. Pour the cooking liquid into a bowl and leave to settle, then pour off carefully, leaving any grit behind. Reserve. Shell half the clams and mussels, discarding the shells.

Put the oil, onion and garlic into a wide pan and cook over a medium heat until the onion is tender. Now add the tomatoes, tomato purée, bay leaf, parsley and chilli and cook for a further 5–10 minutes until thick. Add the rice, the cooking water from the mussels and clams, 900 ml (1½ pints) water, salt and pepper. Bring to the boil and simmer until the rice is tender and the mixture is soupy (if it seems dry, add a splash or two of boiling water). Lay the prawns in the mixture and cook for a few minutes more until they are done. Finally add both the shelled and unshelled mussels and clams, and the coriander, and heat through thoroughly. Taste and adjust the seasoning, then serve.

Sausage and Porcini Risotto

This is one of my favourite risottos, perfect for a cold winter's evening when you need something powerfully full of flavour and comfort to shore you up.

Though you could use any good, meaty pork sausages, it's worth a trip to an Italian deli to get the proper luganega *sausages. For a plainer sausage risotto, omit the mushrooms and use white wine instead of red.*

SERVES 4–6
15 g (½ oz) dried porcini mushrooms
225 g (8 oz) *luganega* sausages
1.2 litres (2 pints) chicken, meat or
   vegetable stock
1 onion, chopped
2 garlic cloves, chopped
25 g (1 oz) butter
1 tablespoon sunflower oil
275 g (10 oz) Arborio or other risotto
   rice
4 sage leaves
Salt and freshly ground black pepper
1 glass dry red wine
3 tablespoons freshly grated Parmesan
   cheese, plus extra to serve

Cover the porcini with hot water, leave to soak for 15 minutes, then pick out the pieces and chop roughly. Leave the soaking water in the bowl to settle. Cut the sausages into pieces about 1 cm (1/2 in) thick.

Heat the stock until it boils, then reduce the heat as low as possible so that it stays hot as you cook.

In a separate, large, heavy-based pan, cook the onion and garlic gently in 15 g (1/2 oz) of the butter and the oil until tender, without browning. Raise the heat, add the sausages and fry until browned. Add the rice, sage, and soaked mushrooms and stir for 1 minute until the rice is translucent. Add salt and pepper, and pour in the wine and soaking liquid from the mushrooms, taking care to stop before you reach the grit at the bottom. Simmer until it has almost all been absorbed, stirring constantly.

Now add a generous ladleful of the hot stock and stir until it has all been absorbed. Repeat until the rice is just cooked, without being soggy. Ideally at this point the risotto should be damp, slightly moist but not swimming in liquid. Draw off the heat and beat in the remaining butter and the Parmesan. Adjust the seasonings and serve with extra Parmesan for those who want it.

Risotto Milanese

This is perhaps the greatest of all risottos. It can be served as a first or main course on its own, though it is also the classic accompaniment to osso buco *(see p. 144). The bone marrow is an optional extra but it does add a marvellous, though virtually unidentifiable, richness. When ordering it from your butcher, explain that you want to extract the marrow from the bones and ask him to saw them into short lengths, 5 cm (2 in) or so, to make this easier. Two bones should give you enough marrow.*

The quantity of saffron depends entirely on your taste and pocket. A full 1/8 teaspoon gives a glorious daffodil-yellow colour, half that reduces it to primrose and a mild hint of saffron. A very generous pinch of saffron threads is about equivalent to 1/16 teaspoon. Dry-fry it briefly to crisp the threads, then pound them to a powder.

SERVES 4–6
1.2 litres (2 pints) chicken stock
1/16–1/8 teaspoon powdered saffron or
**   1–2 generous pinches of saffron**
**   threads (see above)**
75 g (3 oz) butter
50 g (2 oz) beef marrow, roughly
**   chopped**

2 shallots, finely chopped, or 1 1/2
**   tablespoons finely chopped onion**
350 g (12 oz) Arborio or other
**   risotto rice**
120 ml (4 fl oz) dry white wine
50 g (2 oz) freshly grated Parmesan
**   cheese, plus extra to serve**
Salt and freshly ground black pepper

Bring the stock to the boil, turn down the heat and keep it at a low simmer. Pour 2 tablespoons of hot stock over the saffron and leave it to steep.

Melt two-thirds of the butter in a heavy pan. Add the beef marrow and shallots or onion and fry gently until tender, without browning. Add the rice and stir for 1 minute until translucent. Pour in the wine and simmer over a medium-low heat until almost all the liquid has been absorbed, stirring constantly.

Add a generous ladleful of the hot stock and simmer until almost all the liquid has been absorbed, stirring constantly. Repeat, adding 1 ladleful of stock at a time, until the rice is tender but still *al dente,* i.e. firm but not chalky and hard. Add the saffron and its soaking liquid after the risotto has been simmering for about 20 minutes. You may find that you don't need all of the stock, but if you don't have quite enough, finish with hot water; the finished risotto should be creamy and wet, but not swimming in liquid. Stir in the remaining butter (or more!), the Parmesan, pepper and salt to taste. Serve immediately, with extra Parmesan for those who want it.

Rice with Rabbit

This is not a risotto, nor a paella either for that matter. It is a full-flavoured rice and rabbit stew, homely to look at (I can't deny that it has a somewhat murky aspect), but nevertheless very good to eat.

My friend in Spain, Felisa, makes the stew in two stages. When she has a moment during the early part of the day, she simmers the rabbit until very tender, making sure that there is plenty of liquid in the pan. Twenty minutes or so before serving, she re-heats it, adding the rice, so that it is perfectly cooked by the time everyone has gathered around the table.

SERVES 4–6

1 rabbit, cut into small pieces
3 tablespoons olive oil
$^1/_2$ onion, chopped
5 cloves garlic, peeled but whole
1 green pepper, chopped
1 bay leaf
225 g (8 oz) tomatoes, skinned, seeded and chopped
2 tablespoons chopped fresh parsley
1 generous glass white or red wine
Salt and freshly ground black pepper
225 g (8 oz) medium-grain rice

Brown the rabbit in the olive oil in a wide shallow pan, then remove it from the pan and set aside. Add the onion, 3 of the whole garlic cloves, the green pepper and the bay leaf to the pan and cook gently until the onion and pepper are tender. Now return the rabbit to the pan, together with the tomato and parsley. Stir and cook for 5 minutes. Pour in the wine and enough water to cover the rabbit generously, and add salt and pepper. Bring to the boil and simmer gently, covered, for about 1 hour, until the rabbit is very tender. There should still be loads of liquid in the pan. Taste and adjust the seasonings.

Stir the rice into the liquid and simmer, stirring occasionally, for 10–20 minutes, until the rice is tender. When it is almost done, crush the remaining 2 garlic cloves and stir into the rice.

When the rice is cooked, it will have absorbed a considerable amount of liquid, but the dish should still be fairly soupy and wet – if necessary add a little extra water or stock. Serve immediately.

Chicken Liver Pilav

I visited Istanbul for the television series, Travels à la Carte, *and visited Nesrin Ilter at home. As Nesrin cooked, I couldn't help noticing two similarities between the cooking of Sicily and Turkey – at least, of Istanbul. Aubergines play an immensely important role in both, and the pairing of pine nuts and currants re-emerged in this recipe.*

SERVES 6

275 g (10 oz) medium or long-grain rice
Salt and freshly ground black pepper
50 g (2 oz) unsalted butter
1 large onion, chopped
50 g (2 oz) pine nuts
175 g (6 oz) chicken livers, chopped

600 ml (1 pint) hot chicken stock
1 heaped teaspoon ground cinnamon
1 teaspoon ground allspice
1 teaspoon caster sugar
50 g (2 oz) currants
3 tablespoons chopped fresh dill

Pour hot water over the rice, stir in 1 heaped teaspoon salt and leave until cold. Drain and rinse thoroughly. Leave in a sieve to finish draining.

Melt the butter in a large saucepan, and add the onion and pine nuts. Cook until the onion is lightly browned. Add the chicken livers, salt and pepper and cook, stirring, for 2 minutes. Now add the rice and continue to stir for about 4 minutes. Pour in the hot stock and stir in the spices, sugar and currants, and more salt and pepper. Bring to a simmer, reduce the heat and cover tightly. Leave to cook for 15–20 minutes, without stirring, until the rice is just done and all the liquid is absorbed. Only add more stock (or water) if absolutely necessary. Stir in the dill, turn off the heat, cover again and leave to stand for a final 5 minutes before serving.

Tabbouleh

This Moroccan salad is a wonderfully fresh, zingy mixture of couscous (it is usually made with left-over couscous but it's worth preparing a batch from scratch) with oodles of chopped fresh herbs and lots of lemon juice. It is a perfect summer salad, lovely as part of a mixed buffet (and handy, since the flavours improve on keeping for 24 hours) or indeed just as a side dish with cold chicken or grilled prawns, or good cheese and pitta bread. For a more Middle Eastern feel, serve with warm pitta bread, hummus, spiced black olives and taramasalata.

SERVES 6

**150 g (5 oz) quick couscous or
    310 g (11 oz) cooked couscous**
**6 tablespoons finely chopped fresh
    parsley**
3 tablespoons chopped fresh mint

**3 tomatoes, skinned, seeded and very
    finely diced**
1/2 red onion, very finely chopped
Juice of 1 1/2–2 lemons
4 tablespoons olive oil
Salt and freshly ground black pepper

Pour 300 ml (10 fl oz) of boiling water over the couscous and leave for 20 minutes, stirring once or twice, until all the water has been absorbed.

Mix with all the remaining ingredients. Taste and adjust the seasonings. Cover and leave overnight.

Stir and taste again. Serve at room temperature.

Couscous with Roast Tomatoes, Peppers and Goats' Cheese

I've always thought of couscous as a brilliant storecupboard stand-by, ready in minutes but patient enough to hang around if supper has to wait. It is an excellent accompaniment to all kinds of stews and damp dishes, since it soaks up juices in a most encouraging way.

This is a distinctly modern, European way of using couscous, topped with an unctuous, deeply flavoured sauce made from roasted tomatoes and peppers and finished with chunks of roasted onion, pepper and tomatoes and salty goats' cheese. I cannot claim the idea as my own, sadly, since I stole it from a press release for an Italian product and then reworked it to do without the poor product in question. Apologies to the public relations company and the producers and thanks very much for a great idea.

SERVES 4

FOR THE VEGETABLES

8 plum tomatoes, halved

1 red onion, quartered

2 red peppers, seeded and cut into
large chunks

1 fresh red chilli

4 whole garlic cloves

2 fresh thyme sprigs

3 tablespoons olive oil

1 tablespoon sherry vinegar

1 tablespoon caster sugar

Salt and freshly ground black pepper

FOR THE COUSCOUS

300 g (11 oz) couscous

600 ml (1 pint) hot chicken or
vegetable stock

2 tablespoons olive oil

3 tablespoons chopped fresh parsley

TO SERVE

110 g (4 oz) goats' cheese, rinded and
roughly diced

6 fresh basil leaves, shredded

Pre-heat the oven to 220°C/425°F/Gas Mark 7. Oil a large, shallow, ovenproof dish or roasting tin. Place the plum tomatoes in it in a single layer, cut-side up, along with the onion quarters, the peppers, the whole chilli and the garlic. Tuck the thyme sprigs amongst them. Drizzle over the olive oil and the sherry vinegar. Then sprinkle on the sugar, salt and pepper. Bake, uncovered, for 40–50 minutes, until the onions are beginning to brown and catch at the edges.

Meanwhile, put the couscous into a bowl and pour on the steaming hot stock. Leave for 15 minutes, until all the liquid has been absorbed, stirring once or twice. Drizzle over the olive oil and mix well. Cover with foil and keep warm in a moderately hot oven.

When the vegetables are done, pick out about half the tomatoes, peppers and onions and keep warm. Unless you want a hot sauce, remove the chilli. Tip the rest into a food processor, scraping in any juices and caramelized brown goo. Don't worry about the garlic skins. Process until smooth; then sieve. Thin with a little water or stock if necessary. Taste and adjust the seasoning.

Take the couscous out of the oven, add the parsley and fork up a little to mix in the greenery and separate the grains. Pile up in a serving dish. Pour over the sauce, arrange the reserved vegetables on top and scatter with goats' cheese and basil shreds. Serve hot.

Traditional Moroccan Couscous with Seven Vegetables

The traditional method of cooking couscous, steamed and massaged with oil and steamed again, and then finished with aged butter (smen, which you will only find in Moroccan food stores) or ordinary butter, takes time and patience, but it does produce the finest tasting and textured grain of all.

When you can't spare the time to coddle your couscous into its finest state, use one of the quick-cooking types instead, to serve with this most popular stew of lamb and vegetables.

In this version, based on the one cooked for me at the Moroccan Women's Centre in west London, the seven types of vegetable are onions, carrots, swede, cabbage, courgettes, winter squash and tomatoes, but these can be varied according to what is most readily available, as long as there is a good balance of tastes and textures.

SERVES 8

1 kg (2 lb 4 oz) couscous
100 ml (3¹/₂ fl oz) sunflower oil
100 g (3¹/₂ oz) butter or 1 generous
 tablespooon *smen*
2 tablespoons salt

FOR THE STEW
¹/₂ shoulder of lamb, weighing about
 1.5 kg (3 lb), cut into chunks (a good
 7–10 cm/3–4 in across), bone and all
2 large onions, chopped
4 garlic cloves, chopped
2 heaped teaspoons ground ginger
2 teaspoons freshly ground black
 pepper
1 tablespoon ground cumin

A generous pinch of saffron strands
100 ml (3¹/₂ fl oz) sunflower oil
4 large carrots, cut in half lengthways
 and each length halved
1 swede, peeled and cut into 5 cm
 (2 in) chunks
¹/₂ small white cabbage, cut into 6
 chunks
700 g–1 kg (1 lb 8 oz–2 lb 4 oz) orange-
 fleshed winter squash, e.g. onion
 squash, or pumpkin, peeled, seeded
 and cut into 5 cm (2 in) chunks
340 g (12 oz) courgettes, cut into 5 cm
 (2 in) chunks
4 tomatoes, halved
Salt

To cook traditional couscous, with grain that has not been pre-cooked and dried, you will either need a proper *couscoussière* or else you will have to rig up an approximation. First of all the *k'dra* or *barma*, in other words the bottom part of the *couscoussière*. For this, you will need a large, deep saucepan or casserole, preferably one that is comparatively narrow and tower-like, rather than wide and squat, so that less of the juice evaporates off as the stew cooks. And for the top part, the *kesskess*, where the grain itself is cooked, you can get away with a capacious colander lined with muslin that will sit comfortably and safely on top of the saucepan. This means that the rightful lid won't fit properly, so you will also need several large sheets of foil, to cover the whole ensemble as the couscous cooks.

Begin with the stew. Put all the meat, the onions, garlic and spices into the saucepan, with the oil. Add a ladle of water and season with salt. Cook over a moderate heat for about 10 minutes, stirring occasionally. Now add the harder, slower-cooking vegetables, that is, carrots, swede and cabbage, and enough water to cover generously. Bring up to the boil and then simmer gently for 40 minutes.

Meanwhile, tip the couscous into a wide, shallow bowl. Measure out about 300 ml (10 fl oz) of water and start sprinkling it over the couscous with your hands. Turn the couscous as you do it and continue until the water is all used up. Once the stew has been simmering for 40 minutes, place the colander or *kesskess* over the saucepan and add a couple of generous handfuls of the moistened couscous. Spread out on the base of the colander. As soon as steam starts to rise through, add another two handfuls of couscous and spread out again. When the steam rises again, add the remaining couscous and flatten it. Cover and leave for about 20 minutes, until steam rises up through all the couscous. Tip the couscous into a wide bowl and leave to cool for a few minutes. Now drizzle over about 100 ml (3½ fl oz) of oil. Measure out about 300 ml (10 fl oz) of water and add the 2 tablespoons of salt. Stir, then dip your hands into the water and scatter over the grains again. Use your fingers to turn the grains and break up any lumps. Keep going until the couscous is more or less lump-free.

Add all the remaining vegetables to the stew. Return the couscous to the colander, in the same way as before, and cover again. Steam for another 20 minutes, until the couscous is tender. Tip it out again into a large serving bowl and dot with butter or *smen*. With a large slotted spoon, lift the meat and vegetables out of the saucepan and arrange them on the couscous. Pour over a few ladles of the cooking juices, to moisten, and then pour the remaining juices into a separate bowl. Place both bowls on the table, so guests can moisten their own couscous to their liking.

Grilled or Fried Polenta Diamonds with Chicken Liver Ragoût

Straight-cooked polenta can be pretty boring, but beat in a generous knob or two of butter (and I do mean generous) and some freshly grated Parmesan (the more, the merrier) and it is instantly transformed into a purée that is every bit as good as, if not better than, mashed potatoes. Often, people who are not over-enthusiastic about hot polenta mush are won over by grilled or fried polenta. Here, the softness of the cooked polenta is encased in a crisp, browned crust – I happen to like the grilled crust best but I'm fairly partial to the fried version, too. These polenta squares, or diamonds, are the perfect accompaniment to a rich venison stew but they are just as good with, say, a beef, red wine and olive or mushroom casserole. They are also excellent with grilled or roast vegetables, particularly slow-roasted tomatoes, or as the base for a simple canapé of air-dried ham, rocket and Parmesan, perhaps.

One of the best of all toppings for grilled polenta is also one of the cheapest – this ragoût of chicken livers (frozen ones are fine) and tomatoes.

SERVES 6 AS A STARTER,
4 AS A MAIN COURSE

FOR THE POLENTA
200 g (7 oz) polenta
Olive oil for frying or grilling
4 tablespoons freshly grated Parmesan
   cheese
30 g (1 oz) butter
Salt and freshly ground black pepper

FOR THE RAGOÛT
2 shallots, finely chopped
3 garlic cloves, chopped
2 tablespoons olive oil
250 g (8 oz) chicken livers, cleaned and
   fairly finely chopped
1 large fresh rosemary sprig
450 g (1 lb) fresh tomatoes, skinned,
   seeded and chopped
1 generous glass (200 ml/7 fl oz) red
   wine
2 tablespoons sun-dried tomato purée
   or red pesto
$1/2$ tablespoon sugar
3 tablespoons chopped fresh parsley
Salt and freshly ground black pepper
Dash of balsamic vinegar

Line a Swiss roll tin with non-stick baking parchment or grease it well. Cook the polenta according to the packet instructions, adding, if necessary, a little extra hot water as it cooks to give a fairly runny purée. When it is done, stir in the Parmesan, butter, salt and pepper, making sure that it is adequately seasoned. While the polenta is still very hot, pour it into the tin, spreading it out evenly to make a thin, even layer. Leave to cool completely.

To make the ragoût, fry the shallots and garlic gently in the olive oil until tender, without browning. Now add the chicken livers and rosemary and fry for 2 minutes, stirring. Tip the tomatoes into the pan, pour in the red wine, and add the sun-dried tomato purée or pesto, the sugar, half the parsley and salt and pepper. Bring to the boil and then leave to simmer until you have a thick, sauce-like mixture. When it is done remove the rosemary sprig, stir in a splash or two of balsamic vinegar and the remaining parsley. Re-heat when needed, without boiling.

To finish the polenta, cut it into moderately large diamonds, or squares, or fingers or whatever takes your fancy. Either fry in sizzling hot oil until browned on both sides, or brush with oil and grill close to a thoroughly pre-heated grill, until brown and crusty on both sides.

Place a few diamonds of polenta on each plate and top with the ragoût. Serve immediately.

Cold Desserts

Vanilla'd Fruit Salad

Here, vanilla adds sparkle and a unifying note to an exotic fruit salad. The daring amongst you could try adding a sliced, seeded red chilli for extra kick. It is surprisingly good.

SERVES 6

FOR THE SYRUP
110 g (4 oz) caster sugar
150 ml (5 fl oz) water
1 vanilla pod, split open

FOR THE FRUIT SALAD
1 small pineapple, peeled, cored and cubed
1 mango, peeled, stoned and diced
1 papaya, peeled, quartered, seeded and sliced
2 bananas
Juice of 1 lime

Make the syrup first. Put all the ingredients into a saucepan and stir over a moderate heat, until the sugar has dissolved. Bring up to the boil and simmer for 5 minutes, stirring once or twice to help dislodge the vanilla seeds. Leave to cool.

Mix the pineapple, mango and papaya. Peel the bananas, slice them and turn the slices in the lime juice. Add to the salad, with the juice. Pour over the syrup. Turn gently, cover tightly and leave for half an hour or so before serving.

Prunes Cooked in Marsala and Orange

Most of the alcohol is cooked off but the taste remains in this upmarket version of stewed prunes. Stewed really is quite the wrong word in this case, since the prunes are cooked very briefly and then left to absorb the scent of their syrup over a period of time.

SERVES 4
2 oranges
300 ml (10 fl oz) Marsala
140 g (5 oz) demerara sugar
1 cinnamon stick

450 g (1 lb) prunes, weighed with stones in, soaked if necessary

TO SERVE
300 ml (10 fl oz) whipping cream

Pare four strips of orange zest from one of the oranges, then squeeze the juices from both fruit and place in a pan, with the strips of zest, Marsala, sugar and cinnamon stick. Bring to the boil, stirring until the sugar has dissolved. Leave to simmer for

5 minutes and then add the prunes. Simmer for another 5 minutes and then draw off the heat. Tip into a deep serving bowl and leave to cool.

When cold, cover and chill in the fridge for at least 24 hours (the prunes will keep, and improve, for at least 6 days and perhaps longer).

Shortly before serving, whip the cream with 2 tablespoons of the syrup from the prunes, until it just holds its shape. Spoon the prunes into individual glasses or pretty bowls and top with a swirl of whipped cream. Serve at once.

Baked Peaches in Wine

In Portugal, the Herdade de Zambujal is a huge peach-growing (and bull-raising) estate three-quarters of an hour's drive down the coast from Sesimbra. Right through the height of the peach season, there's always a dish of these baked peaches waiting to be eaten in the kitchen of the grand family house. Their cook usually uses white wine, but occasionally substitutes a fruity red.

SERVES 6
6 peaches, skinned but whole
100 g (4 oz) caster sugar
1 cinnamon stick

1/2–3/4 bottle dry white or red wine

TO SERVE
Ground cinnamon

Pre-heat the oven to 180°C/350°F/Gas Mark 4.

Place the peaches close together in a small ovenproof dish. Dredge with the sugar and tuck the cinnamon stick down among them. Pour over enough wine almost to cover. Bake in the oven until tender – about 40–50 minutes, depending on their ripeness and size – turning them once or twice, then leave to cool. Just before serving, dust lightly with cinnamon.

Forced Rhubarb Jellies

A spring tonic, in the best of senses. These jellies slip down like a dream – cool and fresh and scented.

SERVES 6
4 green cardamom pods
675 g (1 lb 7 oz) trimmed weight forced
**   rhubarb, cut into 2.5 cm (1 in)**
**   lengths**
Juice of 2 oranges

140 g (5 oz) caster sugar
1 sachet of powdered gelatine

TO SERVE
150 ml (5 fl oz) single cream

Split open the cardamom pods and extract the black seeds. Crush them finely. Place the rhubarb and cardamom seeds in a pan, with the orange juice and sugar. Cook over a low heat until the juices begin to run and then raise the heat a little and leave to simmer for 5 minutes, or until the rhubarb is collapsing. Tip the contents of the pan into a jelly bag or non-metallic sieve lined with muslin, set over a bowl, and allow to drip without pressing down on the debris. Leave for an hour.

Measure the liquid – you should have about 600 ml (1 pint). If necessary, top up with a little water. Then taste it. It should be sweet enough but retain a mild tartness. This is largely a matter of personal taste so, if you think it needs more sugar, warm it gently with a little extra sugar until you get the right balance.

Put 3 tablespoons of hot water into a small pan and sprinkle the gelatine evenly over. Stir until dissolved. If there are a few stubborn globs that refuse to disappear, warm gently, stirring, without boiling, until they dissolve.

Stir a tablespoon of rhubarb juice into the gelatine and then another and then a third. Finally, pour the whole lot into the remaining rhubarb juice and stir until nicely mixed. Again, if there are blobs of gelatine, warm gently, stirring, until they have dissolved. Pour the jelly into six glasses or small bowls and chill until set.

Just before serving, pour a little single cream over the surface of each jelly.

Passion Fruit and Orange Jellies

I love proper fruit jellies. Light and refreshing, they make a great finale to a rich meal. These orange jellies are boosted with the scent of passion fruit and there is nothing childish about them at all. If you set them in narrow wine or champagne glasses, there will be enough for six small servings. Larger glasses look mean if they are only half-filled so, if that is what you've got, you'll only end up with four servings.

SERVES 4–6
4 passion fruit
3 tablespoons caster sugar
550 ml (1 pint) freshly squeezed orange juice

1 sachet of powdered gelatine

TO SERVE
Single cream

Halve the passion fruit and scrape their innards into a small saucepan. Add the caster sugar and stir over a low heat for a few minutes, until the sugar has dissolved and the fruit is warmed through. Scrape fruit into a sieve set over the bowl of orange juice and press all the juices through, leaving behind little but the black seeds. Save a few of them for decoration.

Heat 3 tablespoons of water in a small pan, until very hot. Draw off the heat and sprinkle the gelatine over. Stir until dissolved. If a few stubborn specks of gelatine remain, warm through gently, stirring constantly, without letting it boil, until they disappear. Cool the gelatine until tepid and then stir in a tablespoon of the orange and passion fruit juice. Then stir in another, and then a third, and then tip the whole lot back into the bowl of juice. Stir to mix well. Pour into stemmed wine glasses, and leave to set in the fridge. To serve, pour a small slick of single cream over the surface and scatter with a few passion fruit seeds.

Fromageon Gascon

From the south-west of France comes this superbly boozy cream to serve with summer fruits, or maybe just on its own in small bowls with crisp almondy biscuits to dip into it.

SERVES 4–6
60 g (2 oz) caster sugar

85 ml (3 fl oz) Armagnac or brandy
280 g (10 oz) young fresh goats' cheese

Beat first the sugar and then the Armagnac or brandy into the cheese. Chill for at least an hour before serving and beat once more before you put it on the table.

Basil Cremets

The sweet nature of basil is often overlooked but it can work well in puddings, if treated with consideration. Here it is folded into the cream and cheese mixture that will be drained to form cremets, *so good with soft summer fruit and/or a raspberry coulis (sieved raspberries sweetened with a little icing sugar).*

SERVES 6
280 g (10 fl oz) cream cheese
150 ml (5 fl oz) fromage frais or Greek
  yoghurt
200 ml (7 fl oz) crème fraîche
  (or whipping cream, lightly
  whipped)

2½ tablespoons caster sugar
3 tablespoons chopped fresh basil
1 egg white

If you have them, line six small *coeurs à la crème* moulds with muslin. Failing that, collect together six small yoghurt or cream pots or clean plastic flowerpots and pierce holes in the bottom with a hot skewer. Rinse the pots and line them with muslin.

Beat the cream cheese with the fromage frais or yoghurt, until smooth. Fold in the crème fraîche or whipped whipping cream, caster sugar and basil. Whisk the egg white until stiff and fold that in last of all. Spoon the mixture into the lined moulds. Stand on a wire rack over a shallow dish, cover and leave overnight in the fridge to drain. Turn out just before serving.

Passion Fruit Syllabub

This is an incredibly rich pudding that can be made very quickly, and tastes divine.

SERVES 4
4 passion fruit
3 tablespoons caster sugar

300 ml (10 fl oz) double cream
Juice of 1 lime
Icing sugar

Extract the passion fruit juice by heating the flesh with the sugar (see Passion Fruit and Orange Jellies, p. 302. Strain and cool. Reserve some of the seeds.

Put the cream into a bowl, and whisk, gradually adding the passion fruit then the lime juice. When it holds its shape softly, taste and stir in a little icing sugar if it is too tart – though syllabubs shouldn't be too sweet. Divide between four glasses, or small bowls, and serve instantly or lightly chilled, scattered with the reserved seeds.

Mango, Lime and Cardamom Fool

Understanding the anatomy of the mango is a help when it comes to cutting. Inside is a long, thin oval stone that runs from stalk end to tip, with two fat cheeks of mango clinging to either side. Slice the two cheeks off and make criss-cross cuts in the cut surface, penetrating almost down to the skin, but without piercing it. Turn inside-out, so the cubes of flesh stand out hedgehog-fashion. Then slice off the cubes with a sharp knife.

This is a very easy, but glamorous, pudding, scented with fragrant cardamom. Evaporated milk, rather than cream, gives it richness though you couldn't tell when eating it. This can be eaten as soon as it is made, but it will thicken a little if left overnight in the fridge. Serve with crisp biscuits, such as Pecan Tuiles (see p. 346).

SERVES 6
3 fresh mangoes, weighing about 300 g (11 oz) each, peeled, stoned and diced
2 limes
4 cardamom pods

4–5 tablespoons light muscovado sugar, to taste
180 ml (6 fl oz) evaporated milk

TO SERVE
1 large mango

Put the mango dice in a food processor. With a zester or a vegetable peeler, take the green zest off one of the limes and shred it finely. Blanch for a minute in boiling water, drain and reserve. Squeeze the juice of the limes and add to the mango. Slit open the cardamom pods, extract the black seeds and crush to a fine powder in a mortar with a pestle. Tip into the processor. Add 3 tablespoons of light muscovado sugar. Process until smooth and then add the evaporated milk and process again, to mix.

Taste and add a little more sugar, if you think it needs it. Divide between six glasses, ramekins or custard cups, cover and leave in the fridge for at least an hour and up to 24 hours, to thicken.

Shortly before serving, sprinkle a little more light muscovado sugar over the top of each fool and finish with a few strands of the reserved lime zest. Take the last mango and slice it, by cutting at right angles to the central stone, to release long, new-moon-shaped slices of flesh. Trim the peel from the slices and serve them alongside the fool.

Coconut Crème Caramel

One of my favourite Thai restaurants serves a crème caramel made with coconut milk instead of cows' milk – an East-meets-West pudding, if ever there was one. I have taken the idea one step further, flavouring the coconut milk with cardamom and cinnamon as well as the more usual vanilla.

SERVES 6–8

FOR THE CARAMEL
140 g (5 oz) granulated or caster sugar

FOR THE CUSTARD
600 ml (1 pint) coconut milk

1 vanilla pod
1 cinnamon stick
2 cardamom pods
4 eggs
30 g (1 oz) caster sugar

Stand either eight 120 ml (4 fl oz) capacity ramekins or six 180 ml (6 fl oz) capacity ramekins in a roasting tin in the oven. Heat the oven to 150°C/300°F/Gas Mark 2.

While the ramekins are heating through, make the caramel. Put the granulated or caster sugar into a saucepan with 5 tablespoons of water. Stir over a moderate heat, until the sugar has completely dissolved, brushing down any sugar crystals stuck to the side of the pan with a brush dipped into cold water. When the syrup is clear, bring up to the boil and boil hard until it caramelizes to a nice hazelnut brown. Don't stir it, but do tilt and swirl the syrup in the pan as it cooks, to even out hot spots. As soon as it is done, whip the ramekins out of the oven. Pour a little of the caramel into each hot ramekin and then quickly tip and tilt them, so that their bottoms and sides are coated in caramel. Once coated, leave the ramekins to cool and then return them to the roasting tin.

To make the custard, put the coconut milk into a pan, with the vanilla pod and cinnamon stick. Slit open the cardamom pods, extract the black seeds and crush coarsely. Add them to the milk, too. Bring gently to the boil and then draw off the heat. Cover and leave to infuse for 15 minutes in a warm place. Whisk the eggs with the caster sugar. Bring the coconut milk back to the boil and then pour on to the eggs, stirring constantly. Strain the mixture into the ramekins. Pour enough hot water into the roasting tin to come about halfway up the ramekins. Carefully transfer to the oven and cook gently for an hour or so, until the coconut custard has just set. Leave the ramekins to cool and then store in the fridge, loosely covered with cling film, until needed.

To serve, invert into shallow bowls and pass around a bowl of cream for those who like to go the whole hog.

Sweet Baked Ricotta

An Australian recipe, though I imagine inspired by Italian ricotta desserts, this comes from the Bather's Pavilion Restaurant, which overlooks the beach at Balmoral, near Sydney. There they serve it with grilled peach halves, though I like it with all manner of fruit. Try quartering some figs, without cutting them right through, dusting them with icing sugar and popping them under the grill for a few minutes and then serving them hot, with the cool baked ricotta.

In the autumn, the ricotta goes well with a compote of blackberries, or poached pears or quinces. In winter and early spring, try it with lightly cooked forced or garden rhubarb.

Whatever you choose to serve it with, bake the ricotta a day in advance, so that it has time to firm up in the fridge. If the dimensions of the tin you use are different from mine, you may need to vary the cooking time a little accordingly, so allow plenty of time and judge whether it is done by eye.

SERVES 8
800 g (1 lb 12 oz) ricotta
2 eggs

1 vanilla pod
200 g (7 oz) icing sugar

Pre-heat the oven to 170°C/325°F/Gas Mark 3. You will need a non-stick loaf tin about 22 × 12 × 6 cm (9 × 5 × 2^1/2 in). If you don't have a non-stick tin, line the one you have with foil and brush the foil with almond or groundnut oil.

Sieve the ricotta and then beat it with the eggs (or process the two together). Slit open the vanilla pod and scrape the seeds out into the ricotta mixture. Sift in the icing sugar and mix thoroughly. Spoon into the loaf tin, smooth down, and cover with foil. Place the tin in a slightly larger baking tin and pour in enough hot water to come about halfway up the sides of the loaf tin. Carefully place in the oven and bake for an hour or so, or until barely firm.

Lift the tin out of its water bath and remove the foil. Leave to cool and then cover with cling film and refrigerate. When it is thoroughly chilled, you ca turn it out of the tin and slice as required. Let it come back to room temperature before you serve it.

Almond, Honey and Ricotta Cheesecake

A virginal white cheesecake with a hint of lime sharpness, and a delicate waft of honey and finely chopped almonds to give it some texture. The crème fraîche topping is one of those easy touches that worries many people as they can't see how it could possibly set solidly. Don't worry – it does set as it cools and gives a silky, rich finish.

SERVES 8

FOR THE CRUST
200 g (7 oz) digestive biscuits, finely crushed
110 g (4 oz) butter, melted

FOR THE FILLING
85 g (3 oz) almonds, toasted
450 g (1 lb) ricotta
3 eggs, separated
5 tablespoons runny honey

2 tablespoons caster sugar
Finely grated zest and juice of 1 lime
1/2 teaspoon vanilla essence
A pinch of salt

FOR THE TOPPING
300 ml (10 fl oz) crème fraîche
1 tablespoon vanilla sugar
Toasted flaked almonds
A few fine strands of lime zest

Pre-heat the oven to 190°C/375°F/Gas Mark 5. Mix the crushed digestives thoroughly with the butter and press them evenly into the base of a 5 cm (2 in) deep, 20–22 cm (8–8 1/2 in) tart tin or cake tin with a removable base, spreading them slightly up the sides. Bake for 10 minutes and then leave to cool.

Grind the almonds to a coarse powder in a food processor. Beat the ricotta until smooth and then beat in the egg yolks, honey, sugar, lime zest and juice, vanilla essence, salt and, finally, the almonds. Whisk the egg whites until they form stiff peaks, then fold into the ricotta mixture. Spoon into the crushed digestive case. Bake the cheesecake for 25–35 minutes, until almost set but with a very minor wobble in the centre. Take out of the oven and let it stand for 5 minutes.

Mix the crème fraîche with the vanilla sugar, then pour over the cheesecake and spread out evenly. Return to the oven for 10 minutes. Leave to cool in the tin and then chill for 4 hours. Run the blade of a knife, dipped first into hot water, around the edge, then unmould. Decorate with flaked almonds and lime zest, and serve.

Hungarian Baked Cheesecake

Use an enriched yeast dough as the base, topped with a blend of soft cheese mixed with soured cream and raisins.

It's important to get the dough stretched out as thinly as possible over the base of the tin, which should, by the way, be more generously greased than usual if you want the dough to be crisp underneath. Inevitably it will rise up unevenly here and there, but that's no disaster.

SERVES 8–10

FOR THE YEAST DOUGH
225 ml (7¹/2 fl oz) milk
25 g (1 oz) fresh yeast or 15 g (¹/2 oz)
   dried yeast
1 tablespoon caster sugar
450 g (1 lb) strong plain flour
Pinch of salt
100 g (4 oz) butter or duck fat
1 egg, beaten

FOR THE FILLING
350 g (12 oz) ricotta or curd cheese
225 ml (7¹/2 fl oz) crème fraîche, or
   double cream mixed with soured
   cream
3 eggs, separated
75 g (3 oz) caster sugar
75 g (3 oz) raisins

First make the yeast dough. Warm the milk to blood temperature (it's about right when you can hold your finger in it for only 10 seconds before it feels too hot). Stir in the crumbled yeast and sugar. Leave in a warm place for 5–10 minutes, until frothing.

Sift the flour with the salt. Rub in the butter or duck fat. Make a well in the centre and add the beaten egg and about two-thirds of the yeast mixture. Mix, gradually drawing in the flour and adding more of the yeast mixture as needed, until you have a soft, slightly sticky dough. Knead vigorously for 10 minutes, until smooth and elastic. Dust with a little flour, cover with a cloth and leave in a warm place until doubled in bulk – about 1–1¹/2 hours.

Punch down, knead again for 5 minutes, then line a thoroughly greased, deep 25 × 35 cm (10 × 14 in) baking tin with the dough, using your hands to spread it evenly over the base and ease it an inch or so up the sides. Persevere – though it has an infuriating habit of slipping back, you will eventually get it to stretch over the tin. Leave in a warm place for 10 minutes while you make the filling.

Preheat the oven to 180°C/350°F/Gas Mark 4. To make the filling, beat the ricotta with the crème fraîche or cream mixture until smooth. Add the egg yolks, sugar and raisins and mix. Whisk the egg whites until they form stiff peaks, then fold into the mixture. Spread lightly and evenly over the prepared base. Bake in the oven for about 30–40 minutes, until the filling is just set. Serve warm or cold.

Chocolate Meringue Cake with Cherries and Mascarpone

It is a shame that Black Forest gateau has been so bastardized and ruined by commerce, since cherries and chocolate are a natural partnership. Raspberries, too, go blissfully well with chocolate. This chocolate cake, slathered with rich mascarpone and fruit, is even more indulgent. The cake is crisp and meringue-like on the outside and fudgey with chocolate on the inside. All in all, an indecently rich and wicked pudding. For an even fudgier interior, but a slightly less crisp top, leave the cake to stand overnight covered with a clean tea-towel. If you don't like mascarpone, serve with whipped cream.

SERVES 8

FOR THE CAKE
110 g (4 oz) plain chocolate
110 g (4 oz) unsalted butter, softened
3 eggs, separated
30 g (1 oz) plain flour
110 g (4 oz) caster sugar

TO SERVE
150 ml (5 fl oz) whipping cream,
  whipped
220 g (8 oz) mascarpone
450 g (1 lb) cherries, stoned, or
  raspberries

Pre-heat the oven to 170°C/325°F/Gas Mark 3. Line the base of a 19–20 cm (7^1/$_2$–8 in) cake tin with a circle of non-stick parchment and butter the sides generously.

For the cake, break the chocolate into squares or chop it in a food processor and melt it. As soon as it has melted, take the bowl off the heat. Beat in half the butter, a little at a time, and then the egg yolks.

Blend the flour with the remaining butter until soft and evenly mixed and stir into the chocolate mixture, until completely amalgamated. Whisk the egg whites until soft, add half the sugar and whisk again, until shiny and thick. Fold in the remaining sugar. Lightly fold the meringue into the chocolate mixture and pour into the cake tin. Stand the tin in a roasting tin half-filled with hot water and bake for 1^1/$_4$ hours. Remove from the oven and leave to cool. Turn out just before serving.

Fold the whipped cream into the mascarpone. Either pile high on the cake and top with a tumble of cherries or raspberries, or arrange slices of cake on individual plates, with a large dollop of mascarpone cream and a generous mound of fruit scattered over. Devour.

Portuguese Rice Pudding

Arroz Doce, *always eaten cold, is to be found on the menu of almost every café and small restaurant in Portugal – at least, in my limited experience. When made well, with good ingredients, it is one of the nicest rice puddings imaginable. The rice is cooked first in water to soften it, then again in milk to make it meltingly tender. Butter and egg yolks render it rich and velvety.*

SERVES 6–8
200 g (7 oz) medium-grain rice
Salt
Generous 600 ml (1 pint) creamy milk
90 g (3^1/$_2$ oz) butter

Zest of 1 lemon, pared off in strips
175 g (6 oz) caster sugar
8 egg yolks
Ground cinnamon

Boil the rice in plenty of water with a pinch of salt, until barely tender. Drain thoroughly and place in a large pan with the milk, butter and lemon zest. Bring to the boil and simmer for about 20 minutes until thick and creamy. Draw off the heat and stir in the sugar and then the egg yolks. Divide between 6–8 bowls, dust generously with ground cinnamon and leave to cool.

Portuguese Custard Tarts

Pastéis de nata are not quite like ordinary custard tarts. For a start the custard is rich and tender, made usually with egg yolks rather than whole eggs. And then there's the pastry, a puff pastry, but rolled out in a most unusual way, so that the pastry case is a mass of fine overlapping layers. The instructions may sound a little confusing, but follow them step by step and you'll soon understand how they work.

MAKES 14
225 g (8 oz) puff pastry

FOR THE FILLING
4 egg yolks
50 g (2 oz) caster sugar

2 teaspoons flour
200 ml (7 fl oz) single cream

TO SERVE
Ground cinnamon
Icing sugar

Roll out the pastry thinly into a rectangle 35 × 20 cm (14 × 8 in). Roll up tightly from one of the short edges to form a plump sausage shape 20 cm (8 in) long. Wrap in foil and chill in the freezer until firm but not frozen solid. Using a sharp knife, cut into discs 1 cm (1/2 in) thick. Using your fingers, press each circle into a deep tartlet tin, easing the pastry up the sides. Prick with a fork and rest for 30 minutes in the refrigerator.

Pre-heat the oven to 230°C/450°F/Gas Mark 8.

Beat the egg yolks with the sugar and the flour. Gradually beat in the cream. Pour into a pan and stir over a gentle heat, without boiling, until you have a thick custard. Cool. Fill the tartlets two-thirds full with custard. Bake in the oven for 10–15 minutes, until the custard has browned. Eat warm or cold, dusted with cinnamon and icing sugar.

Heavenly Bacon

Heavenly bacon, or tocino de cielo, *is one of the best of all the* yemas *(egg-yolk sweets) that abound in Spain and Portugal (where its known as* toucinho do céu). *It varies in thickness from one establishment to another, may be served up in neat squares or turned out of little round moulds, with or without caramel. Essentially, however, this heavenly bacon is a sweet, sticky, baked custard made with sugar syrup rather than cream or milk. In texture it is as smooth and silky as a baby's bottom. Very rich, undoubtedly very wicked and very delicious.*

SERVES 6–8

FOR THE CARAMEL
100 g (4 oz) caster sugar

FOR THE CUSTARD
275 g (10 oz) caster sugar
4 strips of lemon zest
10 egg yolks, lightly beaten

Begin with the caramel. Put the sugar into a heavy-bottomed pan with 3 tablespoons water. Stir constantly over a low–medium heat until the sugar has completely dissolved, without ever letting it boil. Brush down any crystals stuck to the side of the pan with a brush dipped in cold water. Once the syrup is clear, stop stirring. Bring to the boil and boil until the syrup caramelizes to a rich brown. Watch over it carefully, and occasionally tilt the pan, gently swirling the sugar syrup, but don't be tempted to stir. Once it has caramelized, pour the syrup either into an 18 cm (7 in) square tin, tilting to coat the base thoroughly, or into 6 small dariole moulds.

To make the syrup, put the sugar into a pan with 150 ml (5 fl oz) water and the lemon zest and stir over a medium heat until the sugar has completely dissolved without letting it boil. Brush down any crystals clinging to the side of the pan with a brush dipped in cold water. Once the syrup is clear, bring to the boil, then remove the lemon zest. Boil the syrup until it reaches 112°C/234°F, the thread stage. Use a sugar thermometer as a guide if you have one, then test by dipping 2 spoons, held back to back, into the syrup. Quickly lift out and gently pull apart. If long threads of sugar form, you've hit the right point. Quickly take the syrup off the heat and allow it to cool for about 3–4 minutes.

Pre-heat the oven to 160°C/325°F/Gas Mark 3.

Pour the syrup slowly into the beaten egg yolks, beating constantly with a whisk or fork. Strain the mixture into the tin or moulds coated in caramel and cover with foil. Stand in a roasting tin and pour in enough boiling water to come about half-way up the tin or moulds. Bake in the oven until just set, about 30–40 minutes. Cool in the roasting tin.

When cool, turn out of the moulds (if using). If cooked in one tin, cut into squares.

Amalfitana Aubergine and Chocolate Pudding

Yes, honestly! ... and it really is amazingly delicious. I was first introduced to the pudding by the owner of the Al San Vincenzo Restaurant in Bayswater, London, and later came across this recipe for it in a book of Neapolitan desserts. It's best made 24 hours in advance. Try to find good quality candied peel, in whole pieces. It's worth chopping it yourself, as the taste is so much better than the ready-prepared stuff.

SERVES 6–8

3 medium-sized aubergines, sliced
    lengthways
Salt
Olive oil and sunflower oil, for frying
Plain flour
Cocoa powder, to decorate

FOR THE CRÈME PATISSIÈRE
300 ml (10 fl oz) full-cream milk
1 vanilla pod, slit lengthways
3 egg yolks

150 g (5 oz) caster sugar
45 g (1¹/₂ oz) plain flour
A pinch of salt
85 g (3 oz) finely chopped mixed
    candied peel

FOR THE CHOCOLATE CREAM
30 g (1 oz) cocoa powder, sifted
45 g (1¹/₂ oz) plain flour, sifted
60 g (2 oz) caster sugar
300 ml (10 fl oz) full-cream milk
A knob of butter

Sprinkle the aubergine slices lightly with salt and set aside for an hour.

Rinse the slices clean and pat dry. Heat 2.5 cm (1 in) of oil (I use half olive oil and half sunflower oil) in a wide frying-pan. One by one, dust each aubergine slice with flour and fry until golden brown. Drain on kitchen paper.

While the aubergine is being salted, make the *crème patissière* and the chocolate cream. For the *crème patissière*, heat the milk slowly with the vanilla pod, until it starts to boil. Cover, draw off the heat and leave to infuse for 20 minutes. Beat the egg yolks with the sugar, flour and a pinch of salt. Gradually tip in the milk, whisking constantly. Pour back into the pan and stir over a medium heat. Bring to the boil, stirring constantly, and then let it bubble and heave for 3 minutes. Draw off the heat, stir in the candied peel and leave to cool. Remove the vanilla pod.

For the chocolate cream, mix the cocoa, flour and caster sugar in a pan and gradually whisk in the milk. Bring gently up to the boil, stirring constantly. Simmer for 2–3 minutes, until the taste of raw flour has gone. Draw off the heat and beat in the butter.

Cover the base of a deep dish (around 22 cm/9 in or slightly smaller) with a layer of aubergine. Cover with a layer of *crème patissière* (warmed slightly, if necessary, to make it runnier) and then spoon over a layer of chocolate cream. Repeat the layers once or twice, depending on the size of your dish, finishing off with a layer of chocolate cream. Chill for at least 4 hours, or longer if possible.

Dust with cocoa just before serving. Cut into squares with a large knife, and ask your guests to guess what the mystery ingredient is.

Baklava

When I visited Istanbul the pastry room upstairs at the Gullouglu Baklava Bakery was an amazing sight. In a haze of white flour a dozen men were pulling and stretching out the paper-thin dough. They looked like ghosts, covered from head to foot in a fine dusting of flour. Even the telephone high up on the wall looked bizarre – something from a theatrical set perhaps? It was only when I emerged outside that I suddenly looked down and realized that I too had metamorphosed into a ghostly figure.

A quick dust down and it was round to the shop to buy a selection of baklava, those sticky nut-filled pastries with their many layers of crisp buttery filo pastry.

Home-baked baklava are never quite the same as really good professional ones, made by skilled bakers, but they are a pleasure to make for all that. Adjusting the cooking time and temperature to suit your oven is important – the idea is to make sure that every layer of pastry is crisp through to the heart. Treat my instructions as guidelines, and keep an eye on the baklava as they cook. If they seem to be browning far too fast, reduce the temperature slightly and/or cover loosely with foil.

SERVES 12
450 g (1 lb) filo pastry
4 oz (100 g) unsalted butter, melted

FOR THE NUT FILLING
350 g (12 oz) walnuts or pistachios
(or a mixture of the two),
coarsely ground or very finely
chopped

1 tablespoon ground cinnamon

FOR THE SYRUP
10 oz (275 g) granulated sugar
Juice of 1 lemon

Pre-heat the oven to 180°C/350°F/Gas Mark 4.

To prevent the filo drying out, cover it first with a sheet of greaseproof paper then with a tea-towel wrung out in cold water. Brush a 33 × 25 cm (13 × 10 in) baking dish with a little of the butter. Brush half the sheets of filo pastry with butter and lay in the baking dish, one on top of the other. Spread over the filling ingredients, then cover with the remaining pastry sheets, again buttering each one before laying it down.

Using a sharp knife, tuck the edges down neatly round the sides. Brush with the remaining butter. Using the sharp knife, cut into diamonds. Bake in the oven for 25 minutes, then reduce the heat to 150°C/300°F/Gas Mark 2, and bake for a further 30 minutes.

While the baklava is cooking, put the sugar for the syrup into a pan with 300 ml (10 fl oz) water and the lemon juice. Stir over a medium heat until the sugar has dissolved. Bring to the boil and simmer for 5 minutes. Cool. As soon as the baklava comes out of the oven, pour over the syrup, then leave to cool completely.

Strawberry Sorbet

Many of the scruffiest of cafés in the back streets of Palermo in Sicily make their own ice-creams and sorbets, blending and freezing them virtually on the pavement as you watch. They are more than welcome on a hot day, as long as the lack of hygiene doesn't bother you too much.

I gave in to the lure of cooling scoops of strawberry sorbet, intensely flavoured as only a freshly made water-ice, based on sun-ripened fruit, can be. The formula is straightforward – it's the quality of the fruit that counts. You need the best strawberries, their sweet scent balanced with a hint of tartness. If you can find them, throw in a handful of tiny wood strawberries as well, or serve alongside the finished sorbet.

SERVES 4–6
150 g (5 oz) sugar
450 g (1 lb) strawberries, hulled and
 halved
Juice of 1 orange

Put the sugar in a pan with 120 ml (4 fl oz) water and stir over a medium heat until the sugar has dissolved. Bring to the boil, then draw off the heat and cool.

Process the strawberries with the orange juice and about two-thirds of the sugar syrup. Taste and add more syrup if necessary, bearing in mind that the sweetness will be dulled when the sorbet is frozen. The mixture should be a little on the sweet side, but not overwhelmingly sugary.

Freeze in a *sorbetière* if you have one. If not, set the freezer to its coldest setting. Pour the mixture into a shallow freezer container and freeze until the sides have set. Break up, and push into the centre. Freeze again until beginning to set right through. Quickly tip into a food processor and whizz to a smooth slush, or beat vigorously to smooth out the ice crystals. If you have time, repeat this process once more. Finally return the iced slush to the freezer to start freezing. Transfer to the refrigerator to soften slightly about 15 minutes before serving.

VARIATION

The Italians are good at ice-cream and smooth sorbets, everyone knows that, but they are also masters of the wondrous, grainy-but-slushy heaps of crystals known as *granite* (the plural of *granita*), the purest and most elegant of iced desserts. To make Strawberry Granita, prepare as above. Freeze the mixture until the sides are beginning to set. Break up into small granules and push into the centre. Repeat this every 30 minutes or so, until you end up with tiny glittering shards of chilled strawberry ice.

Tropical Sorbet

Mix passion fruit juice with tropical fruits to make an unusually fragrant sorbet.

SERVES 4–6
4 passion fruit
2 tablespoons plus 200 g (7 oz) caster sugar

1/2 medium-sized pineapple, peeled, cored and roughly chopped
2 large bananas, peeled and sliced
Juice of 1 lime

Halve the passion fruit and scrape their innards into a small saucepan. Add 2 table-spoons caster sugar and stir over a low heat for a few minutes, until the sugar has dissolved. Scrape the fruit into a sieve set over a bowl and press all the juices through, leaving behind little but the black seeds. Heat the remaining sugar in a pan with 200 ml (7 fl oz) water until it has completely dissolved. Bring to the boil, then draw off the heat and leave to cool.

Process the passion fruit juice and remaining ingredients to a smooth mush. Gradually add enough of the sugar syrup to sweeten to taste, bearing in mind that freezing dampens down the sweetness.

Freeze the mixture in an ice-cream machine, according to the manufacturer's instructions. If you don't have an ice-cream maker, pour the mixture into a shallow freezer container, cover and freeze at your freezer's lowest setting. Once the sides begin to harden, break them up and push into the centre. Return to the freezer. Repeat once more and then leave in the freezer until the sorbet is just set but not yet rock solid. Scrape into a processor or mixer and whizz fast to smooth out ice crystals. If you are totally lacking in machinery, you'll just have to flex your arm muscles and beat hard. Return the sorbet to the freezer.

Transfer from the freezer to the fridge to soften 20–30 minutes before eating.

Vanilla and Walnut Ice-cream

This recipe makes an absolutely sensational ice-cream but, if you want something a mite plainer, leave out the walnuts to produce a deep, rich, unmistakably classy straight vanilla ice-cream. If you are after nothing more than a neutral, vaguely vanilla flavour backdrop for other puddings, leave the pod whole and untampered with.

SERVES 6
300 ml (10 fl oz) full-cream milk
1 vanilla pod, slit open
3 large egg yolks

110 g (4 oz) caster sugar
85 g (3 oz) chopped walnuts
300 ml (10 fl oz) double cream

Put the milk into a pan, with the vanilla pod, and bring slowly to the boil, stirring every now and then. Draw off the heat, cover and leave to infuse for 20–30 minutes.

Pre-heat the oven to 200°C/400°F/Gas Mark 6. Whisk the egg yolks with the sugar and then whisk in the milk, together with the vanilla pod. Set the bowl over a pan of lazily simmering water, making sure that the base of the bowl does not come into contact with the water. Stir until the custard thickens enough to coat the back of the spoon. Leave to cool and then strain.

Meanwhile, spread the walnuts out on a baking tray and toast in the oven, until they turn a shade or two darker. Allow around 4–7 minutes, checking and shaking them once or twice as they roast. Tip into a metal sieve and shake over a piece of newspaper to dislodge all those flakes of papery skin. Leave to cool.

When the custard is cool, whip the cream lightly and fold in the custard. If you have an ice-cream maker, freeze according to manufacturer's instructions adding the walnut pieces when the mixture is sludgy, but not too thick.

If you don't, pour the mixture, without adding the walnut pieces, into a shallow container. Freeze as for Tropical Sorbet on p. 315. After whizzing in the processor or beating by hand, fold in the walnut pieces and return to the freezer to set solid.

Transfer from the freezer to the fridge to soften about 45 minutes before eating.

Maple and Walnut Parfait

This is a spectacularly good, light, frozen mousse. Maple syrup and walnuts go very well together, but for an all-American parfait you could substitute pecans.

SERVES 6
60 g (2 oz) walnuts
200 ml (7 fl oz) maple syrup

1 egg white
240 ml (9 fl oz) double cream
Salt

Pre-heat the oven to 200°C/400°F/Gas Mark 6. Spread the walnuts out on a baking sheet and toast them in the oven for around 5 minutes or so, until browned, checking once or twice to make sure they don't burn. Tip into a wire sieve and shake off all the loosened, papery skin. Cool and chop roughly.

Heat the maple syrup to boiling point. Meanwhile, whisk the egg white with a pinch of salt until it forms soft peaks. Gradually pour in the very hot syrup, whisking constantly. Continue whisking until you have a thick, stiff meringue. Use an electric whisk, if you have one, as this doesn't happen instantly by any means. Then leave it to cool.

Whip the cream until just stiff and then fold it into the maple meringue. Finally, fold in the nuts. Spoon into a dish and freeze; there's no need to pay it any attention while it freezes because all that whisking and cream guarantees a smooth, creamy ice-cream. Transfer to the fridge to soften half an hour before serving.

Saffron and Honey Ice-cream

Saffron and honey, two of nature's golden foods, are well suited to each other. I've loved the combination ever since I tasted Joyce Molyneux's (of the Carved Angel in Dartmouth) baked honey and saffron custards with gooseberries. Here, they are diluted again by cream but frozen stiff to a rich, ambrosial ice-cream.

SERVES 6
5 egg yolks
300 ml (10 fl oz) milk
150 ml (5 fl oz) single cream

A generous pinch of saffron strands
85 g (3 oz) runny honey
230 ml (8 fl oz) double cream

Whisk the egg yolks in a large bowl. Bring the milk and the single cream to the boil. Draw off the heat and stir in the saffron strands and honey. Quickly pour the hot, milky mixture on to the egg yolks, whisking constantly. Set the bowl over a pan of gently simmering water, making sure the bottom of the bowl doesn't touch the water, and stir until the custard thickens enough to coat the back of the spoon. Lift the bowl off the pan and dunk into a shallow bowl of cold water, to halt cooking. Leave to cool, stirring occasionally to distribute the streaks of colour left by the saffron strands.

Whip the double cream until it is just beginning to hold its shape, but is still floppy. Fold it into the custard and then freeze in an ice-cream maker. If you don't have one, freeze as for Tropical Sorbet on p. 315. After whizzing in the processor or beating by hand, return the ice-cream to the container for the last time, put it back into the freezer and leave it alone to freeze solid.

To serve, transfer from the freezer to the fridge about 40 minutes before serving.

Prune and Armagnac Ice-cream

If prunes suggest nursery food and childhood horrors, this ice-cream will redress the balance. It's strictly for grown-ups, and definitely for dinner parties rather than daily consumption. Soak the prunes for as long as you can, so that they have plenty of time to absorb the flavour of the Armagnac or brandy.

SERVES 6–8
150 g (5 oz) caster sugar
5 tablespoons Armagnac or brandy
450 g (1 lb) prunes (weighed with their
stones)

300 ml (10 fl oz) milk
1 vanilla pod, slit open
4 egg yolks
300 ml (10 fl oz) double cream

Put 75 g (3 oz) of the sugar in a pan with 150 ml (5 fl oz) water. Stir over a moderate heat until dissolved. Bring to the boil, then draw off the heat. Stir in the Armagnac and pour over the prunes. Cover and leave to soak for at least 24 hours, if not 2 or 3 days, then pit the prunes and purée them with their syrup.

Bring the milk and vanilla pod to the boil. Cover and infuse over the lowest possible heat for 10 minutes, then remove the vanilla pod. Whisk the egg yolks lightly with the remaining sugar. Pour on the hot milk, stirring constantly. Set the bowl over a pan of lazily simmering water, making sure that the base does not touch the water. Stir until just thick enough to coat the back of a spoon. Draw off the heat and strain. Stir in the prune purée and cool. Whip the cream lightly and fold in the prune custard.

Freeze in a *sorbetière* if you have one. Otherwise pour into a shallow container and place in the freezer, set to its lowest setting. When half-set, beat hard to break up the crystals. Return to the freezer. Freeze until almost solid, then beat again (in a processor, if you like). Freeze until solid.

Transfer from the freezer to the fridge to soften half an hour before eating.

Coconut Ice-cream with Lemon Grass Syrup

This is a great combination of cool, mild ice-cream with a perfumed sauce. To make it even more sensational, serve with slices of ripe mango. If you are short of time, replace the coconut ice-cream with a scoop of high-quality vanilla ice-cream. Coconut cream is a thick liquid that comes in small 200 ml (7 fl oz) cartons and is not the same as the solid blocks of creamed coconut.

SERVES 4
3 lemon grass stems, trimmed, bruised and thinly sliced
250 g (9 oz) caster sugar

FOR THE COCONUT ICE-CREAM
400 ml (14 fl oz) can coconut milk

200 ml (7 fl oz) carton coconut cream
1 vanilla pod, slit open
4 egg yolks
3 tablespoons light muscovado sugar
250 ml (9 fl oz) double cream

To make the lemon grass syrup, put the lemon grass, sugar and 300 ml (10 fl oz) of water in a pan and stir over a medium heat until the sugar has completely dissolved. Bring to the boil and simmer gently for 5 minutes. Draw off the heat and leave to cool, then strain.

To make the ice-cream, put the coconut milk and coconut cream into a pan with the vanilla pod and bring slowly to the boil. Draw off the heat, cover and leave for 10 minutes.

Bring back to the boil. Whisk the egg yolks with the sugar until pale and frothy and then pour the hot coconut milk onto them, whisking constantly. Set the bowl over a pan of lazily simmering water, making sure that the base of the bowl does not come into contact with the water. Stir until the custard thickens enough to coat the back of the spoon. Take the bowl off the pan and stand it in some cold water, to halt the cooking process. Leave to cool and then remove the vanilla pod.

Whip the cream lightly until it begins to thicken and then stir it into the coconut custard. Freeze in an ice-cream maker, if you have one. If you don't, tip the mixture into a shallow freezer container, cover and freeze as for Tropical Sorbet on p. 315. After whizzing in the processor or beating by hand, return to the freezer to finish freezing.

Transfer the ice-cream to the fridge to soften 45 minutes before eating.

To serve, put two or three scoops of ice-cream on each plate or in each bowl and spoon over some of the syrup.

Chocolate and Chilli Ice-cream with Orange and Cinnamon Sauce

An absolute humdinger of an ice-cream: the first taste reveals a rich chocolatey flavour with just a slight hint of a mysterious tingle. The tingle turns into a mild heat as you eat more, revealing its source and making a brilliant contrast with the cold. The orange sauce is optional but turns it into an even more spicy affair.

SERVES 6
300 ml (10 fl oz) single cream
1 dried red chilli, halved
1 cinnamon stick, halved
4 egg yolks
110 g (4 oz) light muscovado sugar
120 g (4^1/$_2$ fl oz) plain chocolate,
  coarsely grated or finely chopped

250 ml (8 fl oz) double or whipping
  cream

FOR THE SAUCE
2 oranges
1 cinnamon stick
2 cloves
200 g (7 oz) caster sugar

Put the single cream into a pan, with the chilli and cinnamon stick halves. Bring gently to the boil and then draw off the heat, cover and leave to stand for 20 minutes.

Meanwhile, using a hand-held electric beater, whisk the egg yolks with the sugar until pale (relatively speaking: the colour of the sugar means it will never go white) and fluffy. Bring the cream back to the boil, draw off the heat and stir in the chocolate. As soon as it has melted, pour (and scrape – it makes the mixture quite thick) on to the egg yolks, whisking constantly. Place the bowl over a pan of gently simmering water, making sure that the base does not come into contact with the water. Stir for 5 minutes. Lift the bowl off the pan and stand it in a basin of cold water. Leave to cool until tepid and then pick out the bits of chilli and cinnamon.

Whip the double or whipping cream lightly and fold it into the chocolate custard. Freeze in an ice-cream maker. If you don't have an ice-cream maker, pour the mixture into a shallow freezer container, cover and freeze as for Tropical Sorbet on p. 315. After whizzing in the processor or beating by hand, return the ice-cream to the freezer.

Transfer from the freezer to the fridge about an hour before serving.

To make the sauce, pare the zest from the oranges in wide strips and then shred the strips (or use a zester, if you prefer). Blanch the shreds in boiling water for a minute, drain and then repeat. Squeeze the juice of the oranges. Put the juice and the blanched zest into a pan, with the cinnamon stick, cloves, sugar and 200 ml (7 fl oz) of water. Stir over a moderate heat until the sugar has dissolved and then bring to the boil and simmer for about 25 minutes, stirring occasionally. Skim off what scum you can and then leave to cool.

To serve, put two or three small scoops of ice-cream on each plate and spoon a little of the orange sauce, with its zest, around them.

Hot Puddings

Grilled Figs with Orange, Honey and Pecan Sauce

This is a pretty, light pudding for early autumn, when purple or green figs are at their plumpest and most succulent. Blanch the zest and prepare the sauce in advance; then there is precious little to do when it comes to finishing the pudding for serving.

SERVES 4

1 orange

2 tablespoons honey

60 g (2 oz) butter

1 tablespoon icing sugar

5 cm (2 in) fresh rosemary sprig

8 figs, halved

60 g (2 oz) shelled pecans

Single cream, to serve

Pare the zest from the orange and cut it into fine shreds (or use a zester). Blanch the shreds in boiling water for a minute, drain and repeat. Reserve. Squeeze the juice from the orange and place it in a pan with the honey, butter, icing sugar and rosemary. Stir over a low heat for 5 minutes, until smoothly mixed. Set aside until needed.

Shortly before you wish to serve, pre-heat the grill thoroughly. Brush the cut sides of the figs with a little of the sauce and grill until sizzling and lightly browned. Meanwhile, remove the rosemary sprig from the sauce, add the pecans and re-heat. Arrange the figs on individual plates, spoon some of the sauce around them and garnish with the blanched orange zest. Serve immediately, with single cream.

Rhubarb and Honey Compote

If you don't have a microwave, this is probably the simplest way to cook rhubarb without ending up with a collapsing mush. Baked in the oven, sweetened with honey and sugar (or all sugar if you prefer), scented mildly with orange, it just needs an occasional glance to make sure it is not overcooking. Cooking time depends largely on the girth of the stems.

SERVES 6–8

900 g (2 lb) rhubarb, trimmed and cut
    into 2.5 cm (1 in) lengths

5 tablespoons honey

85 g (3 oz) caster sugar

4 strips of orange zest

Juice of 1 orange

Cream or Greek yoghurt, to serve

Pre-heat the oven to 170°C/325°F/Gas Mark 3. Place the rhubarb in a shallow, oven-proof dish. Drizzle over the honey and then sprinkle with sugar. Add the orange zest and juice. Cover with foil. Bake for 25–30 minutes, stirring every now and then, until the rhubarb is tender but not disintegrating. Serve hot, warm or cold, with cream or yoghurt.

Pear and Blackberry Compote with Star Anise

A twist on that old favourite, stewed apple and blackberry. Here it is pears that make the grade, and the compote is flavoured with star anise. One whole star gives a fairly subtle aniseed flavour; use two if you are rather partial to it and would like a bolder presence. Serve the compote hot or cold, with clotted cream, vanilla ice-cream, crème fraîche or Greek yoghurt.

SERVES 6–8

5 pears, peeled, cored and sliced
1–2 star anise

450 g (1 lb) blackberries
250 g (9 oz) caster sugar
1 cinnamon stick

Put all the ingredients in a pan and add about 150 ml (5 fl oz) of water. Cover and cook over a low heat for about 5 minutes, until the blackberry juice begins to flow, stirring once or twice to dissolve the sugar. Simmer until the pear slices are very tender (this may be no more than a few minutes if they were fairly ripe, longer if they were on the hard side). Serve hot or cold.

Baked Quinces

This is the easiest way to cook quinces and probably the best. They look pretty and they taste elegantly and purely of quince and a hint of caramel. Serve with single or double cream.

SERVES 4
4 small quinces
30 g (1 oz) butter
4 tablespoons caster sugar

TO SERVE
Cream

Pre-heat the oven to 200°C/400°F/Gas Mark 6. Cut each quince in half horizontally (not from stalk to stem). Trim a thin slice from the stem end and from the top, so that you can sit the two halves flat, without too much wobbling around. Use about two-thirds of the butter to grease an ovenproof dish generously and arrange the halved quinces in it, trimmed-side down, central cut upwards. Dredge with caster sugar and dot with the remaining butter. Spoon about 3 tablespoons of water around the quinces.

Bake for about 45–60 minutes, until tender. Check occasionally and baste with their own juices once or twice. If the dish threatens to burn dry, add a little more water. Serve the quinces with their syrup and some cream.

Roast Pears with Ginger

Roasting halved pears with butter and ginger concentrates their flavour and cooks them to a tender buttery state. The ginger steers them away from any hint of bland-ness. This is a pretty pudding, which tastes superb.

SERVES 4
4 pears
Juice of 1 lemon
60 g (2 oz) butter
3–4 pieces of preserved stem ginger
   in syrup, drained and chopped

3 tablespoons vanilla sugar or caster
   sugar

TO SERVE
Single cream

Pre-heat the oven to 220°C/425°F/Gas Mark 7. Peel the pears and cut them in half. Turn in the lemon juice, to prevent from browning. Carefully scoop out the core, without breaking each pear half. Slice the pears lengthways, cutting up towards the stem but not quite cutting right through, so that the halves hold together. Lay them in a buttered ovenproof dish, flattening them slightly to fan out the slices. Scatter over the ginger and then the sugar and dot with the remaining butter. Spoon 4 tablespoons of water around the pears (or a little more if the dish is on the large side). Roast for about 30 minutes, basting occasionally, until the pears are very tender and translucent, with the odd hint of brown. Serve piping hot, with single cream.

Flambéd Buttered Plums

This is a lovely pudding, quick to make, mildly boozy and with a hint of drama. Serve with vanilla ice-cream, or just plain single cream.

SERVES 4
450 g (1 lb) dark plums (Victorias work
   well)

50 g (2 oz) butter
75 g (3 oz) sugar
40 ml (1 1/2 fl oz) brandy

Split the plums in half and discard the stones. Melt the butter in a wide frying-pan and add the plum halves in a single layer, cut side up. Sprinkle over the sugar. Cover with a large plate or foil and cook over a low heat for 5 minutes. Turn the plums over, shake the pan gently to help the sugar dissolve, then cover again and cook for a further 5 minutes, still over a low heat. Warm the brandy gently in a small pan without letting it boil.

To serve, either divide the plums and their syrup between 4 shallow plates, or place them in a warmed shallow serving dish. Set light to the warm brandy and pour, flaming gaily, over the plums. Take carefully to the table before the flames die down.

Mango and Cardamom Gratin

This gratin was inspired by a dish from the south-west of France. Replacing the original peaches with mango and cardamom turns it into a most exotic pudding, best eaten warm from the oven.

SERVES 4–6
2 medium-sized mangoes
4 green cardamom pods

75 g (2¹/₂ oz) caster sugar
250 ml (8 fl oz) crème fraîche
1 egg, lightly beaten

Pre-heat the oven to 180°C/350°F/Gas Mark 4. Using a sharp knife, slice the unpeeled mangoes, cutting down towards the stones and easing the slices off, gradually working your way along and around the stones. Trim the skin off the slices and put them into a bowl. Slit open the cardamom pods and extract the black seeds. Crush to a powder with a little of the sugar. Sprinkle over the mango slices, together with about two-thirds of the remaining sugar. Leave to marinate for a few minutes, or up to an hour.

Lay the slices snugly in an oval gratin dish. Beat the cream with the egg and pour over. Let it settle and sprinkle with the rest of the sugar. Bake for 30–40 minutes, until lightly browned.

Baked Vanilla Custard with Apricots

Baked vanilla custard is marvellous in its own right, but can also form the basis of many other puddings. It is what makes the best crème caramel, the best crème brûlée, but, in this recipe, it covers the tartness of a layer of poached apricots, fresh or dried. Other fruit can be substituted in season – gooseberries, currants or rhubarb, perhaps.

The richness of the custard is something that can be varied at will. For a rather plain custard, use milk instead of cream. Single cream is a nice halfway house en route to sheer gluttony; whipping cream takes you a step further along the road and double cream makes baked custards of the most devastatingly indulgent texture in the world. I recommend it.

SERVES 6
6 fresh or 12 dried apricots
140 g (5 oz) caster sugar or vanilla sugar
2 strips of lemon zest

FOR THE CUSTARD
425 ml (15 fl oz) single, whipping or double cream
1 vanilla pod, slit open
4 egg yolks

Skin, quarter and stone fresh apricots. Chop dried ones roughly. Put the caster or vanilla sugar in a pan with 300ml (10 fl oz) of water and stir over a moderate heat until dissolved. Add the apricots and the lemon zest, and poach gently until the fruit is tender. Scoop out the fruit and divide it between six medium-sized ramekins. Boil the liquid down until it's syrupy. Reserve about half of it and spoon the rest over the apricots, discarding the lemon zest.

For the custard, put the cream into a pan, with the vanilla pod, and bring very slowly to the boil, stirring frequently. Draw off the heat, cover and leave to infuse for 20–30 minutes.

Pre-heat the oven to 150°C/300°F/Gas Mark 2. Beat the egg yolks with the reserved syrup and gradually beat in the warm cream. Strain over the apricots. Stand the ramekins in a roasting tin and pour in enough hot water to come about halfway up their sides. Bake for about 40–50 minutes, until just set. Serve warm or chilled.

Buttermilk Pancakes with Maple Syrup

To be frank, there is no better way to enjoy maple syrup than poured straight over hot pancakes, like these American buttermilk ones. They are good plain and possibly even nicer with blueberries. For breakfast, serve sausages as well (that's right – as well as the syrup, though you might be wise to dispense with the blueberries).

SERVES 4-6
220 g (8 oz) plain flour
1 teaspoon baking powder
1 teaspoon bicarbonate of soda
1/4 teaspoon salt
1 tablespoon caster sugar
450 ml (16 fl oz) buttermilk
2 eggs

2 tablespoons melted butter
100 ml (3 1/2 fl oz) milk
200 g (8 oz) blueberries (optional)
Oil or clarified butter, for greasing

TO SERVE
Butter and lots of maple syrup

Sift the flour with the baking powder, bicarbonate of soda and salt. Mix in the sugar. Mix the buttermilk with the eggs and butter. Add the dry ingredients and stir until more or less smooth (don't worry about the odd small lump). Stir in the milk and then the blueberries, if using.

Heat a heavy cast-iron frying-pan or griddle over a medium heat. Brush with a little oil or clarified butter. Ladle about 2 tablespoons of the batter per pancake on to the griddle. Turn when the bubbles are all rising to the surface and bursting and the underneath is nicely browned. Cook briefly on the other side until hazelnut brown. If the pancakes seem a bit flabby and the bubbles are having trouble rising, thin the mixture down with a little water or extra milk. Serve the pancakes piping hot, smeared with butter and smothered in maple syrup.

Blueberry and Cornmeal Grunt

Also known as 'blueberry slump', this is a speciality of Nova Scotia, though it is made in many parts of Canada and America, particularly in blueberry country. It can be cooked on top of the stove or in the oven (my favourite) and I give both methods. Cornmeal is a fancy innovation – the dumplings are usually made of plain flour but cornmeal makes them look and taste even nicer.

SERVES 4–6

FOR THE BLUEBERRY SAUCE
450 g (1 lb) blueberries
1 cinnamon stick
1/4 teaspoon freshly grated nutmeg
150 g (5 oz) caster sugar
2 tablespoons lemon juice
100 ml (3 1/2 fl oz) water

FOR THE DUMPLINGS
75 g (2 1/2 oz) fine cornmeal
85 g (3 oz) plain flour

1 teaspoon baking powder
A pinch of salt
1 tablespoon caster sugar
Finely grated zest of 1/2 lemon
30 g (1/2 oz) butter
Milk

TO SERVE
Cream

To make this on the hob put all the sauce ingredients into a wide pan and bring gently to the boil, stirring until the sugar has dissolved. Simmer gently for about 4 minutes.

To make the dumplings, sift the cornmeal with the flour, baking powder and salt. Stir in the sugar and the lemon zest. Rub in the butter and then add enough milk to make a soft dough that will just drop off the spoon. Drop spoonfuls of the dough into the blueberry sauce, cover tightly and simmer for a further 10–15 minutes, without raising the lid. The dumplings should have puffed up nicely and be cooked through. Serve immediately, with cream – double or whipped or crème fraîche, as the fancy takes you.

To make this in the oven, pre-heat the oven to 190°C/375°F/Gas Mark 5. Spread the berries out in a wide ovenproof dish and tuck the cinnamon stick in amongst them. Sprinkle over the nutmeg and sugar and then pour on the lemon juice and water. Bake, uncovered, for 5–10 minutes, until the juices begin to run.

Make the dough for the dumplings as above. Take the dish out of the oven and raise the oven heat to 220°C/425°F/Gas Mark 7. Drop spoonfuls of the dough into the berries and then return to the oven for 20 minutes, until the dumplings are puffed and patched with brown. Serve immediately, with cream as above.

Prune and Chocolate Tart

This is a tart to dazzle and delight, a grand finale to a dinner party and proof positive, if it is needed, that prunes are no joking matter. On a base of crisp pâte sablée *pastry runs a layer of dark prune purée, covered discreetly with a baked mousse of dark chocolate. Serve it warm or chilled, with whipped cream, crème fraîche or mascarpone.*

SERVES 10–12

FOR THE PASTRY
210 g (7¹/₂oz) plain flour
A pinch of salt
75 g (3 oz) icing sugar
150 g (6 oz) unsalted butter
2 small egg yolks

FOR THE PRUNE PURÉE
280 g (10 oz) stoned, ready-to-eat
   prunes
2 tablespoons brandy

FOR THE CHOCOLATE FILLING
100 g (3¹/₂oz) plain chocolate, broken
   into squares
3 eggs, separated
300 ml (10 fl oz) double cream, lightly
   whipped
90 g (3 oz) caster sugar

TO DECORATE
Icing sugar

To make the pastry, sift the flour with the salt and the icing sugar. Process the dry ingredients, with the butter and egg yolks, to form a soft dough. Scrape the dough out on to a floured work surface and knead it very briefly, to smooth out. Then roll it into a ball, wrap in cling film and chill in the fridge for at least an hour.

Put a baking sheet in the oven and pre-heat it to 180°C/350°F/Gas Mark 4. Roll out the dough on a well-floured surface and use to line a 25–28 cm (10–11 in) tart tin. Don't worry if the pastry tears; just patch up holes or splits with the trimmings and no one will be any the wiser. Prick the pastry base and leave it to rest again in the fridge for half an hour.

Line the pastry case with greaseproof paper or foil, weigh it down with baking beans and bake blind, on the hot baking sheet, for 20 minutes. Remove the paper or foil and beans and return to the oven for about 10 minutes to dry out, without browning.

Meanwhile, make the prune purée by putting the prunes into a pan with barely enough water to cover. Bring to the boil and simmer for 5–10 minutes, until the prunes are very tender. Lift out with a slotted spoon and process the prunes with the brandy and just enough of their cooking liquid to make a thick purée (some 2–3 tablespoons). Spread over the base of the pastry case.

To make the chocolate layer, chop the chocolate roughly and put it in a bowl, set over a pan of gently simmering water, making sure that the base of the bowl does not come into contact with the water. Lift the bowl off the pan as soon as the chocolate has melted. Cool slightly and then beat the egg yolks in, one by one. Fold in the cream. Whisk the egg whites until they form soft peaks. Sprinkle over the sugar and then whisk until pale and glossy. Fold into the chocolate mixture. Pour into the pastry case and smooth down lightly. Bake at the same temperature for about 40 minutes, until puffed, and set around the edges but still very slightly wobbly in the centre. Take out of the oven and serve warm or cold, lightly dusted with icing sugar.

Cranberry Butter Tart

This is an old favourite of mine, which I come back to time and again. The butter in the filling gives the tart a rich translucence, balanced by the tartness of the cranberries.

SERVES 6–8

FOR THE PASTRY
220 g (8 oz) plain flour
A pinch of salt
110 g (4 oz) butter
1 tablespoon caster sugar
Finely grated zest of 1 orange
1 egg

FOR THE FILLING
220 g (8 oz) cranberries
220 g (8 oz) caster sugar
110 g (4 oz) unsalted butter, cut into
    small pieces
2 eggs, beaten
30 g (1 oz) flaked almonds

To make the pastry, stir the flour with the salt and then rub in the butter. Stir in the sugar and orange zest. Make a well in the centre and break in the egg. Mix, adding just enough cold water to form a dough. Knead briefly to smooth out and then wrap in cling film and chill for 30 minutes.

Line a 25 cm (10 in) tart tin with the pastry, prick the base with a fork and leave to rest again in the fridge for half an hour.

Pre-heat the oven to 200°C/400°F/Gas Mark 6. Line the pastry case with grease-proof paper or foil, weigh it down with baking beans and bake blind for 10 minutes. Remove the beans and paper or foil and return to the oven for about 5 minutes, to dry out without browning.

To make the filling, put the cranberries into a pan, with a quarter of the sugar and 2 tablespoons of water. Stir over a low heat until juices begin to run and the sugar has dissolved. Bring to the boil and boil rapidly until the cranberries have all burst. Off the heat, beat in the remaining sugar and the butter. Leave to cool until tepid.

Beat the eggs into the cranberry mixture. Pour the filling into the pastry case, scatter with the almonds and return to the oven for about 30 minutes, until just set. Serve warm.

Rhubarb Meringue Tart

Forced rhubarb is delicate and delicious and a pleasure to cook with. It arrives in January or early February, like a beacon amongst the duller fruit of that time. Though rhubarb is not technically a fruit at all, it has all the attributes of fruit and is welcome as the first home-grown dessert-maker of the year. Like snowdrops, it promises that winter will not last forever. This is one of the best of all rhubarb puddings, with a thick almondy base that soaks up some of the rhubarb juice without becoming unpleasantly soggy, and a finishing swirl of meringue. Looks good, tastes even better.

SERVES 6

FOR THE PASTRY
110 g (4 oz) ground almonds
110 g (4 oz) plain flour, sifted
Pinch of salt
175 g (6 oz) unsalted butter
85 g (3 oz) light muscovado sugar
2 egg yolks, beaten

FOR THE FILLING
450 g (1 lb) forced rhubarb, trimmed
and cut into 2.5 cm (1 in) lengths
60 g (2 oz) raisins
1 1/2 tablespoons cornflour
170 g (6 oz) caster sugar
2 egg whites

To make the pastry, mix the ground almonds, flour and salt and rub in the butter. Stir in the sugar and then add the egg yolks and, if necessary, just enough cold water to make a soft dough. Using your hands, press it into a 20 cm (8 in), loose-bottomed tart tin, to form a fairly thick crust, rising up the sides. Leave to rest for half an hour in the fridge. Pre-heat the oven to 200°C/400°F/Gas Mark 6.

Prick the pastry case with a fork and line it with cooking foil or greaseproof paper, weigh down with baking beans and bake blind for 10 minutes. Remove the beans and foil or paper and return to the oven to dry out, without browning, for about 5 minutes. Leave to cool until tepid.

To make the filling, toss the rhubarb with the raisins, cornflour and 60 g (2 oz) of sugar and then spread the mixture over the tart base and bake for 10 minutes. Meanwhile, whisk the egg whites until they form stiff peaks. Add half the remaining sugar and whisk again, until glossy and smooth. Fold in the last of the sugar and whisk as before. Pile up on top of the rhubarb, making nice swirls with a fork. Return to the oven for 10 minutes, until the meringue is beginning to catch and brown on the crests. Serve warm or cold.

Rhubarb and Pineapple Crisp

I was intrigued to hear a Yorkshire rhubarb grower (forced rhubarb, of course) being interviewed on the radio. It was a fascinating piece, but what I remember above all is his passion for rhubarb and pineapple together. He was absolutely right – the two get on famously. Here they make up a sensational double-act in a fruit crisp – an American sort of crumble. The aniseed flavour of star anise is subtle but suits them well. Later on, when forced rhubarb is long gone and garden rhubarb is plentiful, try it again, replacing the star anise with a sprig or two of sweet cicely if you have it.

SERVES 6
450 g (1 lb) forced rhubarb
1 pineapple, peeled, cored and cubed
Finely grated zest of 1 orange
150 g (5 1/2 oz) caster sugar
2 tablespoons flour
1/2 star anise

FOR THE TOPPING
140 g (5 oz) plain flour
110 g (4 oz) butter, diced
170 g (6 oz) light muscovado sugar
40 g (1 1/2 oz) rolled oats

Trim the rhubarb and cut into 3cm (1 in) lengths. Mix with the pineapple, orange zest, caster sugar and flour. Break the star anise into individual 'petals' and mix that in too. Pile into a shallow baking dish, to give a layer of no more than 3cm (a generous inch) in depth.

For the topping, sift the flour and rub in the butter roughly. Stir in the sugar and oats, then mix with your fingers, rubbing the mixture together to form coarse crumbs. Scatter over the fruit in a thin but even layer, then press down gently. Bake at 190°C/375°F/Gas Mark 5 for about 30–35 minutes until golden brown and crisp on top. Serve hot or warm with cream.

Rich Mascarpone Custard Tart

Mascarpone is a phenomenally rich cream cheese, more like impossibly over-the-top cream than any recognizable cheese. Cheese though it may be, mascarpone is actually used more like cream. It is just soft enough to dollop on top of puddings, like the very best clotted cream. Its taste is sweetish but basically neutral, making it a ready vehicle for other ingredients and an easy way to impart a generous slurp of luxury to all kinds of sweet and savoury dishes. It has become something of an essential in the fashionable world of cooking. No smart menu is complete without at least one item seduced by the velvet touch of mascarpone. Most big supermarkets now sell it – they had to lay in stocks once we discovered tiramisú, that lovely, boozy pudding that has become the Italian restaurant equivalent of Black Forest gateau. On a hot summer's day I discovered that mascarpone can curdle when beaten with other ingredients. Now I make sure that the mascarpone stays cool in the fridge until the moment it is needed.

SERVES 6–8

FOR THE PASTRY
125 g (4 oz) unsalted butter, softened
50 g (2 oz) caster sugar
1 large egg
250 g (8 oz) plain flour
A pinch of salt

FOR THE FILLING
300 ml (10 fl oz) single cream
1 vanilla pod, slit open

5 egg yolks
100 g (3½ oz) caster sugar
100 g (3½ oz) mascarpone
Finely grated zest of 1 lime
1 tablespoon lime juice

TO SERVE
Ground cinnamon or icing sugar

To make the pastry, cream the butter with the sugar in a food processor, until light and fluffy. Add the egg and process until smoothly mixed. Sift the flour with a pinch of salt and add to the processor. Mix until smooth and then gather up into a ball. Wrap in cling film and let the pastry rest in the fridge for half an hour.

Pre-heat the oven to 180°C/350°F/Gas Mark 4. Line a deep 20 cm (8 in) tart tin with the pastry and then leave to relax again in the fridge for half an hour.

Prick the pastry with a fork, line it with greaseproof paper or cooking foil, weigh it down with baking beans and bake blind for 20 minutes.

Remove the beans and paper or foil and return the pastry case to the oven for another 5–10 minutes to dry out, without letting it brown. Reduce the oven temperature to 170°C/325°F/Gas Mark 3.

To make the filling, put the cream into a pan, with the vanilla pod, and bring it gently to the boil. Turn the heat down as low as possible, cover and leave to infuse for 15 minutes.

Beat the egg yolks with the caster sugar until pale and mousse-like. Gradually pour in the hot cream, stirring constantly. Strain a little of the mixture on to the mascarpone and beat it in, to slacken it. Now strain the remainder into the mascarpone, add the lime zest and juice and mix thoroughly but don't overwork. Pour the custard into the pastry case and bake for about 40–50 minutes, until the custard is virtually set but still has a hint of a wobble in the centre. This is best eaten warm but is good cold, too. Either way, dust it lightly with a little cinnamon or icing sugar before serving.

Tarte aux Pignons

There are many versions of the Provençal pine nut tart, some made with shortcrust pastry, some filled with custard. This particular one has to be among the best. It is quite my favourite pine nut dessert, with a soft, gooey, scented filling, studded with browned pine nuts. It comes from an American book by Antoine Bouterin, a Provençal chef, called Cooking Provence.

SERVES 6
250 g (9 oz) puff pastry

FOR THE FILLING
130 g (4¹/₂ oz) ground almonds
Finely grated zest of 1 orange
220 g (8 oz) caster sugar

1 tablespoon orange-flower water
2 tablespoons honey
2 large eggs, beaten
2 tablespoons extra virgin olive oil
115 g (4 oz) pine nuts

Pre-heat the oven to 200°C/400°F/Gas Mark 6. Roll the pastry out very thinly and use it to line a 20–23 cm (8–9 in) tart tin, doubling the pastry over the rim, to make a double-thickness rim, and crimping it securely. Prick the base with a fork and leave it to rest for half an hour in the fridge. Cover the pastry base with a square of buttered cooking foil (butter-side down!), fill the case with baking beans and bake blind for about 10 minutes. Remove the beans and foil and return the pastry case to the oven, for about another 10 minutes to dry out, without colouring. Leave to cool.

For the filling, put the ground almonds in a bowl and add the orange zest and sugar. Mix, make a well in the centre and then add the orange-flower water, honey, eggs and oil. Mix thoroughly, to give a thick, smooth batter. Tip in two-thirds of the pine nuts, pour the mixture into the pastry case and sprinkle evenly with the remaining pine nuts. Bake until browned and almost, but not quite, firm in the centre: about 20–25 minutes.

Apple and Armagnac Filo Tart

Making a genuine croustade *is no easy feat – it takes considerable skill to stretch the dough out so very thin that you can read your watch through it. I have resorted to bought filo pastry for my* croustade. *It's not quite the same, but the results are still impressive. The sheets of filo that I used were fairly large, about 35 × 40 cm (14 × 16 in). If yours are smaller, use two where I have folded mine in half. Choose apples that really are golden and ripe.*

SERVES 8
225 g (8 oz) granulated or caster sugar
150 ml (5 fl oz) Armagnac or brandy
1 teaspoon natural vanilla essence

900 g (2 lb) ripe Golden Delicious apples
100 g (4 oz) unsalted butter, melted
15 sheets filo pastry

The day before you intend to eat the *croustade* make the Armagnac syrup. Put the sugar into a pan with 150 ml (5 fl oz) water, stir over a medium heat until the sugar has dissolved, then bring to the boil. Draw off the heat and stir in the Armagnac and vanilla essence. Leave to cool.

Peel and core the apples, then slice very thinly. Set aside 4 tablespoons of the syrup and pour the rest over the apples, turning the slices gently. Cover with a cloth and leave at room temperature overnight.

Next day, brush a round tart tin 25 cm (10 in) in diameter with butter. To prevent the filo pastry drying out as you work, pile up the sheets, cover with a sheet of greaseproof paper and lay a tea-towel wrung out in cold water over the paper. Put a metal baking sheet in the oven and pre-heat it to 200°C/400°F/Gas Mark 6.

Take the first sheet of filo, brush lightly with butter, fold in half and lay in the tin, one corner inwards, so that it covers about one-third of the base with the ends trailing over the side. Do the same with a second sheet, laying it at right angles to the first. Repeat with a further 6 sheets of filo (making 8 in all so far), gently pressing them down so that they line the tin. Take a 9th sheet, brush with butter and lay it over the entire base, without folding.

Now fill the tart with slices of apple, making sure that they lie flat. Spoon over 2–3 tablespoons of their soaking syrup. Flip the trailing ends of filo over to cover the filling, smoothing them down nicely, but still leaving an inch or so hanging over the edge. Brush another sheet of filo with butter, fold in half and lay it over the top. Trim off the edges close to the tin with a sharp knife or a pair of scissors.

Time for a bit of artistry. Taking a sheet of filo at a time (no need for butter here), scrunch it up gently in your hands, then lay it on top of the *croustade* so that it balloons up in crumpled waves, covering about one-fifth of the surface. Repeat with another 4 sheets, to finish with a casual-looking arrangement of elegantly scrumpled filo covering the entire *croustade*. Dip the brush in melted butter and flick it over the pastry. Don't try to brush on the butter or you'll flatten those chic waves.

Set the *croustade* on the hot baking sheet (this gives an instant blast of heat to the underside, so that it cooks more crisply) and bake for 15 minutes, then reduce the heat to 180°C/350°F/Gas Mark 4, and bake for a further 30 minutes (cover loosely with foil if it threatens to burn). As soon as it comes out of the oven, brush with the reserved Armagnac syrup. Work lightly so as not to crack the filo, but be generous and use it all up. Serve warm (it can be re-heated briefly in the oven).

Caramel Nut Tart

The Engadiner valley is a fair drive from Chur – a small town in Switzerland that I visited for the television series Travels à la Carte. *But it's not too far to go for its famous* nusstorte, *with its rich, caramelized nut filling, enclosed in a double layer of biscuity pastry. Pastry shops, and indeed stall-holders in the market, have plenty to sell to the passer-by, and it's definitely not to be missed. However, if you're not heading in that direction, here's the recipe.*

SERVES 6–8

FOR THE PASTRY
300 g (11 oz) plain flour
Pinch of salt
200 g (7 oz) butter, chilled and diced
100 g (4 oz) sugar
1 egg plus 1 egg yolk

FOR THE FILLING
300 g (11 oz) sugar
300 ml (10 fl oz) double cream
225 g (8 oz) walnuts, chopped
100 g (4 oz) hazelnuts, chopped
100 g (4 oz) almonds, chopped
1 egg yolk mixed with 1 tablespoon
   milk, to glaze

To make the pastry, sift the flour with the salt and rub in the butter. Stir in the sugar. Beat the egg and yolk together and add to the flour. Mix to form a soft dough. Rest the pastry in the refrigerator for 30 minutes. Roll out just over half of it, and line a 23–25 cm (9–10 in) straight-sided tart tin.

To make the filling, put the sugar into a pan with 4 tablespoons water. Stir over a moderate heat, without letting it boil, until the sugar has completely dissolved. Brush down any crystals stuck to the side of the pan with a brush dipped in cold water. Stop stirring. Bring to the boil and boil hard for 5–10 minutes, until it caramelizes to a rich brown.

Draw off the heat and pour in the cream at arm's length (it will spit at you). Swirl it around to dissolve the caramel, then return to the heat. Stir in the nuts and bring back to the boil. Cool for a few minutes until warm rather than hot, then spread in the pastry case.

Roll out the remaining pastry to form a lid. Brush the edges of the case with a little of the egg glaze, then cover with the lid, pressing it gently into place inside the tin. Rest it for 30 minutes in the refrigerator.

Brush the pastry with egg glaze. Place in a cold oven and set to 220°C/ 425°F/Gas Mark 7. After 15 minutes reduce the heat to 180°C/350°F/Gas Mark 4, and bake for a further 20 minutes, until lightly browned.

Linzertorte

Like the Engadiner nusstorte, *or Caramel Nut Tart (see p. 334), linzertorte has travelled to Switzerland (from across the Austrian border) and made a second home for itself there. I bought a particularly good individual linzertorte from a farmer's wife at the Saturday market, fully intending to take only a small nibble for purely professional purposes, but of course I ended up eating the whole thing.*

In essence it is a glorified form of almond shortbread, rolled out thickly to line a tart tin. A thin layer of raspberry jam covers it, topped with a lattice of pastry. The quality of the jam will regulate the quality of the final tart. Home-made is best, but otherwise a really good bought one, made with a high proportion of fruit to sugar, is essential.

Since the dough is very rich, it can be a little tricky to handle. Don't worry. Press the dough into the tin, and use your fingers to smooth over any tears or holes. Lay the dough strips over the jam using a palette knife. If the odd one breaks as you lay it down, just pinch the ends together: as the whole tart is dusted with icing sugar before serving, it won't show too much.

SERVES 6–8
150 g (5 oz) flour
1/2 teaspoon ground cinnamon
Pinch of salt
150 g (5 oz) caster sugar
150 g (5 oz) ground almonds

Finely grated zest of 1 lemon
150 g (5 oz) butter, softened
2 egg yolks
200 g (7 oz) best-quality raspberry jam

TO DECORATE
Icing sugar

Sift the flour with the cinnamon and salt. Mix with the sugar, ground almonds and lemon zest. Make a well in the centre and place the butter and egg yolks in it. Using a palette knife at first, and then the tips of your fingers, work to a dough. Knead briefly to smooth out. Break off about a quarter of the pastry and wrap in cling film. Wrap the larger part in cling film, then chill both for 30 minutes.

Roll out the larger ball of pastry (leave the rest in the refrigerator for the moment) to a thickness of 5 mm (1/4 in) and line a 24 cm (9 1/2 in) buttered and floured tart tin with it. Prick with a fork and spread evenly with the jam. Roll out the remaining pastry and trimmings and cut into long strips 1 cm (1/2 in) wide. Use these to make a lattice pattern over the jam, pressing the ends on to the edge of the pastry case. Rest for 30 minutes in the refrigerator.

Place a baking tray in the oven, and pre-heat to 200°C/400°F/Gas Mark 6. Set the tart on the hot baking tray and cook for 25–30 minutes, until nicely browned. Cool and dust lightly with icing sugar before serving.

Apple and Prune Pie

I first ate this croustade in the Gascony region of France. Only a little further north and the croustade changes character to become a puff-pastry pie, in this case filled with prunes and apples.

SERVES 6–8
785 g (1 lb 12 oz) puff pastry
3 ripe Golden Delicious apples, peeled, cored and thinly sliced
225 g (8 oz) prunes, soaked and then pitted
100 g (4 oz) vanilla sugar, or 100 g (4 oz) caster sugar and 1 teaspoon natural vanilla essence

3 tablespoons *eau-de-vie de prunes* or Armagnac or brandy

FOR THE GLAZE
1 egg yolk, lightly beaten
extra caster sugar

Put a baking sheet in the oven and pre-heat to 220°C/425°F/Gas Mark 7.

Roll out about two-thirds of the pastry and use to line a 25 cm (10 in) loose-bottomed cake tin 5–7.5 cm (2–3 in) deep. Press it down gently into the corners and leave the excess hanging over the sides. Put the apple slices in the pie, then the stoned prunes, then sprinkle over the sugar, vanilla essence (if using) and the *eau-de-vie*. Brush the edges of the pastry with a little of the egg-yolk glaze.

Roll out the remaining pastry and place over the pie. Trim the edges nicely and press firmly together. Make a hole in the centre. Use the trimmings, if you wish, to cut out shapes to decorate the *croustade*, and glue them on with egg-yolk glaze. Rest the pie in the refrigerator for 30 minutes if you have time.

Brush with egg-yolk glaze, sprinkle with caster sugar and set on the piping-hot baking sheet in the oven. After 15 minutes reduce the heat to 180°C/350°F/Gas Mark 4 and bake for a further 25 minutes. Cover loosely with foil if the top is browning too quickly. Cool for a few minutes in the tin, then unmould carefully. Serve hot or warm.

Mango Tatin

The poor old Tatin sisters are probably turning in their grave, if not whirling. Their original upside-down, caramelized apple tart has been twisted and played with, adapted and misused endlessly by cooks and chefs. The original, made with a short, not puff, pastry remains one of the all-time most glorious puddings, one that is impossible to beat. So, I make no claim that this is better – it is just a delicious way of using mangoes and I freely admit to appropriating the name, the caramel and the upside-downness, all for the sake of the exotic mango.

The trick to this pudding is timing and knowing your pan. I make it in a heavy cast-iron frying-pan that holds the heat very efficiently, so I need to draw the pan off the heat as soon as the juices begin to colour, as they will continue to cook and caramelize in the heat of the pan. If you are using a thinner pan, you may have to cook the mango over the heat for a little longer, until the juices are light brown. In short, I would advise that you make it once for the family, before you attempt to dish it up for a smart dinner party.

SERVES 6
250 g (8 oz) puff pastry
100 g (4 oz) butter, cut into thin slivers
200 g (8 oz) vanilla sugar
Juice of 1/2 lime

3–4 mangoes, depending on size, peeled

TO SERVE
Crème fraîche, mascarpone or Greek yoghurt

Pre-heat the oven to 220°C/425°F/Gas Mark 7. Find a heavy-based frying-pan with an ovenproof handle or a handle that can be removed, or a sturdy flameproof and oven-proof tart tin, around 25 cm (10 in) in diameter or very slightly larger. Roll out the pastry thinly and, using your frying-pan as a template, cut out a circle of the same size. Prick all over with a fork and then chill in the fridge for at least half an hour.

Lay slivers of butter all over the base of your frying-pan, and then strew the sugar more or less evenly over the butter. Drizzle about a tablespoon of lime juice over the sugar.

Slice the cheeks off both sides of two (or three if they are small) of the mangoes and then cut into long curved slices, about 6 mm (1/4 in) thick, keeping the slices from each cheek together. Slide a palette knife or a wide-bladed knife underneath, lift up carefully and then turn over on to your hand and lay, curved side down, in the pan. Press down gently, flattening slightly to fan the pieces out. You should be able to fit four cheeks into the pan quite comfortably if the mangoes are large. If they are small, put five cheeks around the edge of the pan and lay the sixth in the centre. Cut up the remaining mango in the same way and use the slices to fill in gaps around the edges and anywhere else. The slices should be quite densely packed.

Place the pan over a moderate heat, raising it to high as the butter melts and the juice begins to run. Continue to cook, letting the juice bubble and boil around the mango slices until it just begins to colour, turning the pan so that it is heated through evenly. Don't stir or you'll ruin all your artistry with the slices!

Draw off the heat. Cover with the pastry. Bake for 12–15 minutes, until the pastry is puffed and nicely browned. Let the tart sit for a minute or two in its pan and then place a large serving plate on top, and quickly invert on to the plate. If any bits of mango are left sticking to the pan, carefully dislodge them and arrange them back in place on the tart – no one will ever know.

Serve the tart hot or warm, with crème fraîche, mascarpone or Greek yoghurt.

Apple Strudel

Though I'm sure many Swiss cooks would protest that strudel and filo dough are not quite the same thing, I've found that filo pastry makes a very good wrapping for a strudel. Lucky, as it happens, since I've never had much success when I've tried my hand at making strudel pastry, always ending up with more holes than anything else.

As with all pastry dishes, strudel is best when it has only recently emerged from the oven, before it has a chance to get soggy and flabby. The breadcrumbs or semolina absorb some moisture from the filling, retarding the process, but they can't stop it altogether.

SERVES 6–8

6 sheets filo pastry, each about
   47.5 × 30 cm (19 × 12 in)
50 g (2 oz) butter, melted and cooled
   until tepid
2 tablespoons dry breadcrumbs or
   semolina
Icing sugar

FOR THE FILLING

750 g (1 lb 8 oz) eating apples, peeled,
   cored and diced small
Finely grated zest and juice of
   $1/2$ lemon
90 g ($3^1/2$ oz) caster sugar
1 heaped teaspoon ground cinnamon
40 g ($1^1/2$ oz) raisins

TO SERVE
Cream

Mix all the filling ingredients together. Pre-heat the oven to 190°C/375°F/Gas Mark 5.

To prevent the filo pastry drying out, lay it in a heap, cover with a sheet of grease-proof paper and cover that with a tea-towel wrung out in cold water. Lay a large (dry) sheet of greaseproof paper on the work surface. Take 1 sheet of filo pastry and lay it out flat in front of you on the greaseproof paper. Brush with melted butter. Take the next sheet and lay it out flat, overlapping the first along the edge by about 7.5 cm (3 in). Brush with butter. The third sheet is laid exactly over the first, then brushed with butter, the fourth over the second, then brushed with butter, and so on until all the pastry is used up.

Sprinkle the dry breadcrumbs or semolina over the top two-thirds of the filo pastry, leaving a 4 cm (1 1/2 in) border. Dollop the apple mixture over the semolina and smooth down lightly to cover. Flip the 4 cm (1 1/2 in) of bare edge over the filling. Now, starting at the top, roll up the pastry round the apple filling, using the greaseproof paper to help you. Carefully lift on to a greased baking tray and curve round into a horseshoe shape. Brush the top with any remaining butter.

Bake in the oven for 30–40 minutes, until lightly browned and crisp. Poke a skewer into the centre of the strudel to see if the apple is tender. Loosen the strudel with a knife, then slide carefully on to a serving dish, dust with icing sugar and serve hot with cream.

Tarte de Cambrai

The recipe for this moist, buttery, pear pudding-cake was given to my mother many years ago, by the woman who ran the droguerie *in the small French town we visit every year. It quickly became a family favourite and I still love it.*

SERVES 6–8
4–5 large, ripe pears
Juice of ¹/2 lemon
60 g (2 oz) butter
Sugar

FOR THE BATTER
110 g (4 oz) self-raising flour
A pinch of salt

80 g (3 oz) vanilla sugar or caster sugar
4 tablespoons sunflower oil
120 ml (4 fl oz) milk
2 eggs, lightly beaten

TO SERVE
Cream

Pre-heat the oven to 200°C/400°F/Gas Mark 6. Grease a 25 cm (10 in) shallow cake tin.

Peel, core and slice the pears then turn them in the lemon juice. To make the batter, sift the flour and salt. Stir in the sugar. Make a well in the centre and add the oil, milk and eggs. Beat together, gradually drawing in the flour and sugar to make a smooth batter. Pour the batter into the prepared tin. Arrange the pear slices on top, and then dot with butter and sprinkle evenly with sugar (around 2 tablespoons should do it). Bake for 50–60 minutes, until golden brown and puffed. Eat warm to get it at its best, with cream.

Bread Pudding with Apples

Bread pudding with apples, or Brødpudding med Epler, *is a delicious Norwegian dish. I can't truthfully claim, however, that this is something I tucked into while I was in the country. If I'm honest, I must admit that it's a recipe I came across, and took a fancy to, in James and Elizabeth White's* Good Food from Denmark and Norway *(Frederick Muller Ltd), published back in 1959, the year I was born! I love bread pudding, and the addition of tart apple purée made this version irresistible.*

SERVES 4–6
350 g (12 oz) cooking apples
Finely grated zest of ¹/2 lemon
100 g (4 oz) caster sugar
8 thin slices of bread

Softened butter
50 g (2 oz) flaked almonds
300 ml (10 fl oz) milk
150 ml (5 fl oz) double cream
2 eggs

Peel and core the apples and cut roughly into chunks. Put into a pan with 2 tablespoons water and the lemon zest, cover and stew over a low heat until the juices begin to run. Raise the heat and cook until the apples have collapsed to a thick purée. Sweeten to taste.

Butter the slices of bread on both sides. Spread with apple purée, quarter, and layer in a baking dish, scattering almonds between the layers. Beat the milk with the cream, about 50 g (2 oz) sugar and the eggs. Pour over the bread and leave for 1 hour, so that the bread can soak up the milk.

Pre-heat the oven to 160°C/325°F/Gas Mark 3. Stand the dish in a roasting tin and pour boiling water around it to a depth of about 2.5 cm (1 in). Bake in the oven for 30–40 minutes, until just set. Serve hot.

Baking

Shortcrust Pastry

This is a simple pastry which gives short and crisp results. You'll need it for several recipes throughout the book.

MAKES 350 g (12 oz)
225 g (8 oz) plain flour
Pinch of salt

100 g (4 oz) chilled butter, diced
1 egg yolk, beaten
Iced water

To make the pastry, sift the flour with the salt. Rub the butter into the flour until it resembles fine breadcrumbs. Make a well in the centre and add the egg yolk and enough iced water to form a soft dough – 1½–2 tablespoons of water should be enough. Mix quickly and lightly, and knead very briefly to smooth out. Wrap and chill for at least 30 minutes in the fridge. Bring back to room temperature before using and cook in a pre-heated oven as required in the individual recipe.

Yorkshire Pudding

When I shared a flat in student days with a Yorkshireman, he insisted that the Yorkshire pudding (which he made to accompany not just beef, but any type of roast meat) must be served before the meat in the traditional style. This was a most delicious economy measure. The pudding, soggy with juices from the joint under which it had been roasted, served to fill up hungry stomachs before the meat arrived. That way a smaller joint could be stretched around many people and with any luck there would still be enough left for the following day.

These days, I like my Yorkshire pudding rather crisper on the surface (though I dislike those little individual puddings which always seem to be all crust and no moist interior at all) so I put it into the oven as the roast comes out. By the time the meat is fully rested and ready to serve, the Yorkshire pud is puffed and browned and ready to dish up.

Crisp, tender Yorkshire pudding also makes a marvellously homely but indulgent dessert, served with lashings of condensed milk or golden syrup and some cream!

SERVES 8
250 g (9 oz) plain flour
A pinch of salt

3 eggs
300 ml (10 fl oz) milk
2–3 tablespoons dripping or oil

Either pre-heat the oven to 220°C/425°F/Gas Mark 7, or turn it up that high when your joint of beef is nearly cooked, if it is being done at a lower temperature. Sift the flour with the salt into a bowl and make a well in the centre. Add the eggs and a generous splosh of milk. Begin to stir in the flour, gradually adding the rest of the milk, then 300 ml (10 fl oz) water until you get a smooth, creamy batter.

Put a baking sheet into the oven. Pour the dripping or oil into a roasting tin or shallow oven-proof dish and place it on the baking sheet in the hot oven. Leave for 10–15 minutes to heat through thoroughly (at this point take the meat out of the oven to rest, assuming it is cooked). Quickly remove the dish from the oven, give the batter a stir and pour it in. Return the dish of batter to the oven, setting it on the baking sheet and bake for 25–30 minutes until well-risen and browned. Serve as soon as possible.

Cracklin' Cornbread

All types of cornmeal are ground down from dried maize. Polenta is usually the coarsest. What is sold as 'coarse cornmeal' is marginally smaller grained. Fine cornmeal is soft and silky smooth. You can swap them around freely in most recipes though, naturally, the texture of the finished article will be affected.

Maize or sweetcorn is native to the New World, so the Americas can lay a far greater historical claim to cornmeal than the Italians. They use it with – dare I say it? – more imagination than the Mediterraneans. They've had more time to play with it, so that's not so surprising. There isn't room here to go into details of the endless recipes using cornmeal from the Deep South, and further down in Central America, nor, for that matter, the delicious dumplings and porridges from the Caribbean. But I do just have space for one real, down-home American treat.

Cracklin' cornbread should be made with real, down-home, pork cracklin', the browned crisp scraps left after rendering down the fat from the family pig. Failing that, fried bacon has to do instead (don't be tempted to try those tough packet cracklings).

For something rather trendier, replace the bacon with sun-dried tomatoes, or add chopped fresh chilli or coriander.

As the American food writer Craig Claiborne says, there are more recipes for cornbread than there are magnolia trees in the South.

SERVES 6
225 g (8 oz) cornmeal
110 g (4 oz) plain flour, sifted
1 teaspoon baking powder
1 teaspoon salt
1/2 tablespoon caster sugar
300 ml (10 fl oz) buttermilk
120 ml (4 fl oz) milk
2 eggs, beaten

80 g (3 oz) unsalted butter, melted and cooled
6–8 bacon rashers, grilled until crisp and roughly chopped
85 g (3 oz) mature Cheddar cheese, diced small (optional)
1/2 teaspoon coarsely crushed black peppercorns (optional)

Pre-heat the oven to 200°C/400°F/Gas Mark 6. Mix the cornmeal with the sifted flour, baking powder, salt and sugar. Make a well in the centre and add the buttermilk, milk, eggs and melted butter. Mix to a batter and then stir in the bacon, and Cheddar and black peppercorns, if using. Pour into a greased 22 × 22 cm (9 × 9 in) or 25 × 20 cm (10 × 8 in) baking tin or ovenproof dish and bake for 25–30 minutes, until the edges are browned. Test in the centre of the cornbread with a skewer or the blade of a knife. If it comes out clean, the bread is done. Cut into squares and serve warm as an accompaniment to a main course or on its own, slathered with butter.

VARIATIONS

Add 1 or 2 fresh red or green chillies, seeded and finely chopped, as well as, or instead of, the bacon. Cheddar is optional, again. Omit the black peppercorns.

Add 3 tablespoons chopped fresh coriander, together with 1 or 2 fresh red or green chillies, seeded and finely chopped, omitting the bacon and black peppercorns. Cheddar is optional.

Add 5 pieces of sun-dried tomato, finely diced, and 2 tablespoons chopped fresh basil or 1 or 2 fresh red or green chillies, seeded and finely chopped, omitting the bacon and black peppercorns. Omit the Cheddar but sprinkle freshly grated Parmesan liberally over the surface, before baking.

Parmesan and Polenta Biscuits

These biscuits have a crisp, grainy texture, thanks to the inclusion of the polenta. Eat warm from the oven, with pre-prandial drinks.

MAKES ABOUT 20
100 g (4 oz) fine polenta or cornmeal, plus a little extra for rolling out
50 g (2 oz) plain flour
60 g (2 oz) Parmesan cheese, grated
80 g (c 3 oz) chilled butter, diced

1 egg, lightly beaten
1 egg yolk

TO DECORATE
Extra grated Parmesan cheese, or sesame or caraway seeds

Pre-heat the oven to 190°C/375°F/Gas Mark 5. Put the polenta or cornmeal, flour and Parmesan in the processor, then add the butter. Process to breadcrumbs, then add enough beaten egg to form a soft, but rollable dough. Wrap in cling film and chill in the fridge for half an hour.

Roll out thinly to a thickness of about 5 mm (1/4 in), on a board sprinkled with polenta or cornmeal (or flour if you prefer). Stamp out circles of dough (I use a 6 cm (2 1/2 in) cutter) and lay them on a baking tray lined with non-stick baking parchment. Mix the egg yolk with 1 tablespoon of cold water, to make an egg wash. Brush the wash over the biscuits and sprinkle them with the Parmesan or seeds. Bake for 10 minutes, until golden brown.

Lift on to a wire rack to cool. Store in an airtight tin if not using immediately.

Sage and Sunflower Seed Rolls

These rolls are heaven-sent for a fine slice of Cheddar or other good British hard cheese, though they are also irresistible warm from the oven, with nothing more than a smear of butter. Guard them jealously if you are making them for a special occasion, as they disappeared in the twinkling of an eye in my household.

MAKES 6 ROLLS

15g (1/2 oz) fresh yeast

1 teaspoon sugar

450g (1 lb) strong white flour

1 1/2 teaspoons salt

1 tablespoon olive oil

30g (1 oz) sunflower seeds

2 tablespoons chopped fresh sage

Milk

Cream the yeast with 150ml (5 fl oz) of warm water and the sugar and leave in a warm place for 5–10 minutes, until it's frothing merrily. Sift the flour with the salt into a large bowl and make a well in the middle. Pour in the yeast mixture and the oil and start mixing, gradually adding more warm water, until you have a soft dough. Knead thoroughly for a good 5 minutes, until the dough is smooth and elastic. Place in a lightly oiled bowl, turn to coat in oil, then cover with a damp tea-towel and leave in a warm place until it has doubled in bulk – about an hour.

Pre-heat the oven to 200°C/400°F/Gas Mark 6. Punch the dough down and gradually knead in the sunflower seeds and sage. Divide into six pieces and roll each one into a ball. Place the balls on a greased baking tray, flattening them slightly to give neat bun shapes. Leave plenty of space between the balls to allow them to expand. Leave in a warm place for about 30 minutes, until they have doubled in size.

Brush lightly with a little milk and bake for 20 minutes, until lightly browned. If they are done, the buns will lift easily off the tray. One final check – tap the under-neath of one of the buns. If it sounds hollow, it really is done. Transfer to a wire rack to cool.

Sun-dried Tomato Bread

To me, sun-dried tomatoes capture some of the essence of southern Italy. They hold memories of hot sun and have the intense, rich, deep, gutsy flavour that character-izes the local cooking. There's nothing fancy about them, even though they have become so fashionable as to be almost commonplace in British bistro-land. They are plain, simple and honest fare.

Sun-dried tomatoes come in several different forms. You can buy them fully dried, in packets, unadorned and plain – they will need to be rehydrated to some degree, which means that you can imprint your own personal stamp on them. However, it is probably easier to buy them ready to use in jars of oil. The best are always stored in olive oil (though the calibre of the oil can vary considerably) and will often be animated with sprigs of herbs and maybe some garlic. Most brands are pretty good but you do get what you pay for. A higher price tag generally indicates a classier sun-dried tomato.

MAKES A 450G (1LB) LOAF
450 g (1 lb) strong white flour
1 1/2 teaspoons salt
1 sachet easy-blend yeast
1 teaspoon sugar

2 tablespoons olive oil, from the jar of
   tomatoes
1/2 jar sun-dried tomatoes, in olive oil,
   drained and chopped

Mix the flour with the salt, yeast and sugar. Add the olive oil and enough water to form a soft dough. It is better to err marginally on the damp side, as the flour absorbs a good deal of water as you knead. If the worst comes to the worst, dust overly sticky dough with extra flour as you knead.

Knead the bread energetically for a good 5 minutes, until it is satin-smooth and elastic. Return to the bowl and cover with a damp tea-towel. Leave in a warm place until it has doubled in bulk, which will take around an hour depending on the room temperature.

Punch the dough down, knead briefly and then spread it out as best you can. Dot with half the sun-dried tomatoes, roll up, knead again briefly and then repeat. Give it another quick kneading, to distribute the pieces of sun-dried tomato evenly. Place in a greased, 500 g (1 lb) loaf tin. Cover with a damp tea-towel and again leave to rise in a warm place, until the dough has risen to fill the tin. Pre-heat the oven to 220°C/425°F/Gas Mark 7.

Bake the loaf for about 25–30 minutes, until it is cooked through. To test, turn the tin upside-down and shake the bread out – it should slide out fairly easily. Tap the bottom: if it sounds hollow, the bread is done. If the loaf sticks mercilessly to the tin, or all you get is a dull thud when you tap it, return to the oven for another 5 minutes or so, to finish cooking. Leave the loaf to cool on a wire rack.

VARIATION

Instead of using pieces of sun-dried tomato, use sun-dried tomato purée and replace the tomato oil in the dough with olive oil. After the dough has had its first rising, knead it for about 3 minutes, to smooth it out. Using the palms of your hands, flatten out the dough and then smear it thickly with the purée. Roll up like a Swiss roll and then settle it as neatly as you can in its tin. Bake as above.

Pecan Tuiles

The pecan is the American nut par excellence. Indigenous to the Mississippi Valley and south down into Mexico, it was known and used appreciatively by Native Americans long before Old World colonists intruded into their land. Now, of course, the pecan has achieved worldwide fame in sticky pecan pie, which we all think of as a quintessential American tart.

Pecan kernels look something like walnuts, though there are obvious differences. The outer shell is a smooth, burnished, red-brown, shaped something like an elongated olive. Being thin, it is easy to crack, and generously filled. Inside, the meat has the double-lobed form of a walnut but stretched out, flattened and with kinks ironed out. They taste sweeter and softer than walnuts, without the hint of bitterness that gives walnuts their edge.

Pecans give these thin, lacy biscuits a subtle, buttery sweetness. Crisp and brittle, they are lovely served with creamy puddings or munched with coffee.

MAKES ABOUT 12

120 g (4 oz) unsalted butter
120 g (4 oz) caster sugar
30 ml (1 fl oz) double cream
1/4 teaspoon vanilla essence

90 g (3 oz) shelled pecans, finely ground
A pinch of salt
60 g (2 oz) plain flour

Pre-heat the oven to 180°C/350°F/Gas Mark 4. Line several baking trays with non-stick baking parchment. Put the butter, sugar, cream, vanilla essence and ground pecans into a pan, with a pinch of salt, and place over a gentle heat. Stir continuously, until the mixture begins to boil. Immediately tip in the flour, mix in evenly and cook for 4 minutes, stirring continuously. Draw off the heat and leave to cool slightly. Drop teaspoonfuls on to the baking trays, leaving a good 7 cm (3 in) gap between dollops, to allow for spreading.

Bake for 9–12 minutes, in relays, leaving a couple of minutes between each tray, until the edges are browned and the centre is a light golden tan. Now you have a choice. The easy route is just to leave the biscuits on the trays for about 3 minutes, until firm, and then lift them on to a wire rack to cool. If you want to be fancy, you can curve them into *tuiles* (the French for curved roof tiles). This second option looks good but demands split-second timing and is bound to leave a few broken biscuits in its wake – cook's perk. If you are aiming at curvaceous *tuiles*, cook only four biscuits on each tray. Once they're out of the oven leave to cool for 1 1/2 minutes. Then, while they are still soft enough to bend without cracking, drape each one over a rolling pin and curve it round. They'll harden up very quickly and can be removed after a minute or two. This is easy, once you get the knack and the right timing. The biscuits can be made in advance and stored in an airtight container.

Paris-Brest

This must be the only cake to be named after a bicycle race. A wheel of almond-studded choux pastry is filled with praline-flavoured buttercream (if you are really pushed for time, you can substitute 300 ml/10 fl oz of double cream, whipped, for the plain buttercream). Sumptuous.

SERVES 8

FOR THE BUTTERCREAM
100 g (3¹/₂ oz) caster sugar or vanilla
   sugar
3 egg yolks, lightly beaten
180 g (6 oz) unsalted butter, softened
200 g (7 oz) Almond Praline powder
   (see p. 375)

FOR THE CHOUX PASTRY
100 g (3¹/₂ oz) butter
150 g (5¹/₄ oz) strong white bread flour
A pinch of salt
4 eggs

TO DECORATE
1 egg, lightly beaten, to glaze
45 g (1¹/₂ oz) flaked almonds
Icing sugar

The buttercream can be made 24 hours in advance. Stir the sugar with 4 tablespoons of water over a medium heat until the sugar has completely dissolved. Brush down any sugar crystals stuck to the side of the pan, with a brush dipped in cold water. Bring up to the boil and boil until the syrup reaches the soft-ball stage, that is 115°C/240°F. To test, drip a little into a glass or bowl of iced water: if it forms a soft, but not sticky, ball, it is done.

Pour the hot syrup slowly into the egg yolks, beating constantly. Keep beating (an electric whisk is a great help) until the mixture is cool and very thick. Cream the butter until it is light and fluffy and then beat in the egg mousse. Fold in the praline powder.

Make the ring of choux pastry only on the day it is to be eaten. Pre-heat the oven to 220°C/425°F/Gas Mark 7. Put the butter and 225 ml (8 fl oz) of water into a pan and bring up to the boil. As soon as it boils, draw off the heat, tip in the flour and salt and beat until thoroughly mixed. Return to a low heat, stirring constantly, until the mixture pulls away from the sides of the pan and spoon. Draw off the heat and beat in the first three eggs, one by one. Beat the last egg lightly in a separate bowl and beat it into the dough gradually, until the dough is smooth and glossy and just slides off the spoon. You may not need all of the last egg.

Line a baking tray with non-stick baking parchment and mark out a 25 cm (10 in) circle. Pipe or dot the mixture all around the circle, smoothing it, if necessary, to form a wheel about 4 cm (1¹/₂ in) wide. Brush with egg glaze and sprinkle with flaked almonds. Bake for 15 minutes.

Reduce the oven heat to 180°C/350°F/Gas Mark 4 for a further 20 minutes, until the pastry is puffed and pleasingly golden brown.

Carefully slice the ring in half horizontally and open it up, so that steam can escape while it cools. Don't worry if you have a few breaks; once the whole lot is reassembled they will hardly show at all.

The last part, best left until the last possible moment, is to pipe or spoon the buttercream into the bottom of the ring. Replace the top carefully, nestle it down, dust lightly with icing sugar and it's ready to go!

Polenta Syrup Cake

This beautiful, burnished-gold cake, soaked in a sweet citrus syrup, is fairly quick to make and perfect for a party, since it needs to be baked a day in advance. It is at its best served with Greek yoghurt, to cut the sweetness, and soft fruit, in season.

SERVES 6–8

FOR THE CAKE
3 eggs
110 g (4 oz) caster sugar
110 g (4 oz) butter, melted and cooled
   until tepid
Juice of 1/2 orange
225 g (8 oz) polenta or fine cornmeal
1/2 tablespoon baking powder
A pinch of salt

Finely grated zest of 1/2 lemon
Finely grated zest of 1 orange
1 teaspoon vanilla essence
Greek yoghurt, to serve
Soft fruit, in season, to serve

FOR THE SYRUP
Juice of 2 oranges
Juice of 1/2 lemon
140 g (5 oz) caster sugar

Pre-heat the oven to 190°C/375°F/Gas Mark 5. Line a 20 cm (8 in) cake tin with non-stick baking parchment. Whisk the eggs with the caster sugar until pale and thick. Beat in the butter and the orange juice. Mix the polenta or cornmeal with the baking powder and salt and gradually beat it into the egg mixture. Stir in the two zests and the vanilla essence. Pour the cake batter into the prepared tin. Place in the oven and immediately reduce the heat to 170°C/325°F/Gas Mark 3. Bake for about 30–40 minutes, until the cake is brown and pulling away from the tin. Test it with a skewer, which should come out clean.

Once the cake is in the oven, make the syrup. Put all the ingredients into a pan and bring to the boil. Simmer gently for 5 minutes. Leave to cool.

When the cake comes out of the oven, make holes in it with a skewer and pour over the cool syrup. Leave to cool. Turn the cake out and serve with Greek yoghurt and soft fruits.

Saffron Tea Bread

If you've ever read anything about saffron, you are bound to know that it is the most expensive spice in the world, worth more than its weight in gold; but, for all that, for its exalted past and honoured present, it is a spice that rewards the user ten fold. A tiny amount, a small fraction of a gram, betrays its presence in any dish with all the grandeur of true nobility, bestowing its pure golden colour streaked sparsely with fiery red and, naturally, its remarkable, incomparable flavour.

Describing the taste of saffron is well-nigh impossible. It's often labelled bitter-sweet. I think it has a surprisingly alluring, metallic edge to it, but the description I like best is 'honey laced with the sea'. This comes not from some romantic Eastern poet but from a commercial grower in North Wales, Caroline Riden, who is quite besotted with the stuff. She says, too, that using it is like cooking with living gold.

Though Caroline's range of saffron recipes spans all the great saffron countries, she particularly likes to use it in baking, an art that still thrives in Wales. This tea bread is lifted instantly out of the ordinary by the addition of saffron. If you want to slice it neatly, you will have to keep it for a day to firm up, but I admit to loving it warm from the oven even if it does crumble hopelessly.

MAKES 1 LOAF
Good pinch of saffron strands
100 g (3¹/₂ oz) butter
100 g (3¹/₂ oz) caster sugar
100 g (3¹/₂ oz) golden sultanas

50 g (1³/₄ oz) glacé cherries, halved
280 g (10 oz) plain flour
2 teaspoons baking powder
A pinch of salt

Put the saffron in a jar or jug and pour in 230 ml (8 fl oz) of hot water. Leave for 20 minutes (or longer if more convenient).

Put the butter and sugar into a pan large enough to take all the ingredients and stir over a moderate heat, until the butter has melted and mixed evenly with the sugar. Now add the sultanas and cherries, give them a quick stir and then pour in the saffron water, complete with all the threads. Return to the heat and simmer gently for 5 minutes. Leave to cool.

Pre-heat the oven to 180°C/350°F/Gas Mark 4. Prepare a 500 g (1 lb) loaf tin by greasing it and then cutting two wide strips of non-stick baking parchment and laying them at right angles in the tin, pressing down against the inside so that one runs the length of the tin and up the ends, with an overhang at each end, while the other runs across the first, over the narrow base of the tin and up the sides again, with an overhang. The idea is to form a sort of cradle, so that the cooked loaf can just be lifted straight out of the tin when it is done.

Sift the flour with the baking powder and salt. Tip into the saffron mixture and stir to form a batter. Pour into the prepared loaf tin and smooth down. Bake for 1–1¹/₄ hours, or until a skewer inserted into the centre comes out clean. Lift out of the tin on to a wire rack and leave to cool. Serve thickly sliced and plentifully buttered.

Sauces, Dressings and Preserves

Beef Stock

Beef stock is always a brown stock, made first by caramelizing the bones and vegetables for both flavour and colour, then finished with lengthy simmering. You can now buy pretty good quality fresh beef stock in tubs in supermarkets, which is infinitely preferable to a stock cube but still can't match a humdinger of a home-made stock.

Buy your bones from the butcher, who should be only too glad to get rid of them. Onion and carrots are essential, but you can omit the celery and/or leek. Never add salt to a stockpot. You may want to reduce the stock down for a sauce so it is far better to season with salt when the stock is being used, rather than when it is being made. If you have a large enough stockpot it is a good idea to make double the quantity (it freezes very well).

This same method can be used for lamb and veal stock. With lamb stock, I often add a good slug of Marsala or Madeira to the pan.

**MAKES ABOUT 1.5 LITRES
    (3 PINTS)**
1.5 kg (3 lb) beef bones
1 large onion
2 carrots, quartered
1 tablespoon oil
1 celery stalk, quartered
1 leek, trimmed and quartered
4 sprigs of parsley
2 bay leaves
1 large sprig of thyme

Put the bones in a roasting tin and roast at 220°C/425°F/Gas Mark 7 until they are richly browned, turning them every now and then. This is a surprisingly slow process and could easily take an hour or more. Keep checking them. Quarter the onion, but don't peel it. Turn the onion and carrots in the oil and add to the roasting tin after half an hour.

Once both bones and vegetables are well browned (but not burnt – take out any pieces that are looking perilously dark), tip them into a large stockpot and add the remaining ingredients. Cover very generously with cold water and bring slowly to the boil, skimming off any scum that rises to the surface. Leave to simmer gently for at least 4 hours, 6 is better. Top up with water as necessary.

Leave to cool, then strain. Chill in the fridge until any fat has congealed on top and scrape it off. If you aren't going to use the stock immediately, either freeze as it is, or, to save space in the freezer, reduce down further.

To freeze, measure the amount of stock you have and make a note of it. Pour it into a wide frying-pan and boil hard until reduced right down to a few spoonfuls. Cool then pour into ice-cube trays and freeze. Divide the amount of stock you started off with by the number of ice-cubes (i.e. if you started off with 1.5 litres/3 pints and you have 6 cubes' worth, then each cube is the equivalent of 250 ml/½ pint of stock).

Then you'll know how much diluted stock each ice-cube represents. Once frozen, drop the ice-cubes into a freezer bag and label.

When needed, take the required number of ice-cubes, place in a measuring jug and top up with enough hot water to make up the original quantity.

Chicken Stock

Making chicken stock is quick and virtually foolproof if you have a microwave. Chicken stock also happens to be the most universally useful of stocks, because although it has plenty of flavour, it is a potentially neutral flavour that enhances rather than overwhelms whatever it is added to. As a result it can form the basis of umpteen sauces and endless soups. You can use the bones left after you've roasted a chicken, but a raw carcass makes the best stock of all. It may be worth asking your butcher to save a few carcasses for you next time he's cutting up chickens and then make a double batch. If you can get the giblets as well, so much the better.

I use exactly the same method for making stock from all sorts of birds – anything from duck, through to game birds such as pheasant, partridge or mallard.

MAKES ABOUT 1.2 LITRES (2 PINTS)

1 chicken carcass and, if available, giblets (not liver) and skin
1 onion, quartered
1 carrot, sliced
2 celery sticks, sliced
1 bay leaf
3 sprigs of parsley
2 sprigs of thyme
6 black peppercorns

Put all the ingredients in a pan and cover generously with water. Bring to the boil, then simmer gently for 2–3 hours, occasionally skimming off any scum that rises to the top. Add more boiling water if the liquid level drops too low. Strain and cool. If you have time, chill overnight in the fridge and lift off the congealed fat from the surface next day. If not, then skim off as much fat as you can.

To microwave, put all the ingredients in the largest microwaveable bowl that you own. Cover with boiling water, then cover tightly with clingfilm. Microwave on full power for 25 minutes, then let it stand for half an hour before straining.

Freeze the stock as for Beef Stock, see p. 352.

Basic Tomato Sauce

This is the basic method, open to a hundred and one variations. Change the herbs, add chilli or fresh ginger, increase the garlic, omit the garlic, throw in a glass of red or white wine or the juice of an orange, leave it slightly rough and chunky, sieve or liquidize to smoothness, enrich with cream, and on and on ad infinitum.

To skin tomatoes, simply cover them with boiling water, leave for a couple of minutes, then drain. The skin should pull away easily. If it still clings stubbornly, repeat the process. Where tomatoes are to be seeded, cut them in half horizontally and either scoop out the seeds with a teaspoon, or squeeze them out if the tomatoes are to be used for a sauce where they'll get crushed anyway and the odd seed isn't going to upset matters.

The length of time you cook a tomato sauce changes the flavour immeasurably. A brief spurt of high heat for a matter of 5–10 minutes or so will give a fresh, sprightly sauce, whereas slower gentle simmering for 30 minutes or more gives it a totally different character, mellow with much more depth. Either way, tomato sauce made with British tomatoes can be a stroke too acidic – you can correct this with a little sugar. To increase the fullness of flavour, add a tablespoon of tomato purée, or a glass of red wine, or even, dare I say it, a generous slurp of tomato ketchup!

SERVES 3–4
2 tablespoons olive oil
1 onion, chopped
1 clove garlic, peeled and chopped
450 g (1 lb) tomatoes, skinned, seeded
   and roughly chopped, or 1 × 400 g
   (14 oz) can tomatoes

1 tablespoon tomato purée
2 sprigs of fresh thyme
Chopped fresh parsley or torn up fresh
   basil leaves
Salt and freshly ground black pepper
1/2 teaspoon caster sugar

Warm the oil in a frying-pan and add the onion and garlic. Cook gently until tender without browning. Add tomatoes, tomato purée, thyme, parsley (if using), salt and pepper. If you are using basil it can be added at this stage, but I prefer to add it right at the end of the cooking time. Either boil hard for 5–10 minutes for a fresh-tasting sauce or simmer gently for 30 minutes until thick and rich for a mellower taste, adding a splash of water if it is drying out too quickly. Taste and adjust the seasoning, adding the sugar if it is too acidic. Stir in the basil (if using).

Sorrel Sauce

Sorrel is the basis for one of the classic sauces for fish (though I like it with chicken and eggs as well). Tart and creamy, it adds a note of luxury. Stir any juices that seep out as the fish cooks into the sauce just before serving. For a lighter sauce, reduce the amount of cream and replace it with fish stock.

SERVES 4
2 handfuls of sorrel
25 g (1 oz) butter
150 ml (5 fl oz) double cream

Juices from cooking fish or a splash of
   fish stock (optional)
Salt and freshly ground black pepper

Snip off the stems of the sorrel leaves and discard. Shred the leaves finely. Heat the butter in a pan, and add the sorrel. Stir over a moderate heat until the sorrel dissolves to a rough purée. Stir in the cream and any cooking juices or a splash of fish stock if using and season. Return to the heat and cook for a few minutes. Serve hot.

Cranberry and Orange Sauce

Fresh cranberries arrive in our shops a few weeks before Thanksgiving at the end of November, and remain prominently in evidence until Christmas, lingering perhaps until the New Year. Then they disappear, quite suddenly. So if you have a taste for them, make the most of it while the going is good – pop the punnet straight into the freezer.

However you use cranberries, they will always demand a considerable load of sugar, even in savoury dishes, since they are naturally tart and bitter. They have an instant affinity with orange and lemon, with warm spices such as cinnamon, cloves and ginger and with port or red wine.

There are endless variations on the cranberry sauce theme – some tempered with orange juice or port, or with this spice or that. This is one version I happen to like, though I tamper with it practically every time. As the sauce keeps well in the fridge, it's worth making a fairly large quantity. Serve it with the turkey, of course, but try it also with ham, or in sandwiches, or with cheese. I love it with roast game – the best partnership of all.

SERVES 8–10
450 g (1 lb) cranberries
Finely grated zest and juice of
   2 oranges

225 g (8 oz) caster sugar
1 cinnamon stick
3 cloves
1 teaspoon ground allspice

Put all the ingredients into a pan and stir over a medium–low heat, until the juices begin to run and the sugar has dissolved. Bring to the boil and simmer for about 5–8 minutes, until the berries have popped. Spoon into a bowl, leave to cool and store, covered, in the fridge.

Vietnamese Dipping Sauce

Simple as a recipe can be, Nuoc Mam Gung, or Vietnamese dipping sauce, is a real joy if you have even the most minimal liking for the flavours of the Far East. It's gingery, sweet, hot, sharp and salty all at once. Try serving it with plainly grilled prawns or chicken. Once you've had a taste, you will probably come up with a hundred and one other ways to use it.

The recipe comes from The Simple Art of Vietnamese Cooking *by Binh Duong and Marcia Kiesel (Simon & Schuster).*

Fish sauce is the south-east Asian equivalent of soy sauce and absolutely essential in the cooking of the region. A thin, clear, mid-brown liquid, it is the salt of Thai or Vietnamese food, but also more than that. It imparts a remarkable, subtle taste that brings out other flavours like magic. Though it is made from fermented fish and salt, it doesn't taste particularly fishy and it doesn't clash with chicken, eggs or vegetables or whatever else forms the principal ingredient of the dish it seasons.

Fish sauce is sold in many supermarkets these days, but you'll get it at a better price and in far prettier bottles in oriental food stores, particularly Thai or Malaysian ones. Look out for bottles labelled nam pla *(from Thailand),* nuoc mam *(from Vietnam), or* ngan-pya-ye *(from Myanmar, formerly known as Burma). The strength may vary a little from one brand to another – Vietnamese* nuoc mam *tends to be more fishy, with a darker colour – so, when it comes to cooking with fish sauce, always use recipe quantities as a rough guide. Taste and add more fish sauce if you think the finished dish needs it.*

MAKES ABOUT 110 ml (4 fl oz)
5 cm (2 in) piece of fresh ginger, peeled
    and finely chopped
2 tablespoons caster sugar
2 small, fiery, fresh red chillies,
    chopped

2 garlic cloves, chopped
1/2 small lime, peeled and sectioned
2 tablespoons fish sauce

Pound the ginger, sugar, chillies and garlic in a mortar with a pestle, to form a syrupy sauce. Add the lime sections and pound again, working them into the mixture. Finally, work in the fish sauce. Serve at room temperature, with rice or as a dipping sauce. The sauce can be kept, in an airtight jar, for up to a week in the fridge.

Garlic and Onion Purée

I use this purée as a sauce, rather than a vegetable dish, serving it with roast meats, or grilled fish. The slowly cooked onions and garlic develop a marvellous sweetness.

SERVES 6
3 heads of garlic
350 g (12 oz) onions, roughly chopped

8 tablespoons olive oil
Salt

Separate the cloves of garlic, but do not peel. Place in a heavy-based pan with the onion and olive oil. Cover and stew very gently over a low heat until both the garlic and onion are meltingly tender – a good 40 minutes or so. Let the mixture cool slightly. Using your hands, squeeze the cooked garlic out of its skins, back into the pan. Liquidize the onions and garlic together, sieve and season. Re-heat when you're ready to serve.

Turkish Garlic and Walnut Sauce

Tarator, a garlic and walnut sauce from Turkey, sauce is a wonderful concoction, pungent and rich, yet marrying well with all kinds of food, particularly fish. It should have the consistency of relaxed mayonnaise, not too thick and not too sloppy either. I happen to like it best made with walnuts, but pine nuts are good too. Use up any left-overs on hot boiled vegetables – delicious.

SERVES 6–8
2 slices of stale white bread – about 65 g (2¹/2 oz) – crusts removed
3 cloves garlic, crushed
1–2 tablespoons white wine vinegar

50 g (2 oz) walnuts or pine nuts, finely ground
Salt
6 tablespoons olive oil

Soak the bread in water for 10 minutes. Drain and gently squeeze out the water.

To make the sauce in a liquidizer or processor, whizz the bread with the garlic, vinegar, nuts and salt until smooth, then gradually drizzle in the olive oil. Taste and adjust the seasoning.

Without a processor, pound the bread with the garlic, nuts and salt in a mortar until you have a smooth paste. Work in the vinegar, then the oil a little at a time. Taste and adjust the seasoning.

Horseradish and Walnut Sauce

Neat creamed horseradish is one of the classic accompaniments to roast beef, but if you've got a really good joint in the oven, take a little time to make this most luxurious horseradish sauce.

SERVES 8
75 g (3 oz) shelled walnuts
350 ml (12 fl oz) whipping cream
1¹/2 tablespoons creamed horseradish

1¹/2–2¹/2 teaspoons lemon juice
¹/2 teaspoon sugar
Salt and freshly ground black pepper

Pre-heat the oven to 200°C/400°F/Gas Mark 6. Spread the walnuts out on a baking sheet and roast in the oven for 4–7 minutes, shaking once or twice, until they turn a shade or two darker. Tip into a metal sieve and shake to remove the loose papery skin. Cool and chop.

Whip the cream and mix with the remaining ingredients, then fold in the walnuts. Taste and adjust the flavourings. It should be punchy, but not hot enough to take the roof off your mouth.

French Canadian Roast Apple Sauce

This is one of the best of all versions of apple sauce, with the added bonus of a crisp, caramelized crust on top. It comes from Nicola Cox's Game Cookery *– a marvellous book – published by Gollancz. Serve the sauce with roast pork, goose or any fatty meat. If you add just a little more sugar, it also makes a most delicious pudding!*

SERVES 4–6
675 g (1 lb 8 oz) tart cooking apples
2 cloves
Demerara sugar

Finely grated zest and juice of 1 lemon
1 tablespoon dark rum (optional)
A pinch of ground cloves
1/4 teaspoon ground cinnamon

Pre-heat the oven to 180°C/350°F/Gas Mark 4. Peel, core and slice the apples thickly. Cram into a baking dish, adding the cloves, about 3 tablespoons of demerara sugar and the lemon zest as you go. Pour over the lemon juice and a tablespoon or so of water. Bake in the oven for 45 minutes or until tender (if you like, it can go into the same oven as your roast pork, 45 minutes before the end of cooking time).

Now splash on the rum, if using, and sprinkle with cloves and cinnamon and an even layer of demerara sugar. Whip under a pre-heated grill and cook until the sugar caramelizes. Mash up the softened apple as you serve so that it becomes more sauce-like.

Spiced Apple Sauce

This is a more conventional apple sauce, perked up with a few spices, but nothing more fancy than that. If you wish to serve the sauce cold, leave out the butter.

SERVES 6
675 g (1 lb 8 oz) cooking apples
1 large cinnamon stick
3 cloves
1 blade of mace

3 allspice berries, bruised
40 g (1 1/2 oz) butter
Freshly ground black pepper
Sugar, to taste

Peel and core the apples, then chop roughly. Put into a heavy-based pan with the spices and enough water to dampen the base. Cover and place over a low–medium heat until the juices begin to run. Raise the heat a little and cook until the apples have collapsed to a purée, stirring once or twice to make sure it isn't catching on the base. If it threatens to burn, lower the heat and add another spoonful of water.

Fish out the spices if you can find them, then add the butter, pepper and a couple of spoonfuls of sugar. Beat with a wooden spoon to smooth out and mix. Taste and add more sugar if needed. Serve warm or cold with roast pork.

Basic Vinaigrette

Please don't waste your money on bottles of ready-made French dressing. They are ridiculously expensive and not terribly good either. Making a proper vinaigrette or French dressing is child's play. Of course, you'll have to invest in a decent bottle of oil, either extra virgin olive oil or plainer groundnut oil, and another of wine vinegar, but they can be used for other things too.

Any left-over vinaigrette will keep in a screwtop jar in the fridge for several weeks. In fact, I usually make double or treble quantities, so that there's plenty left to use at a moment's notice.

**ENOUGH FOR A GENEROUS
6-PERSON SALAD**
1 tablespoon wine vinegar
1/2 teaspoon Dijon mustard (optional)

Salt and freshly ground black pepper
**4–5 tablespoons olive oil or groundnut
oil**

In a salad bowl, mix the vinegar with the mustard, if using, salt and pepper. Whisk in the oil, a tablespoon at a time. After the fourth spoonful, taste – if it is on the sharp side, whisk in the last spoonful of oil and more if necessary. Adjust the seasonings.

Alternatively put all the ingredients into a screw-top jar, close tightly and shake to mix. Taste and adjust the seasoning or add more oil, as necessary.

My Favourite Salad Dressing

This is the dressing that I use time and again on my salads, and I never tire of it. Friends often ask for the recipe, but there is really nothing much to it, as long as you have either good sherry vinegar or balsamic vinegar and a bottle of kecap manis, Indonesian sweet soy sauce.

Sherry vinegar is made from young sherry that is set aside because of its naturally high acidity and then aged in old sherry casks. It has clear parallels with the creation of Italian balsamic vinegar, though the Spanish barrels will usually be made of oak. The results, however, are very different in character. Good sherry vinegar can be as viscous as balsamic vinegar but it tends to be sharper, with a clear scent of sherry and an underlying oak flavour. It varies considerably in quality, as you might expect, but the best sherry vinegar is probably the finest of all wine vinegars.

With balsamic vinegar, you get exactly what you pay for. The cheap stuff is sharper, less subtle, rougher, though not without charm. You can throw it around with gay abandon, slugging it into salad dressings, stews and roast dishes, without worrying about wanton extravagance. It really is worth splashing out, just once, on a flask of more mature vinegar, twelve years old or more, to find out why people get so excited about the stuff.

Kecap manis has a sweet, salt flavour that enhances no end of Western dishes as well as its own Indonesian cuisine. I use it in this salad dressing and in home-made beefburgers or meatballs and drizzle it over pan-fried salmon fillet.

I sometimes use a little lemon oil mixed with ordinary extra virgin olive oil. Open a bottle of lemon olive oil, take one whiff and you are transported straight to the Mediterranean. Bottled sunshine, that's what it is … though it is actually pressed in late autumn or winter. Since it is the essential oil of the lemons, and not the juice, that perfumes the extra virgin olive oil, there is no sharpness, just a marvellous aroma and taste. I use it primarily in salad dressings, but perhaps even nicer is lemon olive oil drizzled over freshly steamed or fried or grilled fish – excellent, in particular, with skate. It can be used on vegetables or chicken too, but always treat it as a condiment, for adding last-minute zip. This is not an oil for frying!

This recipe makes enough salad dressing for a bowl of green leaves for three to four people.

SERVES 3–4

1/2 tablespoon sherry or balsamic
   vinegar
1/2 tablespoon *kecap manis*

Salt and freshly ground black pepper
2–3 tablespoons olive oil or
   1–1 1/2 tablespoons each of olive oil
   and lemon olive oil

Mix the vinegar and *kecap manis* and season with a teensy bit of salt and a good grinding of pepper. Whisk in the oil(s) and then taste and adjust the balance of flavours.

Sauce Rougette

In Brittany, where a huge quantity of top-grade artichokes are grown, the locals serve them with this shallot vinaigrette.

SERVES 4

1 1/2 tablespoons red wine vinegar
Salt and freshly ground black pepper

8 tablespoons groundnut or olive oil
3 shallots, finely chopped

Mix the vinegar with salt and pepper and whisk in the olive oil a little at a time. Add the shallots and serve.

Anchovy Dressing

This is a powerfully flavoured dressing so save it to use on robust salads. I love it with slightly bitter frisée and rocket, with a scattering of diced tomato.

**ENOUGH FOR A GENEROUS
6-PERSON SALAD**
4 anchovy fillets, chopped
1 small clove garlic, peeled

**1 tablespoon sherry vinegar or red
wine vinegar**
Freshly ground black pepper
4–5 tablespoons olive oil

In a mortar or small bowl pound the chopped anchovy fillets and garlic to a paste. Add the vinegar and pound and mix until creamy. Season with plenty of pepper and beat in the oil a tablespoon at a time. Taste and the adjust seasonings, adding more oil if needed.

Serve with a salad of frisée, and finely chopped tomato.

Pesto

Pesto is the most renowned way of using basil. There's not much nicer than a steaming hot dish of pasta, drenched with pesto made with good basil. If you want to do things properly, as they do in Genoa, throw some diced potato, sliced carrots and maybe some green beans into the pan before you add the pasta, which, if it isn't the Genoese trenette, should be spaghetti or at least tagliatelle (jiggle timings to fit). The idea is that vegetables and pasta should be cooked at more or less the same time. Drain together and toss with the pesto and, if necessary, a little extra olive oil to lubricate. Serve with more Parmesan or pecorino if you want it.

SERVES 4 ON PASTA
75 g (2¹/₂ oz) fresh basil
**60 g (2 oz) Parmesan and/or hard
pecorino cheese, broken up into
chunks**

60 g (2 oz) pine nuts
2–3 garlic cloves, roughly chopped
100 ml (3¹/₂ fl oz) olive oil
Salt (optional)

Strip the leaves off the basil and place in the food processor. Add the cheese, pine nuts and garlic and process to a paste. Gradually trickle in the olive oil, to give a creamy sauce. Add salt to taste if you wish.

You want to do it properly? OK. Pound the garlic to a paste with a pinch or two of salt in the mortar. Add the basil and nuts and keep pounding until you have a paste. Work in the cheese, constantly grinding and pounding, and then enough olive oil to give a creamy sauce. I bet you feel smugly virtuous after all that!

Sun-dried Tomato and Toasted Walnut Pesto

You can buy red pestos galore in jars from big supermarkets these days, but it is very easy to make your own. This version, held together with roasted walnuts, is superb, though I say it myself. Stir it plentifully into hot pasta for a quick supper – you might like to scatter a few torn-up basil leaves over the top as well – and use any left-over pesto to boost the flavours of tomatoey sauces or stews. I sometimes stir it into mince for something like a cottage pie, or a bastardized version of a bolognese sauce.

You don't have to use the chilli but I reckon it's a good idea. A medium-hot red chilli won't turn it into a fire-raising sauce but it does give an extra lift.

SERVES 4–6 ON PASTA
60 g (2 oz) walnuts
100 g (3¹/₂ oz) drained sun-dried tomatoes in oil
3 garlic cloves, roughly chopped
60 g (2 oz) Parmesan cheese, broken into chunks

1 fresh red chilli, seeded and roughly chopped (optional)
Oil from the jar of tomatoes
Olive oil

Pre-heat the oven to 200°C/400°F/Gas Mark 6. Spread the walnuts on a tray and toast them in the oven for 3–4 minutes, shaking once or twice, until browned. Keep an eye on them, as they burn quite easily and then they will be good for nothing but the bin. Tip the browned nuts into a wire sieve and shake the sieve over a sheet of newspaper, to remove loose flakes of papery skin. Leave to cool.

Once cooked, tip the nuts into a food processor and add the sun-dried tomatoes, garlic, Parmesan and chilli, if using. Process until smooth and then, with the motor still running, trickle in enough oil (I use a mixture of tomato oil and olive oil) to give a creamy sauce.

If you want to store the pesto, spoon it into a screw-topped jar, smooth down and cover with a thin layer of olive oil. Screw the lid on tightly and keep in the fridge, where it will last for at least two weeks as long as you remember to cover it anew with olive oil every time you dip into it. It will probably last a good deal longer, in fact, but I can't be sure, because we always eat it up pretty quickly.

Tapenade

Olive pastes, pâtés and purées abound in delis and supermarkets these days but Provençal tapenade is the granddaddy of them all. It has many uses, the simplest being as a relish spread thinly on slices of toasted bread, or as a dip with crudités. It can be dolloped on grilled fish or chicken, or smeared thinly over a whole fish to be baked in the oven. For a softer flavour, mash hard-boiled egg yolks with an equal quantity of tapenade and pile back into the halved egg whites to make oeufs à la tapenade or use tapenade to flavour mayonnaise or butter.

There are innumerable variations on the basic idea, though all of them include black olives and capers (from which the purée takes its name). Brandy goes into some but not others. Odder ingredients include dried figs, or roasted tomatoes. Adding the tuna mutes the flavour slightly but it is by no means essential. Ideally, small, black, wrinkled Niçoise olives should be used but be warned: they are a pig to pit. Note that '220 g (8 oz) black olives, pitted' means 220 g black olives weighed with their pits or stones still in situ, not weighed after you have removed the pits. If possible, chew on one of the olives before you buy, to make quite certain that you really like its taste. Don't buy them in a jar or tin, unless you know that you like the taste of the brand. When Niçoise olives are not on the cards, I find that the big juicy Greek Kalamatas make a good tapenade.

SERVES 8
220 g (8 oz) black olives, pitted
1–2 garlic cloves, roughly chopped
30 g (1 oz) drained and rinsed capers
45 g (1¹/₂ oz) canned or salted anchovy fillets, or salted pilchard fillets, roughly chopped
60 g (2 oz) canned tuna fish (optional)
1 tablespoon lemon juice
1 tablespoon brandy (optional)
8 tablespoons olive oil
Pepper

To make in a processor, blend all the ingredients together, gradually trickling on the olive oil as the blades whirr.

Without a processor, chop all the solid ingredients together and then pound to a paste in a mortar, with a pestle, gradually incorporating the lemon juice, brandy and finally the olive oil. Either way, be generous with the pepper.

Sweetcorn and Tomato Salsa

Though the word salsa literally translates as sauce, in the past few years it has come to mean a cold, finely chopped relish, usually made with raw vegetables and fruit, that is served as if it were a sauce proper with grilled fish and poultry. This sweetcorn and tomato salsa is fresh and zippy, and can be made in a couple of shakes. I like to serve it with barbecued chicken. Any left-overs can be stored in the fridge for up to 24 hours. Two heads of sweetcorn will yield about 225 g (8 oz) of kernels.

To cut the kernels from the cobs, stand the cobs upright and slice down close to the tough core, so that the kernels fall off in wide sheets. Scrape the cob over the pan to squeeze out the juice left in the severed bases of the kernels. Add the whole kernels to the pan with a generous knob of butter and salt, cover tightly and cook over a low heat until tender.

SERVES 6

225 g (8 oz) sweetcorn kernels, fresh or
    frozen

350 g (12 oz) ripe tomatoes, skinned,
    seeded and finely diced

1–2 fresh green or red chillies, seeded
    and very finely diced

6 spring onions, sliced very thinly

2 tablespoons chopped fresh coriander
    or fresh basil

Salt and freshly ground black pepper

Juice of 1/2–1 lime

If you are using fresh corn, put it into a saucepan with a tablespoon of water, cover tightly and cook over a low heat for 5 minutes or so until just tender but still slightly crisp. With frozen sweetcorn, just let it thaw. Drain thoroughly, and chop the sweetcorn roughly.

Mix the sweetcorn with all the remaining ingredients, adding lime juice to taste. Cover and leave for at least 1 hour. Stir, taste again and adjust the seasoning. Serve at room temperature.

Pineapple, Lovage and Avocado Salsa

This fruity salsa goes particularly well with grilled or roast duck, neatly counter-pointing the richness of the meat.

SERVES 6–8

1 lime

1 medium-sized pineapple

1 avocado

5 fresh lovage leaves, finely chopped

1 red onion, finely chopped

1 fresh red chilli, seeded and finely
    chopped

Salt

Pare the zest from the lime in long strips. Blanch in boiling water for a minute. Drain well, dry and chop. Squeeze the lime juice. Peel and core the pineapple and dice the flesh finely. Mix with the lime juice and zest. Peel and dice the avocado finely and add to the pineapple, along with the remaining ingredients. Turn quickly and carefully, to mix without battering the avocado to a pulp. Cover and leave for at least half an hour, for the flavours to blend.

Taste and adjust the seasonings, adding a little more lovage if you think the salsa could take it.

Indian Raw Onion Chutney

This uncooked 'chutney' takes only a few minutes to make and is a fine accompaniment to any curry, along with a bowl of mango chutney and sour lime pickles. It's more like a salsa than a pickle and should be served fresh. I usually use a red onion which has a sweeter taste than ordinary white ones.

SERVES 4

1 large red onion, finely chopped

1 heaped teaspoon ground cumin

$1/4$–$1/2$ teaspoon chilli powder

$1/2$ teaspoon sweet paprika

2 tablespoons lemon juice

Mix all the ingredients. Taste and add a little more cumin or chilli if it needs it.

Raw Vegetable Pickles

These delicious Japanese pickles are best made 24–48 hours in advance. The red of the pepper and radishes (if you use red-skinned ones, that is) is gradually released to colour the turnip an enchanting shade of pink. Covered, they will keep for up to a week in the fridge.

MAKES ABOUT 900 G (2 LB)

20 pink summer radishes, sliced, or 225 g (8 oz) piece of oriental radish (such as mooli, daikon or white radish), peeled and cut into matchsticks

2 large carrots, peeled and cut into matchsticks

2 turnips, peeled, halved and thinly sliced

1 cucumber, cut into matchsticks

1 red pepper, cut into thin strips

1 tablespoon salt

2 tablespoons sesame seeds

175 ml (6 fl oz) rice vinegar or white wine vinegar

Mix all the vegetables in a large bowl. Sprinkle with salt, and mix thoroughly with your hands to make sure that all the vegetables are evenly coated. Set aside for 15 minutes.

In a small heavy frying-pan, dry-fry the sesame seeds over a high heat, shaking the pan gently, until they begin to jump and give off a delicious nutty smell. Tip into a bowl and leave to cool.

Go back to the vegetables. Knead with your hands for a minute or two, then tip into a colander. Squeeze out as much liquid as you can, and transfer to a clean bowl. Add the vinegar and sesame seeds and mix well. Cover and leave in the fridge for at least 30 minutes, and up to 3 days, stirring occasionally.

Mixed Salad Pickles

When I visited Hungary, a little dish of mixed salad pickles was put before each person at almost every meal I ate. In hotels and restaurants they are often the only attempt at 'fresh' vegetables, and luckily they are good enough to stand in loco.

Though any number of different vegetables can be used, the main ones should be cabbage (shredded as thinly as is humanly possible) and cucumber, with green peppers ranking second in importance. Carrots are there more for a splash of colour than anything else, so should by no means predominate. Red peppers can be used but will discolour the green of the other vegetables.

**MAKES ENOUGH TO FILL A
1.75 LITRE (3 PINT)
PRESERVING JAR**
About 1.5 g (3 lb 8 oz) mixed
    vegetables (cucumber, cabbage,
    green peppers, carrots, etc.)

450 g (1 lb) onions, finely sliced
100 g (4 oz) coarse sea salt
350 g (12 oz) granulated sugar
300 ml (10 fl oz) distilled malt vinegar

Peel and slice the cucumber as thinly as possible. Quarter the cabbage, remove the tough stalk, then shred very finely. Seed the peppers, discard the white membranes, then cut into thin strips. Peel or scrape the carrots and slice paper-thin.

Mix the cabbage with the onions and a handful of the salt. Weigh down with a plate and leave for 24 hours in a cool place, turning occasionally. Salt the cucumber, carrots and peppers in the same way, keeping them separate.

Put the sugar and vinegar in a pan and stir over a medium heat until the sugar has completely dissolved. Leave to cool.

Next day, drain all the vegetables, rinse and drain again, squeezing them with your hands to expel excess water. Pack them tightly into sterilized jars, building up layers of different vegetables, and tucking discs of carrot in a ring around the outer edge of the central layer, so that they show decoratively through the glass. Pour over the marinade, filling right up to the top. Cover with a clean tea-towel and leave for 24 hours. Top up with marinade if necessary, so that the vegetables are totally covered. Seal tightly with non-corrosive lids and leave in a cool dark place for at least a week before using. The pickles can be stored for up to 3 months or even longer, though the colours will deteriorate.

Bread and Butter Pickles

I adore these pickles, but I've often wondered how they got their name. I don't know for sure, but I suspect it is merely because they are good enough to eat with nothing more than thickly buttered bread. Mind you, a slice of mature cheese goes down well alongside.

Use a red onion if you can, for the colour as well as the taste. I always peel the cucumber for these pickles – it looks nicer and has a better texture – but it's not absolutely necessary. The pickles can be eaten after 3 or 4 days, but they will taste even better after 3 weeks.

**MAKES ENOUGHT TO FILL
    TWO–THREE 450 G (1 LB) JARS**
1 large cucumber
1 red or white onion, very thinly sliced
1 green pepper, seeded and cut into
    strips
1 1/2 tablespoons coarse sea salt

300 ml (10 fl oz) white wine vinegar
275 g (10 oz) caster sugar
1 tablespoon mustard seed
1 teaspoon celery seed or dill seed
5 cm (2 in) stick of cinnamon
6 allspice berries
Pinch of cayenne pepper

Peel the cucumber if you wish and slice it into discs about 3 mm (1/8 in) thick. Mix with the onion, pepper and salt in a bowl. Sit a plate or saucer on top, weigh down with a can or weights and leave in the fridge for 4–12 hours or overnight. Drain, and rinse under the cold tap. Taste the cucumber and if it seems too salty rinse again. Drain thoroughly.

Now sterilize the jars. Wash them in warm soapy water then rinse in hot water. Without touching the insides, set on a wire rack in the oven, set to 110°C/225°F/Gas Mark 1/2. Leave for at least half an hour, until the chutney is ready to be potted.

Place all the remaining ingredients in a large saucepan and stir over a medium heat until the sugar has dissolved. Simmer for 1 minute. Add the drained, salted vegetables, stir once, and bring to a bare simmer without boiling. Spoon into the hot sterilized jars and seal tightly. Store in a cool, dark, dry place for up to 4 months.

Peppered Tarragon Peaches

Serve these peach slices, flavoured with the hot aroma of pepper and the aniseed scent of tarragon, with cold meats or even with a curry instead of a chutney. Try to get freestone peaches which come easily away from the stone. Clingstones will be harder to slice neatly and you will end up with a bit of a mush, even though the taste won't be impaired.

MAKES ENOUGH TO FILL THREE 250 ML (9 FL OZ) JARS
1.5 kg (3 lb) just-ripe peaches or nectarines
300 ml (10 fl oz) white wine vinegar
500 g (1 lb 2 oz) caster or granulated sugar

3 × 5 cm (2 in) pieces of cinnamon stick
2 teaspoons black peppercorns, coarsely crushed
3–6 fresh tarragon sprigs

Try skinning the peaches. Sometimes, if they are of the right type and right degree of ripeness, the skin will just pull away with little need for encouragement. If it sticks fast, bring a pan of water up to the boil and, one by one, dip the peaches into it for about 30 seconds and then strip off the skins if they are sufficiently loosened. Pop the peaches back in for another 30 seconds if need be, but don't just leave them idling in hot water – you don't want them half-cooked and mushy. Quarter the skinned peaches, discarding the stones. Cut out and discard any bruised or damaged patches.

Put all the remaining ingredients, except the tarragon, into a saucepan and stir over a moderate heat, until the sugar has completely dissolved. Bring to the boil and simmer for 3 minutes. Add the peaches and simmer very, very gently over a low heat until they are tender and slightly translucent. Turn them once or twice, if you have to, but don't stir or you'll damage their shape. As soon as they are cooked, lift out with a slotted spoon and pack into sterilized jam jars or Kilner jars (see Bread and Butter Pickles, p. 367 for sterilizing method), tucking a sprig or two of tarragon in with them and making sure that a piece of cinnamon and some of the peppercorns make their way into each jar. Reduce the syrup by about half and immediately pour it over the peaches, completely submerging them. Seal with non-corrosive lids and label. When cold, store in a cool dark cupboard for at least three weeks before eating.

Cranberry and Ginger Relish

If I have a little time on my hands before Christmas, I make this whole cranberry relish baked slowly in the oven. Stored in sterilized jars, it will keep for a month or more in a cool, dark place. A good stand-by for unexpected guests, and a great present.

MAKES ABOUT 650 G (1 LB 6 OZ)
450 g (1 lb) cranberries
225 g (8 oz) caster sugar
Finely grated zest and juice of
  1/2 orange

3 pieces of preserved stem ginger in syrup, drained and finely chopped

Pre-heat the oven to 180°C/350°F/Gas Mark 4. Spread the cranberries in a single layer in an ovenproof dish or roasting tin. Sprinkle evenly with the remaining ingredients and cover with foil. Bake for about 45 minutes, stirring twice. Spoon into hot sterilized jars (see Bread and Butter Pickles, p. 369, for sterilizing method).

Torshi Lift

The Middle Eastern torshi lift is a turnip pickle but beetroot is an essential element, colouring the dull chunks of turnip a brilliant, beautiful pink, as well as imparting a beetrooty sweetness. The final pickle is remarkably delicious. It is so good that you might well just want to serve the pieces of pink turnip and beetroot as pre-dinner nibbles. It's not subtle, I'll grant you that, but it's extremely moreish, and excellent too, served with decent bread and butter and a traditional hard British cheese.

MAKES ENOUGHT TO FILL A
  1 LITRE (1 3/4 PINT) JAR
1 kg (2 lb 4 oz) small turnips
1 large raw beetroot, weighing about
  200 g (7 oz)

4 garlic cloves, thinly sliced
A small bunch of celery leaves
4 tablespoons sea salt
350 ml (12–13 fl oz) white wine vinegar

Peel the turnips and cut them in halves or quarters, depending on their size. Peel the beetroot, cut in half and slice. Pack in sterilized jar(s) (see Bread and Butter Pickles,

p. 367, for sterilizing method), alternating layers of turnip and beetroot, adding the garlic slices and celery leaves every now and then. Put the salt into a pan with 1 litre (1¾ pints) of water and bring to the boil, stirring until the salt has dissolved. Add the vinegar and then pour over the vegetables, making sure that they are completely covered. Seal with a non-corrosive lid(s).

Store the jar(s) in a warm but not hot place. On a shelf in a warm kitchen will do. The pickles will be ready to eat in 10–12 days. Once they are suitably softened and pickled, and suffused with pink, transfer to a cool place, where they will keep for another month or so.

Aubergines Preserved in Olive Oil

This is a preserve I'm particularly fond of – strips of aubergine preserved in oil with a handful of aromatics. As they sit in their jars, the purple of the skins gradually creeps into the pale flesh. A beautiful sight. Serve them as part of an antipasto with plates of salami, cured ham, olives, cheese, and plenty of crusty bread.

SERVES 6–8
450 g (1 lb) aubergine
Salt
150 ml (15 fl oz) white wine vinegar
150–200 ml (5–7 fl oz) extra virgin olive oil

150–200 ml (5–7 fl oz) sunflower oil
4 cloves garlic, peeled and finely chopped
1–3 fresh red chillies, finely chopped
Leaves of 2 sprigs of fresh thyme or ½ teaspoon dried

Slice the aubergine into discs about 2.5 cm (1 in) thick, and then into strips 2.5 cm (1 in) wide. Layer in a large colander, sprinkling each layer with salt. Set aside for 4 hours, turning occasionally. Rinse under the cold tap.

Place the aubergine strips in a pan with the vinegar and just enough water to cover. Bring to the boil and simmer gently for 5–10 minutes until tender. Drain thoroughly and pat dry with kitchen paper.

Mix 150 ml (5 fl oz) olive oil with an equal quantity of sunflower oil. Mix garlic, chilli and thyme together. Into a sterilized preserving jar (see Bread and Butter Pickles, p. 367) pour enough of the oil mixture to cover the base. Sprinkle with a little of the garlic, chilli and thyme mixture. Add a layer of aubergines, sprinkle with a little more of the garlic, chilli and thyme, and pour in enough oil to cover. Repeat until all the aubergine is used up, covering the final layer generously with oil. You may find that you need a little extra oil.

Cover loosely and leave to stand in a cool place for 1–2 hours to settle. If necessary add more oil to cover completely. Seal tightly and keep in a cool, dry, dark place for at least a week and up to 6 months.

Honey Fudge Sauce

This honey fudge sauce is outrageously silky, rich and gooey. Try it over ice-cream or sliced bananas, with a slick of cream to cap it all.

Small jars of honey fudge sauce make very welcome presents.

SERVES 6–8
110 g (4 oz) raisins
4 tablespoons rum
60 g (2 oz) butter

85 g (3 oz) caster sugar
60 g (2 oz) light muscovado sugar
110 g (4 oz) honey
100 ml (3½ fl oz) evaporated milk

Soak the raisins in the rum for at least 24 hours – if you have time, soak them in enough rum to cover in a sealed jar for a month or two.

Put the butter into a heavy-bottomed pan with the caster sugar, muscovado sugar and honey. Stir over a low heat, until the butter has melted and the sugar has dissolved and everything is evenly mixed. Stir for about 4 minutes, always over a low heat. Stir in the evaporated milk, a little at a time, and then stir in the drained raisins. Bring back to the boil, still stirring, and then draw off the heat and stir for a minute or two more. If not using immediately, spoon into a hot, sterilized jam jar (see Bread and Butter Pickles, p. 369), seal tightly and leave to cool. Once opened, store in the fridge where it will keep for up to 2 weeks (or possibly longer, but I couldn't tell you because we couldn't keep our hands off it any longer).

Canadiana Sauce

This is an almost instant sauce from the Ontario Maple Syrup Producers' booklet of maple syrup recipes. Use real, 100 per cent pure maple syrup – truly, it is like nothing else.

SERVES 6
300 ml (10 fl oz) whipping cream

130 ml (4½ fl oz) maple syrup
85 ml (3 fl oz) rye whiskey

Whip the cream and slowly fold in the maple syrup and rye whiskey. Serve over hot puddings.

Fig Jam

This confiture de figues was inspired by the breakfast jams of Mme Manet at the Hôtel des Trois Lys in Condom, France. A brush with Weight Watchers induced her to reduce the sugar content of her home-made jams, and they taste all the better for it. However, less sugar means that this jam won't reach a firm set, always remaining more runny than the usual British style of jam.

MAKES ABOUT 1.5 KG (3 LB 8 OZ)

900 g (2 lb) purple or green figs, not too ripe

2 lemons

3 cloves

450 g (1 lb) granulated or caster sugar

Nip the hard stems off the figs, then quarter the fruit. Grate the zest of the lemons finely. Squeeze the juice, and reserve the pips. Tie the pips and the cloves in a square of muslin. Put the figs in a pan with the lemon juice, pips and 150 ml (5 fl oz) water. Bring gently to a simmer and simmer for 15 minutes until the figs are tender. Now add the sugar and lemon zest and stir until the sugar has completely dissolved. Bring back to the boil and boil until thick and syrupy – about 40 minutes.

Remove the muslin bag and let the jam settle for 5 minutes. Ladle into hot sterilized jam jars (see Bread and Butter Pickles, p. 369), cover and seal as normal. Store in a cool dark place and use within 3 months. Store the jars, once opened, in the refrigerator.

Quince Jelly

One of my all-time favourite jellies, with its glowing amber colour and heavenly perfume. First, though, you must find your quinces. If you don't grow any yourself, it's worth asking around to see if any neighbours have a tree hidden away in their garden. With luck you will be able to scrounge a few windfalls (but do be careful to remove all blemishes and bruises before using the quinces), and if necessary you can eke them out by adding a couple of cooking apples.

I haven't included any quantities here. It's up to you how much jelly you wish to make, and is probably dependent on how many quinces you can lay your hands on.

Quinces

Granulated sugar

Wash the quinces and rub off the fine fluff. Cut out and discard any blemished or bruised patches. Chop up the rest of the quinces, peel, core and all, and throw into a large heavy pan, adding enough water to come about half-way up the fruit. Bring to the boil and boil hard until the fruit is very tender and pulpy. Stir, and mush down occasionally as it cooks.

Tip the contents of the pan into a jelly bag, or a non-metallic sieve lined with a double layer of muslin, and let the juice drip through. Don't press down on the pulp or you'll end up with a cloudy jelly. Leave it to drip into a bowl for at least 2 hours or overnight.

Measure the quantity of juice, and for each 600 ml (1 pint) weigh out 450 g (1 lb) sugar. Stir together, in a clean pan, over a moderate heat until the sugar has dissolved. Bring to the boil and boil hard until setting point is reached. If you have one, use a sugar thermometer as a guide to the setting point, but don't rely on it absolutely. Always back it up by testing manually; drip a drop of the jam on to a chilled saucer. Cool for a few minutes, then nudge with your finger nail. If the surface wrinkles, the jam is ready; if it doesn't, repeat a few minutes later.

When the jam is ready, ladle it into hot sterilized jars (see Bread and Butter Pickles, p. 367), seal and label. Store in a cool dry place for up to six months. Refrigerate once opened.

Almond Brittle and Almond Praline

From one recipe, two outcomes. Almond brittle makes a lovely sweet. Ground to a powder it becomes praline. In Sicily, they use the cut-side of a halved lemon to smooth and flatten down the cooked brittle. It's a clever trick, obvious when you have lots of lemons to hand, as they do there, but still worth borrowing here, where we don't.

MAKES 200 G (7 OZ)
100 g (4 oz) whole blanched almonds
100 g (4 oz) caster sugar

Pre-heat the oven to 190°C/375°F/Gas Mark 5. Oil a cool marble surface, if you have one, or a baking tray if you haven't. Spread the almonds out on another baking tray and toast them in the oven, until they are a fairly light golden brown, shaking them every couple of minutes. This should take around 6 minutes but check frequently.

Put the sugar into a pan with 4 tablespoons of water. Stir over a moderate heat until the sugar has completely dissolved, brushing down the sides with a brush dipped in water, to remove any sugar crystals that adhere to the pan. Raise the heat and let the syrup boil, without stirring. Swirl the pan now and then to even out the effects of odd hot spots. As soon as the syrup has caramelized to a rich brown, draw the pan off the heat and instantly add the almonds. Pour on to the prepared surface, smooth down with a cut lemon, if you have one to spare (see above), and leave to cool. Break up into bits, and you have a delicious heap of almond brittle.

Grind the bits to a powder, either in a food processor or with a pestle in a mortar, and you have equally delicious praline powder. Either will keep for up to a month as long as they are stored in an airtight container, well away from moisture.

Index